Kaplan Publishing are constantly finding new ways to support students looking for exam success and our online resources really do add an extra dimension to your studies.

This book comes with free MyKaplan online resources so that you can study anytime, anywhere. **This free online resource is not sold separately and is included in the price of the book.**

Having purchased this book, you have access to the following online study materials:

CONTENT	AAT	
	Text	Kit
Electronic version of the book	✓	✓
Knowledge Check tests with instant answers	✓	
Mock assessments online	✓	✓
Material updates	✓	✓

How to access your online resources

Received this book as part of your Kaplan course?
If you have a MyKaplan account, your full online resources will be added automatically, in line with the information in your course confirmation email. If you've not used MyKaplan before, you'll be sent an activation email once your resources are ready.

Bought your book from Kaplan?
We'll automatically add your online resources to your MyKaplan account. If you've not used MyKaplan before, you'll be sent an activation email.

Bought your book from elsewhere?
Go to **www.mykaplan.co.uk/add-online-resources**
Enter the ISBN number found on the title page and back cover of this book.
Add the unique pass key number contained in the scratch panel below.
You may be required to enter additional information during this process to set up or confirm your account details.

This code can only be used once for the registration of this book online. This registration and your online content will expire when the examinations covered by this book have taken place. Please allow one hour from the time you submit your book details for us to process your request.

Please scratch the film to access your unique code.

Please be aware that this code is case-sensitive and you will need to include the dashes within the passcode, but not when entering the ISBN.

FINANCIAL ACCOUNTING: PREPARING FINANCIAL STATEMENTS

STUDY TEXT

Qualifications and Credit Framework

Q2022

This Study Text supports study for the following AAT qualifications:

AAT Level 3 Diploma in Accounting

AAT Level 3 Certificate in Bookkeeping

AAT Diploma in Accounting at SCQF Level 7

FINANCIAL ACCOUNTING: PREPARING FINANCIAL STATEMENTS

KAPLAN PUBLISHING'S STATEMENT OF PRINCIPLES

LINGUISTIC DIVERSITY, EQUALITY AND INCLUSION

We are committed to diversity, equality and inclusion and strive to deliver content that all users can relate to.

We are here to make a difference to the success of every learner.

Clarity, accessibility and ease of use for our learners are key to our approach.

We will use contemporary examples that are rich, engaging and representative of a diverse workplace.

We will include a representative mix of race and gender at the various levels of seniority within the businesses in our examples to support all our learners in aspiring to achieve their potential within their chosen careers.

Roles played by characters in our examples will demonstrate richness and diversity by the use of different names, backgrounds, ethnicity and gender, with a mix of sexuality, relationships and beliefs where these are relevant to the syllabus.

It must always be obvious who is being referred to in each stage of any example so that we do not detract from clarity and ease of use for each of our learners.

We will actively seek feedback from our learners on our approach and keep our policy under continuous review. If you would like to provide any feedback on our linguistic approach, please use this form (you will need to enter the link below into your browser).

https://forms.gle/U8oR3abiPpGRDY158

We will seek to devise simple measures that can be used by independent assessors to randomly check our success in the implementation of our Linguistic Equality, Diversity and Inclusion Policy.

British Library Cataloguing-in-Publication Data

A catalogue record for this book is available from the British Library.

Published by:

Kaplan Publishing UK
Unit 2 The Business Centre
Molly Millar's Lane
Wokingham
Berkshire
RG41 2QZ

ISBN: 978-1-83996-874-7

© Kaplan Financial Limited, 2024

The text in this material and any others made available by any Kaplan Group company does not amount to advice on a particular matter and should not be taken as such. No reliance should be placed on the content as the basis for any investment or other decision or in connection with any advice given to third parties. Please consult your appropriate professional adviser as necessary. Kaplan Publishing Limited, all other Kaplan group companies, the International Accounting Standards Board, and the IFRS Foundation expressly disclaim all liability to any person in respect of any losses or other claims, whether direct, indirect, incidental, consequential or otherwise arising in relation to the use of such materials. Printed and bound in Great Britain.

Acknowledgements

This product contains copyright material and trademarks of the IFRS Foundation®. All rights reserved. Used under licence from the IFRS Foundation®. Reproduction and use rights are strictly limited. For more information about the IFRS Foundation and rights to use its material please visit www.ifrs.org.

Disclaimer: To the extent permitted by applicable law the Board and the IFRS Foundation expressly disclaims all liability howsoever arising from this publication or any translation thereof whether in contract, tort or otherwise (including, but not limited to, liability for any negligent act or omission) to any person in respect of any claims or losses of any nature including direct, indirect, incidental or consequential loss, punitive damages, penalties or costs.

Information contained in this publication does not constitute advice and should not be substituted for the services of an appropriately qualified professional.

IFRS

The IFRS Foundation logo, the IASB logo, the IFRS for SMEs logo, the 'Hexagon Device', 'IFRS Foundation', 'eIFRS', 'IAS', 'IASB', 'IFRS for SMEs', 'IASs', 'IFRS', 'IFRSs', 'International Accounting Standards' and 'International Financial Reporting Standards', 'IFRIC', NIIF® and 'SIC' are **Trade Marks** of the IFRS Foundation.

IFRS

Trade Marks

The Foundation has trade marks registered around the world (**'Trade Marks'**) including 'IAS®', 'IASB®', 'IFRIC®', 'IFRS®', the IFRS® logo, 'IFRS for SMEs®', IFRS for SMEs® logo, the 'Hexagon Device', 'International Financial Reporting Standards®', NIIF® and 'SIC®'.

Further details of the Foundation's Trade Marks are available from the Licensor on request.

FINANCIAL ACCOUNTING: PREPARING FINANCIAL STATEMENTS

CONTENTS

	Page number
Introduction	P.7
Unit guide	P.11
The assessment	P.27
Unit link to the synoptic assessment	P.28
Study skills	P.29

STUDY TEXT

Chapter

1	Double entry bookkeeping	1
2	Accounting for VAT and payroll	63
3	Capital and revenue expenditure	81
4	Depreciation	99
5	Disposal of capital assets	133
6	The extended trial balance – an introduction	165
7	Underlying accounting principles	169
8	Accounting for inventory	195
9	Irrecoverable and doubtful debts	217
10	Control account reconciliations	245
11	Bank reconciliations	277
12	Accruals and prepayments	289
13	Suspense accounts and errors	313
14	The extended trial balance – in action	339
15	Preparation of accounts for a sole trader	387
16	Partnership accounts	433
17	Incomplete records	477
18	The interpretation of profitability ratios	545
19	Appendix 1 – International accounting terminology and the alternatives	563

Mock Assessment Questions	575
Mock Assessment Answers	593
References	613
Index	I.1

This document references IFRS® Standards and IAS® Standards, which are authored by the International Accounting Standards Board (the Board), and published in the 2023 IFRS Standards Red Book.

INTRODUCTION

HOW TO USE THESE MATERIALS

These Kaplan Publishing learning materials have been carefully designed to make your learning experience as easy as possible and to give you the best chance of success in your AAT assessments.

They contain a number of features to help you in the study process.

The sections on the Unit Guide, the Assessment and Study Skills should be read before you commence your studies.

They are designed to familiarise you with the nature and content of the assessment and to give you tips on how best to approach your studies.

STUDY TEXT

This study text has been specially prepared for the revised AAT qualification introduced in February 2022.

It is written in a practical and interactive style:

- key terms and concepts are clearly defined
- all topics are illustrated with practical examples with clearly worked solutions based on sample tasks provided by the AAT in the new examining style
- frequent activities throughout the chapters ensure that what you have learnt is regularly reinforced
- 'pitfalls' and 'examination tips' help you avoid commonly made mistakes and help you focus on what is required to perform well in your examination
- 'Test your understanding' activities are included within each chapter to apply your learning and develop your understanding.

FINANCIAL ACCOUNTING: PREPARING FINANCIAL STATEMENTS

ICONS

The chapters include the following icons throughout.

They are designed to assist you in your studies by identifying key definitions and the points at which you can test yourself on the knowledge gained.

Definition

These sections explain important areas of Knowledge which must be understood and reproduced in an assessment.

Example

The illustrative examples can be used to help develop an understanding of topics before attempting the activity exercises.

Test your understanding

These are exercises which give the opportunity to assess your understanding of all the assessment areas.

Foundation activities

These are questions to help ground your knowledge and consolidate your understanding on areas you're finding tricky.

Extension activities

These questions are for if you're feeling confident or wish to develop your higher level skills.

Quality and accuracy are of the utmost importance to us so if you spot an error in any of our products, please send an email to mykaplanreporting@kaplan.com with full details.

Our Quality Co-ordinator will work with our technical team to verify the error and take action to ensure it is corrected in future editions.

FINANCIAL ACCOUNTING: PREPARING FINANCIAL STATEMENTS

Progression

There are two elements of progression that we can measure: first how quickly students move through individual topics within a subject; and second how quickly they move from one course to the next. We know that there is an optimum for both, but it can vary from subject to subject and from student to student. However, using data and our experience of student performance over many years, we can make some generalisations.

A fixed period of study set out at the start of a course with key milestones is important. This can be within a subject, for example 'I will finish this topic by 30 June', or for overall achievement, such as 'I want to be qualified by the end of next year'.

Your qualification is cumulative, as earlier papers provide a foundation for your subsequent studies, so do not allow there to be too big a gap between one subject and another.

We know that exams encourage techniques that lead to some degree of short term retention, the result being that you will simply forget much of what you have already learned unless it is refreshed (look up Ebbinghaus Forgetting Curve for more details on this). This makes it more difficult as you move from one subject to another: not only will you have to learn the new subject, you will also have to relearn all the underpinning knowledge as well. This is very inefficient and slows down your overall progression which makes it more likely you may not succeed at all.

In addition, delaying your studies slows your path to qualification which can have negative impacts on your career, postponing the opportunity to apply for higher level positions and therefore higher pay.

You can use the following diagram showing the whole structure of your qualification to help you keep track of your progress.

FINANCIAL ACCOUNTING: PREPARING FINANCIAL STATEMENTS

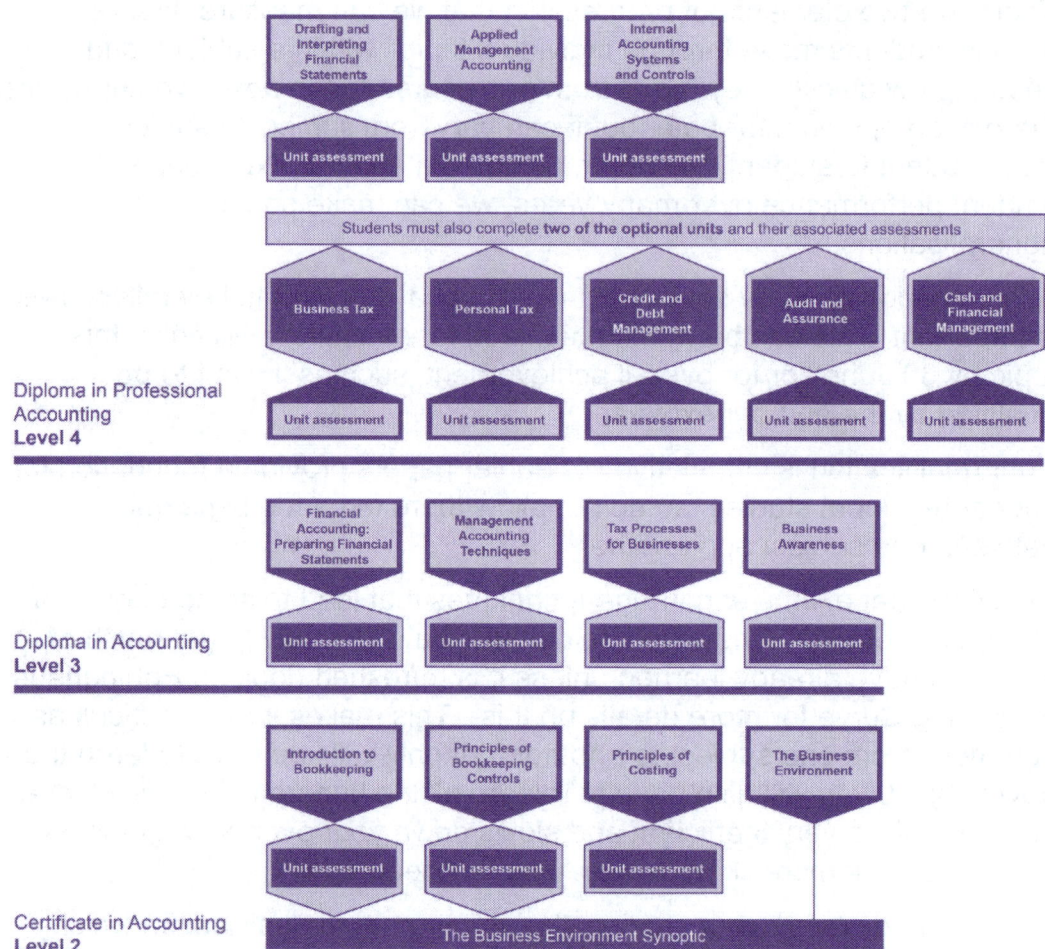

FINANCIAL ACCOUNTING: PREPARING FINANCIAL STATEMENTS

UNIT GUIDE

Introduction

This unit provides students with the skills required to produce statements of profit or loss and statements of financial position for sole traders and partnerships using a trial balance. In employment, students may be required to prepare a portion of, or all, the final accounts and this unit will give them the theoretical knowledge needed to complete that task. It will also allow them to understand how final accounts have been produced, either manually or automatically through use of accounting software.

Students will gain the double-entry bookkeeping skills needed to record financial transactions into an organisation's accounts, using a manual bookkeeping system. They will take this forward to carry out adjustments, ensuring that the accounts will conform to the accruals basis of accounting. Students will understand depreciation, where the loss of value of a non-current asset during a period is reflected in the profit figure for that period. They will also learn to account for allowances for doubtful receivables where account is taken of the likelihood that not all the credit customers will pay in full. These adjustments are regularly carried out by employers to ensure accounts give a more accurate view of both the profitability and the financial stability of the organisation.

By developing an awareness of how the final accounts are used, and by whom, students will appreciate how to produce useful accounting records, sometimes from incomplete information. They will learn about the format of both the statement of profit or loss and the statement of financial position. Students will also learn how to use their double-entry bookkeeping skills to analyse and correct errors that have been made in the ledgers. Students will also be required to check the accuracy of the balances on key accounts within the accounting system by carrying out reconciliations with independent documents, such as bank statements. Accounting ratios to assess the profitability of sole traders will also be introduced. This will allow students to interpret financial statements more effectively.

The application of ethical principles is threaded throughout this unit. All work must be carried out with integrity, objectivity and a high degree of professional competence.

FINANCIAL ACCOUNTING: PREPARING FINANCIAL STATEMENTS

Learning outcomes

On completion of this unit the learner will be able to:

- Understand the accounting principles underlying final accounts preparation
- Understand the principles of advanced double-entry bookkeeping
- Implement procedures for the acquisition and disposal of non-current assets
- Prepare and record depreciation calculations
- Record period end adjustments
- Produce and extend the trial balance
- Produce financial statements for sole traders and partnerships
- Interpret financial statements using profitability ratios
- Prepare accounting records from incomplete information

Scope of content

To perform this unit effectively you will need to know and understand the following:

                                                                                           Chapter

1   Understand the accounting principles underlying final accounts preparation

1.1   The primary users of final accounts   7

Learners need to know:

- the primary users of final accounts: - existing and potential investors - lenders - other creditors
- how final accounts are used by the primary users.

FINANCIAL ACCOUNTING: PREPARING FINANCIAL STATEMENTS

1.2 The framework of accounting underlying the preparation of final accounts — 7

Learners need to understand:

- the accounting principles:
    - accruals
    - going concern
    - business entity
    - materiality
    - consistency
    - prudence
    - money measurement.

1.3 Qualities of useful financial information — 7

Learners need to know:

- the fundamental qualitative characteristics:
    - relevance representation
    - faithful representation
- the enhancing qualitative characteristics:
    - comparability
    - verifiability
    - timeliness
    - understandability
- the importance of ensuring financial statements are free from material misstatement
- the importance of the accountant's fundamental ethical principles and professional scepticism when preparing financial statements for users.

2 Understand the principles of advanced double-entry bookkeeping

2.1 Use of the accounting equation — 1

Learners need to understand:

- the importance of the accounting equation for keeping accounting records
- the effect of accounting transactions on elements of the accounting equation:
  - capital
  - assets
  - liabilities.

Learners need to be able to:

- calculate the different elements of the accounting equation:
  - capital
  - assets
  - liabilities.

2.2 Classification of ledger accounts — 1

Learners need to know:

- the classification of general ledger accounts into:
  - assets: non-current (tangible, intangible) and current
  - liabilities: non-current and current
  - equity (capital)
  - income
  - expenses.

2.3 Purpose and use of books of prime entry and ledger accounting — 1, 2, 10

Learners need to understand:

- the daybooks (books of prime entry): sales, sales returns, purchases, purchases returns, discounts allowed, discounts received, cash book and journal (including narratives)

FINANCIAL ACCOUNTING: PREPARING FINANCIAL STATEMENTS

- information recorded in each type of daybook
- how daybooks are used to update ledger account records, including dealing with value added tax (VAT)
- the different ledgers and how they interact: the general ledger and the memorandum (subsidiary) ledgers (receivables ledger and payables ledger)
- control accounts:
  - receivables ledger
  - payables ledger
  - wages and salaries
  - VAT
- that accounting software automates the transfer of data into the control accounts.

Learners need to be able to:

- prepare ledger accounts using double-entry principles.

2.4 Carry out financial period end routines

1, 6, 10, 11, 14

Learners need to understand:

- that at the end of the period accounts are balanced off differently depending on their classification in terms of income, expense, asset, liability or capital
- that accounting software automates the period end routine.

Learners need be able to:

- verify general ledger balances by using relevant sources of information and performing reconciliations where appropriate: physical checks, inventory records, supplier and bank statements, receivables and payables ledgers (memorandum ledger accounts), non-current asset register
- transfer balances or carry down balances on ledger accounts as appropriate
- determine whether transactions are genuine and valid for inclusion in the organisation's records.

FINANCIAL ACCOUNTING: PREPARING FINANCIAL STATEMENTS

3 **Implement procedures for the acquisition and disposal of non-current assets**

3.1	**Importance of prior authority for capital expenditure**	3

Learners need to understand:

- why authorisation is necessary
- the appropriate person in an organisation to give authority

3.2	**The importance of classifying expenditure into capital or revenue expenditure**	3, 4

Learners need to understand:

- that International Financial Reporting Standards (IFRS) exist that are relevant to non-current assets (NCA): IAS 16
- the definitions of cost, useful life, residual value, depreciable amount, carrying amount
- which items can be included in the cost of NCA under the current IFRS (capital expenditure)
- that revenue expenditure should be excluded from the value of NCA
- the importance of only capitalising expenditure in excess of the level specified in the organisation's policy
- the effect of capitalisation on the statement of profit or loss (SPL) and statement of financial position (SFP).

Learners need to be able to:

- categorise items into revenue and capital expenditure for the purposes of accounting for non-current assets.

3.3	**Record acquisitions and disposals of non-current assets**	3, 5

Learners need to understand:

- the purpose and content of the non-current asset register, including assisting physical verification and reconciling with general ledger entries and balance

FINANCIAL ACCOUNTING: PREPARING FINANCIAL STATEMENTS

- the meaning of any balance on the disposals account
- that part-exchange is a different form of funding to cash or credit
- that non-current asset registers can be part of accounting software or held independently on spreadsheets
- how gains and losses on disposal are treated at the period end.

Learners need to be able to:

- update the non-current asset register for acquisitions and disposals
- record acquisitions and disposals in the general ledger (including part-exchanges)
- treat VAT according to the registration status of the acquiring organisation.

    Excluded: VAT treatment of part exchanges

4 Prepare and record depreciation calculations

4.1 Calculate depreciation   4

Learners need to understand:

- that accounting for depreciation is an application of the accruals principle of accounting
- that the depreciable amount of the NCA should be allocated over the relevant period of its useful life
- that depreciation can be calculated automatically by accounting software or independently through spreadsheets then journaled-in.

Learners need to be able to:

- calculate the depreciation charge for an asset, using the straight-line method of depreciation, according to organisational policy, in terms of: - using either a given percentage or the useful life calculation method - dealing with cases when a residual value is expected or where no residual value is expected - depreciating for a full year or pro-rata for part of a year

FINANCIAL ACCOUNTING: PREPARING FINANCIAL STATEMENTS

	• calculate the depreciation charge for an asset, using the diminishing balance method of depreciation for a full year with a given percentage.	
4.2	**Record depreciation** Learners need to be able to: • record depreciation in the: - non-current asset register - general ledger, including producing relevant journal entries • reconcile the NCA register to the appropriate general ledger balances.	4
5	**Record period end adjustments**	
5.1	**Record accruals and prepayments of income and expenditure** Learners need to understand: • that adjustments for accruals and prepayments are an application of the accruals principle of accounting • why there can be a difference between the amount paid or received during the period and the amount recognised in the statement of profit or loss for that period • how adjustments for accruals and prepayments for the current period and the reversal of adjustments for the previous period affect ledger accounts • that accrued and prepaid income and expense balances are recognised as either assets or liabilities • that adjustments for accruals and prepayments are an application of the accruals principle of accounting • that accounting software automates recurring entries including for accruals and prepayments. Learners need to be able to: • calculate the amount of a prepayment or accrual adjustment to be made • account for accruals and prepayments by making entries in the general ledger, including using the journal	12

- account for the reversal of accruals and prepayments from a previous period by making entries in the general ledger, including using the journal.

5.2 Record irrecoverable debts and allowances for doubtful receivables   9

Learners need to understand:

- that allowances for doubtful receivables are an application of the accruals principle of accounting

- the differences between irrecoverable debts, allowances for specific doubtful receivables and general allowances for doubtful receivables

- Learners need to be able to:

- account for the writing-off of an irrecoverable debt and for the recovery of an irrecoverable debt previously written off in the ledgers

- calculate new allowances for doubtful receivables and adjustments to existing allowances for doubtful receivables in accordance with organisational policy

- use the journal to record irrecoverable debts and adjustments to allowances for doubtful receivables.

5.3 Record inventory   8

Learners need to understand:

- that accounting for inventory is an application of the accruals basis of accounting.

- the effect that changes in valuation of inventory have on profit/loss for a period

- that IFRS exist that are relevant to inventory valuation: IAS 2

- that inventory must be valued at the lower of cost and net realisable value (NRV) on an individual item basis

- which types of expenditure can be included in the valuation of inventory

FINANCIAL ACCOUNTING: PREPARING FINANCIAL STATEMENTS

- that accounting software automates the process of recording, tracking and valuing inventory.

Learners need to be able to:

- determine the closing inventory figure in accordance with current accounting standards
- make entries in the journal to record the value of closing inventory.

5.4 Considerations for recording period end adjustments

7, 14

Learners need to understand:

- that when making period end adjustments:
  - there is scope to significantly affect the reported results of the organisation
- that when making period end adjustments:
  - there is scope to significantly affect the reported results of the organisation
  - accounting software requires the user to enter dates accurately
- the need to apply professional scepticism, integrity and objectivity to prevent misleading and inaccurate information
- the effects of including misleading or inaccurate period end adjustments (non-compliance with regulations, misinformed decision making by users of the final accounts)
- how to respond appropriately to period end pressures:
  - time pressure
  - pressure to report favourable results
  - pressure from authority.

6 Produce and extend the trial balance

6.1 Prepare an initial trial balance

1, 6, 13, 14

Learners need to understand:

- that certain accounts can carry either a debit or a credit balance: VAT, disposals, bank, irrecoverable debts expense

FINANCIAL ACCOUNTING: PREPARING FINANCIAL STATEMENTS

- the importance of producing the trial balance to check for errors
- the limitations of the trial balance as a check for errors
- that accounting software completes the transfer of data into the trial balance.

Learners need to be able to:

- transfer balances from ledger accounts, a list of balances or written data into the correct debit or credit columns of the initial trial balance
- correct errors that are not shown by the initial trial balance
- correct errors that are shown by the initial trial balance by the use and clearing of the suspense account.

6.2 Prepare an adjusted trial balance 1, 6, 13, 14

Learners need to understand:

- that accounting software automatically recalculates balances after adjustments.

Learners need to be able to:

- place the following adjustments correctly into the adjustments columns of the adjusted trial balance so that it balances:
    - closing inventory
    - accruals of income or expenses
    - prepayments of income or expenses
    - corrections of errors
    - depreciation
    - irrecoverable debts
    - allowances for doubtful receivables
    - disposals of NCA including part-exchange.

FINANCIAL ACCOUNTING: PREPARING FINANCIAL STATEMENTS

6.3 Complete the extended trial balance (ETB) — 6, 14

Learners need to understand:

- the importance of the fully extended trial balance for the preparation of financial statements
- the difference between entries in the ETB for sole traders and partnerships.

Learners need to be able to:

- complete the SPL and SFP columns of the ETB, for sole traders, by extending figures: - from the ledger balances and adjustments columns of the adjusted trial balance - to the relevant SPL and SFP columns
- balance off the ETB, for sole traders, by calculating the profit/loss figure and entering it into the relevant SPL and SFP columns.

Excluded: completion of the ETB for partnerships

7 Produce financial statements for sole traders and partnerships

7.1 Prepare financial statements for sole traders — 15

Learners need to understand:

- the purpose of SPLs
- the purpose of SFPs
- how the financial statements are linked to the accounting equation
- how the SPL and SFP are related
- terminology:
  - sales revenue = sales – sales returns
  - net purchases = purchases – purchases returns + carriage inwards
  - cost of sales = opening inventory + net purchases – closing inventory

Learners need to be able to:

- prepare SPLs
- prepare SFPs using the net assets presentation

FINANCIAL ACCOUNTING: PREPARING FINANCIAL STATEMENTS

7.2 Opening and closing capital for sole traders 15

Learners need to understand:

- the reasons for movements in the capital balance during a period.

Learners need to be able to:

- account for drawings of cash, goods and services, capital injections and profits or losses during a period in order to complete the capital account.

7.3 Produce the SPL for partnerships 16

Learners need to understand:

- why the difference between the SPL for a partnership and for a sole trader is the appropriation account
- the purpose and content of the partnership appropriation account
- how the SPL is linked to the partnership appropriation account.

Learners need to be able to:

- prepare an appropriation account:
  - interest on capital (calculation not required)
  - interest on drawings (calculation not required)
  - salaries or commission paid to partners
- calculate each partner's share of any residual profit/loss according to the profit-sharing ratio
- prepare a partnership's SPL.

7.4 Produce the SFP for partnerships 16

Learners need to understand:

- why the difference between the SFP for a partnership and for a sole trader is the partners' capital and current accounts
- the difference between the partners' current accounts and the appropriation account
- the difference between the partners' current accounts and the partners' capital account

Learners need to be able to:

- account for drawings in the form of cash, goods or services
- prepare partners' current accounts:
    - interest on capital (calculation not required)
    - interest on drawings (calculation not required)
    - salaries or commission paid to partners
    - drawings
- prepare a partnership's SFP using the net assets presentation.

8 Interpret financial statements using profitability ratios

8.1 Calculate profitability ratios 18

Learners need to understand:

- the relationship between the SPL and SFP regarding net profit
- the link between gross profit margin and mark-up
- the meaning of profitability ratios.

Learners need to be able to:

- calculate the following profitability ratios to assist with interpretation of the financial statements:
    - ROCE (return on capital employed): formula used = profit for the year / capital employed × 100 (where capital employed = capital + non-current liabilities)
    - gross profit margin: formula used = gross profit / sales revenue × 100 - net profit margin: formula used = profit for the year / sales revenue × 100
    - net profit margin: formula used = profit for the year / sales revenue × 100

FINANCIAL ACCOUNTING: PREPARING FINANCIAL STATEMENTS

– expense/revenue percentage (specified expense including cost of sales as a % of sales revenue): formula used = specified expense / sales revenue × 100).

| 8.2 | **The interpretation of profitability ratios** | 18 |

Learners need to understand:

- why calculating ratios can aid planning, decision making and control for businesses
- factors that may cause changes in a business's ratios and differences between businesses' ratios
- whether a ratio is better or worse than a comparative ratio; comparisons can be made with:
    – a different organisation
    – a different time period
    – an industry standard
- the importance of professional scepticism to the interpretation of financial information.

9 Prepare accounting records from incomplete information

| 9.1 | **Identify missing figures** | 17 |

Learners need to be able to:
- calculate missing figures relating to income, expenses, assets, liabilities and capital by:
    – selecting relevant data
    – using daybooks
    – using the cash book
    – reconstructing ledger accounts: receivables and payables ledger control accounts, VAT control account and the bank account
    – calculating and labelling the missing figures of reconstructed accounts
    – calculating opening and closing balances
    – adjusting for VAT.

FINANCIAL ACCOUNTING: PREPARING FINANCIAL STATEMENTS

9.2 Mark-up and margin   17

Learners need to understand:

- the difference between margin and mark-up.

Learners need to be able to:

- calculate margin and mark-up to determine missing figures
- use cost of sales calculations to determine missing figures.

9.3 Reasonableness of figures when information is incomplete   17

Learners need to understand:

- whether a given figure is reasonable
- why an actual balance and a calculated balance can be different
- the importance of checking information produced by accounting software for accuracy
- when and how to apply professional scepticism

Delivering this unit

This unit links with:

- Level 2 Introduction to Bookkeeping
- Level 2 Principles of Bookkeeping Controls
- Level 3 Business Awareness
- Level 3 Tax Processes for Businesses
- Level 4 Drafting and Interpreting Financial Statements

FINANCIAL ACCOUNTING: PREPARING FINANCIAL STATEMENTS

THE ASSESSMENT

Test specification for this unit assessment

Assessment type	Marking type	Duration of exam
Computer based unit assessment	Computer marked	2 hours and 30 minutes

The assessment for this unit consists of 6 compulsory, independent, tasks.

The competency level for AAT assessment is 70%.

	Learning outcomes	Weighting
1	Understand the accounting principles underlying final accounts preparation	5%
2	Understand the principles of advanced double-entry bookkeeping	10%
3	Implement procedures for the acquisition and disposal of non-current assets	10%
4	Prepare and record depreciation calculations	10%
5	Record period end adjustments	10%
6	Produce and extend the trial balance	15%
7	Produce financial statements for sole traders and partnerships	20%
8	Interpret financial statements using profitability ratios	10%
9	Prepare accounting records from incomplete information	10%
	Total	100%

FINANCIAL ACCOUNTING: PREPARING FINANCIAL STATEMENTS

APPRENTICESHIP LEARNERS ONLY

UNIT LINK TO THE END POINT ASSESSMENT (EPA)

To achieve the Assistant Accountant apprenticeship leaners must pass all of the assessments in the Diploma in Accounting, complete a portfolio and reflective discussion and complete a synoptic/knowledge assessment.

The synoptic/knowledge assessment is attempted following completion of the individual AAT units and it draws upon knowledge and understanding from those units. It will be appropriate for learners to retain their study materials for individual units until they have successfully completed the synoptic assessment for that apprenticeship level.

With specific reference to this unit, the following learning objectives are also relevant to the knowledge assessment:

LO1 Understand the accounting principles underlying final accounts preparation.

LO2 Understand the principles of advanced double-entry bookkeeping.

LO3 Implement procedures for the acquisition and disposal of non-current assets.

LO4 Prepare and record depreciation calculations.

LO5 Record period end adjustments.

LO6 Produce and extend the trial balance.

LO7 Produce financial statements for sole traders and partnerships.

LO9 Prepare accounting records from incomplete information.

STUDY SKILLS

Preparing to study

Devise a study plan

Determine which times of the week you will study.

Split these times into sessions of at least one hour for study of new material. Any shorter periods could be used for revision or practice.

Put the times you plan to study onto a study plan for the weeks from now until the assessment and set yourself targets for each period of study – in your sessions make sure you cover the whole course, activities and the associated Test your understanding activities.

If you are studying more than one unit at a time, try to vary your subjects as this can help to keep you interested and see subjects as part of wider knowledge.

When working through your course, compare your progress with your plan and, if necessary, re-plan your work (perhaps including extra sessions) or, if you are ahead, do some extra revision/practice questions.

Effective studying

Active reading

You are not expected to learn the text by rote, rather, you must understand what you are reading and be able to use it to pass the assessment and develop good practice.

A good technique is to use SQ3Rs – Survey, Question, Read, Recall, Review:

1. **Survey the chapter**

    Look at the headings and read the introduction, knowledge, skills and content, so as to get an overview of what the chapter deals with.

2. **Question**

    Whilst undertaking the survey ask yourself the questions you hope the chapter will answer for you.

3   Read

Read through the chapter thoroughly working through the activities and, at the end, making sure that you can meet the learning objectives highlighted on the first page.

4   Recall

At the end of each section and at the end of the chapter, try to recall the main ideas of the section/chapter without referring to the text. This is best done after short break of a couple of minutes after the reading stage.

5   Review

Check that your recall notes are correct.

You may also find it helpful to re-read the chapter to try and see the topic(s) it deals with as a whole.

Note taking

Taking notes is a useful way of learning, but do not simply copy out the text.

The notes must:

- be in your own words
- be concise
- cover the key points
- be well organised
- be modified as you study further chapters in this text or in related ones.

Trying to summarise a chapter without referring to the text can be a useful way of determining which areas you know and which you don't.

Three ways of taking notes:

1   Summarise the key points of a chapter

2   Make linear notes

A list of headings, subdivided with sub-headings, listing the key points.

If you use linear notes, you can use different colours to highlight key points and keep topic areas together.

Use plenty of space to make your notes easy to use.

3   **Try a diagrammatic form**

   The most common of which is a mind map.

   To make a mind map, put the main heading in the centre of the paper and put a circle around it.

   Draw lines radiating from this to the main sub-headings which again have circles around them.

   Continue the process from the sub-headings to sub-sub-headings.

Annotating the text

You may find it useful to underline or highlight key points in your study text – but do be selective.

You may also wish to make notes in the margins.

Revision phase

Kaplan has produced material specifically designed for your final examination preparation for this unit.

These include pocket revision notes and an exam kit that includes a bank of revision questions specifically in the style of the new syllabus.

Further guidance on how to approach the final stage of your studies is given in these materials.

Further reading

In addition to this text, you should also read the 'Accounting Technician' magazine every month to keep abreast of any guidance from the examiners.

FINANCIAL ACCOUNTING: PREPARING FINANCIAL STATEMENTS

Double-entry bookkeeping

Introduction

A sound knowledge of double entry underpins many of the learning outcomes and skills required for Financial Accounting: Preparing Financial Statements. It is essential knowledge in order to pass this unit and learners will be assessed on double-entry bookkeeping in the examination and so this must be very familiar ground. Although much of the content of this chapter should be familiar, it is essential that it is covered in order to build upon this basic knowledge in later Chapters.

ASSESSMENT CRITERIA

Use of the accounting equation (2.1)

Classification of ledger accounts (2.2)

Purpose and use of books of prime entry and ledger accounting (2.3)

Carry out financial period end routines (2.4)

Prepare an initial trial balance (6.1)

Prepare an adjusted trial balance (6.2)

CONTENTS

1. Principles behind double-entry bookkeeping
2. Overview of the accounting system
3. Rules of double-entry bookkeeping
4. Double entry – cash transactions
5. Double entry – credit transactions
6. The trial balance and balancing a ledger account
7. The financial statements
8. Digital bookkeeping systems

1 Principles behind double-entry bookkeeping

1.1 Introduction

Double-entry bookkeeping is based upon three basic principles:

- the dual effect principle
- the separate entity principle
- the accounting equation.

1.2 The dual effect

Definition – The dual effect principle

The principle of the dual effect is that each and **every** transaction that a business makes has **two** effects.

For example, if a business buys goods for cash then the two effects are that cash has decreased and that the business now has made purchases. The principle of double-entry bookkeeping is that each of these effects must be shown in the ledger accounts by a **debit entry** in one account and an equal **credit entry** in another account.

Each and every transaction that a business undertakes has **two equal and opposite effects.**

1.3 The separate entity concept

Definition – The separate entity concept

The separate entity concept is that the business is a completely separate accounting entity from the owner.

Therefore, if the owner pays personal money into a business bank account this becomes the capital of the business which is owed back to the owner. Similarly, if the owner takes money out of the business in the form of drawings then the amount of capital owed to the owner is reduced.

The business itself is a completely separate entity in accounting terms from the owner of the business.

1.4 The accounting equation

At its simplest, the accounting equation simply says that:

Assets = Liabilities

If we treat the owner's capital as a special form of liability then the accounting equation is:

Assets = Liabilities + Capital

Or, rearranging:

Assets – Liabilities = Capital

Profit will increase the owner's capital and drawings will reduce it, so that we can write the equation as:

Assets – Liabilities = Capital + Profit – Drawings

1.5 Definitions

Definition – Asset

An asset is a resource with economic value that is owned or controlled, with an expectation that it will provide a future benefit.

Assets are classified as either non-current assets or current assets. They may be tangible physical items or intangible items with no physical form.

Definition – Non-current assets

Non-current assets are those that will be used within the business over a long period (usually greater than one year), e.g. property, plant and equipment.

Definition – Current assets

Current assets are those that are expected to be realised within the business in the normal course of trading (usually a period less than one year) e.g. inventory.

Double-entry bookkeeping: Chapter 1

 Definition – Liability

A liability is an obligation to something of value (such as an asset) as a result of past transactions or events. For example, owing a balance to a credit supplier is a liability.

 Definition – Current liabilities

Current liabilities are the short-term payables of a business. This means payables that are due to be paid within twelve months of the statement of financial position date e.g. trade payables.

 Definition – Non-current liabilities

Non-current liabilities are payables that will be paid over a longer period, which is in excess of one year of the statement of financial position date, e.g. loans.

Test your understanding 1

Place the following account names under the correct headings.

Receivables
Bank overdraft
VAT payable
Motor van
Land

Inventory
Payables
Computers
Cash

Non-current assets	Current assets	Current liabilities

FINANCIAL ACCOUNTING: PREPARING FINANCIAL STATEMENTS

 Definition – Equity

This is the 'residual interest' in a business and represents what is left when the business is wound up, all the assets sold and all the outstanding liabilities paid. It is effectively what is paid back to the owners when the business ceases to trade.

 Definition – Income

This is the recognition of the inflow of economic benefit to the entity in the reporting period. This can be achieved, for example, by earning sales revenue.

 Definition – Expense

This is the recognition of the outflow of economic benefit from an entity in the reporting period. This can be achieved, for example, by purchasing goods or services.

 Test your understanding 2

Heather Simpson notices an amount of £36,000 on the trial balance of her business in an account called 'capital'. She does not understand what this account represents.

Briefly explain what a capital account represents.

Double-entry bookkeeping: Chapter 1

 Test your understanding 3

Musgrave starts in business with capital of £20,000, in the form of cash £15,000 and non-current assets of £5,000.

In the first three days of trading Musgrave has the following transactions:

- Purchases inventory £4,000 on credit terms, supplier allows one month's credit.
- Sells some inventory costing £1,500 for £2,000 and allows the customer a fortnight's credit.
- Purchases a motor vehicle for £6,000 and pays by cash.

The accounting equation at the start would be:

Assets less liabilities	=	Ownership interest
£20,000 – £0	=	£20,000

Required:

Re-state in values the accounting equation after all the transactions had taken place.

2 Overview of the accounting system

2.1 Overview of the accounting system

A business may enter into a large number of transactions on a daily basis. It is quite clear that keeping track of all transactions can be a detailed process.

To ensure that a business does keep track of all sales earned, purchases and expenses incurred, the transactions are recorded in an accounting system.

FINANCIAL ACCOUNTING: PREPARING FINANCIAL STATEMENTS

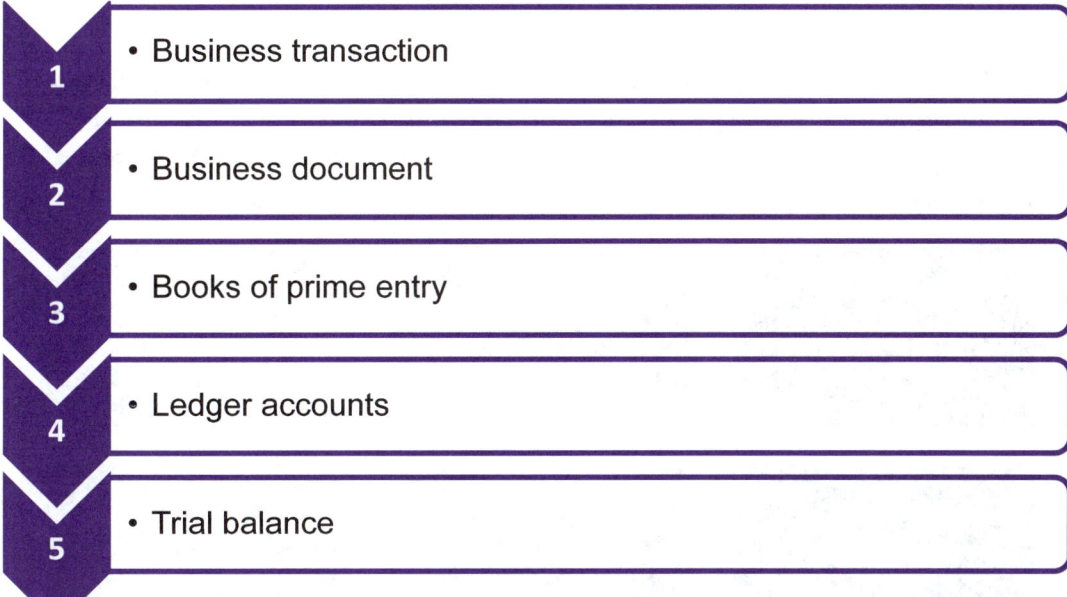

1. Initially a **business transaction** will take place; a credit sale, a credit purchase, a cash sale, a cash purchase, another expense either paid from the bank or by cash, cash paid into the bank, withdrawal of cash from the bank and owner's drawings.

2. A **business document** will be produced e.g. an invoice.

3. The transaction and details from the business document will be entered into the **books of prime entry**. A book of prime entry is where a transaction is first recorded. There are several books of prime entry which may also be referred to as 'day books'.

4. The transactions that have been recorded in the books of prime entry are transferred into **ledger accounts** as part of the **general ledger** on a regular basis. Ledger accounts are used as part of the double-entry accounting system.

5. An initial **trial balance** is a list of all of the ledger accounts in the accounting system and is used as a control to check that transactions have been recorded correctly in the double-entry system prior to the preparation of the financial statements.

2.2 Books of prime entry

A book of prime entry is the place where the transaction (which is detailed on a business document) is first recorded in the books of the business. Books of prime entry may also be referred to as day books. There are several day books which will be briefly reviewed in this chapter:

- Sales day book
- Purchases day book
- Sales returns day book
- Purchases returns day book
- Cash book
- Petty cash book
- Discounts allowed day book
- Discounts received day book
- Journal

Definition – Sales day book

The sales day book is simply a list of the sales invoices that are to be processed for a given period (e.g. a week).

Definition – Sales returns day book

The sales returns day book is simply a list of the credit notes that are to be processed for a given period (e.g. a week).

Definition – Purchases day book

The purchases day book is simply a list of the purchases invoices that are to be processed for a given period (e.g. a week).

FINANCIAL ACCOUNTING: PREPARING FINANCIAL STATEMENTS

Definition – Purchases returns day book

The purchases returns day book is simply a list of the credit notes that have been received from suppliers for a given period (e.g. a week).

Definition – Cash book

A cash book is a record of cash receipts and payments that can form part of the double-entry bookkeeping system as well as being a book of prime entry.

Definition – Discounts allowed day book

The discounts allowed day book is used to record the discounts that have not been deducted at the point of the invoice being recorded within the sales day book but instead were offered on a conditional basis i.e. prompt payment discount.

Definition – Discounts received day book

The discounts received day book is used to record the discounts that have not been deducted at the point of the invoice being recorded in the purchases day book but instead were offered on a conditional basis i.e. prompt payment discount.

Definition – Petty cash book

A petty cash book is one in which all petty or small payments made through the petty cash fund are recorded systematically.

Definition – Journal

A journal is a record of transactions which do not occur regularly and which are not recorded in any other book of prime entry. For example, the acquisition of property, plant or equipment or the recognition of an accrual of expense. The accounting adjustment would be accompanied by a narrative to explain what the adjustment is for.

2.3 The general ledger

> **Definition – General ledger**
>
> A general ledger contains all the ledger accounts for recording transactions occurring within an entity.
> **Note:** The AAT's preferred term is 'general ledger' but the general ledger may also be referred to as the 'main' or 'nominal' ledger.

2.4 The memorandum (subsidiary) ledger

> **Definition – Memorandum (subsidiary) ledger**
>
> A memorandum (subsidiary) ledger provides details behind the entries in the general ledger. Memorandum ledgers are maintained for individual receivables and payables.

> **Definition – Receivables ledger**
>
> Memorandum (subsidiary) receivables ledger may also be referred to as the 'sales ledger'. It is a set of accounts for individual receivables.

> **Definition – Payables ledger**
>
> Memorandum (subsidiary) payables ledger may also be referred to as the 'purchases ledger'. It is a set of accounts for individual payables.

3 Rules of double-entry bookkeeping

3.1 Double-entry bookkeeping rules

There are a number of rules that can help to determine which two accounts are to be debited and credited for a transaction:

- When money is paid out by a business this is a credit entry in the cash or bank account.

- When money is received by a business this is a debit entry in the cash or bank account.

- An asset or an increase in an asset is always recorded on the debit side of its account.
- A liability or an increase in a liability is always recorded on the credit side of its account.
- An expense is recorded as a debit entry in the expense account.
- Income is recorded as a credit entry in the income account.

3.2 The golden rules

Every debit has an equal and opposite credit.

Ledger account	
A debit entry represents	**A credit entry represents**
An increase to an asset	An increase to a liability
A decrease to a liability	A decrease to an asset
An item of expense	An item of income

For increases we can remember this as DEAD CLIC

Ledger account	
Debits increase:	Credits increase:
Expenses	Liabilities
Assets	Income
Drawings	Capital

4 Double entry – cash transactions

4.1 Introduction

For this revision of double-entry bookkeeping we will start with accounting for cash transactions – remember that money paid out is a credit entry in the cash account and money received is a debit entry in the cash account.

Cash/Bank account	
DEBIT	**CREDIT**
Money in	Money out

Example 1

Dan Baker decides to set up in business as a sole trader by paying £20,000 into a business bank account. The following transactions are then entered into:

(i) purchase of a van for deliveries by writing a cheque for £5,500

(ii) purchase of goods for resale by a cheque for £2,000

(iii) payment of shop rental in cash, £500

(iv) sale of goods for cash of £2,500

(v) Dan took £200 of cash for his own personal expenses.

Note that cash received or paid is normally deemed to pass through the bank account.

State the two effects of each of these transactions and record them in the relevant ledger accounts.

Solution

Money paid into the business bank account by Dan:

- increase in cash
- capital now owed back to Dan.

    Double entry:

    - a debit to the bank account as money is coming in
    - a credit to the capital account.

Bank account			
	£		£
Capital	20,000		

Capital account			
	£		£
		Bank	20,000

FINANCIAL ACCOUNTING: PREPARING FINANCIAL STATEMENTS

(i) Purchase of a van for deliveries by writing a cheque for £5,500

- cash decreases
- the business has a non-current asset, the van.

Double entry:

- a credit to the bank account as cash is being paid out
- a debit to an asset account, the van account.

Bank account

	£		£
Capital	20,000	Van	5,500

Van account

	£		£
Bank	5,500		

(ii) Purchase of goods for resale by a cheque for £2,000

- decrease in cash
- increase in purchases.

Double entry:

- a credit to the bank account as money is paid out
- a debit to the purchases account, an expense account.

Purchases of inventory are always recorded in a purchases account and never in an inventory account. The inventory account is only dealt with at the end of each accounting period and this will be dealt with in a later Chapter.

Bank account

	£		£
Capital	20,000	Van	5,500
		Purchases	2,000

Purchases account

	£		£
Bank	2,000		

(iii) Payment of shop rental in cash, £500

- decrease in cash
- expense incurred.

Double entry:

- a credit to the bank account as money is paid out
- a debit to the rent account, an expense.

Bank account

	£		£
Capital	20,000	Van	5,500
		Purchases	2,000
		Rent	500

Rent account

	£		£
Bank	500		

(iv) Sale of goods for cash of £2,500

- cash increases
- sales increase.

Double entry:

- a debit to the bank account as money is coming in
- a credit to the sales account, income.

Bank account

	£		£
Capital	20,000	Van	5,500
Sales	2,500	Purchases	2,000
		Rent	500

Sales account

	£		£
		Bank	2,500

(v) Dan took £200 of cash for his own personal expenses

- cash decreases
- drawings increase (money taken out of the business by the owner).

Double entry:

- a credit to the bank account as money is paid out
- a debit to the drawings account.

Bank account

	£		£
Capital	20,000	Van	5,500
Sales	2,500	Purchases	2,000
		Rent	500
		Drawings	200

Drawings account

	£		£
Bank	200		

5 Double entry – credit transactions

5.1 Introduction

We will now introduce sales on credit and purchases on credit and the receipt of money from receivables and payment of money to payables. For the sales and purchases on credit there is no cash increase or decrease therefore the cash account rule cannot be used. Remember an increase in income is a credit entry and an increase in an expense is a debit entry.

Example 2

Dan now makes some further transactions:

(i) purchases are made on credit for £3,000

(ii) sales are made on credit for £4,000

(iii) Dan pays £2,000 to the credit suppliers

(iv) £2,500 is received from the credit customers

(v) Dan returned goods costing £150 to a supplier

(vi) goods were returned by a customer which had cost £200.

State the two effects of each of these transactions and write them up in the appropriate ledger accounts.

Solution

(i) Purchases are made on credit for £3,000

- increase in purchases
- increase in payables (PLCA).

Double entry:

- a debit entry to the purchases account, an expense
- a credit to the payables account, a liability.

Purchases account

	£		£
Bank	2,000		
Payables	3,000		

Payables account (PLCA)

	£		£
		Purchases	3,000

(ii) Sales are made on credit for £4,000

- increase in sales
- increase in receivables.

Double entry:

- a credit entry to the sales account, income
- a debit entry to the receivables account, an asset.

Sales account

	£		£
		Bank	2,500
		Receivables	4,000

Receivables account (RLCA)

	£		£
Sales	4,000		

(iii) Dan pays £2,000 to the suppliers

- decrease in cash
- decrease in payables.

Double entry:

- a credit entry to the bank account as money is paid out
- a debit entry to payables as the liability is reduced.

Bank account

	£		£
Capital	20,000	Van	5,500
Sales	2,500	Purchases	2,000
		Rent	500
		Drawings	200
		Payables	2,000

Payables account (PLCA)

	£		£
Bank	2,000	Purchases	3,000

(iv) £2,500 is received from the credit customers

- increase in cash
- decrease in receivables.

Double entry:

- a debit entry in the bank account as money is received
- a credit entry to receivables as they are reduced.

Bank account

	£		£
Capital	20,000	Van	5,500
Sales	2,500	Purchases	2,000
Receivables	2,500	Rent	500
		Drawings	200
		Payables	2,000

Receivables account (RLCA)

	£		£
Sales	4,000	Bank	2,500

(v) Dan returned goods costing £150 to a supplier

- purchases returns increase
- payables decrease.

Double entry:

- a debit entry to the payables account as payables are now decreasing
- a credit entry to the purchases returns account (the easiest way to remember this entry is that it is the opposite of purchases which are a debit entry).

Payables account (PLCA)

	£		£
Bank	2,000	Purchases	3,000
Purchases returns	150		

Purchases returns account

	£		£
		Payables	150

(vi) Goods were returned by a customer which had cost £200

- sales returns increase
- receivables decrease.

Double entry:

- a credit entry to the receivables account as receivables are now decreasing
- a debit entry to sales returns (the opposite to sales which is a credit entry).

FINANCIAL ACCOUNTING: PREPARING FINANCIAL STATEMENTS

Receivables account (RLCA)			
	£		£
Sales	4,000	Bank	2,500
		Sales returns	200

Sales returns account			
	£		£
Receivables	200		

6 The initial trial balance and balancing a ledger account

6.1 Introduction

Definition – The initial trial balance

An initial trial balance is the list of the balances on all of the ledger accounts in an organisation's general (main, nominal) ledger.

6.2 Trial balance

When entries have been made in the ledger accounts for a period, the balance for each ledger account will be extracted and a trial balance can be prepared.

The trial balance appears as a list of debit balances and credit balances depending upon the type of account. If the double entry has been correctly carried out then the debit balance total should be equal to the credit balance total. If the trial balance does not balance, i.e. the debit and credit totals are not equal then some errors have been made in the double entry (this will be covered in more detail in a later Chapter).

In a computerised system, the order of the trial balance will be based on the account code assigned to each ledger account. This means that related items such as different types of non-current assets will normally be listed together.

A trial balance lists all of the ledger account balances in the general ledger. Before we can prepare the initial trial balance, we need to balance each ledger account first.

6.3 Procedure for balancing a ledger account

The following steps should be followed:

Step 1

Total both the debit and credit columns to find the higher total – enter this figure as the total for both the debit and credit columns.

Step 2

For the side that does not add up to this total put in the figure that makes it add up and call it the balance carried down, or 'bal c/d.'

Step 3

Enter the balance brought ('bal b/d') down on the opposite side below the totals.

Example 3

We will now balance Dan's bank ledger account

Bank account

	£		£
Capital	20,000	Van	5,500
Sales	2,500	Purchases	2,000
Receivables	2,500	Rent	500
		Drawings	200
		Payables	2,000

The bank ledger account below shows steps 1, 2 and 3 being performed.

Bank account

	£		£
Capital	20,000	Van	5,500
Sales	2,500	Purchases	2,000
Receivables	2,500	Rent	500
		Drawings	200
		Payables	2,000
		Balance c/d **Step 2**	14,800
Step 1	25,000	**Step 1**	25,000
Balance b/d **Step 3**	14,800		

FINANCIAL ACCOUNTING: PREPARING FINANCIAL STATEMENTS

 Example 4

Given below are the initial transactions for Mr Smith, a sole trader. Enter the transactions in the ledger accounts using a separate account for each receivable and payable. Produce the trial balance for this sole trader at the end of 12 January 20X1.

On 1 Jan 20X1	Mr Smith put £12,500 into the business bank account.
On 2 Jan 20X1	He bought goods for resale costing £750 on credit from J Oliver. He also bought on the same basis £1,000 worth from K Hardy.
On 3 Jan 20X1	Sold goods for £800 to E Morecombe on credit.
On 5 Jan 20X1	Mr Smith returned £250 worth of goods bought from J Oliver, being substandard goods.
On 6 Jan 20X1	Sold goods on credit to A Wise for £1,000.
On 7 Jan 20X1	Mr Smith withdrew £100 from the bank for his personal use.
On 8 Jan 20X1	Bought a further £1,500 worth of goods from K Hardy, again on credit.
On 9 Jan 20X1	A Wise returned £200 worth of goods sold to him on the 6th.
On 10 Jan 20X1	The business paid J Oliver £500 by cheque, and K Hardy £1,000 also by cheque.
On 12 Jan 20X1	Mr Smith banked a cheque for £800 received from E Morecombe.

Solution

Step 1

Enter the transactions into the ledger accounts and then balance each ledger account. Use a separate ledger account for each receivable and payable.

(Note that in most examinations you will be required to complete the double entry for receivables and payables in the receivables and payables ledger control accounts, but for practice we are using the separate accounts.)

Step 2

Balance each of the ledger accounts.

Capital account

	£			£
		1 Jan	Bank	12,500

Sales account

		£			£
			3 Jan	E Morecombe	800
	Balance c/d	1,800	6 Jan	A Wise	1,000
		1,800			1,800
				Balance b/d	1,800

Purchases account

		£			£
2 Jan	J Oliver	750			
2 Jan	K Hardy	1,000			
8 Jan	K Hardy	1,500		Balance c/d	3,250
		3,250			3,250
	Balance b/d	3,250			

Purchases returns account

	£			£
		5 Jan	J Oliver	250

Sales returns account

		£		£
9 Jan	A Wise	200		

Drawings account

		£		£
7 Jan	Bank	100		

FINANCIAL ACCOUNTING: PREPARING FINANCIAL STATEMENTS

Bank account

		£			£
1 Jan	Capital	12,500	7 Jan	Drawings	100
12 Jan	E Morecombe	800	10 Jan	J Oliver	500
				K Hardy	1,000
				Balance c/d	11,700
		13,300			13,300
	Balance b/d	11,700			

E Morecombe account

		£			£
3 Jan	Sales	800	12 Jan	Bank	800

A Wise account

		£			£
6 Jan	Sales	1,000	9 Jan	Sales returns	200
				Balance c/d	800
		1,000			1,000
	Balance b/d	800			

J Oliver account

		£			£
5 Jan	Purchases returns	250	2 Jan	Purchases	750
10 Jan	Bank	500			
		750			750

K Hardy account

		£			£
10 Jan	Bank	1,000	2 Jan	Purchases	1,000
	Balance c/d	1,500	8 Jan	Purchases	1,500
		2,500			2,500
				Balance b/d	1,500

Note that accounts with only one entry do not need to be balanced as this entry is the final balance on the account.

Step 3

Produce the trial balance by listing each balance brought down as either a debit balance or a credit balance.

Make sure that you use the balance brought down below the total line as the balance to list in the trial balance.

Step 4

Total the debit and credit columns to check that they are equal.

Trial balance as at 12 January 20X1

	Debits £	Credits £
Capital		12,500
Sales		1,800
Purchases	3,250	
Purchases returns		250
Sales returns	200	
Drawings	100	
Bank	11,700	
A Wise	800	
K Hardy		1,500
	16,050	16,050

Note: E Morecombe and J Oliver have a nil balance so have not appeared in the trial balance.

We often need to account for adjustments (e.g. for omissions, errors or period end journals) after the trial balance has been extracted. These adjustments must be recorded in the general ledger accounts using adjustment journals. After the adjustment journals have been posted, rather than extracting another trial balance, we can instead adjust the initial trial balance. This is the basis for preparing an extended trial balance (see later in this text) and finally the financial statements of the organisation.

6.4 Debit or credit balance?

When you are balancing a ledger account it is easy to see which side, debit or credit, the balance brought down is on. However, if you were given a list of balances rather than the account itself then it is sometimes difficult to decide which side the balance should be shown in the trial balance, the debit or the credit?

There are some rules to help here:

- assets are debit balances
- expenses are debit balances
- liabilities are credit balances
- income is a credit balance.

This can be remembered using the 'DEAD CLIC' mnemonic.

6.5 Balancing off a ledger account

Before the financial statements can be prepared at the accounting period end, the ledger accounts need to be balanced off. Although computerised accounting systems can automatically balance off the ledger accounts, you need to understand the process.

For asset, liability and capital accounts, the balance on the account is carried down and brought down to give the opening balance for the next accounting period. For income or expense accounts, the balance is transferred to a statement of profit or loss ledger account, leaving a nil balance in the income or expense account.

To prepare the statement of profit or loss, all the income and expense account balances are transferred to a new ledger account in the general ledger, called the profit and loss ledger account. The balance on this account is the profit/(loss) for the period. The information summarised in the profit and loss ledger account is transferred to the vertical statement of profit or loss format.

It is unlikely that you will see a profit and loss ledger account within a computerised accounting system as the transfer of the relevant account balances to the statement of profit or loss occurs automatically at the point at which the financial statements are being prepared.

Test your understanding 4

(a) Show by means of ledger accounts how the following transactions would be recorded in the books of Bertie Dooks, a seller of second-hand books:

   (i)   paid in cash £5,000 as capital
   (ii)   took the lease of a stall and paid six months' rent – the yearly rental was £300
   (iii) spent £140 cash on the purchase of books from W Smith
   (iv)   purchased on credit from J Fox books at a cost of £275
   (v)   paid an odd-job man £25 to paint the exterior of the stall and repair a broken lock
   (vi)   put an advertisement in the local paper at a cost of £2
   (vii) sold three volumes containing The Complete Works of William Shakespeare to an American for £35 cash
   (viii) sold a similar set on credit to a local schoolmaster for £3
   (ix)   paid J Fox £175 on account for the amount due to him
   (x)   received £1 from the schoolmaster
   (xi)   purchased cleaning materials at a cost of £2 and paid £3 to a cleaner
   (xii) took £5 from the business to pay for his own groceries.

(b) Balance off the ledgers, clearly showing balance carried down (c/d) and balance brought down (b/d) or the amount to transfer to the statement of profit or loss.

FINANCIAL ACCOUNTING: PREPARING FINANCIAL STATEMENTS

Test your understanding 5

The following balances have been extracted from the books of Fitzroy at 31 December 20X2:

Prepare a trial balance at 31 December 20X2.

	£	Debit	Credit
Capital on 1 January 20X2	106,149		
Freehold factory at cost	360,000		
Motor vehicles at cost	126,000		
Inventories at 1 January 20X2	37,500		
Receivables	15,600		
Cash in hand	225		
Bank overdraft	82,386		
Payables	78,900		
Sales	318,000		
Purchases	165,000		
Rent and rates	35,400		
Discounts allowed	6,600		
Insurance	2,850		
Sales returns	10,500		
Purchase returns	6,300		
Loan from bank	240,000		
Sundry expenses	45,960		
Drawings	26,100		
TOTALS			

Test your understanding 6

Enter the following details of transactions for the month of May 20X6 into the appropriate books of account. You should also extract a trial balance as at 1 June 20X6. Open a separate ledger account for each receivable and payable, and also keep separate 'cash' and 'bank' ledger accounts. Balance off each account and prepare a trial balance.

20X6

1 May	Started in business by paying £6,800 into the bank.
3 May	Bought goods on credit from the following: J Johnson £400; D Nixon £300 and J Agnew £250.
5 May	Cash sales £300.
6 May	Paid rates by cheque £100.
8 May	Paid wages £50 in cash.
9 May	Sold goods on credit: K Homes £300; J Homes £300; B Hood £100.
10 May	Bought goods on credit: J Johnson £800; D Nixon £700.
11 May	Returned goods to J Johnson £150.
15 May	Bought office fixtures £600 by cheque.
18 May	Bought a motor vehicle £3,500 by cheque.
22 May	Goods returned by J Homes £100.
25 May	Paid J Johnson £1,000; D Nixon £500, both by cheque.
26 May	Paid wages £150 by cheque.

FINANCIAL ACCOUNTING: PREPARING FINANCIAL STATEMENTS

Test your understanding 7

1. The bank account for January is as follows:

Bank account

	£		£
Balance b/d	1,900	Payables	7,000
Receivables	2,500		
Cash sales	500		

At the end of the month there is a **debit/credit** balance of **£7,000/4,900/2,100**.

Circle the correct answer

2. True or false, to increase a liability a debit entry is made.
   - True
   - False

Tick the correct answer for task 2

Circle the correct answer for task 3, 4, 5, 6 and 7

3. When a sole trader uses goods for resale for personal use the drawings account is **Debited / Credited** and the purchases account is **Debited / Credited**.

4. When a supplier is paid the bank account is **Debited / Credited** and the supplier account is **Debited / Credited**.

5. When goods are sold to a receivable, the sales account is **Debited / Credited** and the receivable account is **Debited / Credited**.

6. A bank overdraft is a **Debit / Credit** account in the trial balance.

7. Discounts received are a **Debit / Credit** balance in the trial balance.

Test your understanding 8

Tony

Tony started a business selling tapes and CDs. In the first year of trading he entered into the following transactions:

(a) Paid £20,000 into a business bank account.
(b) Made purchases from Debbs for £1,000 cash.
(c) Purchased goods costing £3,000 from Gary for cash.
(d) Paid £200 for insurance.
(e) Bought storage units for £700 cash from Debbs.
(f) Paid £150 cash for advertising.
(g) Sold goods to Dorothy for £1,500 cash.
(h) Paid the telephone bill of £120 in cash.
(i) Sold further goods to Dorothy for £4,000 cash.
(j) Bought stationery for £80 cash.
(k) Withdrew £500 cash for himself.

Required:

Show how these transactions would be written up in Tony's ledger accounts and balance off the accounts. Note you should enter bank and cash transactions into one ledger account.

 Test your understanding 9

Dave

Dave had the following transactions during January 20X3:

1 Introduced £500 cash as capital.
2 Purchased goods on credit from A Ltd worth £200.
3 Paid rent for one month, £20.
4 Paid electricity for one month, £50.
5 Purchased a car for cash, £100.
6 Sold half of the goods on credit to X Ltd for £175.
7 Drew £30 for his own expenses.
8 Sold the remainder of the goods for cash, £210.

Required:

Write up the relevant ledger accounts necessary to record the above transactions and balance off the accounts.

FINANCIAL ACCOUNTING: PREPARING FINANCIAL STATEMENTS

 Test your understanding 10

Audrey Line

Audrey Line started in business on 1 March, opening a toy shop and paying £6,000 into a business bank account.

made the following transactions during her first six months of trading:

	£
Payment of six months' rent	500
Purchase of shop fittings	600
Purchase of toys on credit	2,000
Payments to toy supplier	1,200
Wages of shop assistant	600
Electricity	250
Telephone	110
Cash sales	3,700
Drawings	1,600

All payments were made by cheque and all inventories had been sold by the end of August.

Required:

Record these transactions in the relevant accounts.

 Test your understanding 11

1   The final figure calculated in the trading account is known as?

   Assets   Net profit   Gross profit   Cost of sales

   Circle the correct answer

2   State the accounting equation.

Double-entry bookkeeping: Chapter 1

 Test your understanding 12

Peter

From the following list of balances, you are required to draw up a trial balance for Peter at 31 December 20X8:

	£
Fixtures and fittings	6,430
Delivery vans	5,790
Cash at bank (in funds)	3,720
General expenses	1,450
Receivables	2,760
Payables	3,250
Purchases	10,670
Sales revenue	25,340
Wages	4,550
Drawings	5,000
Lighting and heating	1,250
Rent, rates and insurance	2,070
Capital	15,100

FINANCIAL ACCOUNTING: PREPARING FINANCIAL STATEMENTS

Test your understanding 13

Lara

The following transactions took place in July 20X6:

1 July	Lara started a business selling cricket boots and put £200 in the bank.
2 July	Marlar lent her £1,000.
3 July	Bought goods from Greig Ltd on credit for £296.
4 July	Bought motor van for £250 cash.
7 July	Made cash sales amounting to £105.
8 July	Paid motor expenses £15.
9 July	Paid wages £18.
10 July	Bought goods on credit from Knott Ltd, £85.
14 July	Paid insurance premium £22.
25 July	Received £15 commission as a result of successful sales promotion of MCC cricket boots.
31 July	Paid electricity bill £17.

Required:

(a) Write up the ledger accounts in the books of Lara.

(b) Extract a trial balance at 31 July 20X6.

Test your understanding 14

Peter Wall

Peter Wall started business on 1 January 20X8 printing and selling astrology books. He introduced £10,000 capital and was given a loan of £10,000 by Oswald. The following is a list of his transactions for the three months to 31 March 20X8:

1 Purchased printing equipment for £7,000 cash.

2 Purchased a delivery van for £400 on credit from Arnold.

3 Bought paper for £100 on credit from Butcher.

4 Bought ink for £10 cash.

5 Paid £25 for one quarter's rent and rates to 31 March 20X8.

6   Paid £40 for one year's insurance premium.

7   Sold £200 of books for cash and £100 on credit to Constantine.

8   Paid Oswald £450 representing the following:

   (i)   Part repayment of principal.

   (ii) Interest calculated at an annual rate of 2% per annum for three months.

9   Received £60 from Constantine.

10 Paid £200 towards the delivery van and £50 towards the paper.

11 Having forgotten his part payment for the paper he then paid Butcher a further £100.

Required:

(a) Write up all necessary ledger accounts, including cash.

(b) Extract a trial balance at 31 March 20X8 (before period-end accruals).

7 The financial statements

7.1 What are financial statements?

Periodically all types of businesses will produce financial statements in order to show how it has performed and what assets and liabilities it has.

The two principal financial statements are the statement of profit or loss and the statement of financial position.

7.2 Statement of profit or loss

  Definition – Statement of profit or loss

The statement of profit or loss summarises the transactions of a business over an accounting period and determines whether the business has made a profit or a loss for that accounting period of time.

The trading account section matches sales to the cost of the goods sold to determine gross profit for the accounting period.

7.3 Statement of financial position

> **Definition – Statement of financial position**
>
> The statement of financial position is a summary of all of the assets and liabilities of the business on the last day of the accounting period.

Note that the statement of financial position is split into two sections.

(a) The top part of the statement of financial position lists all of the assets and liabilities of the business. This is then totalled by adding together all of the asset values and deducting the liabilities.

Current assets are always listed in the reverse order of liquidity, which means how easily they are converted into their liquid or cash form. To this end inventory is shown first, then receivables and then bank and cash balances.

(b) The bottom part of the statement of financial position shows how the business is funded. For a sole trader this is made up of the capital at the start of the year plus the net profit for the year less any drawings that the owner has taken during the year.

This part of the statement of financial position is also totalled and it should have the same total as the top part of the statement of financial position.

The production of both the statement of profit or loss and the statement of financial position will be considered for sole traders and partnerships in later Chapters.

8 Digital bookkeeping systems

8.1 Digital bookkeeping

With the introduction of affordable and reliable information technology, organisations have been able to computerise their bookkeeping systems. It is rather rare to find an organisation which does not use some form of computer to aid the day-to-day record keeping that is an essential part of running a business, whether large or small.

A simple spreadsheet to record monies in and out of the business may suffice for small organisations. A larger, or more complex, business may benefit from the introduction of a fully computerised bookkeeping system.

Definition – Digital bookkeeping

Digital bookkeeping means storing your accounting records online, either on a local server or in the cloud.

Definition – The cloud

The cloud is the internet; it refers to all that can be accessed remotely via the internet.

There are many digital bookkeeping packages on the market, each of which work in a similar way. However, they will each offer different approaches to data entry, presentation of reports and so on, as well as different 'extras' such as stock management modules, budgeting and tax planning. Some systems, including Sage Business Cloud Accounting, also allow a business to integrate a computerised payroll function.

Digital bookkeeping systems can import transactions from a number of sources: bank records, csv files, third party software.

Definition – CSV file

A Comma Separated Values (CSV) file is a plain text file that contains a list of data. A CSV file is used to exchange data between different applications.

The structure of a CSV file is fairly simple. It is a list of data that is separated by commas.

Customer name, email, contact number
Simone Supplies, admin@simonesupplies.com, 0141 382 9291
TJK, accounts@tjk.co.uk, 01827 361 111

A CSV file may be more complicated, with thousands of lines, more entries on each lines or even long strings of text.

8.2 Benefits of using digital bookkeeping systems

- Simple data entry and efficiency
- Automatic generation of reports
- Automation of tasks
- Reduction of errors
- Integration with other systems

Simple data entry and efficiency

- Manual data entry is more time consuming than processing transactions digitally.

Automatic generation of reports

- Automatically creates a trial balance from the general ledger accounts.

Automation of tasks

- Processes recurring entries.

 Definition – Recurring entries

A recurring entry is a journal entry that is recorded in every accounting period.

- Makes duplication of automated and manual entries possible.
- Automatically balances the cash book.
- Automatically completes the transfer of data from the books of prime entry to the ledgers.
- Automatically completes the transfer of data into the control accounts.
- Automatically reconciles the receivables and payables ledgers to their respective control accounts.

Reduction of errors

- Transferring data manually is more likely to result in errors. However this does not mean that digital systems eliminate errors altogether.

Integration with other systems

- Connecting individual systems into a one single larger system that functions as one.
- The goal is to get various systems to 'talk' to each other, to speed up information flow and reduce operational costs for the organisation.
- System integration can be used to connect both internal and third party systems that the organisation operates with, such as suppliers for example.

8.3 Drawbacks of using digital bookkeeping systems

Cost	Implementation and support
Potential errors	Specialised needs

Cost

- The package cost is more expensive than a paper-based system.

Implementation and support

- Some assistance may be required when setting up accounting software. The system provider will usually charge for this service.
- The purchase of annual maintenance contracts and a support package may be required.

Potential errors

- If the amount or frequency of a recurring entry changes it may create errors.
- Although the system is able to automatically balance ledgers, it doesn't mean the entries made are necessarily correct. If the underlying data which has been input is incorrect, then the automatic balances will also be incorrect.

Specialised needs

- Specialist businesses may need to tailor a digital package or change the processes to use the software successfully.

8.4 The importance of ensuring bookkeeping transactions are entered accurately

Accounting records should be accurate and up to date. Inaccuracies will ultimately lead to incorrect information being held within the accounting system. This may lead to a variety of consequences, depending on what type of system is being used.

Manual systems

- Human errors are inevitable, especially where there are large volumes of data being processed. For example, an incorrect entry on a suppliers' account, or an omission of an invoice, may result in a supplier not being paid on time, or being paid the wrong amount.
- Identifying the source of an error may be more difficult and time consuming in a manual system, as all prime books of entry would need to be reviewed manually.
- Incorrect information could be provided to stakeholders, i.e. the owners, lenders and customers.

Digital systems

- Sometimes, there are so many codes that the accountants do not know which code to enter for which transaction. This can often lead to confusion when two or more codes refer to closely related transactions.
- If the accounts system is integrated with other systems, both internal and external to the organisation, then errors in one system could have knock-on effects on all systems.
- If the accounts system automatically balances all ledgers, the errors may go unnoticed for a long period of time.

- If staff aren't adequately trained in the system they may not have the technical understanding to find the source of any errors.
- If the system is set up to automatically pay suppliers, for example, then incorrect payments could be made if the original entries on to the system were incorrect. This may go undetected for a long period of time if it is in the supplier's favour.
- Incorrect information could be provided to stakeholders, i.e. the owners, lenders and customers.

9 Summary

In this opening chapter the basic principles of double-entry bookkeeping have been revised from your basic accounting studies.

The basic principles of double-entry bookkeeping are of great importance for this unit and in particular all leaners should be able to determine whether a particular balance on an account is a debit or a credit balance in the trial balance.

Test your understanding answers

Test your understanding 1

Non-current assets	Current assets	Current liabilities
Land	Inventory	Bank overdraft
Motor van	Receivables	VAT payable
Computers	Cash	Payables

Test your understanding 2

The balance on the capital account represents the investment made in the business by the owner. It is a special liability of the business, showing the amount payable to the owner at the statement of financial position date.

Test your understanding 3

Assets		
	Non-current assets (5,000 + 6,000)	11,000
	Cash (15,000 – 6,000)	9,000
	Inventory (4,000 – 1,500)	2,500
	Receivables	2,000
		24,500

Assets – Liabilities = Ownership interest

£24,500 – £4,000 = £20,500

Ownership interest has increased by the profit made on the sale of inventory.

Test your understanding 4

Ledger accounts

Cash account

	£		£
Capital account (i)	5,000	Rent (six months) (ii)	150
Sales (vii)	35	Purchases (iii)	140
Receivables (x)	1	Repairs (v)	25
		Advertising (vi)	2
		Payables (ix)	175
		Cleaning (xi)	5
		Drawings (xii)	5
		Balance c/d	4,534
	5,036		5,036
Balance b/d	4,534		

Payable account (J Fox)

	£		£
Cash (ix)	175	Purchases (iv)	275
Balance c/d	100		
	275		275
		Balance b/d	100

Receivable account (School master)

	£		£
Sales (viii)	3	Cash (x)	1
		Balance c/d	2
	3		3
Balance b/d	2		

Capital account

	£		£
Balance c/d	5,000	Cash (i)	5,000
	5,000		5,000
		Balance b/d	5,000

Sales account

	£		£
		Cash (vii)	35
Statement of profit or loss	38	Receivables (Schoolmaster) (viii)	3
	38		38

Purchases account

	£		£
Cash (iii)	140	Statement of profit or loss	415
Payable (J Fox) (iv)	275		
	415		415

Rent account

	£		£
Cash (ii)	150	Statement of profit or loss	150
	150		150

Repairs account

	£		£
Cash (v)	25	Statement of profit or loss	25
	25		25

Advertising account

	£		£
Cash (vi)	2	Statement of profit or loss	2
	2		2

Cleaning account

	£		£
Cash (xi)	5	Statement of profit or loss	5
	5		5

Drawings account

	£		£
Cash (xii)	5	Balance c/d	5
	5		5
Balance b/d	5		

FINANCIAL ACCOUNTING: PREPARING FINANCIAL STATEMENTS

Test your understanding 5

Trial balance at 31 December 20X2

	Dr £	Cr £
Capital on 1 January 20X2		106,149
Freehold factory at cost	360,000	
Motor vehicles at cost	126,000	
Inventories at 1 January 20X2	37,500	
Receivables	15,600	
Cash in hand	225	
Bank overdraft		82,386
Payables		78,900
Sales		318,000
Purchases	165,000	
Rent and rates	35,400	
Discounts allowed	6,600	
Insurance	2,850	
Sales returns	10,500	
Purchase returns		6,300
Loan from bank		240,000
Sundry expenses	45,960	
Drawings	26,100	
	831,735	831,735

Test your understanding 6

Cash account

		£			£
5 May	Sales	300	8 May	Wages	50
			31 May	Balance c/d	250
		300			300
1 June	Balance b/d	250			

Bank account

		£			£
1 May	Capital	6,800	6 May	Rates	100
			15 May	Office fixtures	600
			18 May	Motor vehicle	3,500
			25 May	J Johnson	1,000
				D Nixon	500
			26 May	Wages	150
			31 May	Balance c/d	950
		6,800			6,800
1 June	Balance b/d	950			

J Johnson account

	£			£
11 May Purchase returns	150	3 May	Purchases	400
25 May Bank	1,000	10 May	Purchases	800
31 May Balance c/d	50			
	1,200			1,200
		1 June	Balance b/d	50

D Nixon account

	£			£
25 May Bank	500	3 May	Purchases	300
31 May Balance c/d	500	10 May	Purchases	700
	1,000			1,000
		1 June	Balance b/d	500

J Agnew account

	£		£
31 May Balance c/d	250	3 May Purchases	250
		1 June Balance b/d	250

K Homes account

	£		£
9 May Sales	300	31 May Balance c/d	300
	300		300
1 June Balance b/d	300		

J Homes account

	£		£
9 May Sales	300	22 May Sales returns	100
		31 May Balance c/d	200
	300		300
1 June Balance b/d	200		

B Hood account

	£		£
9 May Sales	100	31 May Balance c/d	100
1 June Balance b/d	100		

Capital account

	£		£
31 May Balance c/d	6,800	1 May Bank	6,800
		1 June Balance b/d	6,800

Purchases account

	£		£
3 May J Johnson	400		
D Nixon	300		
J Agnew	250		
10 May J Johnson	800		
D Nixon	700	31 May Statement of profit or loss	2,450
	2,450		2,450

Sales account

	£			£
		5 May	Cash	300
		9 May	K Homes	300
			J Homes	300
31 May Statement of profit or loss	1,000		B Hood	100
	1,000			1,000

Rates account

	£			£
6 May Bank	100	31 May	Statement of profit or loss	100

Wages account

	£			£
8 May Cash	50			
26 May Bank	150	31 May	Statement of profit or loss	200
	200			200

Purchase returns account

	£			£
31 May Statement of profit or loss	150	11 May	J Johnson	150

Office fixtures account

	£			£
15 May Bank	600	31 May	Balance c/d	600
1 June Balance b/d	600			

Motor vehicle account

	£		£
18 May Bank	3,500	31 May Balance c/d	3,500
1 June Balance b/d	3,500		

Sales returns account

	£		£
22 May J Homes	100	31 May Statement of profit or loss	100

Trial balance as at 30 May 20X6

	Dr £	Cr £
Cash	250	
Bank	950	
J Johnson		50
D Nixon		500
J Agnew		250
K Homes	300	
J Homes	200	
B Hood	100	
Capital		6,800
Purchases	2,450	
Sales		1,000
Rates	100	
Wages	200	
Purchase returns		150
Office fixtures	600	
Motor vehicles	3,500	
Sales returns	100	
	8,750	8,750

Double-entry bookkeeping: Chapter 1

Test your understanding 7

1   The bank account for January is as follows:

Bank account

	£		£
Balance b/d	1,900	Payables	7,000
Receivables	2,500		
Cash sales	500		
Balance c/d	2,100		
	7,000		7,000
		Balance b/d	2,100

The correct answer is **CREDIT** of **£2,100**.

2   False.

3   When a sole trader uses goods for resale for personal use the drawings account is **Debited** and the purchases account is **Credited**.

4   When a supplier is paid the bank account is **Credited** and the supplier account is **Debited**.

5   When goods are sold to a receivable, the sales account is **Credited** and the receivable account is **Debited**.

6   A bank overdraft is a **Credit** balance in the trial balance.

7   Discounts received are a **Credit** balance in the trial balance.

FINANCIAL ACCOUNTING: PREPARING FINANCIAL STATEMENTS

Test your understanding 8

Tony

Cash

	£		£
Capital (a)	20,000	Purchases (b)	1,000
Revenue (g)	1,500	Purchases (c)	3,000
Revenue (i)	4,000	Insurance (d)	200
		Storage units (e)	700
		Advertising (f)	150
		Telephone (h)	120
		Stationery (j)	80
		Drawings (k)	500
		Balance c/d	19,750
	25,500		25,500
Balance b/d	19,750		

Capital

	£		£
Balance c/d	20,000	Cash (a)	20,000
	20,000		20,000
		Balance b/d	20,000

Purchases

	£		£
Cash (b)	1,000	Statement of profit or loss	4,000
Cash (c)	3,000		
	4,000		4,000

Insurance

	£		£
Cash (d)	200	Statement of profit or loss	200
	200		200

Storage units – cost

	£		£
Cash (e)	700	Balance c/d	700
	700		700
Balance b/d	700		

Advertising

	£		£
Cash (f)	150	Statement of profit or loss	150
	150		150

Telephone

	£		£
Cash (h)	120	Statement of profit or loss	120
	120		120

Revenue

	£		£
Statement of profit or loss	5,500	Cash (g)	1,500
		Cash (i)	4,000
	5,500		5,500

Stationery

	£		£
Cash (j)	80	Statement of profit or loss	80
	80		80

Drawings

	£		£
Cash (k)	500	Balance c/d	500
	500		500
Balance b/d	500		

FINANCIAL ACCOUNTING: PREPARING FINANCIAL STATEMENTS

Test your understanding 9

Dave

Cash

	£		£
Capital	500	Rent	20
Revenue	210	Electricity	50
		Drawings	30
		Car	100
		Balance c/d	510
	710		710
Balance b/d	510		

Capital

	£		£
Balance c/d	500	Cash	500
	500		500
		Balance b/d	500

Purchases

	£		£
Payables (A Ltd)	200	Statement of profit or loss	200
	200		200

Payables

	£		£
Balance c/d	200	Purchases	200
	200		200
		Balance b/d	200

Revenue

	£		£
Statement of profit or loss	385	Receivables (X Ltd)	175
		Cash	210
	385		385

Receivables

	£		£
Revenue	175	Balance c/d	175
	175		175
Balance b/d	175		

Electricity

	£		£
Cash	50	Statement of profit or loss	50
	50		50

Rent

	£		£
Cash	20	Statement of profit or loss	20
	20		20

Motor car

	£		£
Cash	100	Balance c/d	100
	100		100
Balance b/d	100		

Drawings

	£		£
Cash	30	Balance c/d	30
	30		30
Balance b/d	30		

Test your understanding 10

Audrey Line

Cash

	£		£
Capital	6,000	Rent	500
Revenue	3,700	Shop fittings	600
		Payables	1,200
		Wages	600
		Electricity	250
		Telephone	110
		Drawings	1,600
		Balance c/d	4,840
	9,700		9,700
Balance b/d	4,840		

Capital

	£		£
		Cash	6,000

Revenue

	£		£
		Cash	3,700

Shop fittings

	£		£
Cash	600		

Rent

	£		£
Cash	500		

Telephone

	£		£
Cash	110		

Drawings

	£		£
Cash	1,600		

Purchases

	£		£
Payables	2,000		

Payables

	£		£
Cash	1,200	Purchases	2,000
Balance c/d	800		
	2,000		2,000
		Balance b/d	800

Wages

	£		£
Cash	600		

Electricity

	£		£
Cash	250		

Test your understanding 11

1 Gross profit

2 Assets – Liabilities = Capital + Profit – Drawings

FINANCIAL ACCOUNTING: PREPARING FINANCIAL STATEMENTS

Test your understanding 12

Peter

Trial balance at 31 December 20X8

	£	£
Fixtures and fittings	6,430	
Delivery vans	5,790	
Cash at bank	3,720	
General expenses	1,450	
Receivables	2,760	
Payables		3,250
Purchases	10,670	
Revenue		25,340
Wages	4,550	
Drawings	5,000	
Lighting and heating	1,250	
Rent, rates and insurance	2,070	
Capital		15,100
	43,690	43,690

Test your understanding 13

Lara

(a)

Cash

	£		£
Capital	200	Motor van	250
Marlar – loan account	1,000	Motor expenses	15
Revenue	105	Wages	18
Commission	15	Insurance	22
		Electricity	17
		Balance c/d	998
	1,320		1,320
Balance b/d	998		

Purchases

	£		£
Payables	296	Statement of profit or loss	381
Payables	85		
	381		381

Capital

	£		£
Balance c/d	200	Cash book	200
	200		200
		Balance b/d	200

Marlar – loan

	£		£
Balance c/d	1,000	Cash book	1,000
	1,000		1,000
		Balance b/d	1,000

Motor van

	£		£
Cash book	250	Balance c/d	250
	250		250
Balance b/d	250		

Sales revenue

	£		£
Statement of profit or loss	105	Cash book	105
	105		105

Motor expenses

	£		£
Cash book	15	Statement of profit or loss	15
	15		15

Wages

	£		£
Cash book	18	Statement of profit or loss	18
	18		18

Insurance

	£		£
Cash book	22	Statement of profit or loss	22
	22		22

Commission received

	£		£
Statement of profit or loss	15	Cash book	15
	15		15

Electricity

	£		£
Cash book	17	Statement of profit or loss	17
	17		17

Payables

	£		£
Balance c/d	381	Purchases	296
		Purchases	85
	381		381
		Balance b/d	381

(b)

Lara

Trial balance at 31 July 20X6

	£	£
Cash	998	
Purchases	381	
Capital		200
Loan		1,000
Motor van	250	
Sales revenue		105
Motor expenses	15	
Wages	18	
Insurance	22	
Commission received		15
Electricity	17	
Payables		381
	1,701	1,701

Test your understanding 14

Peter Wall

(a)

Cash

	£		£
Capital	10,000	Equipment	7,000
Loan	10,000	Ink	10
Revenue	200	Rent and rates	25
Receivables	60	Insurance	40
		Loan	400
		Loan interest	50
		Payables	200
		Payables	50
		Payables	100
		Balance c/d	12,385
	20,260		20,260
Balance b/d	12,385		

Payables

	£		£
Cash	200	Van	400
Cash	50	Purchases of paper	100
Cash	100		
Balance c/d	150		
	500		500
		Balance b/d	150

Capital

	£		£
		Cash	10,000

Loan account

	£		£
Cash	400	Cash	10,000
Balance c/d	9,600		
	10,000		10,000
		Balance b/d	9,600

Equipment

	£		£
Cash	7,000		

Van

	£		£
Payables (Arnold)	400		

Purchases of paper

	£		£
Payables (Butcher)	100		

Ink

	£		£
Cash	10		

Rent and rates

	£		£
Cash	25		

Loan interest

	£		£
Cash	50		

Insurance

	£		£
Cash	40		

Revenue

	£		£
Balance c/d	300	Cash	200
		Receivables (Constantine)	100
	300		300
		Balance b/d	300

Receivables

	£		£
Revenue	100	Cash	60
		Balance c/d	40
	100		100
Balance b/d	40		

(b) **Trial balance at 31 March 20X8**

	Debit £	Credit £
Cash	12,385	
Payables		150
Capital		10,000
Loan		9,600
Equipment	7,000	
Van	400	
Purchases of paper	100	
Purchases of ink	10	
Rent and rates	25	
Loan interest	50	
Insurance	40	
Revenue		300
Receivables	40	
	20,050	20,050

FINANCIAL ACCOUNTING: PREPARING FINANCIAL STATEMENTS

Accounting for VAT and payroll

Introduction

When dealing with the accounts of sole traders and partnerships it is highly likely that they will be registered for sales tax (called VAT in the UK) unless they are a very small sole trader. Therefore, it is important to consider the accounting for VAT and the rules that apply.

The payroll function and the accounting entries required for the wages and salaries cost and appropriate payroll deductions are also reviewed within this chapter.

ASSESSMENT CRITERIA	CONTENTS
Purpose and use of books of prime entry and ledger accounting (2.3)	1 The operation of VAT (sales tax) 2 VAT and discounts 3 Payroll

Accounting for VAT and payroll: Chapter 2

1 The operation of VAT (sales tax)

1.1 Introduction

This chapter will begin with just a brief reminder of how the VAT (sales tax) system operates.

1.2 What is VAT (sales tax)?

VAT is:

- an indirect tax
- charged on most goods and services supplied within the UK
- is borne by the final consumer, and
- collected by businesses on behalf of HM Revenue and Customs.

VAT is an indirect tax because it is paid indirectly when you buy most goods and services, rather than being collected directly from the taxpayer as a proportion of their income or gains.

VAT is charged by **taxable persons** when they make **taxable supplies** in the course of their business. VAT is not generally charged on non-business transactions.

1.3 Taxable persons

 Definition – Taxable person

Taxable persons are businesses which are (or should be) registered for VAT (sales tax).

1.4 Registration and non-registration for VAT (sales tax)

When a business reaches a set annual turnover level, then it must register for VAT (sales tax). If turnover is below this limit, the business can, if it wishes, register voluntarily. If a business is registered it must:

- charge VAT on its sales or services to its customers
- recover the VAT charged on its purchases and expenses rather than having to bear these costs as part of the business.

In such cases, as the VAT charged and incurred is neither revenue nor expense, the revenues and costs of the business are entered in books at their net of VAT value, and the VAT is entered in the VAT account.

If the business is not registered for VAT then the cost of purchases and expenses must include the VAT as these amounts are said to be irrecoverable. Thus, the costs of the business are entered in the books at their gross (VAT inclusive value) and there is no VAT account.

A person can be an individual or a legal person such as a company.

1.5 Taxable supplies

Taxable supplies or outputs, are most sales made by a taxable person. Taxable supplies can also include gifts and goods taken from the business for personal use.

1.6 Output VAT

Definition – Output VAT

The VAT charged on sales or taxable supplies is called **output VAT**.

1.7 Input VAT

When a business buys goods or pays expenses (inputs), then it will also be paying VAT on those purchases or expenses.

Definition – Input VAT

VAT paid by a business on purchases or expenses is called **input VAT**.

Businesses are allowed to reclaim their input tax. They do this by deducting the input tax they have paid from the output tax which they owe, and paying over the net amount only. If the input tax exceeds the output tax, then the balance is recoverable from HMRC.

1.8 Rates of VAT

In the UK, VAT is currently charged at two main rates, the standard rate of 20% and the zero rate 0%. The zero rate of VAT applies to items such as food, drink, books, newspapers, children's clothes and most transport.

1.9 Standard rated activities

Any taxable supply which is not charged at the zero or reduced rates is charged at the standard rate.

This is calculated by taking the VAT exclusive amount and multiplying by 20%.

If you are given the VAT inclusive rate then calculate the VAT amount by **20/120**.

The following VAT structure can also be used to calculate VAT, VAT inclusive or VAT exclusive figures.

	%
VAT inclusive	120
VAT	20
VAT exclusive	100

 Example 1

Suppose that a business makes sales on credit of £1,000 and purchases on credit of £400 (both amounts exclusive of any VAT). How would these be accounted for in the ledger accounts?

Solution

The sales and purchases must be shown net and the VAT entered in the VAT account. As the sales and purchases were on credit the full double entry would be as follows:

Dr	Receivables account	£1,200
Cr	Sales account	£1,000
Cr	VAT control account	£200

Dr	Purchases account	£400
Dr	VAT control account	£80
Cr	Payables account	£480

Sales account

	£		£
		Receivables	1,000

Receivables account

	£		£
Sales and VAT	1,200		

Purchases account

	£		£
Payables	400		

Payables account

	£		£
		Purchases and VAT	480

VAT control account

	£		£
Payables	80	Receivables	200
Balance c/d	120		
	200		200
		Balance b/d	120

The amount due to HM Revenue and Customs is the balance on the VAT account, £120. We know it is due to HM Revenue Customs as it is brought down on the credit side of the VAT control account – representing a liability.

If a business is not registered for VAT then it will not charge VAT on its sales, and its expenses must be recorded at the gross amount (inclusive of VAT).

If a business is registered for VAT then it will charge VAT on its sales, although they will be recorded as sales at their net amount, and its expenses will also be recorded at the net amount. The output and input VAT is recorded in the VAT account and the difference paid over to HM Revenue and Customs.

1.10 Zero-rated activities

If a business is registered for VAT and sells zero-rated products or services then it charges no VAT on the sales but can still reclaim the input VAT on its purchases and expenses. Such a business will normally be owed VAT by HM Revenue and Customs each quarter.

Example 2

Suppose that a business makes sales on credit of £1,000 plus VAT and purchases on credit of £400 plus VAT. How would these be accounted for if the rate of VAT on the sales was zero, whereas the purchases were standard rated?

Solution

Dr	Receivables	£1,000
Cr	Sales	£1,000
Dr	Purchases	£400
Dr	VAT (400 × 20%)	£80
Cr	Payables	£480

This would leave a debit balance on the VAT control account which is the amount that can be claimed back from HM Revenue and Customs by the business. A debit balance on the VAT control account represents a receivable i.e. a refund is due from HM Revenue and Customs.

1.11 Exempt activities

Certain supplies are exempt from VAT such as financial and postal services.

If a business sells such services then not only is no VAT charged on the sales of the business but also no input VAT can be reclaimed on purchases and expenses.

 Example 3

Suppose that a business makes sales on credit of £1,000 plus VAT and purchases on credit of £400 plus VAT. How would these be accounted for if the sales are exempt activities, whereas the purchases were standard-rated?

Solution

Dr	Receivables	£1,000
Cr	Sales	£1,000
Dr	Purchases	£480
Cr	Payables	£480

There is no VAT on sales due to HM Revenue and Customs and the business cannot claim the £80 from HM Revenue and Customs. However, the seller of the purchases should pay the £80 of VAT over to HM Revenue and Customs.

FINANCIAL ACCOUNTING: PREPARING FINANCIAL STATEMENTS

 Test your understanding 1

A business that is registered for VAT makes credit sales of £110,000 in the period and credit purchases of £75,000. Each of these figures is net of VAT at the standard rate of 20%.

Show how these transactions should be entered into the ledger accounts and state how much VAT is due to HM Revenue and Customs.

1.12 Differences between zero rated and exempt supplies

You must be careful to distinguish between traders making zero rated and exempt supplies.

	Exempt	Zero rated
Can register for VAT?	No	Yes
Charge output VAT to customers?	No	Yes at 0%
Can recover input tax?	No	Yes

 Test your understanding 2

Robbie's business bank account shows administrative expenses of £27,216 which is inclusive of VAT at the standard rate 20%.

Calculate the administrative expenses to be included in the trial balance.

Calculate the VAT figure on administrative expenses for inclusion in the VAT control account.

Update the VAT control account below and find the closing balance figure for VAT.

VAT control account

	£		£
VAT on purchases	35,000	Balance b/d	5,000
Paid to HMRC	5,000	VAT on sales	26,250

KAPLAN PUBLISHING

2 VAT and discounts

2.1 Discounts

A discount is a reduction to the price of the sales of goods or services. There are different types of discounts that may be offered for different reasons. Before we see how discounts impact the calculation of VAT we will review the different types of discounts.

- Trade discount
- Bulk discount
- Prompt payment discount

2.2 Trade discounts

Definition – Trade discount

A trade discount is a definite amount that is deducted from the list price of the goods for the supplies to some customers, with the intention of encouraging and rewarding customer loyalty.

The actual calculation of the trade discount on the face of the invoice should be checked and it should be agreed that the correct percentage of trade discount has been deducted. The deduction of a trade discount will appear on the invoice.

2.3 Bulk discounts

Definition – Bulk discount

A bulk discount is similar to a trade discount in that it is deducted from the list price of the goods and disclosed on the invoice. However, a bulk discount is given by a supplier for sales orders above a certain quantity.

A bulk discount must be checked to the agreement between customer and supplier, to ensure that the correct discount has been deducted. The deduction of a bulk discount will appear on the invoice.

2.4 Prompt payment discount

Definition – Prompt payment discount

Prompt payment discounts (also known as settlement or cash discounts) are offered to customers in order to encourage early payment of invoices.

The details of the prompt payment discount will normally be shown at the bottom of the sales invoice and it is up to the customer to decide whether to pay the invoice early enough to benefit from the prompt payment discount or whether to delay payment and ignore the prompt payment discount. No deduction will occur for a prompt payment discount on the invoice, it will just be offered to the customer.

The agreement between the customer and supplier should be checked to confirm that the correct percentage of prompt payment discount according to the terms has been offered.

A trade discount or a bulk discount is a definite reduction in price from the list price whereas a prompt payment discount is only a reduction in price if the organisation decides to take advantage of it by making early payment.

2.5 VAT calculations and discounts

VAT is calculated after trade and bulk discounts have been deducted from the original list price.

Prompt payment discounts are only offered on an invoice so it does not impact the VAT calculation at the point of the invoice preparation.

If the customer goes on to take advantage of a prompt payment discount offered, the VAT amount is adjusted.

3 Payroll

3.1 Overview of the payroll function

The responsibilities of payroll staff within an organisation include:

- calculating correctly the amount of pay due to each employee,
- ensuring each employee is paid on time with the correct amount,
- ensuring amounts due to external parties such as HM Revenue and Customs are correctly determined and paid on time.

Definition – Gross pay

Gross pay is the wage or salary due to the employee for the amount of work done in the period.

Once the gross pay for each employee has been determined then a number of deductions from this amount will be made to arrive at the net pay for the employee.

Definition – Net pay

Net pay is the amount that the employee will actually receive after appropriate deductions have been made.

Some deductions are compulsory or statutory:

- Income tax in the form of PAYE

Definition – PAYE

The PAYE scheme is a national scheme whereby employers withhold tax and other deductions from their employees' wages and salaries when they are paid. The deductions are then paid over monthly to HM Revenue and Customs by the employer.

- National Insurance Contributions (NIC) which can also be referred to as social security payments

> **Definition – National Insurance**
>
> National Insurance is a state scheme run by HM Revenue and Customs which pays certain benefits including; retirement pensions, widow's allowances and pensions, jobseeker's allowance, incapacity benefit and maternity allowance. The scheme is funded by people who are currently in employment and have earnings above a certain level.

Other deductions are at the choice of the employer or employee and are therefore non-statutory:

- Save as you earn
- Give as you earn
- Pension contributions.

Once the net pay has been determined then each employee must be paid the correct amount, by the most appropriate method at the correct time.

Employers deduct income tax and NIC from each employee's wages or salaries and the employer must also pay its own NIC contribution for each employee. This is done by making payment to HM Revenue and Customs on a regular basis and this is therefore another responsibility of the payroll function.

The payroll staff must ensure that the calculations are made with total accuracy. Not only is the amount that each individual will be paid dependent upon these calculations but there is a statutory duty to make the correct deductions from gross pay and to pay these over to HM Revenue and Customs. Accounting software automates many of the calculations required and the transfer of data into the general ledger.

Payroll staff deal with confidential and sensitive information about individuals such as the rate of pay for an individual. It is of the utmost importance that such details are kept confidential and are not made public nor allowed to be accessed by unauthorised personnel.

3.2 Ledger accounts for wages and salaries

The ledger accounts used to record wages and salaries are:

> The **wages and salaries control account** which acts as a control over the entries in the accounts. All transactions for payroll pass through this account. The control account should have a nil balance when all entries have been dealt with.

Accounting for VAT and payroll: **Chapter 2**

> The **wages expense account** which shows the full cost of employing the staff – the employees' gross pay, the employer's National Insurance Contributions and the employer's pension and voluntary contributions (if applicable).

> The **HMRC liability account** which shows the amount to be paid to HM Revenue and Customs for income tax (PAYE) and National Insurance Contributions.

> The **pension liability account** which records amounts payable to external pension funds – may include both employee and employer contributions.

Note that in the event of there being any other voluntary deductions such as trade union fees there would also be a payable account to reflect this.

3.3 Accounting entries for wages and salaries

Payroll transactions are recorded by journal entries which traces the accounting entry from the payroll record to the journal book to being entered into the general ledger.

The accounting entries for wages and salaries are as follows:

> 1   Dr Wages expense account
>
>   Cr Wages and salaries control account
>
>   with the total expenses relating to the business (gross pay plus employer's NIC).

> 2   Dr Wages and salaries control account
>
>   Cr Bank account
>
>   with the net wages paid to the employees.

> 3   Dr Wages and salaries control account
>
>   Cr HMRC liability
>
>   with those deductions made from the employees which are payable to the HM Revenue and Customs.

FINANCIAL ACCOUNTING: PREPARING FINANCIAL STATEMENTS

If applicable it may also be necessary to record a payable to the pension fund and any other voluntary deductions that are made.

> 4   Dr Wages and salaries control account
>
>   Cr Pension/Other voluntary deduction liability
>
>   with those deductions made from the employees which are payable to the pension fund or other voluntary deduction.

Example 4

The wages and salaries information for an organisation for a week is given as follows:

	£
Gross wages	40,000
PAYE deducted	(8,400)
NIC deducted	(6,600)
Net pay	25,000
Employer's NIC	8,800

Write up the relevant ledger accounts in the general ledger to reflect this.

Solution

Wages and salaries control account

		£			£
2	Bank account	25,000	1	Wages expense account	48,800
3	HMRC Liability (PAYE)	8,400			
3	HMRC Liability (ees NIC)	6,600			
3	HMRC Liability (ers NIC)	8,800			
		48,800			48,800

Wages expense account

		£			£
1	Wages and salaries control	48,800			
				Bal c/d	48,800
		48,800			48,800

HMRC Liability

	£			£
		3 Wages and salaries control		8,400
		3 Wages and salaries control		6,600
Bal c/d	23,800	3 Wages and salaries control		8,800
	23,800			23,800
		Bal b/d		23,800

(a) The wages and salaries control account controls the total gross wages plus the employer's NIC and the amounts paid to the employees, and other organisations (e.g. HM Revenue and Customs for PAYE and NIC). The total gross pay is taken from the company payroll as are the deductions. Assuming that the payroll schedule reconciles and no errors are made when posting the payroll totals to the account, the account should have a nil balance.

(b) The wages expense account shows the total cost to the employer of employing the workforce (£48,800). This is the gross wages cost plus the employer's own NIC cost.

(c) The HMRC Liability account shows the amount due to be paid over to HMRC, i.e. PAYE, employee's NIC plus the employer's NIC.

Test your understanding 3

Given below is a summary of an organisation's payroll details for a week.

	£
Gross wages	54,380
PAYE	11,760
Employee's NIC	8,930
Employer's NIC	12,470

You are required to prepare the journals to enter the figures in the general ledger accounts and to state the balance on the control account, once the net amount has been paid to the employees.

FINANCIAL ACCOUNTING: PREPARING FINANCIAL STATEMENTS

 Test your understanding 4

Rena earns £39,000 per annum. Her deductions for the month are:

	£
PAYE	560
Employee's NIC	285
Employer's pension contributions	120
Employee contribution to pension	110
Employer's NIC	320

Based on the information given, write up the wages expense, wages control, HMRC liability and pension liability accounts.

 ## 4 Summary

For this unit in most cases you will be dealing with VAT registered businesses and therefore you will need to be able to account for VAT and deal with the amount of VAT that is due either to or from HM Revenue and Customs.

In particular you must understand what is meant by the balance on the VAT control account in the trial balance.

We have also reviewed the payroll function and what accounting entries are required. It is important to know, regardless of whether the accounting system is manual or if automated software is used, the ledger accounting entries are the same.

Test your understanding answers

Test your understanding 1

Sales account

	£		£
		RLCA	110,000

Receivables ledger control account

	£		£
Sales + VAT (110,000 + 22,000)	132,000		

Purchases account

	£		£
PLCA	75,000		

VAT control account

	£		£
PLCA (75,000 × 20/100)	15,000	RLCA (110,000 × 20/100)	22,000
Balance c/d	7,000		
	22,000		22,000
		Balance b/d	7,000

Payables ledger control account

	£		£
		Purchases + VAT (75,000 + 15,000)	90,000

The amount due to HM Revenue and Customs is the balance on the VAT control account, £7,000.

Test your understanding 2

1 The amount that should be included in the trial balance is the net amount. As £27,216 is the VAT inclusive amount, the net is calculated as follows:

£27,216 × 100/120 = £22,680 (or £27,216/1.2)

2 The VAT can be calculated using the gross figure £27,216 × 20/120 = £4,536

3 The VAT control would be completed as follows:

VAT control account

	£		£
VAT on purchases	35,000	Balance b/d	5,000
Paid to HMRC	5,000	VAT on sales	26,250
VAT on expenses	**4,536**	**Balance c/d**	**13,286**
	44,536		44,536
Balance b/d	**13,286**		

A debit balance represents a refund due from HMRC.

Test your understanding 3

1 Dr Wages expense account

   Cr Wages and salaries control account

With the total expense of £66,850

2 Dr Wages and salaries control account

   Cr HMRC Liability account

with the PAYE of £11,760, and with the employee's NIC of £8,930 and with the employer's NIC of £12,470

Once the net amount to be paid to the employee has been posted by debiting the wages and salaries control account and crediting the bank account with £33,690 the balance on the control account will be nil.

Test your understanding 4

Solution

Wages and salaries control account

	£		£
Bank account	2,295	Wages expense account	3,690
HMRC Liability (PAYE + both NIC)	1,165		
Pension	230		
	3,690		3,690

Wages expense account

	£		£
Wages and salaries control (Gross + Er's NIC + Er's pension)	3,690	Bal c/d	3,690
	3,690		3,690

HMRC liability

	£		£
		Wages and salaries control	1,165
Bal c/d	1,165		
	1,165		1,165

Pension liability

	£		£
		Wages and salaries control	230
Bal c/d	230		
	230		230

FINANCIAL ACCOUNTING: PREPARING FINANCIAL STATEMENTS

Capital and revenue expenditure

Introduction

In this chapter we will start to look at the details of authorising and accounting for capital expenditure. We will progress this syllabus area by covering accounting for non-current asset acquisitions, depreciation and disposals.

ASSESSMENT CRITERIA	CONTENTS
Importance of prior authority for capital expenditure (3.1)	1 Capital and revenue expenditure
The importance of classifying expenditure into capital or revenue expenditure (3.2)	2 Recording the purchase of non-current assets
Record acquisitions and disposals of non-current assets (3.3)	3 Types of non-current assets
	4 Non-current assets register

1 Capital and revenue expenditure

1.1 Introduction

In the statement of financial position, assets are split between non-current assets and current assets.

1.2 Non-current assets

Definition – Non-current asset

The non-current assets of a business are the assets that were purchased with the intention of long-term use within the business.

Examples of non-current assets include buildings, machinery, motor vehicles, office fixtures and fittings and computer equipment.

1.3 Capital expenditure

Definition – Capital expenditure

Capital expenditure is expenditure on the purchase or improvement of non-current assets.

The purchase of non-current assets such as property, plant and equipment are known as capital expenditure. This means that the cost of the non-current asset is initially taken to the statement of financial position rather than the statement of profit or loss. We will see in a later Chapter how this cost is then charged to the statement of profit or loss over the life of the non-current asset by the process of depreciation.

1.4 Revenue expenditure

Definition – Revenue expenditure

Revenue expenditure is all other expenditure incurred by the business other than capital expenditure.

When determining whether a purchase should be treated as capital or revenue expenditure it is important to consider how significant the cost is i.e. materiality. For example, an item of stationery such as a stapler may be used for a long time within a business but the cost is rather insignificant.

Revenue expenditure is charged as an expense to the statement of profit or loss in the period that it is incurred.

Capital expenditure is shown as a non-current asset in the statement of financial position.

1.5 Authorising capital expenditure

There are different factors that need to be considered with capital expenditure:

Non-current assets can be expensive – Many types of non-current assets are relatively expensive. Most non-current assets will be used to generate income for the business for several years into the future. Therefore, they are important purchases.

Funding options – Timing may also be critical. It may be necessary to arrange a bank overdraft or a loan, or alternatively capital expenditure may have to be delayed in order to avoid a bank overdraft.

Process for authorisation – For these reasons, most organisations have procedures whereby capital expenditure must be authorised by an appropriate person such as a director.

The method of recording the authorisation is also likely to vary according to the nature and size of the organisation, and according to the type of non-current asset expenditure it normally undertakes. In a small business, there may be no formal record other than a signature on a cheque.

In a large company, the directors may record their approval of significant expenditure in the minutes of a board meeting. Other possibilities include the use of requisition forms and signing of the invoice.

In most organisations, disposals of non-current assets must also be authorised in writing.

Where standard forms are used, these will vary from organisation to organisation, but the details for acquisition of an asset are likely to include:

- date
- description of asset
- reason for purchase
- supplier
- cost/quotation

- details of quotation (if applicable)
- details of lease agreement (if applicable)
- authorisation
- method of financing.

Levels of authorisation – In small organisations, most non-current asset purchases are likely to be authorised by the owner of the business. In large organisations, there is normally a system whereby several people have the authority to approve capital expenditure up to a certain limit which depends on the person's level of seniority. The number of signatures required will vary according to the organisation's procedures.

Test your understanding 1

When authorising the purchase of a new machine, choose the most suitable policy.

New machinery purchases should be authorised by:

(a) The office assistant

(b) The accounting technician

(c) The machine operator

(d) A director of the business

2 Recording the purchase of non-current assets

2.1 Introduction

We have seen that the cost of a non-current asset will appear in the statement of financial position as capitalised expenditure. Therefore, it is important that the correct figure for cost is included in the correct ledger account.

IAS 16 – Property, Plant & Equipment

This standard sets out the accounting treatment for property, plant and equipment. It is important to know what can be included in the cost of a non-current asset and what cannot.

Key features of IAS 16 include the definition of terms that you will encounter throughout your studies of non-current assets including depreciation.

2.2 Cost

The cost figure that will be used to record the non-current asset is the full purchase price of the asset. Care should be taken when considering the cost of some assets, in particular motor cars, as the invoice may show that the total amount paid includes some revenue expenditure, for example petrol and road fund licences. These elements of revenue expenditure must be written off to the statement of profit or loss and only the capital expenditure included as the cost of the non-current asset.

 Definition – Cost

Cost should include the cost of the asset and the cost of getting the asset to its current location and into working condition. Therefore, cost is:

Purchase price + additional costs*

*Additional costs may include delivery costs, legal and professional fees, installation costs (site preparation and construction) and test runs.

2.3 Ledger accounts

If a non-current asset is paid for via bank payment or cheque, the double entry is:

    Dr   Non-current asset account
    Cr   Bank account

If the non-current asset was bought on credit the double entry is:

    Dr   Non-current asset account
    Cr   Payables/loan account

Capital and revenue expenditure: Chapter 3

In practice most organisations will have different non-current asset accounts for the different types of property, plant and equipment, for example:

- land and buildings account
- plant and machinery account
- motor vehicles account
- office fixtures and fittings account
- computer equipment account.

Test your understanding 2

When a business purchases disks for a new computer, the amount of the purchase is debited to computer equipment (cost) account.

(a) Is this treatment correct?
(b) If so, why; if not, why not?

Test your understanding 3

Stapling machine

When a business purchases a new stapler so that the office staff can staple together relevant pieces of paper, the amount of the purchase is debited to the fittings and equipment (cost) account.

(a) Is this treatment correct?
(b) If so, why; if not; why not?

Test your understanding 4

Office equipment

A business bought a small item of computer software costing £32.50. This had been treated as office equipment. Do you agree with this treatment?

Give brief reasons.

FINANCIAL ACCOUNTING: PREPARING FINANCIAL STATEMENTS

 Test your understanding 5

Engine

If an airline replaces one of its plane's engines, which are depreciated at a different rate to the rest of the plane's components, at a cost of £1,800,000 would this represent capital or revenue expenditure? Give brief reasons.

2.4 Purchase of non-current assets and VAT

When most non-current assets are purchased VAT will be added and this can normally be recovered from HMRC as input VAT. Therefore, the cost of the non-current asset is the amount net of VAT.

 Test your understanding 6

A piece of machinery has been purchased on credit from a supplier for £4,200 plus VAT.

How will this purchase be recorded?

	Account name	Amount £
Dr	Machinery/Building/Fixtures	4,200/5,040
Dr	Machinery/VAT/Payables	5,040/840
Cr	Bank /Payables/VAT	4,200/5,040

Circle the correct account name and the amount.

2.5 Purchase of cars and VAT

As a general rule, when new cars are purchased it is not possible for the VAT to be recovered, unless it is an excepted car. Therefore, the cost to be capitalised for the car must include the VAT.

An excepted car is one used exclusively for business use and is not available for any private use.

Example 1

Kenji has just purchased a new car for his business, paying by bank transfer and an extract from the invoice shows the following:

	£
Cost of car	18,000
Road fund licence	155
	18,155
VAT on cost of car (£18,000 × 20%)	3,600
Total cost	21,755

Record this cost in the ledger accounts of the business.

Motor cars account

	£		£
Bank (18,000 + 3,600)	21,600		

Motor expenses account

	£		£
Bank	155		

Bank account

	£		£
		Motor vehicle + expenses	21,755

Note that only the motor cars account balance would appear in the statement of financial position, i.e. be capitalised, while the motor expenses account balance would appear in the statement of profit or loss as an expense for the period.

2.6 The journal

Non-current asset acquisitions do not normally take place frequently in organisations and many organisations will tend to record the acquisition in the journal day book.

 Definition – Journal day book

The journal day book is a primary record which is used for transactions that do not appear in the other primary records of the business.

The journal will tend to take the form of an instruction to the bookkeeper as to which accounts to debit and credit and what this transaction is for.

An example of a journal for the purchase of an item of property, plant and equipment is given below.

Journal entry			No: 02714
Date	20 May 20X1		
Prepared by	C Jones		
Authorised by	F Peters		
Account	**Code**	**Debit £**	**Credit £**
Computers: Cost	0120	5,000	
VAT	0138	1,000	
Bank	0163		6,000
Totals		6,000	6,000

Capital and revenue expenditure: Chapter 3

 Test your understanding 7

Below is an invoice for the purchase of a motor car purchased on the 1 June 20X1. The payment was made by bank transfer.

The business's year end is 31 December 20X1

	£
Cost of car	20,000
Road fund licence	165
	20,165
VAT on cost of car (£20,000 × 20%)	4,000
	24,165

Note that in the assessment you may be given different forms to fill in for journal entries, and may be told to ignore any reference columns for the entry. Complete the journal entries to record the purchase of the asset.

Ref	Account name	Dr (£)	Cr (£)

2.7 Non-current assets produced internally

In some instances, a business may make its own non-current assets. For example, a construction company may construct a new head office for the organisation.

Where non-current assets are produced internally then the amount that should be capitalised as the cost is the production cost of the asset.

 Definition – Production cost

Production cost is the direct cost of production (materials, labour and expenses) plus an appropriate amount of the normal production overheads relating to production of this asset.

2.8 Capitalising subsequent expenditure

It is frequently the case that there will be further expenditure on a non-current asset during its life in the business. In most cases this will be classed as revenue expenditure and will therefore be charged to the statement of profit or loss. However, in some cases the expenditure may be so major that it should also be capitalised as an addition to the cost of the non-current asset.

IAS 16 Property, Plant and Equipment states that subsequent expenditure should only be capitalised in three circumstances:

- where it enhances the value of the asset
- where a major component of the asset is replaced or restored
- where it is a major inspection or overhaul of the asset.

2.9 Financing non-current asset acquisitions

Non-current assets generally cost a lot of money and are purchased with the intention that they be used over a period of years. For most businesses the full purchase cost cannot be funded from cash available in the business, and so other financing methods must be found. These may include borrowing, leasing or part exchanging an existing asset.

Factors such as the availability of finance, the overall cost of each finance method, the cash flow requirements to meet repayments and any required security for the debt would be considered as part of the authorisation process, prior to making the purchase.

3 Types of non-current assets

3.1 Introduction

We have seen how the non-current assets of a business will be classified between the various types, e.g. buildings, plant and machinery, etc. However, there is a further distinction in the classification of non-current assets that must be considered. This is the distinction between tangible non-current assets and intangible non-current assets.

3.2 Tangible non-current assets

 Definition – Tangible non-current asset

Tangible non-current assets are assets which have a tangible, physical form.

Tangible non-current assets therefore are all of the types of assets that we have been considering so far such as machinery, cars, computers, etc.

3.3 Intangible non-current assets

 Definition – Intangible non-current asset

Intangible non-current assets are assets for long-term use in the business that have no physical form e.g. patents, licences and goodwill.

 Definition – Goodwill

Goodwill is the asset arising from the fact that a going concern business is worth more in total than the total value of its tangible net assets. Goodwill can arise from many different factors including good reputation, good location, quality products and quality after sales service.

4 Non-current assets register

4.1 Introduction

The non-current assets of a business will tend to be expensive items that the organisation will wish to have good control over. In particular the organisation will wish to keep control over which assets are kept where and check on a regular basis that they are still there.

Most organisations that own a significant number of non-current assets will tend to maintain a non-current assets register as well as the ledger accounts that record the purchase of the non-current assets. A non-current asset register may be part of the accounting software or it may be held independently on a spreadsheet. It forms a record from which control can be maintained through physical verifications and reconciliations with the ledger accounts.

4.2 Layout of a non-current assets register

The purpose of a non-current assets register is to record all relevant details of all of the non-current assets of the organisation. The format of the register will depend on the organisation and the accounting software used, but the information to be recorded for each non-current asset of the business will probably include the following:

- asset description
- asset identification code/barcode
- asset location/member of staff the asset has been issued to
- date of purchase
- purchase price
- supplier name and address
- invoice number
- any additional enhancement expenditure
- depreciation method
- estimated useful life
- estimated residual value
- accumulated depreciation to date
- carrying amount
- disposal details.

A typical format for a non-current assets register is shown below.

4.3 Example of a non-current assets register

Date of purchase	Invoice number	Serial number	Item	Cost	Accum'd depreciation b/f at 1.1.X8	Date of disposal	Dep'n charge in 20X8	Accum'd depreciation c/f	Disposal proceeds	Loss/gain on disposal
				£	£		£	£	£	£
3.2.X5	345	3488	Chair	340						
6.4.X6	466	–	Bookcase	258						
10.7.X7	587	278	Chair	160						
				───						
				758						
				───						

There may also be a further column or detail which shows exactly where the particular asset is located within the business. This will facilitate checks that should be regularly carried out to ensure all of the assets the business owns are still on the premises.

Test your understanding 8

Record the cost of the motor car in the non-current assets register below for the previous Activity 7.

Date of purchase	Invoice number	Serial number	Item	Cost	Accum'd depreciation b/f at 1.1.X8	Date of disposal	Depreciation charge in 20X8	Accum'd depreciation c/f	Disposal proceeds	Loss/gain on disposal
				£	£		£	£	£	£
				——						
				——						

Test your understanding 9

1. Purchase of a motor van is classified as **revenue / capital** expenditure?

2. Decorating the office is an example of **revenue / capital** expenditure.

3. Other than its actual purchase price, what additional costs can be capitalised as part of the cost of the non-current asset?

4. What are the three occasions where subsequent expenditure on a non-current asset can be capitalised according to IAS 16?

5. Goodwill is an example of **a tangible asset / a current asset / an intangible asset**?

5 Summary

In this chapter we have considered the acquisition of non-current assets. The acquisition of property, plant and equipment must be properly authorised and the most appropriate method of funding will be considered as part of this process. The correct cost figure must be used when capitalising the non-current asset and care should be taken with VAT and the exclusion of any revenue expenditure in the total cost. The details of the acquisition of the asset should also be included in the non-current assets register.

Test your understanding answers

Test your understanding 1

The answer is D.

Test your understanding 2

(a) No.

(b) Although, by definition, the computer disks may be considered as non-current assets, their treatment would come within the remit of the concept of materiality and would probably be treated as office expenses – revenue expenditure.

Test your understanding 3

Stapling machine

(a) No.

(b) Although, by definition, since the stapler will last a few years, it might seem to be a non-current asset, its treatment would come within the remit of the concept of materiality as it is likely to be an insignificant cost and would be treated as office expenses.

Test your understanding 4

Office equipment

The item will have value in future years and could therefore be regarded as a non-current asset. However, the stronger argument is that this is not justified by the relatively small amount involved and the concept of materiality would suggest treatment as an expense of the year.

Test your understanding 5

Engine

This would typically represent capital expenditure. As the engine is being depreciated separately from the rest of the plane it is effectively an asset in its own right. The replacement of the separate component is like the purchase of a new asset.

If, on the other hand, the engine was depreciated as part of the plane as a whole it is likely that the replacement cost would simply be treated as a repair/refurbishment cost and would be accounted for as an expense.

Test your understanding 6

	Account name	Amount £
Dr	Machinery	4,200
Dr	VAT	840
Cr	Payables	5,040

Test your understanding 7

Ref	Account name	Dr (£)	Cr (£)
	Motor car	24,000	
	Motor expenses	165	
	Bank		24,165

FINANCIAL ACCOUNTING: PREPARING FINANCIAL STATEMENTS

Test your understanding 8

Date of purchase	Invoice number	Serial number	Item	Cost	Accum'd depreciation b/f at 1.1.X8	Date of disposal	Depreciation charge in 20X8	Accum'd depreciation c/f	Disposal proceeds	Loss/gain on disposal
				£	£		£	£	£	£
1 Jun X1			Motor car	24,000						
				24,000						

Test your understanding 9

1 Capital expenditure.

2 Revenue expenditure.

3 The full purchase price of the asset plus the cost of getting the asset to its location and into working condition.

4 Where the expenditure enhances the economic benefits of the asset.

   Where the expenditure is on a major component which is being replaced or restored.

   Where the expenditure is on a major inspection or overhaul of the asset.

5 Intangible asset.

FINANCIAL ACCOUNTING: PREPARING FINANCIAL STATEMENTS

Depreciation

Introduction

This chapter reviews how to prepare and record depreciation calculations.

You need to be able to:

- understand the purpose of depreciation
- choose and use appropriate methods and rates of depreciation, considering the expected pattern of usage of the asset and the estimated useful life of the acquisition
- record depreciation in the non-current assets register and the general ledger using the following accounts: depreciation charges, non-current asset and non-current asset accumulated depreciation.

ASSESSMENT CRITERIA	CONTENTS
Calculate depreciation (4.1)	1 The purpose of depreciation
Record depreciation (4.2)	2 Calculating depreciation
	3 Assets acquired during an accounting period
	4 Accounting for depreciation
	5 Depreciation in the non-current assets register

1 The purpose of depreciation

1.1 Introduction

We have already seen that property, plant and equipment are capitalised in the accounting records which means that they are treated as capital expenditure and their cost is initially recorded in the statement of financial position and not charged to the statement of profit or loss. However, this is not the end of the story and this cost figure must eventually go through the statement of profit or loss by means of the annual depreciation charge.

1.2 Accruals principle

The need to depreciate arises from the accruals principle. The amount spent on an asset must be charged against profits. However, if the asset contributes to the generation of income over a number of periods it would not be appropriate to charge any single period with the whole cost. Instead we find a way to spread the cost of the asset over its useful life.

1.3 What is depreciation?

Definition – Depreciation

Depreciation is the measure of the cost of the economic benefits of the tangible non-current assets that have been consumed during the period.

Depreciation does not provide for the loss in value of an asset, it is an accrual accounting technique that allocates the depreciable amount of the asset to the periods expected to benefit from the use of the asset.

Definition – Depreciable amount

The depreciable amount is the cost of an asset less any residual value. This is the amount that will be depreciated in full by the end of the estimated useful life.

1.4 How does depreciation work?

The basic principle of depreciation is that a proportion of the cost of the non-current asset is charged to the statement of profit or loss each period and deducted from the cost of the non-current asset in the statement of financial position. This is to follow the pattern of the consumption of benefits from the use of the asset. Over an asset's useful life, its value in the statement of financial position reduces and each year the statement of profit or loss is charged with this proportion of the initial cost.

> **Definition – Carrying amount**
>
> The carrying amount is the cost of the non-current asset less the accumulated depreciation to date.

	£
Cost	X
Less: Accumulated depreciation	(X)
Carrying amount	X

The carrying amount will probably have little relation to the actual market value of the asset at each statement of financial position date. The important aspect of depreciation is that it is a charge to the statement of profit or loss to reflect the amount of economic benefit consumed by the business from the use of the property, plant or equipment during the year.

2 Calculating depreciation

2.1 Introduction

There are two methods of depreciation you are required to be able to calculate by the assessment criteria of Financial Accounting: Preparing Financial Statements.

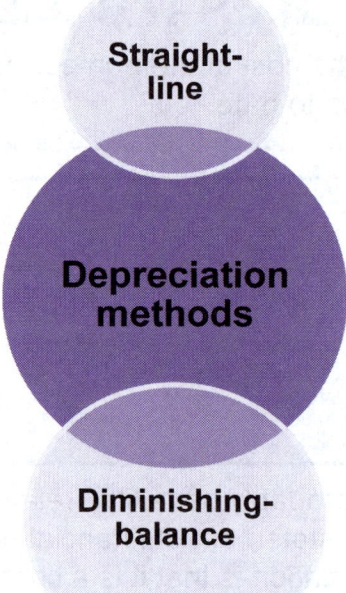

Each of these methods will be reviewed within this chapter. The principles behind each method are relatively the same. In practice, depreciation can be calculated automatically by accounting software or independently using spreadsheets and preparing journals.

2.2 Factors affecting depreciation

There are three factors that affect the depreciation of a non-current asset:

- the **cost** of the asset (dealt with in Chapter 3 Capital and Revenue Expenditure)
- the length of the **useful life** of the asset
- the **estimated residual value** of the asset.

2.3 Useful life

Definition – Useful life

The useful life of an asset is the estimated life of the asset for the current owner. This can be defined in time (number of years) or in output (activity).

This is the estimated number of years or estimated activity level that the business will be using the asset for and therefore the number of years / output level over which the cost of the asset must be spread via the depreciation charge.

The length of the useful life of the asset for the straight-line and diminishing-balance method is considered to be in terms of time. There are alternative methods such as the units of production method where the useful life is in terms of output i.e. activity level.

One particular point to note here is that land is viewed as having an infinite life and therefore no depreciation charge is required for land. However, any buildings on the land should be depreciated.

2.4 Estimated residual value

Many assets will be sold for a form of scrap value at the end of their useful lives.

Definition – Residual value

The estimated residual value of a non-current asset is the amount that is estimated the asset will be sold for when it is no longer of use to the business.

The aim of depreciation is to write off the cost of the non-current asset less the estimated residual value over the useful life of the asset.

2.5 The straight-line method of depreciation

 Definition – Straight-line method

The straight-line method calculates a consistent amount of depreciation over the life of the asset.

The method of calculating depreciation under this method is:

$$\text{Annual depreciation charge} = \frac{\text{Cost} - \text{estimated residual value}}{\text{Useful life}}$$

It should be noted that it is possible to multiply the depreciable amount by a percentage, e.g. instead of dividing by four years you can multiply by 25%; instead of dividing by five years you can multiply by 20%.

 Example 1

An asset has been purchased by an organisation for £400,000 and is expected to be used in the organisation for 6 years. At the end of the six-year period it is currently estimated that the asset will be sold for £40,000.

What is the annual depreciation charge using the straight-line basis?

Solution

$$\text{Annual depreciation charge} = \frac{400,000 - 40,000}{6}$$

$$= £60,000$$

2.6 The diminishing balance method

 Definition – Diminishing-balance method

The diminishing-balance method of depreciation allows a higher amount of depreciation to be charged in the early years of an asset's life compared to the later years. This reflects the increased levels of usage of such assets in the earlier periods of their lives.

The depreciation is calculated using this method by multiplying the carrying amount of the asset at the start of the year by a fixed percentage.

Annual depreciation charge = Carrying amount × %

FINANCIAL ACCOUNTING: PREPARING FINANCIAL STATEMENTS

 Example 2

A non-current asset has a cost of £100,000.

It is to be depreciated using the diminishing-balance method at 30% over its useful life of four years, after which it will have an estimated residual value of £24,000.

Show the amount of depreciation charged for each of the four years of the asset's life.

Solution

	£
Cost	100,000
Year 1 depreciation 30% × 100,000	(30,000)
Carrying amount at the end of year 1	70,000
Year 2 depreciation 30% × 70,000	(21,000)
Carrying amount at the end of year 2	49,000
Year 3 depreciation 30% × 49,000	(14,700)
Carrying amount at the end of year 3	34,300
Year 4 depreciation 30% × 34,300	(10,290)
Carrying amount at the end of year 4	24,010

 Test your understanding 1

A business buys a motor van for £20,000 and depreciates it at 10% per annum using the diminishing-balance method.

Calculate:

- The depreciation charge for the second year of the motor van's use.
- Calculate the carrying amount at the end of the second year.

Depreciation: Chapter 4

Solution

	£
Cost	
Year 1 depreciation	_____
Carrying amount at the end of year 1	
Year 2 depreciation	_____
Carrying amount at the end of year 2	_____

2.7 Choice of method

Whether a business chooses the straight-line method of depreciation or the diminishing-balance method (or indeed any of the other methods which are outside the scope of this syllabus) is the choice of the management. An assessment of suitability should be made.

The straight-line method is the simplest method to use. Often, the Diminishing-balance method is chosen for assets which do in fact reduce in value more in the early years of their life than the later years. This is often the case with cars and computers and the diminishing-balance method is often used for these assets.

Once the method of depreciation has been chosen for a particular class of non-current assets then this same method should be used each year in order to satisfy the accounting objective of comparability. The management of a business can change the method of depreciation used for a class of non-current assets but this should only be done if the new method shows a truer picture of the consumption of the cost of the asset than the previous method.

Test your understanding 2

Give one reason why a business might choose diminishing-balance as the method for depreciating its delivery vans?

(a) It is an easy method to apply.

(b) It is the method applied for non-current assets for which higher benefits are consumed in the earlier years with reducing benefits as the years of use pass by.

(c) It is the method that is most consistent.

3 Assets acquired during an accounting period

3.1 Introduction

So far in our calculations of the depreciation charge for the year we have ignored precisely when in the year the non-current asset was purchased. Pro rata calculations for the straight-line method of depreciation will be required only when the organisational policy stipulates.

There are two main methods of expressing a depreciation policy and both of these will now be considered.

3.2 Calculations on a monthly basis

The policy may state that depreciation is to be charged on a monthly basis. This means that the annual charge will be calculated using the depreciation method given and then pro-rated for the number of months in the year that the asset has been owned.

Example 3

A piece of machinery is purchased on 1 June 20X1 for £20,000. It has a useful life of 5 years and zero scrap value. The organisation's accounting year ends on 31 December.

What is the depreciation charge for 20X1? Depreciation is charged on a monthly basis using the straight-line method.

Solution

Annual charge = $\dfrac{£20,000}{5}$ = £4,000

Charge for 20X1: £4,000 × 7/12 (i.e. June to Dec) = £2,333

Depreciation: **Chapter 4**

 Test your understanding 3

A business buys a machine for £40,000 on 1 January 20X3 and another one on 1 July 20X3 for £48,000.

Depreciation is charged at 10% per annum on cost, and calculated on a monthly basis.

What is the total depreciation charge for the two machines for the year ended 31 December 20X3?

3.3 Acquisition and disposal policy

The second method of dealing with depreciation in the year of acquisition is to have a depreciation policy as follows:

'A full year's depreciation is charged in the year of acquisition and none in the year of disposal.'

Ensure that you read the instructions in any question carefully as in the exam you will always be given the depreciation policy of the business.

 Test your understanding 4

A business purchased a motor van on 7 August 20X3 at a cost of £12,640.

It is depreciated on a straight-line basis using an expected useful life of five years and estimated residual value of zero.

Depreciation is charged with a full year's depreciation in the year of purchase and none in the year of sale.

The business has a year end of 30 November.

Required:

What is the carrying amount of the motor van at 30 November 20X4?

What does this amount represent?

FINANCIAL ACCOUNTING: PREPARING FINANCIAL STATEMENTS

4 Accounting for depreciation

4.1 Introduction

Now we have seen how to calculate depreciation we must now learn how to account for it in the ledger accounts within the general ledger.

4.2 Dual effect of depreciation

The two effects of the charge for depreciation each year are:

- there is an expense to the statement of profit or loss and therefore a debit entry to a depreciation charges account
- there is a requirement to create a provision for accumulated depreciation by crediting this account.

Definition – Provision for accumulated depreciation

The provision for accumulated depreciation account (sometimes referred to as accumulated depreciation) is used to reduce the value of the non-current asset in the statement of financial position.

Example 4

An asset has been purchased by an organisation for £400,000 and is expected to be used in the organisation for six years.

At the end of the six-year period it is currently estimated that the residual value will be £40,000.

The asset is to be depreciated on the straight-line basis.

Show the entries in the ledger accounts for the first two years of the asset's life and how this asset would appear in the statement of financial position at the end of each of the first two years.

Solution

Step 1

Record the purchase of the asset in the non-current asset account.

Non-current asset account

	£		£
Year 1 Bank	400,000		

Step 2

Record the depreciation expense for Year 1.

$$\text{Depreciation charge} = \frac{£400,000 - £40,000}{6}$$

$$= £60,000 \text{ per year}$$

Dr Depreciation charges account
Cr Accumulated depreciation account

Depreciation charges account

	£		£
Year 1 Accumulated depreciation	60,000		

Accumulated depreciation account

	£		£
		Dep'n charges	60,000

Note the statement of financial position will show the cost of the asset and the accumulated depreciation is then deducted to arrive at the carrying amount of the asset.

Step 3

Show the entries for the year 2 depreciation charge

Depreciation charges account

	£		£
Year 2 Accumulated depreciation	60,000		

Accumulated depreciation account

	£		£
		Balance b/d	60,000
		Dep'n charges	60,000

Note that the expense account has no opening balance as this was transferred to the statement of profit or loss at the end of year 1.

However, the accumulated depreciation account being a statement of financial position account is a continuing account and does have an opening balance being the depreciation charged so far on this asset.

Step 4

Balance off the accumulated depreciation account and show how the non-current asset would appear in the statement of financial position at the end of year 2.

Accumulated depreciation account

	£		£
		Balance b/d	60,000
Balance c/d	120,000	Dep'n charges	60,000
	120,000		120,000
		Balance b/d	120,000

Statement of financial position extract

	Cost £	Accumulated depreciation £	Carrying amount £
Non-current asset	400,000	120,000	280,000

KAPLAN PUBLISHING

Test your understanding 5

The following task is about recording non-current asset information in the general ledger.

A new asset has been acquired. VAT can be reclaimed on this asset.

- The cost of the asset excluding VAT is £85,000 and this was paid for by bank transfer.
- The residual value is expected to be £5,000 excluding VAT.
- The asset is to be depreciated using the straight-line basis and the assets useful life is 5 years.

Make entries to account for:

(a) The purchase of the new asset.

(b) The depreciation on the new asset.

Asset at cost account

£	£

Accumulated depreciation

£	£

Depreciation charges

£	£

4.3 Carrying amount

As you have seen from the statement of financial position extract the non-current assets are shown at their carrying amount. As previously stated, the carrying amount is made up of the cost of the asset less the accumulated depreciation on that asset or class of assets.

The carrying amount is purely an accounting value for the non-current asset. It is not an attempt to place a market value or current value on the asset and it in fact often bears little relation to the actual value of the asset.

 Test your understanding 6

At 31 March 20X3, a business owned a motor vehicle which had a cost of £12,100 and accumulated depreciation of £9,075.

Complete the statement of financial position extract below.

	Cost	Accumulated depreciation	Carrying amount
Motor vehicle			

4.4 Ledger entries

No matter what method of depreciation is used whether it is the straight-line method, or the diminishing-balance method, the ledger entries are always the same.

 Example 5

On 1 April 20X2 a machine was purchased for £12,000 with an estimated useful life of 4 years and estimated scrap value of £4,920. The machine is to be depreciated at 20% diminishing-balance.

The ledger accounts for the years ended 31 March 20X3, 31 March 20X4 and 31 March 20X5 are to be written up.

Show how the non-current asset would appear in the statement of financial position at each of these dates.

Solution

Step 1

Calculate the depreciation charge.

			£
Cost			12,000
Year-end March 20X3 – depreciation	12,000 × 20%	=	2,400
			9,600
Year-end March 20X4 – depreciation	9,600 × 20%	=	1,920
			7,680
Year-end March 20X5 – depreciation	7,680 × 20%	=	1,536
			6,144

Step 2

Enter each year's figures in the ledger accounts bringing down a balance on the machinery account and accumulated depreciation account but clearing out the entry in the expense account to the statement of profit or loss.

Machinery account

	£		£
April 20X2 Bank	12,000	Mar 20X3 Balance c/d	12,000
April 20X3 Balance b/d	12,000	Mar 20X4 Balance c/d	12,000
April 20X4 Balance b/d	12,000	Mar 20X5 Balance c/d	12,000
April 20X5 Balance b/d	12,000		

Depreciation charges account

	£		£
Mar 20X3 Accumulated dep'n a/c	2,400	Mar 20X3 SPL	2,400
Mar 20X4 Accumulated dep'n a/c	1,920	Mar 20X4 SPL	1,920
Mar 20X5 Accumulated dep'n a/c	1,536	Mar 20X5 SPL	1,536

Machinery: accumulated depreciation account

	£		£
Mar 20X3 Balance c/d	2,400	Mar 20X3 Depreciation charges	2,400
		Apr 20X3 Balance b/d	2,400
Mar 20X4 Balance c/d	4,320	Mar 20X4 Depreciation charges	1,920
	4,320		4,320
		Apr 20X4 Balance b/d	4,320
Mar 20X5 Balance c/d	5,856	Mar 20X5 Depreciation charges	1,536
	5,856		5,856
		Apr 20X5 Balance b/d	5,856

Statement of financial position extract

Non-current assets		Cost £	Accumulated depreciation £	Carrying amount £
At 31 Mar 20X3	Machinery	12,000	2,400	9,600
At 31 Mar 20X4	Machinery	12,000	4,320	7,680
At 31 Mar 20X5	Machinery	12,000	5,856	6,144

Make sure that you remember to carry down the accumulated depreciation at the end of each period as the opening balance at the start of the next period.

> **Test your understanding 7**
>
> ABC Co owns the following assets as at 31 December 20X6:
>
> | | £ |
> |---|---|
> | Plant and machinery | 5,000 |
> | Office furniture | 800 |
>
> Depreciation is to be provided as follows:
>
> (a) plant and machinery, 20% diminishing-balance method
>
> (b) office furniture, 25% on cost per year, straight-line method.
>
> The plant and machinery were purchased on 1 January 20X4 and the office furniture on 1 January 20X5.
>
> **Required:**
>
> Show the ledger accounts for the year ended 31 December 20X6 necessary to record the transactions.

5 Depreciation in the non-current assets register

5.1 Introduction

In the previous Chapter we considered how the cost of non-current assets and their acquisition details should be recorded in the non-current assets register.

5.2 Recording depreciation in the non-current assets register

Let us now look at recording depreciation in the non-current assets register. Remember this may be recorded on a spreadsheet or the register may form part of accounting software.

Example 6

Date of purchase	Invoice number	Serial number	Item	Cost	Accum'd depreciation b/f at 1.1.X8	Date of disposal	Depreciation charge in 20X8	Accum'd depreciation c/f	Disposal proceeds	Loss/ gain on disposal
				£	£		£	£	£	£
3.2.X5	345	3488	Chair	340						
6.4.X6	466	–	Bookcase	258						
10.7.X7	587	278	Chair	160						
				758						

Using the example from the previous Chapter, reproduced above, we have now decided that fixtures and fittings (including office furniture) should be depreciated at 10% per annum using the straight-line method.

A full year's depreciation is charged in the year of purchase and none in the year of disposal.

The current year is the year to 31 December 20X8.

The chair acquired on 10.7.X7 was sold on 12.7.X8. A new table was purchased for £86 on 30.8.X8.

Do not worry at this stage about the disposal proceeds. We will look at disposals in the next Chapter.

Solution

Date of purchase	Invoice number	Serial number	Item	Cost	Accum'd depreciation b/f at 1.1.X8	Date of disposal	Depreciation charge in 20X8	Accum'd depreciation c/f	Disposal proceeds	Loss/ gain on disposal
				£	£		£	£	£	£
3.2.X5	345	3488	Chair	340	102 (W1)		34	136		
6.4.X6	466	–	Bookcase	258	52 (W2)		26	78		
10.7.X7	587	278	Chair	160	16 (W3)	12.7.X8	– (W4)	–		
30.8.X8	634	1,228	Table	86			9	9		
				844	170		69	223		

Workings:

(W1) 3 years' depreciation — £340 × 10% × 3 years = £102

(W2) 2 years' depreciation — £258 × 10% × 2 years = £52

(W3) 1 year's depreciation — £160 × 10% = £16

(W4) No depreciation in year of sale

Note how the depreciation charge is calculated for each asset except the one disposed of in the year as the accounting policy is to charge no depreciation in the year of sale. If the policy was to charge depreciation even in the year of disposal, then the charge would be calculated and included in the total.

The total accumulated depreciation should agree with the balance carried forward on the accumulated depreciation ledger account in the general ledger.

Depreciation: Chapter 4

 Test your understanding 8

A business called Stig Trading has asked your advice on improving their accounting system. They would like your advice on how to improve the records of non-current assets.

The business produces fashion clothing. They have the following information on the sewing machines in the business.

Machine number	Cost £
SEW 789367	15,500
ING 401388	25,000
MAC 402765	21,500

(a) Which accounting record would you suggest that the business should keep to record the details of these machines?

(b) Name three additional items that you would suggest to the business that they should keep a record of, regarding the machines?

(c) Name one advantage of recording the machines in the record that you have suggested in part (a).

 Test your understanding 9

Mead is a sole trader with a 31 December year end. He purchased a car on 1 January 20X3 at a cost of £12,000. He estimates that its useful life is four years, after which he will trade it in for £2,400. The annual depreciation charge is to be calculated using the straight-line method.
Task

Write up the motor car cost and accumulated depreciation accounts and the depreciation charges account for the first three years, bringing down a balance on each account at the end of each year.

FINANCIAL ACCOUNTING: PREPARING FINANCIAL STATEMENTS

Test your understanding 10

S Telford purchases a machine for £6,000. He estimates that the machine will last eight years and its scrap value then will be £1,000.

Tasks

1. Prepare the machine cost and accumulated depreciation accounts for the first three years of the machine's life, and show the statement of financial position extract at the end of each of these years charging depreciation on the straight-line method.
2. What would be the carrying amount of the machine at the end of the third year if depreciation was charged at 20% on the diminishing-balance method?

Test your understanding 11

Hillton

(a) Hillton started a veggie food manufacturing business on 1 January 20X6. During the first three years of trading he bought machinery as follows:

January	20X6	Chopper	Cost	£4,000
April	20X7	Mincer	Cost	£6,000
June	20X8	Stuffer	Cost	£8,000

Each machine was bought for cash.

Hillton's policy for machinery is to charge depreciation on the straight-line basis at 25% per annum. A full year's depreciation is charged in the year of purchase, irrespective of the actual date of purchase.

Required:

For the three years from 1 January 20X6 to 31 December 20X8 prepare the following ledger accounts:

(i) Machinery account

(ii) Accumulated depreciation account (machinery)

(iii) Depreciation charges account (machinery)

Bring down the balance on each account at 31 December each year.

Tip – *Use a table to calculate the depreciation charge for each year.*

(b) Over the same three-year period Hillton bought the following motor vehicles for his business:

January 20X6	Metro van	Cost £3,200
July 20X7	Transit van	Cost £6,000
October 20X8	Astra van	Cost £4,200

Each vehicle was bought for cash.

Hillton's policy for motor vehicles is to charge depreciation on the diminishing-balance basis at 40% per annum. A full year's depreciation is charged in the year of purchase, irrespective of the actual date of purchase.

Required:

For the three years from 1 January 20X6 to 31 December 20X8 prepare the following ledger accounts:

(i) Motor vehicles account

(ii) Accumulated depreciation account (motor vehicles)

(iii) Depreciation charges account (motor vehicles).

Bring down the balance on each account at 31 December each year.

Tip – Use another depreciation table.

Test your understanding 12

On 1 December 20X2 Infortec Computers owned motor vehicles costing £28,400. During the year ended 30 November 20X3 the following changes to the motor vehicles took place:

		£
1 March 20X3	Sold vehicle – original cost	18,000
1 June 20X3	Purchased new vehicle – cost	10,000
1 September 20X3	Purchased new vehicle – cost	12,000

Depreciation on motor vehicles is calculated on a monthly basis at 20% per annum on cost.

Complete the table below to calculate the total depreciation charge to profits for the year ended 30 November 20X3.

	£
Depreciation for vehicle sold 1 March 20X3	
Depreciation for vehicle purchased 1 June 20X3	
Depreciation for vehicle purchased 1 September 20X3	
Depreciation for other vehicles owned during the year	
Total depreciation for the year ended 30 November 20X3	

6 Summary

This chapter considered the manner in which the cost of non-current assets is charged to the statement of profit or loss over the life of the non-current assets, known as depreciation. There are a variety of different methods of depreciation including the straight-line and diminishing-balance methods.

The accounting entries in the general ledger are the same regardless of the method of depreciation selected. The statement of profit or loss recognises an expense for the depreciation charge and the statement of financial position recognises the accumulated depreciation over the life of the asset to date.

The accumulated balance is netted off against the cost of the non-current asset in the statement of financial position in order to show the non-current asset at its carrying amount.

Finally, the depreciation must also be entered into the non-current assets register each year.

Test your understanding answers

Test your understanding 1

	£
Cost	20,000
Year 1 depreciation	(2,000)
Carrying amount at the end of year 1	18,000
Year 2 depreciation	(1,800)
Carrying amount at the end of year 2	16,200

Test your understanding 2

The answer is B

The diminishing-balance method is used to equalise the combined costs of depreciation and maintenance over the vehicle's life (i.e. in early years, depreciation is high, maintenance low; in later years, depreciation is low, maintenance is high).

The diminishing-balance method is used for non-current assets for which higher benefits are consumed in the earlier years with reducing benefits as the years of use pass by.

Test your understanding 3

		£
Machine 1	£40,000 × 10%	4,000
Machine 2	£48,000 × 10% × 6/12	2,400
		6,400

Test your understanding 4

Annual depreciation = $\frac{£12,640}{5}$ = £2,528

CA = £12,640 − (2 × £2,528) = £7,584

This is the cost of the van less the accumulated depreciation to date. It is the amount remaining to be depreciated in the future. It is not a market value.

Test your understanding 5

Annual depreciation charge = $\frac{85,000 - 5,000}{5}$

= £16,000

Asset at cost account

	£		£
Bank	85,000	Balance c/d	85,000
	85,000		**85,000**

Accumulated depreciation

	£		£
Balance c/d	16,000	Depreciation charges	16,000
	16,000		**16,000**

Depreciation charges

	£		£
Accumulated depreciation	16,000	Statement of profit or loss	16,000
	16,000		**16,000**

Depreciation: Chapter 4

Test your understanding 6

Statement of financial position extract below.

	Cost	Accumulated depreciation	Carrying amount
Motor vehicle	12,100	9,075	3,025

Test your understanding 7

Plant and machinery account

Date		£	Date		£
1.1.X6	Balance b/d	5,000	31.12.X6	Balance c/d	5,000
1.1.X7	Balance b/d	5,000			

Office furniture account

Date		£	Date		£
1.1.X6	Balance b/d	800	31.12.X6	Balance c/d	800
1.1.X7	Balance b/d	800			

Depreciation charges account

Date		£	Date		£
31.12.X6	Accumulated dep'n a/c – plant and machinery	640	31.12.X6	SPL	840
31.12.X6	Accumulated dep'n a/c – office furniture	200			
		840			840

FINANCIAL ACCOUNTING: PREPARING FINANCIAL STATEMENTS

Accumulated depreciation account – Plant and machinery

Date		£	Date		£
31.12.X6	Balance c/d	2,440	1.1.X6	Balance b/d	1,800
			31.12.X6	Dep'n charges	640
		2,440			2,440
			1.1.X7	Balance b/d	2,440

Accumulated depreciation account – Office furniture

Date		£	Date		£
31.12.X6	Balance c/d	400	1.1.X6	Balance b/d	200
			31.12.X6	Dep'n expense	200
		400			400
			1.1.X7	Balance b/d	400

The opening balance on the accumulated depreciation account is calculated as follows:

		Plant and machinery	Office furniture
		£	£
20X4	20% × £5,000	1,000	–
20X5	20% × £(5,000 – 1,000)	800	
	25% × £800		200
Opening balance 1.1.X6		1,800	200

The depreciation charge for the year 20X6 is calculated as follows:

	Plant and machinery	Office furniture	Total
	£	£	£
20% × (5,000 – 1,800)	640		
25% × £800		200	840

Test your understanding 8

1. Non-current assets register
2. Any of the following:
   - Asset description
   - Asset identification code
   - Asset location
   - Date of purchase
   - Purchase price
   - Supplier name and address
   - Invoice number
   - Any additional enhancement expenditure
   - Estimated useful life
   - Estimated residual value
   - Accumulated depreciation to date
   - Carrying amount
   - Disposal details
3. It would be easy to locate the machine.

Test your understanding 9

Motor car cost

	£		£
20X3		20X3	
1 Jan Purchase ledger control	12,000	31 Dec Balance c/d	12,000
20X4		20X4	
1 Jan Balance b/d	12,000	31 Dec Balance c/d	12,000
20X5		20X5	
1 Jan Balance b/d	12,000	31 Dec Balance c/d	12,000
20X6			
1 Jan Balance b/d	12,000		

$$\text{Annual depreciation charge} = \frac{12,000 - 2,400}{4}$$

$$= £2,400$$

Motor car – accumulated depreciation account

	£		£
20X3		20X3	
31 Dec Balance c/d	2,400	31 Dec Depreciation charges	2,400
20X4		20X4	
31 Dec Balance c/d	4,800	1 Jan Balance b/d	2,400
		31 Dec Depreciation charges	2,400
	4,800		4,800
20X5		20X5	
31 Dec Balance c/d	7,200	1 Jan Balance b/d	4,800
		31 Dec Depreciation charges	2,400
	7,200		7,200
		20X6	
		1 Jan Balance b/d	7,200

Depreciation charges account

	£		£
20X3		20X3	
31 Dec Motor car accumulated depreciation	2,400	31 Dec SPL	2,400
20X4		20X4	
31 Dec Motor car accumulated depreciation	2,400	31 Dec SPL	2,400
20X5		20X5	
31 Dec Motor car accumulated depreciation	2,400	31 Dec SPL	2,400

Test your understanding 10

1 Straight-line method

$$\text{Annual depreciation} = \frac{\text{Cost} - \text{Scrap value}}{\text{Estimated life}}$$

$$= \frac{£6,000 - £1,000}{8 \text{ years}}$$

$$= £625 \text{ p.a.}$$

Machine account

	£		£
Year 1: Cost	6,000		

Accumulated depreciation

	£		£
Year 1: Balance c/d	625	Year 1: Depreciation charges	625
Year 2: Balance c/d	1,250	Year 2: Balance b/d	625
		Depreciation charges	625
	1,250		1,250
Year 3: Balance c/d	1,875	Year 3: Balance b/d	1,250
		Depreciation charges	625
	1,875		1,875
		Year 4: Balance b/d	1,875

Statement of financial position extract:

		Cost	Accumulated depreciation	Carrying amount
		£	£	£
Non-current asset:				
Year 1	Machine	6,000	625	5,375
Year 2	Machine	6,000	1,250	4,750
Year 3	Machine	6,000	1,875	4,125

2 Diminishing-balance method

		£
Cost		6,000
Year 1	Depreciation 20% × £6,000	1,200
		4,800
Year 2	Depreciation 20% × £4,800	960
		3,840
Year 3	Depreciation 20% × £3,840	768
Carrying amount		3,072

Test your understanding 11

Hilton

(a)

Workings

		Chopper £	Mincer £	Stuffer £	Total £
Cost		4,000	6,000	8,000	18,000
Depreciation	20X6 – 25%	(1,000)			(1,000)
Depreciation	20X7 – 25%	(1,000)	(1,500)		(2,500)
Depreciation	20X8 – 25%	(1,000)	(1,500)	(2,000)	(4,500)
CA at 31 Dec 20X8		1,000	3,000	6,000	10,000

Machinery

	£		£
20X6		20X6	
Cash – chopper	4,000	Balance c/d	4,000
20X7		20X7	
Balance b/d	4,000		
Cash – mincer	6,000	Balance c/d	10,000
	10,000		10,000
20X8		20X8	
Balance b/d	10,000		
Cash – stuffer	8,000	Balance c/d	18,000
	18,000		18,000
20X9			
Balance b/d	18,000		

Accumulated depreciation (machinery)

	£		£
20X6 Balance c/d	1,000	20X6 Depreciation charges (25% × £4,000)	1,000
20X7 Balance c/d	3,500	20X7 Balance b/d	1,000
		Depreciation charges (25% × £10,000)	2,500
	3,500		3,500
20X8 Balance c/d	8,000	20X8 Balance b/d	3,500
		Depreciation charges (25% × £18,000)	4,500
	8,000		8,000
		20X9 Balance b/d	8,000

Depreciation expense (machinery)

	£		£
20X6 Accumulated depreciation	1,000	20X6 Statement of profit or loss	1,000
20X7 Accumulated depreciation	2,500	20X7 Statement of profit or loss	2,500
20X8 Accumulated depreciation	4,500	20X8 Statement of profit or loss	4,500

(b)

Workings

	Metro £	Transit £	Astra £	Total £
Cost	3,200	6,000	4,200	13,400
Depreciation 20X6 – 40%	(1,280)			(1,280)
CA 31.12.X6	1,920			
Depreciation 20X7 – 40%	(768)	(2,400)		(3,168)
CA 31.12.X7	1,152	3,600		
Depreciation 20X8 – 40%	(461)	(1,440)	(1,680)	(3,581)
CA at 31 Dec 20X8	691	2,160	2,520	5,371

Motor vehicles

	£		£
20X6		**20X6**	
Cash – Metro	3,200	Balance c/d	3,200
20X7		**20X7**	
Balance b/d	3,200		
Cash – Transit	6,000	Balance c/d	9,200
	9,200		9,200
20X8		**20X8**	
Balance b/d	9,200		
Cash – Astra	4,200	Balance c/d	13,400
	13,400		13,400
20X9			
Balance b/d	13,400		

Accumulated depreciation (motor vehicles)

	£		£
20X6		**20X6**	
Balance c/d	1,280	Depreciation charge	1,280
	1,280		1,280
20X7		**20X7**	
		Balance b/d	1,280
Balance c/d	4,448	Depreciation charge	3,168
	4,448		4,448
20X8		**20X8**	
		Balance b/d	4,448
Balance c/d	8,029	Depreciation charge	3,581
	8,029		8,029
		Balance b/d	8,029

Depreciation charges (motor vehicles)

	£		£
20X6 Accumulated depreciation	1,280	20X6 Statement of profit or loss	1,280
20X7 Accumulated depreciation	3,168	20X7 Statement of profit or loss	3,168
20X8 Accumulated depreciation	3,581	20X8 Statement of profit or loss	3,581

Test your understanding 12

	£
Depreciation for vehicle sold 1 March 20X3 (18,000 × 20% × 3/12)	900
Depreciation for vehicle purchased 1 June 20X3 (10,000 × 20% × 6/12)	1,000
Depreciation for vehicle purchased 1 September 20X3 (12,000 × 20% × 3/12)	600
Depreciation for other vehicles owned during the year ((28,400 – 18,000) × 20%)	2,080
Total depreciation for the year ended 30 November 20X3	4,580

FINANCIAL ACCOUNTING: PREPARING FINANCIAL STATEMENTS

Disposal of capital assets

Introduction

When a capital asset or a non-current asset such as property, plant or equipment is disposed of there are a variety of accounting calculations and entries that need to be made.

The asset being disposed of must be removed from the accounting records as it is no longer controlled. In most cases the asset will be disposed of for either more or less than its carrying amount leading to a profit or a loss on disposal which must be accounted for. The disposal of the asset must be recorded in the non-current assets register.

You will be required to put through the accounting entries for the disposal of property, plant and equipment and to record the disposal in the non-current assets register.

The method of acquiring a new non-current asset, with an old asset as a part-exchange will be covered in detail in this chapter.

The purpose of the non-current assets register and how it can be used to regularly check that all of the non-current assets owned by the business are in place, must be understood.

ASSESSMENT CRITERIA	CONTENTS
Record acquisitions and disposals of non-current assets (3.3)	1 Accounting for the disposal of capital assets 2 Part-exchange of assets 3 Authorising disposals 4 Disposals and the non-current assets register 5 Reconciliation of physical assets to the non-current assets register

1 Accounting for the disposal of capital assets

1.1 Introduction

When an item of property, plant and equipment is sold there are two main aspects to the accounting for this disposal:

- the existing entries in the ledger accounts for the asset being disposed of must be removed, as the asset is no longer controlled.

- the profit or loss on disposal must be calculated and accounted for.

1.2 Removal of existing ledger account balances

When an asset is sold, the balances in the ledger accounts that relate to that asset must be removed. There are two such balances:

1   the original cost of the asset in the non-current asset cost account

2   the depreciation to date on the asset in the accumulated depreciation account.

To remove these balances, we open up a disposal account.

Definition – Disposal account

The disposal account is the account which is used to make all of the entries relating to the disposal of the asset and also determines the profit or loss on disposal.

1.3 Profit or loss on disposal

The value that the non-current asset is recorded at in the books of the organisation is the carrying amount, i.e. cost less accumulated depreciation. This is unlikely to be exactly equal to the amount for which the asset is actually sold. The difference between the sales proceeds and the carrying amount is the profit or loss on disposal.

	£
Cost of asset	X
Less: accumulated depreciation	(X)
Carrying amount	X
Disposal proceeds	(X)
(Profit)/loss on disposal	X

If the disposal proceeds are greater than the carrying amount a profit has been made, if the proceeds are less than the carrying amount a loss has been made.

1.4 Steps to disposing of a non-current asset

Step 1

Remove the original cost of the disposed asset from the asset's cost account:

Debit Disposal ledger account

Credit Non-current asset cost account

Step 2

Remove the accumulated depreciation of the disposed asset from the accumulated depreciation account:

Debit Non-current asset accumulated depreciation account

Credit Disposal ledger account

Step 3

Enter the sales proceeds received/receivable for the disposed asset:

Debit Bank/Receivables

Credit Disposal ledger account

Step 4

Balance off the ledger accounts and calculate whether a profit or loss has been made on disposal.

Example 1

A non-current asset cost £14,000

The accumulated depreciation on this asset is £9,600.

This asset has just been sold for £3,800 with the proceeds paid via bank transfer.

(a) What is the profit or loss on disposal?

(b) Write up the relevant ledger accounts to record this disposal.

Solution

(a)

	£
Cost	14,000
Accumulated depreciation	(9,600)
Carrying amount	4,400
Proceeds	(3,800)
Loss on disposal	600

(b) **Step 1**

Remove the original cost of the disposed asset from the asset's cost account.

Debit Disposal ledger account £14,000

Credit Non-current asset cost account £14,000

Non-current asset cost

	£		£
Balance b/d	14,000	Disposal	14,000

Disposal

	£		£
Non-current asset cost	14,000		

Step 2

Remove the accumulated depreciation of the disposed asset from the accumulated depreciation account

Debit Non-current asset accumulated depreciation account £9,600

Credit Disposal ledger account £9,600

Accumulated depreciation

	£		£
Disposal	9,600	Balance b/d	9,600

Disposal

	£		£
Non-current asset cost	14,000	Accumulated dep'n	9,600

Steps 3 and 4

Enter the sales proceeds received/receivable for the disposed asset

Debit Bank £3,800

Credit Disposal ledger account £3,800

Balance off the ledger accounts and calculate whether a profit or loss has been made on disposal.

Disposal

	£		£
Non-current asset cost	14,000	Accumulated dep'n	9,600
		Bank	3,800
		Loss – SPL	600
	14,000		14,000

Note 1: The loss of £600 is credited to the disposal account to balance the account. The corresponding debit is in the statement of profit or loss and represents the loss on the disposal.

Note 2: The profit or loss on disposal can actually be calculated as the balancing figure in the disposal account:

- if there is a debit entry to balance the account then this is a profit on disposal which is credited to the SPL as income

- if there is a credit entry to balance the account then this is a loss on disposal which is debited to the SPL as an additional expense.

Example 2

Nigel sells a van for £700 cash.

It originally cost £2,000 and so far, depreciation has amounted to £1,500.

Record this transaction in the disposals account.

Show the journal entries required to account for this disposal.
Solution

Disposal account

	£		£
MV cost (step 1)	2,000	MV accumulated depreciation (step 2)	1,500
SPL – profit on disposal (step 4)	200	Cash (step 3)	700
	2,200		2,200

Now for each of the journal entries:

Step 1
To remove the motor van cost from the books of the business.

| Dr | Disposals | 2,000 |
| Cr | Motor van cost | 2,000 |

Step 2
To remove the associated depreciation from the books of the business.

| Dr | Motor van accumulated depreciation | 1,500 |
| Cr | Disposals | 1,500 |

Note: These two entries together effectively remove the carrying amount of the van to the disposals account.

Step 3
To record the cash proceeds.

| Dr | Cash | 700 |
| Cr | Disposals | 700 |

Step 4
Balance the disposal account

The resulting balance is the profit on sale. The disposal account balance is then transferred to the statement of profit or loss.

| Dr | Disposals | 200 |
| Cr | Statement of profit or loss | 200 |

FINANCIAL ACCOUNTING: PREPARING FINANCIAL STATEMENTS

 Test your understanding 1

A business buys a car for £20,000 on 15 January 20X2 and expects it to have a useful life of five years.

It depreciates the car at 50% reducing balance and sells on 20 December 20X5 for £10,000. The depreciation policy of the business is to charge a full year's depreciation in the year of acquisition and none in the year of disposal.

Record the ledger entries for the four years 20X2 to 20X5. The financial year of the business is 1 January to 31 December.

Clearly show the profit or loss on disposal.

Car cost

	£		£

Car accumulated depreciation

	£		£

Disposal of capital assets: **Chapter 5**

Disposal account

£		£

1.5 Journal

As with the acquisition of non-current assets, the journal or journal voucher is used as the book of prime entry. The journal voucher for the disposal featured in example 2 is shown below:

Journal entry			No: 234
Date	4 July 20X8		
Prepared by	J Allen		
Authorised by	A Smith		
Account	**Code**	**Debit £**	**Credit £**
Disposals	0240	2,000	
Motor vehicles cost	0130		2,000
Motor vehicles acc. dep'n	0140	1,500	
Disposals	0240		1,500
Cash at bank (receipts)	0163	700	
Disposals	0240		700
Totals		4,200	4,200

Test your understanding 2

Complete the journal voucher below for the following information:

A company buys a car for £20,000.

The depreciation charged to date is £7,500.

The car is sold for £10,000 at the end of three years.

FINANCIAL ACCOUNTING: PREPARING FINANCIAL STATEMENTS

Using the information above and the following account names and codes, complete the journal voucher below:

0130 Motor vehicles cost

0140 Motor vehicles accumulated depreciation

0163 Cash at bank (receipts)

0240 Disposals

Journal entry No 235			
Date	13 June 20X8		
Prepared by	A Tech		
Authorised by	B Jones		
Account	**Code**	**Debit £**	**Credit £**

Test your understanding 3

Spanners has a car it wishes to dispose of. The car cost £12,000 and has accumulated depreciation of £5,000. The car is sold for £4,000.

Tasks

(a) Clearly state whether there is a profit or a loss on disposal.

(b) Show the entries in the motor car cost account, motor car accumulated depreciation account and disposal account.

> **Test your understanding 4**
>
> **Baldrick's venture**
>
> On 1 April 20X6, Baldrick started a business growing turnips and selling them to wholesalers. On 1 September 20X6 Baldrick purchased a turnip-digging machine for £2,700, the machine was sold on 1 March 20X9 for £1,300.
>
> Baldrick's policy for machinery is to charge depreciation on the diminishing balance method at 25% per annum. A full year's charge is made in the year of purchase and none in the year of sale.
>
> **Required:**
>
> For the three years from 1 April 20X6 to 31 March 20X9 prepare the following ledger accounts:
>
> (a) Machinery cost account
>
> (b) Machinery accumulated depreciation account
>
> (c) Depreciation expense account (machinery)
>
> (d) Disposals account
>
> Bring down the balance on each account at 31 March each year.

2 Part-exchange of assets

2.1 Introduction

There is an alternative to selling a non-current asset for cash, particularly if a new asset is to be purchased to replace the one being sold. This is often the case with cars or vans where the old asset may be taken by the seller of the new asset as part of the purchase price of the new asset. This is known as a part-exchange deal.

2.2 Part-exchange deal value

When a part-exchange deal takes place the seller of the new asset will place a value on the old asset and this will be its part-exchange value.

Example 3

A new car is being purchased for a list price of £18,000. An old car of the business has been accepted in part-exchange and the payment required for the new car is £14,700.

What is the part-exchange value of the old car?

Solution

	£
List price of new car	18,000
Payment required	14,700
Part-ex value against old car	3,300

The part-exchange value has two effects on the accounting records:

1   it is effectively the sale proceeds of the old asset

2   it is part of the full cost of the new asset together with the balance paid (whichever method of payment is applicable).

2.3 Steps to disposing of a non-current asset through part-exchange

Step 1

Remove the original cost of the disposed asset from the asset's cost account:

Debit Disposal ledger account

Credit Non-current asset cost account

Step 2

Remove the accumulated depreciation of the disposed asset from the asset account:

Debit Non-current asset accumulated depreciation account

Credit Disposal ledger account

Step 3

Enter the part-exchange allowance received for the 'old' non-current asset/part of the value of the 'new' non-current asset:

Debit Non-current asset cost account

Credit Disposal ledger account

Note: NCA cost is debited as the part-exchange value is part of the total cost of the new asset.

The part-exchange balance is also credited to the disposal account as it represents the effective proceeds of the old asset.

Step 4

Account for the remaining balance due on the 'new' non-current asset being acquired:

Debit Non-current asset cost account

Credit Bank/payables

Step 5

Balance off the ledger accounts and calculate whether a profit or loss has been made on the part-exchange.

Note: Steps 3 and 4 can be combined so that the overall resulting accounting entries would be:

Debit Non-current asset cost account

(With the full capitalisation value of the new non-current asset)

Credit Disposal ledger account

(With the part-exchange value of the transaction)

Credit Bank/payables

(With the remaining balance due on the new non-current asset acquired).

 Example 4

Suppose Nigel had part-exchanged the van for a new one.

The old van had cost £2,000 and accumulated depreciation amounted to £1,500.

The garage gave Nigel an allowance of £700 against the price of the new van which was £5,000. Nigel paid the balance by cheque.

Show all the accounting entries for the disposal of the old van and the acquisition of the new van.

Solution

Steps 1 and 2

Transfer balances from the old van cost and accumulated depreciation accounts to the disposal account.

Old van – cost

	£		£
Balance b/d	2,000	Disposal	2,000
	2,000		2,000

Old van – accumulated depreciation

	£		£
Disposal	1,500	Balance b/d	1,500
	1,500		1,500

Disposal

	£		£
Old van – cost	2,000	Accumulated depreciation	1,500

Note: We have closed off the old van cost and accumulated depreciation account to make the entries clearer.

Steps 3 and 4

Open a new van account and enter in it:

(a) the part-exchange value (£700) from the disposal account; and

(b) the balance of the cost of the new van (£4,300).

These values may be shown separately or may be combined as one amount as discussed in the entries in section 2.3.

The £700 part-exchange value is also credited to the disposal account as the effective proceeds of the old van.

Disposal

	£		£
Old van – cost	2,000	Accumulated depreciation	1,500
		New van – cost	700

New van – cost

	£		£
Disposal	700		
Bank	4,300		

Step 5

Balance the accounts

(a) Close the disposal account to the statement of profit or loss with a profit of £200 being recorded.

(b) Bring down the total cost of the new van of £5,000.

Disposal

	£		£
Old van – cost	2,000	Accumulated depreciation	1,500
SPL – profit on disposal – old van	200	New van – cost	700
	2,200		2,200

New van – cost

	£		£
Disposal	700	Balance c/d	5,000
Bank	4,300		
	5,000		5,000
Balance b/d	5,000		

Note 1: You could put all the entries in one van cost account. It would look like this:

Motor van – cost

	£		£
Balance b/d	2,000	Disposal	2,000
Disposal	700	Balance c/d	5,000
Bank	4,300		
	7,000		7,000
Balance b/d	5,000		

FINANCIAL ACCOUNTING: PREPARING FINANCIAL STATEMENTS

Test your understanding 5

On 30 September 20X3 a business part-exchanged a van which it bought on 1 January 20X0 for £6,000 and has depreciated each year at 25% pa by the straight-line method (assuming nil residual value). The business charges a full year's charge in the year of acquisition and none in the year of disposal. The financial year end of the business is 31 December.

It traded this van in for a new one costing £10,000 and pays the supplier £9,200 by cheque.

1   Record the entries in ledger accounts for the disposal of the OLD van.

2   Record the entries in ledger accounts for the addition of the NEW van.

3   Complete the disposal account and calculate the profit/loss on disposal.

Test your understanding 6

A motor vehicle which had originally been purchased on 31 October 20X1 for £12,000 was part-exchanged for a new vehicle on 31 May 20X3. The new vehicle cost £15,000 and was paid for using the old vehicle and a cheque for £5,000.

Prepare a disposals account for the old vehicle showing clearly the transfer to the statement of profit or loss. (Depreciation for motor vehicles is calculated on a monthly basis at 20% per annum straight-line method assuming no residual value.)

Disposals account

3 Authorising disposals

3.1 Introduction

It is important that disposals of non-current assets are properly controlled. For most organisations, this means that there must be some form of written authorisation before a disposal can take place. In some ways, authorisation is even more important for disposals than for additions.

3.2 Importance of authorisation

Disposals can easily be made without the knowledge of management and are difficult to detect from the accounting records alone. Sales of assets are often for relatively small amounts of cash and they may not be supported by an invoice (for example, if they are to an employee of the business). Although the transaction itself may not be significant, failure to detect and record the disposal correctly in the accounting records may result in the overstatement of non-current assets in the accounts.

3.3 Requirements of valid authorisation

Possibilities for written authorisation include board minutes (for material disposals), memos or authorisation forms. The following information is needed:

- date of purchase
- date of disposal
- description of asset
- reason for disposal
- original cost
- accumulated depreciation
- sale proceeds
- authorisation (number of signatures required will depend upon the organisation's procedures).

FINANCIAL ACCOUNTING: PREPARING FINANCIAL STATEMENTS

4 Disposals and the non-current assets register

4.1 Introduction

When a non-current asset is disposed of then this must be recorded not only in the ledger accounts but also in the non-current assets register.

 Example 5

Date of purchase	Invoice number	Serial number	Item	Cost	Accum'd depreciation b/f at 1.1.X8	Date of disposal	Depreciation charge in 20X8	Accum'd depreciation c/f	Disposal proceeds	Loss/ gain on disposal
				£	£		£	£	£	£
3.2.X5	345	3488	Chair	340	102		34	136		
6.4.X6	466	–	Bookcase	258	52		26	78		
10.7.X7	587	278	Chair	160	16	12.7.X8	–			
30.8.X8	634	1228	Table	86			9	9		
				844	170		69	223		

Using the non-current assets register example from the previous two Chapters (reproduced above) we will now complete the entries for the chair (serial number 278) being disposed of.

The disposal proceeds are £15.

The profit or loss must also be entered into the non-current assets register and the total of all of the profits or losses should equal the amount transferred to the statement of profit or loss for the period.

Solution

(W1)

	£
Cost	160
Accumulated depreciation	(16)
Carrying amount	144
Proceeds	(15)
Loss	129

Disposal of capital assets: Chapter 5

Date of purchase	Invoice number	Serial number	Item	Cost	Accum'd depreciation b/d at 1.1.X8	Date of disposal	Depreciation charge in 20X8	Accum'd depreciation c/d	Disposal proceeds	Loss/gain on disposal
				£	£		£	£	£	£
3.2.X5	345	3488	Chair	340	102		34	136		
6.4.X6	466	–	Bookcase	258	52		26	78		
10.7.X7	587	278	Chair	160	16	12.7.X8	–		15	(129)(W1)
30.8.X8	634	1228	Table	86			9	9		
				───	───					
				844	170					
12.7.X8		278	Chair	(160)	(16)					
				───	───		───	───		───
				684	154		69	223		(129)
				───	───					───

The result will be that the disposed of asset will have a zero balance in the non-current assets register at the end of the accounting period.

5 Reconciliation of physical assets to the non-current assets register

5.1 Introduction

One of the purposes of the non-current assets register is to allow control over the non-current assets of a business. Many non-current assets are extremely valuable and some are also easily moved, especially assets such as personal computers and cars. On a regular basis the organisation should carry out random checks to ensure that the non-current assets recorded in the non-current assets register are actually on the premises.

5.2 Details in the non-current assets register

The non-current assets register will show the purchase cost, depreciation and disposal details of the non-current assets that the business owns and have recently disposed of.

The non-current assets register should also detail the location of the assets. This will either be by an additional column in the non-current assets register or by grouping assets in each department or area of the business together. This enables periodic checks to be carried out to ensure that the physical assets in each department agree to the non-current assets register.

5.3 Discrepancies

A variety of possible discrepancies might appear between the physical assets and the book records.

Issue:	Possible reason:
An asset recorded in the non-current assets register is not physically present.	The asset has been disposed of but not recorded in the non-current assets register.
	The asset has been moved to another location and this has not been detailed.
	The asset has been stolen or removed without authorisation.
An asset existing that is not recorded in the non-current assets register.	The non-current asset register is not up to date.
	The asset has been moved from another location and this has not been detailed.

Whatever type of discrepancy is discovered it must be either resolved or reported to the appropriate person in the organisation so that it can be resolved.

5.4 Agreement of accounting records to non-current assets register

The ledger accounts for the non-current assets should also be agreed on a regular basis to the non-current assets register.

The total cost less any disposals should agree to the totals of non-current asset at cost accounts.

The accumulated depreciation column total for each class of assets should also agree to the accumulated depreciation account balance for each class of asset.

Any total in the loss or gain on disposals column should also agree to the amount charged or credited to the statement of profit or loss.

On a regular basis the non-current assets register details should be agreed to the physical assets held and to the ledger accounts.

Test your understanding 7

Leilani

The following transactions have been made by Leilani's business, in relation to plant and machinery.

1 January 20X7	Lathe machine purchased for £10,000. It is to be depreciated on a straight-line basis with no expected scrap value after four years.
1 April 20X7	Cutting machine purchased for £12,000. It is estimated that after a five-year working life it will have a scrap value of £1,000.
1 June 20X8	Laser machine purchased for £28,000. This is estimated to have a seven-year life and a scrap value of £2,800.
1 March 20X9	The cutting machine purchased on 1 April 20X7 was given in part-exchange for a new micro-cutter with a purchase price of £20,000. A part-exchange allowance of £3,000 was given and the balance paid by cheque. It is estimated that the new machine will last for five years with a scrap value of £3,000. It will cost £1,500 to install.

The accounting year end is 31 December. The company depreciates its machines on a straight-line basis, charging a full year in the year of purchase and none in the year of sale.

At 31 December 20X6 the plant register had shown the following:

Date of purchase	Machine	Cost £	Anticipated residual value £	Rate of depreciation
1 June 20X5	Piece machine	10,000	Nil	Straight line over 5 years
1 January 20X6	Acrylic machine	5,000	1,000	Straight line over 5 years
1 June 20X6	Heat seal machine	6,000	Nil	Straight line over 5 years

Required:

Write up the plant and machinery account, the accumulated depreciation account and the disposal accounts for 20X7, 20X8 and 20X9. Show the relevant extracts from the financial statements.

6 Summary

The two main aspects to accounting for disposals of non-current assets are to remove all accounting entries for the asset disposed of and to account for any profit or loss on disposal. This can all be done by using a disposal account.

Some assets will not be sold outright but will be transferred as a part-exchange deal when purchasing a new asset. The part-exchange value is not only equivalent to the proceeds of sale but is also part of the cost of the new asset being purchased.

Control over the disposal of non-current assets is extremely important and as such authorisation of a disposal and whether it is as a sale or a part-exchange is key to this. Allied to this is the control feature of the non-current assets register.

All purchases and disposals of non-current assets should be recorded in the non-current assets register and the actual physical presence of the non-current assets should be checked on a regular basis to the non-current assets register details.

Test your understanding answers

Test your understanding 1

	£	Depreciation
Cost	20,000	
20X2 depreciation (20,000 × 50%)	(10,000)	10,000
	10,000	
20X3 depreciation (10,000 × 50%)	(5,000)	5,000
	5,000	
20X4 depreciation (5,000 × 50%)	(2,500)	2,500
Total depreciation charged		17,500

(No depreciation is charged in 20X5 as this is the year of disposal – as per the policy stated).

Car cost

	£		£
01/X2 Bank	20,000	12/X2 Balance c/d	20,000
	20,000		20,000
01/X3 Balance b/d	20,000	12/X3 Balance c/d	20,000
	20,000		20,000
01/X4 Balance b/d	20,000	12/X4 Balance c/d	20,000
	20,000		20,000
01/X5 Balance b/d	20,000	12/X5 Disposal a/c	20,000
	20,000		20,000

Car accumulated depreciation

	£		£
12/X2 Balance c/d	10,000	12/X2 Dep'n charges	10,000
	10,000		10,000
12/X3 Balance c/d	15,000	01/X3 Balance b/d	10,000
		12/X3 Dep'n charges	5,000
	15,000		15,000
12/X4 Balance c/d	17,500	01/X4 Balance b/d	15,000
		12/X4 Dep'n charges	2,500
	17,500		17,500
12/X5 Disposal a/c	17,500	01/X5 Balance b/d	17,500
	17,500		17,500

Disposal account

	£		£
12/X5 Car cost	20,000	12/X5 Car accum dep'n	17,500
12/X5 Profit on disposal	7,500	12/X5 Proceeds	10,000
	27,500		27,500

Test your understanding 2

Journal entry No 235			
Date	13 June 20X8		
Prepared by	A Tech		
Authorised by	B Jones		
Account	Code	Debit £	Credit £
Disposals	0240	20,000	
MV cost	0130		20,000
MV acc dep'n	0140	7,500	
Disposals	0240		7,500
Cash at bank	0163	10,000	
Disposals	0240		10,000
Totals		37,500	37,500

Test your understanding 3

(a) **Profit or loss on disposal**

	£
Cost	12,000
Accumulated depreciation	(5,000)
Carrying amount	7,000

Comparing the carrying amount of £7,000 with the sale proceeds of £4,000, there is a loss of (7,000 – 4,000) = £3,000.

(b) **Ledger account entries**

Disposal of non-current assets account

	£		£
Car cost	12,000	Accumulated depreciation	5,000
		Cash at bank a/c (sales proceeds)	4,000
		Loss on disposal	3,000
	12,000		12,000

Car account

	£		£
Balance b/d	12,000	Disposal a/c	12,000

Car accumulated depreciation account

	£		£
Disposal a/c	5,000	Balance b/d	5,000

Cash at bank account

	£		£
Disposal a/c	4,000		

Test your understanding 4

Machinery cost

	£		£
20X7 Cash	2,700	20X7 Balance c/d	2,700
20X8 Balance b/d	2,700	20X8 Balance c/d	2,700
20X9 Balance b/d	2,700	20X9 Disposals account	2,700

Machinery accumulated depreciation

	£		£
20X7 Balance c/d	675	20X7 Depreciation expense (25% × £2,700)	675
20X8 Balance c/d	1,181	20X8 Balance b/d	675
		Depreciation expense (25% × (£2,700 − £675))	506
20X9 Disposals account	1,181	20X9 Balance b/d	1,181

Depreciation expense (machinery)

	£		£
20X7 Accumulated depreciation	675	20X7 Statement of profit or loss	675
20X8 Accumulated depreciation	506	20X8 Statement of profit or loss	506

Disposals

	£		£
20X9 Machinery – cost	2,700	20X9 Accumulated depreciation	1,181
		Cash	1,300
		SPL – loss on disposal	219
	2,700		2,700

Test your understanding 5

Van cost account

	£		£
Cost b/d	6,000	Disposals account	6,000
Disposal account	800		
Bank	9,200	Balance c/d	10,000
	16,000		16,000
Balance b/d	10,000		

Van accumulated depreciation

	£		£
Disposal account	4,500	Balance b/d (£6,000 × 25% × 3 years)	4,500
Balance c/d	2,500	Depreciation charge (£10,000 × 25%)	2,500
	7,000		7,000
		Balance b/d	2,500

Disposal account

	£		£
Van	6,000	Accumulated depreciation	4,500
		Part-exchange allowance	800
		Loss on disposal	700
	6,000		6,000

Test your understanding 6

Disposals account

	£		£
MV cost	12,000	MV accumulated depreciation	3,800
Profit on disposal	1,800	MV cost – part ex	10,000
	13,800		13,800

Accumulated depreciation = £12,000 × 20% × 19/12 = 3,800

Test your understanding 7

Leilani

1. Calculate the Balance b/d position at 1 January 20X7:

	Cost	Annual depreciation		Accumulated depreciation at 1 Jan 20X7
	£		£	£
Piece machine (1 June 20X5)	10,000	$\dfrac{£10,000}{5}$	2,000	4,000
Acrylic machine (1 Jan 20X6)	5,000	$\dfrac{£5,000 - £1,000}{5}$	800	800
Heat seal machine (1 June 20X6)	6,000	$\dfrac{£6,000}{5}$	1,200	1,200
	21,000		4,000	6,000

2 Calculate the annual depreciation on the new assets:

	Cost	Annual depreciation	
	£		£
20X7			
Lathe machine (1 Jan 20X7)	10,000	$\dfrac{£10,000}{4}$	2,500
Cutting machine (1 Apr 20X7)	12,000	$\dfrac{£12,000 - £1,000}{5}$	2,200
Assets b/d at 1 January 20X7	(calc from part 1)		4,000
Charge for the year (20X7)			8,700
20X8			
Lathe machine			2,500
Cutting machine			2,200
Laser machine (1 Jun 20X8)	28,000	$\dfrac{£28,000 - £2,800}{7}$	3,600
Assets b/d at 1 January 20X7			4,000
Charge for the year (20X8)			12,300
20X9			
Lathe machine			2,500
Cutting machine – disposed of			–
Laser machine			3,600
Micro-cutter (1 Apr 20X9)	20,000		
Add: Installation	1,500		
	21,500	$\dfrac{£21,500 - 3,000}{5}$	3,700
Assets b/d at 1 January 20X7			4,000
Charge for the year (20X9)			13,800

3 Show the ledger accounts

Plant and machinery cost account

	£		£
20X7			
Assets Balance b/d	21,000		
Lathe machine	10,000		
Cutting machine	12,000	Balance c/d 31.12.X7	43,000
	43,000		43,000
20X8			
Assets Balance b/d	43,000		
Laser machine	28,000	Balance c/d 31.12.X8	71,000
	71,000		71,000
20X9			
Assets Balance b/d	71,000	Disposal account	12,000
Micro-cutter			
Disposal 3,000			
Bank account 17,000			
Installation costs 1,500	21,500	Balance c/d 31.12.X9	80,500
	92,500		92,500

Plant and machinery accumulated depreciation

	£		£
20X7		**20X7**	
		Balance b/d (1)	6,000
Balance c/d	14,700	Depreciation account (2)	8,700
	14,700		14,700
		20X8	
		Balance b/d	14,700
Balance c/d	27,000	Depreciation account	12,300
	27,000		27,000
		20X9	
Disposal account (4)	4,400	Balance b/d	27,000
Balance c/d	36,400	Depreciation account	13,800
	40,800		40,800

4 Calculate the accumulated depreciation on the cutting machine disposed of:

Cutting machine   purchased   1 April 20X7
                   disposed   1 March 20X9

Therefore depreciation should have been charged for 20X7 and 20X8 and none in 20X9, the year of sale.

Accumulated depreciation is £2,200 × 2 = £4,400.

Debit   Accumulated depreciation account   £4,400
Credit Disposal account   £4,400

Depreciation expense

	£		£
20X7		**20X7**	
Accumulated depreciation	8,700	Statement of profit or loss	8,700
20X8		**20X8**	
Accumulated depreciation	12,300	Statement of profit or loss	12,300
20X9		**20X9**	
Accumulated depreciation	13,800	Statement of profit or loss	13,800

Disposals

	£		£
20X9			
Plant and machinery cost	12,000	Accumulated depreciation	4,400
		Part-exchange – plant and machinery account	3,000
		Loss on disposal (bal fig)	4,600
	12,000		12,000

5   Disposal journal entries for part-exchange:

Debit	Plant and machinery account	£3,000	
Credit	Disposal account		£3,000

Part-exchange allowance.

Debit	Statement of profit or loss	£4,600	
Credit	Disposal account		£4,600

Loss on sale

Debit	Plant and machinery		
Cost	(£20,000 – £3,000)	£17,000	
Installation		£1,500	
		£18,500	
Credit	Bank account		£18,500

Balance on cost of new machine – micro-cutter

6   Show extracts from financial statements:

Statement of profit or loss extracts

	20X7 £	20X8 £	2009 £
Depreciation	8,700	12,300	13,800
Loss on disposal	–	–	4,600

Statement of financial position extracts

		Cost £	Accumulated depreciation £	Carrying amount £
Non-current assets				
20X7	Plant and machinery	43,000	14,700	28,300
20X8	Plant and machinery	71,000	27,000	44,000
20X9	Plant and machinery	80,500	36,400	44,100

FINANCIAL ACCOUNTING: PREPARING FINANCIAL STATEMENTS

The extended trial balance – an introduction

Introduction

The examination will contain an exercise involving preparation or completion of an extended trial balance. You need to be familiar with the technique for entering adjustments to the initial trial balance and extending the figures into the statement of financial position and statement of profit or loss columns.

The relevant adjustments you may be required to make are accruals, prepayments, depreciation charges, disposals of non-current assets, irrecoverable and doubtful receivables, errors and closing inventory.

In this chapter we introduce the purpose and layout of the extended trial balance. The skills that are detailed below will be achieved once all the adjustments have been reviewed and once the extended trial balance in action has been studied.

ASSESSMENT CRITERIA	CONTENTS
Prepare an initial trial balance (6.1)	1 From trial balance to extended trial balance
Prepare an adjusted trial balance (6.2)	
Complete the extended trial balance (ETB) (6.3)	

The extended trial balance – an introduction: Chapter 6

1 From trial balance to extended trial balance

1.1 Introduction

A trial balance is prepared regularly in order to provide a check on the double-entry bookkeeping in the accounting system. Accounting software may be used to complete the transfer of data into the trial balance. It is important to distinguish between an initial trial balance and an adjusted trial balance. An initial trial balance provides an initial summary of the general ledger accounts prior to entering any adjusting entries. One of the main purposes of a trial balance is to serve as a check on the double entry. If the trial balance does not balance, i.e. the debit and credit totals are not equal then some errors have been made in the double entry (this will be covered in more detail in a later Chapter).

An adjusted trial balance is prepared after all the adjusting entries have been posted into the appropriate general ledger accounts. The adjusted trial balance is completed to ensure that the financial statements will be accurate and in balance. The trial balance can also serve as the basis for preparing an extended trial balance and finally the financial statements of the organisation. The extended trial balance and preparation of financial statements is introduced in this chapter.

1.2 The purpose of the extended trial balance

Definition – Extended trial balance

An extended trial balance is a working paper which allows the initial trial balance to be converted into all of the figures required for preparation of the final accounts.

The extended trial balance brings together the balances on all of the general ledger accounts and includes all of the adjustments that are required in order to prepare the final accounts.

1.3 Layout of a typical extended trial balance

A typical extended trial balance (ETB) will have eight columns for each ledger account as follows:

Account name (e.g.)	Trial balance		Adjustments		Statement of profit or loss		Statement of financial position	
	Dr £	Cr £	Dr £	Cr £	Dr £	Cr £	Dr £	Cr £
Sales								
Non-current asset cost								

1.4 Procedure for preparing an extended trial balance

Step 1

Each ledger account name and its balance are initially entered in the trial balance columns.

Total the debit and credit columns to ensure they equal i.e. that all balances have been transferred across. Any difference should be put to a suspense account.

Step 2

The adjustments required are then entered into the column for adjustments. The typical adjustments required are:

- correction of any errors
- depreciation charges for the period
- write off any irrecoverable debts
- increase or decrease in allowance for doubtful receivables
- accruals or prepayments of income and expense
- closing inventory.

Note: it is always important to ensure that all adjustments have an equal and opposite debit and credit. Never enter a one-sided journal.

Step 3

Total the adjustments columns to ensure that the double entry has been correctly made in these columns.

Step 4

All the entries on the line of each account are then cross-cast and the total is entered into the correct column in either the statement of profit or loss columns or statement of financial position columns.

Step 5

The statement of profit or loss column totals are totalled in order to determine the profit (or loss) for the period. This profit (or loss) is entered in the statement of profit or loss columns as the balancing figure.

Step 6

The profit (or loss) for the period calculated in step 5 is entered in the statement of financial position columns and the statement of financial position columns are then totalled.

2 Summary

This chapter has introduced the purpose and layout of the extended trial balance. The Chapters that follow will review the different accounting adjustments you may need to make. These adjustments will include closing inventory, depreciation, disposals, irrecoverable and doubtful receivables, accruals and prepayments. These can all be conveniently put through on the extended trial balance. Remember depreciation and disposals were considered in Chapters 4 and 5.

Once the adjustments have been reviewed, Chapter 14 looks in detail at the extended trial balance in action.

FINANCIAL ACCOUNTING: PREPARING FINANCIAL STATEMENTS

Underlying accounting principles

Introduction

In this chapter we consider the primary users of final accounts and what the possible reasons are for their interest in the financial performance and position of a business.

We must first establish an understanding of the accounting principles underlying final accounts preparation. Not only do we need to be aware of these underlying principles, we must also take into consideration the fundamental and enhancing qualities of the information that is presented within those accounts.

The application of ethical principles is threaded throughout this unit. Learners must understand the importance of those ethical principles and professional scepticism when preparing financial statements for users.

ASSESSMENT CRITERIA

The primary users of final accounts (1.1)

The framework of accounting underlying the preparation of final accounts (1.2)

Qualities of useful financial information (1.3)

Considerations for recording period end adjustments (5.4)

CONTENTS

1. The primary users of final accounts
2. The framework of accounting which underlies the preparation of final accounts
3. Qualities of useful financial information
4. Ethical principles

Underlying accounting principles: Chapter 7

1 The primary users of final accounts

1.1 Introduction

The main purpose of financial statements is to provide information to a wide range of users. Many different groups of people may use financial statements and each group will need particular information for different reasons. The users rely on the accuracy of the financial accounts.

1.2 Primary users of the accounts

The table below summarises the main users of financial statements along with their needs for that information.

User	Needs
Investors / owners	Investors are better able to make decisions regarding their investment if they have relevant information. Investors can include both existing and potential owners. They require information concerning the performance of the business for example, in terms of profitability.
Management and other internal users	Internal users such as management and members of the accounts department require information to assist in the performance of duties, such as maintaining and updating accounting records and other information.
Lenders	Lenders such as banks are interested in the ability of the business to pay interest and repay loans.
Employees	This includes current and potential employees. They require information relating to the ability to pay wages and pensions on a continuing basis. Employees are also interested in future prospects in terms of job security and development opportunities.
Customers	Customers will be concerned to ensure the entity has the ability to provide goods and/or services requested and to continue to provide similar services in the future.
Suppliers	Suppliers need to know if they will be paid. New suppliers may also require reassurance about the financial health of a business before agreeing to supply goods.

| Government | This includes the taxation authorities to calculate and collect taxes due. Also, other government agencies and departments to collect economic and financial data and to measure economic performances such as employment rates. |

In the event of inaccurate or misleading information being provided to users of the financial accounts, uninformed or incorrect decisions may be taken, red flags may be missed, there may be an impact on the creditability of the business or the business may be under or overvalued.

2 The framework of accounting which underlies the preparation of final accounts

2.1 Introduction

There are a number of accounting principles that underpin the preparation of financial statements. We will now consider each in turn.

2.2 Going concern

Definition

The going concern basis presumes that the entity will continue in operation for the foreseeable future and has neither the need nor the intention to liquidate or significantly reduce the scale of its operations.

If the business is no longer considered to be a going concern, the assets of the business would need to be recognised at the amount which is expected from selling them. Liabilities would be recognised at the amounts that they are likely to be settled for.

Example 1

A business presents non-current assets and non-current liabilities as they are deemed to continue in business for the foreseeable future, otherwise they could not be recognised as non-current.

2.3 Accruals basis

Definition

The accruals basis states that transactions should be reflected in the financial statements for the period in which they occur. This means that income should be recognised as it is earned and expenses when they are incurred, rather than when cash is received or paid.

Example 2

Sales revenue should be recognised when goods and services have been supplied; costs are incurred when goods and services have been received.

2.4 Business entity

From an accounting perspective the business is treated as being separate from its owners. Therefore, the information presented in the financial statements relates only to the activities of the business and not to those of the owner(s).

Example 3

An owner withdraws goods from their supplies for their own personal use. This should be recorded as a withdrawal of capital.

2.5 Materiality

Definition

Materiality relates to the significance of transactions, balances and errors that may be within the financial statements.

An item is regarded as material if its omission or misstatement is likely to change the perception or understanding of the users of that information. In other words, the user should not be led to make inappropriate decisions based upon misstated information.

We must recognise that considering something to be material is a subjective assessment. Deeming something as being material, or not, is based on opinions of those who prepare the financial statements.

Example 4

If a large business (such as a company listed on the stock exchange) has its bank balance misstated by £1 in the statement of financial position, this may not be regarded as a material misstatement.

This is because the misstatement by £1 would not significantly distort the relevance and reliability of the financial statements. However, if the bank balance was misstated by £100,000, this is more likely to be regarded as a material misstatement as it significantly distorts the information included in the financial statements.

2.6 The importance of ensuring financial statements are free from material misstatements

Financial statements should be free of material misstatements.

Definition

A material misstatement is incorrect or inaccurate information in a financial statement that could affect the financial decisions of a user who relies on those financial statements.

Materiality relates to the significance of transactions, balances and errors that are within the financial statements. It can be defined as the threshold after which the financial information becomes relevant to the needs of the users when making financial decisions.

Examples of material misstatements include the overstatement or understatement of profits and overvaluation or undervaluation of assets liabilities.

Example 5

If an asset has been overvalued, a lender will have less security for a loan than suggested in the financial statements. This increases the potential risk of loss should the borrower default on the loan.

Example 6

The overstatement or understatement of profit may lead current investors or potential investors to make a decision, which would not be the same if the misstatement had not occurred. For example, an investor may decide to retain their shareholding based upon overstated profits.

2.7 Consistency

Users of financial statements need to be able to compare the performance of a business over a number of years. The presentation and classification of items in the financial statements should remain the same from one period to the next. There are two exceptions; a change in circumstances or the requirements of a new accounting standard.

Consistency of accounting treatment and presentation relates not only from one accounting period to the next, but also within an accounting period, so that similar transactions are accounted for in a similar way throughout the accounting period.

Example 7

Transactions and valuation methods are treated the same way from period to period. Meaning that users of accounts can, therefore, make more meaningful comparisons of financial performance from year to year.

2.8 Prudence

You can be described as prudent if you show good and careful judgement. Those who prepare financial statements should exercise prudence as assets and income should not be overstated and liabilities and expenses should not be understated.

Care must be given to ensure there is not deliberate misstatement of assets, liabilities, income and expenses, as that would introduce bias into the financial statements. Applying the principle of prudence helps to ensure that financial statements are fairly stated and can be relied upon by users.

However, it does not require a deliberate overstatement of liabilities and expenses, or a deliberate understatement of assets and income. The application of prudence should eliminate any bias but it should not reduce the reliability of the information.

Example 8

Inventory is recorded at the lower of cost or net realisable value, rather than the expected selling price. This ensures profit on the sale of inventory is only realised when the sale takes place. We will consider the valuation of inventory, in accordance with IAS 2 in more detail in Chapter 8.

Example 9

Costs are 'provided for' in the accounts as soon as there is a reasonable expectation that such costs will be incurred in the future.

Test your understanding 1

Inventory which costs £2,000 should be recorded at its net realisable value of £3,000.

True or false?

2.9 Money measurement

The money measurement concept states that an accounting transaction should only be recorded if it can be expressed in terms of money.

Examples of items that cannot be recorded, as they cannot be expressed in terms of money include: the skill level of an employee, working conditions of an employee, the level of efficiency of an administration process, the quality of customer support or the durability of a product. However, all of these factors are indirectly reflected in the financial results of a business. They may impact revenues, expenses, assets or liabilities.

Underlying accounting principles: **Chapter 7**

Example 10

Consider the impact of high-quality customer support. This leads to customers making repeat purchases and in turn, increasing revenues.

Example 11

Poor working conditions lead to a higher employee turnover as employees leave and new employees recruited which would potentially increase labour-related expenses, such as recruitment and induction

Test your understanding 2

The business of one of your clients, Olivia Ryan, has made quite substantial losses for the last 6 years, which accounting concept is relevant to preparing the accounts for this client?

- None
- Going concern
- Accruals
- Prudence

3 Qualities of useful financial information

3.1 Introduction

The Conceptual Framework for Financial Reporting identifies two fundamental qualitative characteristics of useful financial information and four enhancing qualitative characteristics:

Fundamental qualitative characteristics:			
Relevance		Faithful representation	
Enhancing qualitative characteristics:			
Comparability	Verifiability	Timeliness	Understandability

3.2 Definitions of the qualitative characteristics

 Definitions

Relevance

Financial information is regarded as relevant if it is capable of influencing the decisions of users.

Faithful representation

This means that financial information must be complete, neutral and free from error.

Comparability

It should be possible to compare an entity over time and with similar information about other entities.

Verifiability

If information can be verified (e.g. through an audit) this provides assurance to the users that it is both credible and reliable.

Timeliness

Information should be provided to users within a timescale suitable for their decision-making purposes.

Understandability

Information should be understandable to those who may want to review and use it. This can be facilitated through appropriate classification, characterisation and presentation of information.

 **Ethical principles**

4.1 Introduction

 Definition – Ethics

Ethics can be defined as the "moral principles that govern a person's behaviour or the conducting of an activity".

The Oxford English Dictionary

Ethics is concerned with how one should act in a certain situation, ensuring that the 'right thing' is being done. You are required to understand how to apply ethical principles whilst working in an accounting function.

Business ethics is the application of ethical principles to the problems typically encountered in a business setting. Applying ethics to a business situation is not separate to a consideration of normal moral judgements.

Typical issues that are addressed include:

- misrepresenting financial performance and position with 'creative accounting' or 'window dressing'
- using legal loopholes to avoid paying tax
- data protection and privacy
- corporate governance
- corporate crime, including insider trading and price fixing
- whistle blowing
- product issues such as patent and copyright infringement, planned obsolescence, product liability and product defects.

4.2 The Code of Ethics for Professional Accountants

The Code of Ethics for Professional Accountants, published by The International Federation of Accountants (IFAC), forms the basis for the ethical codes of many accountancy bodies, including the AAT, ICAEW, ACCA and CIMA.

The Code adopts a principles-based approach. It does not attempt to cover every situation where a member may encounter professional ethical issues, prescribing the way in which he or she should respond. Instead, it adopts a value system, focusing on fundamental professional and ethical principles which are at the heart of proper professional behaviour. Those principles should then be applied to the circumstances faced by the member.

4.3 The importance of fundamental ethical principles and professional scepticism when preparing financial statements

When preparing financial statements, we must ensure that they are prepared accurately and without material misstatement. Complying with the ethical principles is fundamental to this being achieved.

Professional scepticism prompts accountants to critically evaluate information, question assumptions and seek evidence in order to reduce the risk of errors and fraud. Together, the ethical principles and professional scepticism safeguard the reliability of financial information which enables users to make informed decisions.

We will now consider each of the five key ethical principles in turn, in order to see how behaving ethically impacts upon the preparation of the financial statements.

4.4 Five key principles

4.5 Integrity

 Definition

Integrity means that a member must be straightforward and honest in all professional and business relationships. Integrity also implies fair dealing and truthfulness.

Accountants are expected to present financial information fully, honestly and professionally and so that it will be properly understood in its context.

Example 12

A professional accountant should not be associated with reports where the information:

- contains a materially false or misleading statement
- contains statements or information furnished recklessly
- has errors or omissions that make it misleading.

Accountants should abide by relevant law and regulations and remember that, as well as legal documents, letters and verbal agreements may constitute a binding arrangement.

Accountants should strive to be fair and socially responsible and respect cultural differences when dealing with overseas colleagues or contacts. Promises may not be legally binding but repeatedly going back on them can destroy trust, break relationships and lose co-operation.

To maintain integrity, members have the following responsibilities:

4.6 Objectivity

 Definition

Objectivity means that a member must not allow bias, conflict of interest or the undue influence of others to override professional or business judgements.

> **Example 13**
>
> Suppose that you are part of an audit team at a major client:
>
> - If you also own shares in the client company, then this could be viewed as a conflict of interest.
>
> - If you receive excessive hospitality and discounts from the client then this could be seen as an attempt to influence (bribe) you and compromise your objectivity.

Objectivity can also be defined as the state of mind which has regard to all considerations relevant to the task in hand but no other. It is closely linked to the concept of independence.

Whatever capacity members serve in, they should demonstrate their objectivity in different circumstances.

Objectivity is a distinguishing feature of the profession. Members have a responsibility to:

- Communicate information fairly and objectively.

- Disclose fully all relevant information that could reasonably be expected to influence an intended user's understanding of the reports, comments, and recommendations presented.

4.7 The importance of objectivity in accounting

A member must not allow bias, conflict of interest or undue influence of others to override professional or business judgements.

These can include self-interest threats and other conflicts of interest.

Personal threats to independence

Self-interest threats to independence can arise when:

- holding a financial interest in a client, such as owning shares

- having undue dependence on total fees from a client

- receiving excessive hospitality and gifts from a client.

Similarly, familiarity threats to independence can arise when:

- having a close business relationship with a client

- having personal and family relationships with a client.

Threats to independence can also occur due to undue pressures from authority and workload.

Conflict of interest

Threats to objectivity due to a conflict of interest may be created when

- a member in practice competes directly with a client
- a member in practice has a joint venture with a major competitor of a client.
- a member in practice performs services for clients whose interests are in conflict (e.g. they may be competitors in the same industry).
- a member in practice performs services for clients who are in dispute with each other in relation to the matter or transaction in question.

Test your understanding 3

Helen, an AAT member working in an accounting practice, has been offered a job by one of her audit clients.

In order to maintain her independence, what course of action should Helen take?

- Resign immediately.
- Inform the partners of her current employer and be removed from the audit of the client.
- Nothing – it is just an offer.

4.8 Professional competence and due care

Definition

Professional competence means that a member has the knowledge and ability to discharge their responsibilities in accordance with current developments in working practice, legislation and technique.

Definition

Due care means that a member must act diligently and in accordance with applicable technical and professional standards when providing professional services i.e. must not be negligent.

In agreeing to provide professional services, a professional accountant implies that there is a level of competence necessary to perform those services and knowledge, skill and experience will be applied with reasonable care and diligence.

FINANCIAL ACCOUNTING: PREPARING FINANCIAL STATEMENTS

 Example 14

Suppose that you are a junior member of the accounts department of a business. Your normal role is to deal with credit control issues. The payroll clerk has been absent for the past few weeks and so the office manager has asked you to process the payroll for the month.

What are the ethical issues associated with this situation?

You may not have the competence to take on this work responsibly. If you are not aware of the bookkeeping requirements associated with accounting for payroll, you may make errors if you do the work without supervision or training.

If you were to do this work, and then make errors, it could be suggested that you had fallen short of the standard expected from a person working in an accounting environment, even though you are not yet suitably experienced or qualified.

What action could be taken?

You could suggest to the office manager that you are willing to learn to do this work, but that you would need appropriate training and supervision.

Professional accountants must refrain from performing any services that they are not competent to carry out, unless appropriate advice and assistance is obtained to ensure that services are performed satisfactorily.

Professional competence may be divided into two separate phases:

1. **Gaining professional competence** – for example, by training to gain the AAT qualification.

2. **Maintaining professional competence** – accountants need to keep up to date with developments in the accountancy profession including relevant national and international pronouncements on accounting, auditing and other relevant regulations and statutory requirements.

Members have a responsibility to:

- Maintain an appropriate level of professional competence by ongoing development of their knowledge and skills.

- Maintain technical and ethical standards in areas relevant to their work through continuing professional development.

- Perform their professional duties in accordance with relevant laws, regulations, and technical standards.
- Prepare complete and clear reports and recommendations after appropriate analysis of relevant and reliable information.

Members should adopt review procedures that will ensure the quality of their professional work is consistent with relevant national and international pronouncements that are issued from time to time.

Due professional care applies to the exercise of professional judgement in the conduct of work performed and implies that the professional approaches matters requiring professional judgement with proper diligence.

Test your understanding 4

Peter, an AAT member, has been asked by his friend Kristopher to complete a tax self-assessment form for him. Unfortunately, Peter has never completed such a return.

Potentially, which fundamental principle is threatened?

4.9 Confidentiality

Definition

A member must, in accordance with the law, respect the confidentiality of information acquired as a result of professional and business relationships and not disclose any such information to third parties without proper and specific authority unless there is a legal or professional right or duty to disclose.

Confidential information acquired as a result of professional and business relationships must not be used for the personal advantage of the member or third parties.

Confidentiality is not only a matter of disclosure of information. It also concerns using information for personal advantage or for the advantage of a third party.

Example 15

Suppose that you are an accountant in practice and you discover that the client has just won a major contract. This has yet to be publicised. When a press release is made, the share price is expected to rise significantly.

If you buy the (undervalued) shares, you have breached the principle of confidentiality. You used confidential information with the expectation of making a personal gain.

Members should:

- be prudent in the use and protection of information acquired in the course of their duties. The duty of confidentiality continues even after the end of the relationship between the member and the employer or client.

- not use information for any personal gain or in any manner that would be contrary to the law or detrimental to the legitimate and ethical objectives of the business.

- inform those in control about the confidentiality of information acquired in the course of their work. Activities should be monitored to assure that confidentiality is maintained.

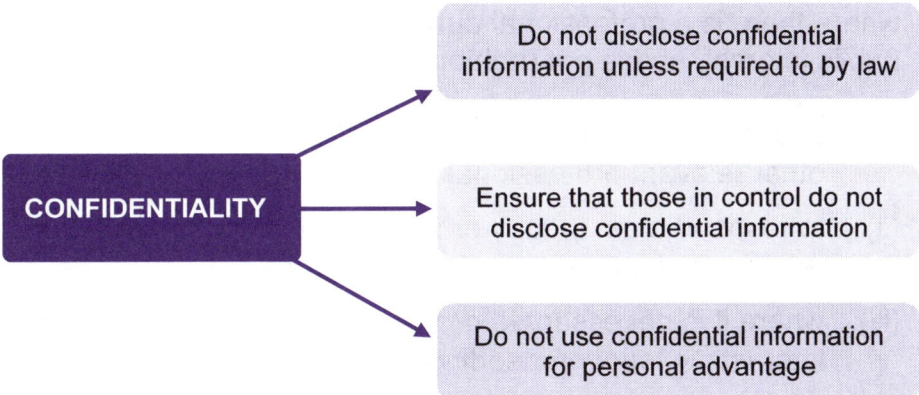

Underlying accounting principles: Chapter 7

A member must take care to maintain confidentiality even in a social environment. The member should be alert to the possibility of accidental disclosure, particularly in circumstances involving close or personal relationships, associates and long-established business relationships.

Note that the duty of confidentiality within an organisation. For example, working in an accounting and finance environment provides you with access to information which may not be known outside of your department, such as payroll information. This should be regarded as confidential and not disclosed to others within the organisation without appropriate authorisation.

There are circumstances when disclosure of confidential information may be permitted or even mandatory:

- if permitted by law and is authorised by the client or the employer
- if required by law, for example:
    (i) production of documents or other provision of evidence in the course of legal proceedings or
    (ii) disclosure to the appropriate public authorities (for example, HMRC) of infringements of the law that come to light or
    (iii) disclosure of actual or suspected money laundering or terrorist financing to the member's firm's MLRO (Money Laundering Reporting Officer) or to SOCA (Serious Organised Crime Authority.
- where there is a professional duty or right to disclose, which is in the public interest, and is not prohibited by law. For example:
    (i) to comply with the quality review of an IFAC member body or other relevant professional body
    (ii) to respond to an inquiry or investigation by the AAT or a relevant regulatory or professional body
    (iii) where it is necessary to protect the member's professional interests in legal proceedings or
    (iv) to comply with technical standards and ethics requirements.

In deciding whether to disclose confidential information, members should consider the following points:

- whether the interests of all parties, including third parties, could be harmed even though the client or employer (or other person to whom there is a duty of confidentiality) consents to the disclosure of information by the member

- whether all the relevant information is known and substantiated, to the extent that this is practicable. When the situation involves unsubstantiated facts, incomplete information or unsubstantiated conclusions, professional judgement should be used in determining the type of disclosure to be made, if any

- the type of communication or disclosure that may be made and by whom it is to be received; in particular, members should be satisfied that the parties to whom the communication is addressed are appropriate recipients.

Test your understanding 5

You work in the payroll department of a large business. Your friend Emma has been working in the admin office for the past few months and wants to know what her colleague Alisha earns. Alisha is always buying new clothes and booking holidays to exotic places!

What should you do?

- Provide Emma with the information she wants – she should be able to know whether she's being treated fairly!

- Tell Emma that you are unable to provide her with that information as it is confidential.

4.10 Professional behaviour

Definition

A professional accountant should comply with relevant laws and regulations and should avoid any action that discredits the profession.

Professional behaviour is distinguished by certain characteristics:

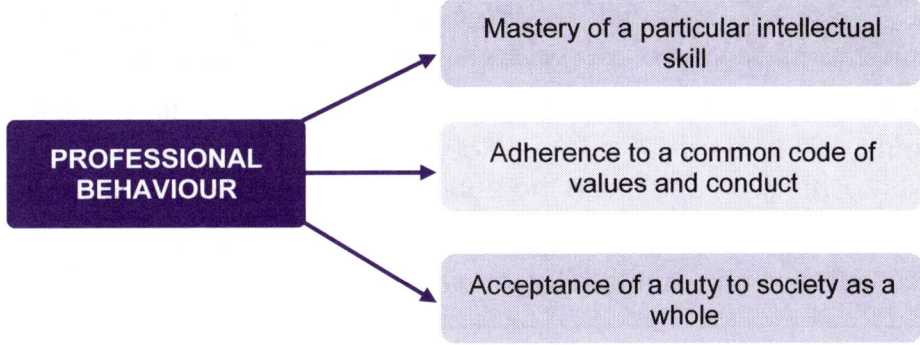

Underlying accounting principles: Chapter 7

The objectives of the accountancy profession are to work to the highest standards of professionalism, to attain the highest levels of performance and generally to meet the public interest requirement. These objectives require four basic needs to be met:

(i) **Credibility** – there is a need for credibility in information and information systems.

(ii) **Professionalism** – there is a need to be clearly identified by employers, clients and other interested parties as a professional person in the accountancy field.

(iii) **Quality of services** – assurance is needed that all services obtained from a professional accountant are carried out to the highest standards of performance.

(iv) **Confidence** – users of the services of professional accountants should be able to feel confident that there is a framework of professional ethics to govern the provision of services.

Example 16

Suppose that you are working as an accounting technician in practice and your client is very keen for the final accounts to be completed for an upcoming meeting which will discuss the future of the business. Upon review of your work, your manager shows concern about the recoverability of a number of debts, potentially showing an understatement in the irrecoverable debts figure.

Further investigation would cause a delay in the completion of the accounts, which would mean the accounts would not be ready for the client's meeting.

The appropriate action, regardless of pressure from the client, is to investigate the recoverability of these debts as any adjustment required could impact the outcome of the meeting.

Test your understanding 6

Leo is an AAT student working for an accountancy practice. Leo is currently working on the audit of Robson Ltd and has been told by his senior to 'hurry up and finish the audit as the available budget is close to being exceeded'.

Discuss the comment made by the senior.

What is understood by the term 'professionalism' will depend on the context and culture of the business.

It should include:

- **Professional/client relationship:**
  - the client presumes the needs will be met without having to direct the process
  - the professional decides which services are actually needed and provides them
  - the professional is trusted not to exploit the authority for unreasonable profit or gain.

- **Professional courtesy** – this is a bare minimum requirement of all business communication.

- **Expertise** – professionalism implies a level of competence that justifies financial remuneration.

- **Marketing and promoting services** – accountants should not make exaggerated or defamatory claims in their marketing.

4.11 The importance of transparency and fairness

Definition

Transparency means openness (say, of discussions), clarity and lack of withholding of relevant information unless necessary.

Decisions are made based upon financial accounts and reports. Therefore investors, amongst other stakeholders want transparent information about a business. It is the quality of the financial reports that enables informed decisions to be made.

Definition

Fairness means a sense of even-handedness and equality. Acting fairly is an ability to reach an equitable judgement in a given ethical situation.

If we act fairly we encourage strong organisational goals and develop strong relationships within a business.

Auditors may refer to financial information as being 'true and fair'. Fair implies that the financial statements present the information faithfully without any element of bias.

> **Test your understanding 7**
>
> You are a trainee accountant in your second year of training within a small practice. A more senior trainee has been on sick leave, and you are due to go on study leave.
>
> You have been told by your manager that, before you go on leave, you must complete a complicated task that the senior trainee was supposed to do. The deadline suggested appears unrealistic, given the complexity of the work.
>
> You feel that you are not sufficiently experienced to complete the work alone but your manager appears unable to offer the necessary support. You feel slightly intimidated by your manager, and also feel under pressure to be a 'team player' and help out.
>
> However, if you try to complete the work to the required quality but fail, you could face repercussions upon your return from study leave.
>
> **Required:**
>
> Analyse the scenario to determine the following:
>
> (a)   Which fundamental ethical principles are involved?
>
> (b)   What possible courses of action could be taken?

5   Summary

Financial statements provide a number of different users with information for their different needs. You should have an appreciation for the different users and what they wish to know about the financial performance and position of a business.

We have reviewed a number of accounting concepts which you must understand and see their application in practical terms. You also need to know the two fundamental qualitative characteristics of financial information which are: relevance and faithful representation and the four enhancing qualitative characteristics of financial information which are: comparability, verifiability, timeliness and understandability.

The importance of ethical behaviour in an accounting environment needs to be understood. This unit introduced the ethical principles that need to be applied when working in an accounting environment. The five key principles which make up the code of ethics are: integrity, objectivity, professional competence, confidentiality and professional behaviour.

Test your understanding answers

Test your understanding 1

False. In accordance with the prudence concept and IAS 2. Inventory is recorded at the lower of cost or net realisable value, rather than the expected selling price. This ensures profit on the sale of inventory is only realised when the sale takes place.

Test your understanding 2

- Going concern

Test your understanding 3

Helen should inform her current employers and should be removed from the audit of the client.

Test your understanding 4

Professional competence and due care.

Test your understanding 5

Tell Emma that you are unable to provide her with that information as it is confidential. Regardless of Emma being your friend, you have a duty of confidentiality which must not be breached.

Test your understanding 6

It may be that Leo is working slower than expected, in which case the comment may be simply an attempt at motivation.

However, the comment to hurry up the audit may mean that the job is not done to the correct standard, thus compromising the ethical principle of professional behaviour and due care.

If the senior puts undue pressure on Leo, then this could be viewed as intimidation which threatens objectivity.

Test your understanding 7

Fundamental ethical principles affected

(a) **Integrity**: Can you be open and honest about the situation?

(b) **Professional competence and due care**: Would it be right to attempt to complete work that is technically beyond your abilities, without proper supervision? Is it possible to complete the work within the time available and still act diligently to achieve the required quality of output?

(c) **Professional behaviour**: Can you refuse to perform the work without damaging your reputation within the practice? Alternatively, could the reputation of the practice suffer if you attempt the work?

(d) **Objectivity**: Pressure from your manager, combined with the fear of repercussions, gives rise to an intimidation threat to objectivity.

Possible course of action

You should explain to your manager that you do not have sufficient time and experience to complete the work to a satisfactory standard.

However, you should demonstrate a constructive attitude, and suggest how the problem may be resolved. (Your professional body is available to advise you in this respect.) For example, you might suggest the use of a subcontract bookkeeper.

Explore the possibility of assigning another member of staff to supervise your work.

If you feel that your manager is unsympathetic or fails to understand the issue, you should consider how best to raise the matter with the person within the practice responsible for training. It would be diplomatic to suggest to your manager that you raise the matter together, and present your respective views.

It would be unethical to attempt to complete the work if you doubt your competence.

However, simply refusing to, or resigning from your employment, would cause significant problems for both you and the practice. You could consult your professional body. If you seek advice from outside the practice (for example legal advice), then you should be mindful of the need for confidentiality as appropriate.

You should document, in detail, the steps that you take in resolving your dilemma, in case your ethical judgement is challenged in the future.

FINANCIAL ACCOUNTING: PREPARING FINANCIAL STATEMENTS

Accounting for inventory

Introduction

In this chapter we will learn how to account for inventory, including recording purchases, opening and closing inventory and the issues that surround valuing and recording closing inventory.

As well as being able to enter a valuation for closing inventory correctly in the extended trial balance and financial statements, we will consider other aspects of inventory valuation from IAS 2.

This will include:

- a closing inventory reconciliation
- valuing inventory at the lower of cost and net realisable value
- determining the cost of inventory and its net realisable value
- various methods of costing inventory units.

ASSESSMENT CRITERIA	CONTENTS
Record inventory (5.3)	1 Inventory 2 Closing inventory reconciliation 3 Valuing inventories 4 Accounting for inventories

1 Inventory

1.1 Purchasing inventory

When inventory is purchased it is accounted for within purchases, no adjustment is made to the inventory account until the year end. The accounting entry to record the purchase of inventory is:

Dr Purchases

Cr Bank/trade payables

You will be required to calculate inventory at the end of an accounting period and post it to the ledger system by way of a journal entry.

Most businesses will have a variety of different types of inventory. For a retail business this will be the goods that are in inventory and held for resale. In a manufacturing business there are likely to be raw material inventories (that will be used to make the business's products), partly finished products (known as work in progress) and completed goods ready for sale (known as finished goods). The inventories held are assets of the business.

1.2 Counting closing inventory

At the end of the accounting period an inventory count (known as a stock take) will normally take place where the quantity of each line of inventory is counted and recorded. The organisation will then know the number of units of each type of inventory that it has at the year end. Accounting software can be used to automate the process of recording and tracking inventory. The next stage is to value the inventory.

1.3 Closing inventory and the financial statements

Once the inventory has been counted and valued it must then be included in the financial statements. The valuation and accounting for this will be considered later in the chapter.

1.4 Statement of financial position

The closing inventory is an asset of the business and as such will appear on the statement of financial position. It is a current asset and will normally be shown as the first item in the list of current assets, as it is the least liquid of the current assets. Liquidity refers to the ease of converting an asset into cash.

1.5 Statement of profit or loss

Inventory appears as part of the cost of sales in the statement of profit or loss:

	£	£
Revenue		X
Less: cost of sales		
Opening inventory	X	
Plus: purchases	X	
	X	
Less: closing inventory	(X)	
		(X)
Gross profit		X

As you will see the 'cost of sales' figure is made up of the opening inventory, plus the purchases of the business for the period, less the closing inventory.

The opening inventory is the figure included in the accounts as last year's closing inventory.

The purchases figure is the balance on the purchases account.

The closing inventory figure is then deducted in order to determine the cost of the goods actually sold in the period.

The items included in the closing inventory have not yet been sold, they cannot be used to determine the cost of the sales within the current year, and so, are deducted. This is an application of the accruals basis of accounting.

Closing inventory appears in both the statement of financial position and the statement of profit or loss.

2 Closing inventory reconciliation

2.1 Introduction

Before the inventory of a business can be valued, the physical amount of inventory held must be counted and the amounts that exist checked to records. Any discrepancies must be investigated. This is known as a closing inventory reconciliation. Accounting software can be used to automate the process of recording, tracking and valuing inventory, such as software used within supermarkets.

2.2 Stores records

For each line of inventory, the stores department would maintain a record such as a 'bin card' or 'inventory card'. The following details are maintained:

- the quantity of inventory received from suppliers (sourced from delivery notes or goods received notes). This should be netted off by any goods returned to the suppliers (sourced from credit notes or despatch notes)

- the quantity issued for sale or use in manufacture (sourced from store requisitions)

- any amounts returned to the stores department (sourced from goods returned notes), and

- the amount/balance of units that should be on hand at that time.

At any point in time the balance on the stores record should agree with the number of items of that line of inventory physically held by the stores department.

2.3 Possible reasons for differences

If there is a difference between the quantity physically counted and the records this could be for a variety of reasons:

- Goods may have been delivered and therefore have been physically counted but the records have not yet been updated to reflect the delivery.

- Goods may have been returned to suppliers and therefore will not have been counted but again the records have not yet been updated.

- Goods may have been issued for sales or for use in manufacturing, therefore they are not in the stores department but the records do not yet reflect this issue.
- Some items may have been stolen so are no longer physically in inventory.
- Errors may have been made, either in counting the number of items held, or in entering details in the records or system.

Example 1

At 30 June 20X4 a sole trader carried out an inventory count and compared the quantity of each line of inventory to the inventory records. In most cases the actual inventory quantity counted agreed with the records but, for three lines of inventory, the sole trader found differences.

	Inventory code		
	FR153	JE363	PT321
Quantity counted	116	210	94
Inventory record quantity	144	150	80

The inventory records and documentation were thoroughly checked for these inventory lines and the following was discovered:

- On 28 June, 28 units of FR153 had been returned to the supplier as they were damaged. A credit note has not yet been received and the despatch note had not been recorded in the inventory records.

- On 29 June, a goods received note showed that 100 units of JE363 had arrived from a supplier but this had not yet been entered in the inventory records.

- Also, on 29 June, 14 units of PT321 had been recorded as an issue to sales, however they were not physically dispatched to the customer until after the inventory was counted.

- On 28 June, the sole trader had taken 40 units of JE363 out of inventory in order to process a rush order for a customer and had forgotten to update the inventory record.

The closing inventory reconciliation must now be performed and the actual quantities for each line of inventory must be determined.

Solution

Closing inventory reconciliation – 30 June 20X4

FR153	Quantity
Inventory record	144
Less: Returned to supplier	(28)
Counted	116

When valuing the FR153 inventory line, the actual quantity counted of 116 should be used. There should also be a journal entry to reflect the purchase return:

Debit   Payables ledger control account

Credit   Purchases returns

JE363	Quantity
Inventory record	150
Add: GRN not recorded	100
Less: Sales requisition	(40)
Counted	210

The quantity to be valued should be the quantity counted of 210 units. If the sale has not been recorded then an adjustment will be required for the value of the sales invoice:

Debit   Receivables ledger control account

Credit   Sales account

In addition, if the purchase has not been recorded then an adjustment will be required for the value of the purchase invoice:

Debit   Purchases

Credit   Payables ledger control account

PT321	Quantity
Inventory record	80
Add: Subsequent sale	14
Counted	94

In this case the amount to be valued is the inventory record amount of 80 units and if the sale has not been recorded then an adjustment must be made at the selling price of the 14 units, (note that this is done as the inventory was sold on 30th June, pre-period end, but after the inventory count):

Debit   Receivables ledger control account

Credit   Sales account

3 Valuing inventories

3.1 Introduction

Now that we know how many units of inventory we have from the inventory count, we will consider how the units of inventory are valued.

3.2 IAS 2

IAS 2 *Inventory* deals with the way in which inventories should be valued for inclusion in the financial statements. The basic rule from IAS 2 is that inventories should be valued at: '**the lower of cost and net realisable value**', [IAS 2, para 9].

Definition – Cost of inventory

IAS 2 *Inventories* defines cost as comprising '**all costs of purchase, costs of conversion and other costs incurred in bringing the inventories to their present location and condition**' [IAS 2, para 10].

3.3 Cost

Purchase cost includes the purchase price, import duties, transport and handling costs and any other directly attributable costs, less trade discounts, rebates and subsidies.

Accounting for inventory: Chapter 8

Costs of conversion includes:

- direct production costs
- production overheads, and
- other overheads attributable to bringing the product to its present location and condition.

This means the following:

- Only **production overheads** – not those for marketing, selling and distribution – should be included in cost.
- Exceptional spoilage, idle capacity and other abnormal costs are not part of the cost of inventories.
- General management and non-production related administration costs should not be included in inventory cost.

The **cost of inventory** can be summarised as:

- the purchase price from the supplier, less any trade discounts
- any delivery costs to get it to its current location, and
- the production cost of any work performed on it since it was purchased.

This means that different items of the same inventory held in different locations may have different costs.

Test your understanding 1

A business had to pay a special delivery charge of £84 on a delivery of urgently required games software it had purchased for resale. This amount had been debited to office expenses account.

(a) This treatment is incorrect. Which account should have been debited? (Tick)

    Purchases account ☐

    Inventory account ☐

    Returns Inwards account ☐

(b) Give the journal entry to correct the error.

In many cases organisations buy goods at different times and at different prices, therefore when determining the cost of inventory held, assumptions have to be made about the movement of inventory into and out of the business.

The methods of determining the purchase price of the goods is examined in the Management Accounting Techniques unit. In that Unit you will learn about two methods of costing.

The first in, first out (FIFO) method of costing inventory assumes that the goods going out of the warehouse are the earliest purchases. Therefore, the inventory items left are the most recent purchases.

The weighted average cost (AVCO) method values inventory at the weighted average of the purchase prices each time inventory is issued. This means that the total purchase price of the inventory is divided by the number of units of inventory, but this calculation must be carried out before every issue out of the warehouse.

3.4 Net realisable value

Definition – Net realisable value

Net realisable value (NRV) is the actual or estimated selling price (net of trade but before settlement discounts) less all further costs to completion and all costs to be incurred in marketing, selling and distributing.

NRV can be summarised as the actual or estimated selling price less any future costs that will be incurred before the product can be sold.

Example 2

Jenny manufactures widgets. Details of the basic version are given below:

	Cost £	Selling price £	Selling cost £
Basic widgets	5	10	2

What value should be attributed to each widget in inventory?

Solution

Inventory valuation	£
Cost	5
Net realisable value (£10 – £2)	8

Therefore, inventory should be valued at £5 per widget, the lower of cost and NRV.

It is wrong to add the selling cost of £2 to the production cost of £5 and value the inventory at £7 because it is not a production cost.

3.5 Separate items or groups of inventories

When determining whether inventory should be valued at cost or net realisable value each item of inventory or groups of similar items should be considered separately.

FINANCIAL ACCOUNTING: PREPARING FINANCIAL STATEMENTS

 Example 3

A business has three lines of inventory A, B and C. The details of cost and NRV for each line is given below:

	Cost £	NRV £
A	1,200	2,000
B	1,000	800
C	1,500	2,500
	3,700	5,300

What is the value of the closing inventory of the business?

Solution

It is incorrect to value the inventory at £3,700, the total cost, although it is clearly lower than the total NRV. Each line of inventory must be considered separately.

	Cost £	NRV £	Inventory value £
A	1,200	2,000	1,200
B	1,000	800	800
C	1,500	2,500	1,500
	3,700	5,300	3,500

You will see that the NRV of B is lower than its cost and therefore the NRV is the value that must be included for B.

Make sure that you look at each inventory line separately and do not just take the total cost of £3,700 as the inventory value.

Test your understanding 2

A business owned by Kit sells three products: A, B and C. At the year-end, inventories were held as follows:

	Cost £	Selling price £
A	1,200	1,500
B	6,200	6,100
C	920	930

At sale a 5% commission is payable to an agent.

What is the total value of these inventories in the business's accounts?

Complete the following table.

	Cost £	Selling price £	NRV £
A			
B			
C			

Total inventory valuation =

3.6 Adjustment to the closing inventory valuation

If closing inventory has been valued at cost and it is subsequently determined that some items have a net realisable value which is lower than cost, then the valuation of the closing inventory must be reduced.

4 Accounting for inventories

4.1 Accounting for closing inventory

In order to determine the valuation of closing inventory the cost must be compared to the net realisable value. We have seen how cost is defined and the major element of cost will be the purchase price of the goods.

Once the inventory has been counted and valued, it must be included in the accounting records.

FINANCIAL ACCOUNTING: PREPARING FINANCIAL STATEMENTS

At the period end, adjustments must be made to account for closing inventory in the statement of profit or loss (SPL) and the statement of financial position (SFP).

The journal required is:

Dr   Inventory SFP – as it is an asset on the SFP

Cr   Inventory SPL – closing inventory in the cost of sales

4.2 Accounting for opening inventory

This is the balance on the inventory SFP account, being the closing inventory figure for the previous accounting period. Inventory brought forward is assumed to have been used to generate assets for sale.

No entries are put through this inventory account until the period end; this is why opening inventory appears in the trial balance. Remember that all purchases of goods are accounted for in the purchases account, they should never be entered directly into the inventory account.

The opening inventory balance must be removed from inventory assets and recognised as an expense as part of the cost of sales in the statement of profit or loss.

The double entry for this is:

Dr   Inventory SPL – opening inventory in the cost of sales

Cr   Inventory SFP – as it no longer an asset on the SFP

This opening inventory balance has now been removed from the inventory account in the statement of financial position.

Example 4

A business has a figure for opening inventory of £10,000. The opening inventory would be presented as follows:

Inventory – SFP

	£		£
Balance b/d – opening inventory	10,000		

As inventory is an asset, this is currently shown as a debit balance in the inventory asset (SFP) account. At the end of the year, the opening inventory must be removed from assets and the expense recognised as follows:

Dr Inventory SPL £10,000

Cr Inventory SFP £10,000

Accounting for inventory: Chapter 8

Inventory – SFP

	£		£
Balance b/d – opening inventory	10,000	Opening inventory – SPL	10,000

Inventory – SPL

	£		£
Opening inventory - SFP	10,000		

Next, the closing inventory for the year of £12,000 must be recognised using the following adjustment:

Dr Inventory SFP £12,000

Cr Inventory SPL £12,000

Inventory – SFP

	£		£
Balance b/d – opening inventory	10,000	Opening inventory – SPL	10,000
Closing inventory	12,000		

Inventory – SPL

	£		£
Opening inventory - SFP	10,000	Closing inventory – SFP	12,000

The inventory in the SFP is the closing inventory valuation of £12,000, closing inventory is classified as a current asset.

Within the SPL, the opening inventory and closing inventory form part of the cost of sales. Shown below is how the opening and closing inventory balances would appear as part of the cost of sales:

Opening inventory	£10,000
Plus: purchases	X
	X
Less: closing inventory	(£12,000)

Opening inventory forms part of the expense of cost of sales as it is assumed to be used to generate assets for sale. After adding the purchases expense for the year, which increases the cost of sales, the closing inventory is deducted so that the cost of sales does not include costs of goods that remain unsold.

Test your understanding 3

1. Where will the closing inventory appear in the statement of financial position? (Tick)

    Non-current assets ☐

    Current assets ☐

2. Where will the closing inventory appear in the statement of profit or loss? (Tick)

    Expenses ☐

    Cost of sales ☐

3. A line of inventory has been counted and the inventory count shows that there are 50 units more in the inventory room than is recorded on the inventory card. What possible reasons might there be for this difference?

    _____

    _____

    _____

    _____

4. Complete the following sentence.

    Inventory should be valued at the _____ of _____ and _____

5. The closing inventory of a sole trader has been valued at cost of £5,800 and recorded in the trial balance. However, one item of inventory which cost £680 has a net realisable value of £580. What is the journal entry required for this adjustment? (Tick)

Debit	**Credit**	
Closing inventory SFP	Closing inventory SPL	☐
Closing inventory SPL	Closing inventory SFP	☐

Accounting for inventory: Chapter 8

 Test your understanding 4

Phil Townsend is the proprietor of Infortec and he sends you the following email:

'I have been looking at the inventory valuation for the year end and I have some concerns about the Mica40z PCs.

We have ten of these in inventory, each of which cost £500 and are priced to sell to customers at £580. Unfortunately, they all have faulty hard drives which will need to be replaced before they can be sold. The cost is £100 for each machine.

However, as you know, the Mica40z is now out of date and having spoken to some computer retailers I am fairly certain that we are going to have to scrap them or give them away for spares. Perhaps for now we should include them in the closing inventory figure at cost. Can you please let me have your views.'

Required:

Write an email in response to Phil email. You should refer to alternative inventory valuations and to appropriate accounting standards.

A pro forma email has been provided below.

To:	Re:
From:	Date: X-X-20XX

FINANCIAL ACCOUNTING: PREPARING FINANCIAL STATEMENTS

 Test your understanding 5

Melanie Langton trades as 'Explosives'.

You have received an email from Melanie Langton:

'I have been looking at the draft financial statements you have produced. In the valuation of the closing inventory you have included some of the jeans at less than cost price. The figure you used is net realisable value and this has effectively reduced the profit for the period.

The closing inventory will be sold in the next financial period and my understanding of the accruals concept is that the revenue from selling the inventory should be matched against the cost of that inventory.

This is not now possible since part of the cost of the inventory has been written off in reducing the closing inventory valuation from cost price to net realisable value.'

Required:

Write a suitable response to Melanie Langton in the form of an email.

Your answer should include references to relevant accounting concepts and to IAS 2.

A pro forma email has been provided below.

To:	Re:
From:	Date: X-X-20XX

5 Summary

In this chapter we have covered the valuation of inventory and how to record opening and closing inventory adjustments, in accordance with accounting standard IAS 2.

Test your understanding answers

Test your understanding 1

(a) Purchases account

			£	£
(b)	Dr	Purchases a/c	84	
	Cr	Office expenses a/c		84

Test your understanding 2

Inventory is valued at the lower of cost and net realisable value (costs to be incurred 5% in selling inventory are deducted from selling price in computing NRV).

	Cost £	Selling price £	NRV £
A	1,200	1,500	1,425
B	6,200	6,100	5,795
C	920	930	884

Total inventory values (1,200 + 5,795 + 884) = **£7,879**

Accounting for inventory: Chapter 8

 Test your understanding 3

1. As a current asset.
2. As a reduction to cost of sales.
3.
   - A delivery has not yet been recorded on the inventory card.
   - A return of goods from a customer has not yet been recorded on the inventory card.
   - An issue to sales has been recorded on the inventory card but not yet despatched.
   - A return to a supplier has been recorded on the inventory card but not yet despatched.
4. Inventory should be valued at the lower of cost and NRV (net realisable value).
5.

Debit	Closing inventory – SPL	£100
Credit	Closing inventory – SFP	£100

 Test your understanding 4

To: Phil Townsend
From: Accounting Technician

Re: Valuation of inventory
Date: X-X-20XX

I note your observations concerning the inventory valuation and the issue of the Mica 40z PCs.

IAS 2 Inventory, states that inventory should be valued at the lower of cost and net realisable value. The NRV of a Mica 40z is £480.

If we were confident that we could sell them at that price then that would be the value for inventory purposes as this is lower than their cost of £500.

However, as you feel we are likely to scrap these computers, then I recommend we write them off to a zero-inventory valuation immediately as the net realisable value is, in effect, zero.

Test your understanding 5

To: Melanie Langton **Re:** Closing inventory valuation
From: Accounting Technician **Date:** X-X-20XX

I refer to your recent note concerning the valuation of the closing inventory. As far as the accounting concepts are concerned, the cost of inventory would normally be matched against income in compliance with the accruals concept (i.e. purchase costs of inventory are recognised in the same period as the revenue from selling those items). Most of your inventory will be valued at cost rather than net realisable value, as the latter is usually higher than cost due to the need to achieve profit margins, and IAS 2 requires inventory to be valued at the lower of cost and net realisable value. If, however, the estimated selling price were to fall below cost (for example if market conditions changed or if the goods became damaged) then the IAS 2 principle just identified would require you to impair the value of inventory down to the estimated NRV.

I hope this fully explains the points raised in your note.

FINANCIAL ACCOUNTING: PREPARING FINANCIAL STATEMENTS

Irrecoverable and doubtful debts

Introduction

When producing a trial balance or extended trial balance, and eventually a set of final accounts, a number of adjustments are often required to the initial trial balance figures.

One of these adjustments may be to the receivables balance in order to either write off any irrecoverable debts or to provide for any allowance for doubtful receivables.

ASSESSMENT CRITERIA	CONTENTS
Record irrecoverable debts and allowances for doubtful receivables (5.2)	1 Problems with receivable accounts 2 Irrecoverable debts 3 Doubtful receivables 4 Types of allowances for doubtful receivables 5 Writing off a debt already provided for 6 Money received from irrecoverable and doubtful receivables

1 Problems with receivable accounts

1.1 Introduction

When sales are made to credit customers the double entry is to debit the receivables account (receivables ledger control account) and credit the sales account. Therefore, the sale is recorded in the accounts as soon as the invoice is sent out to the customer on the basis that the customer will pay for these goods.

1.2 Conditions of uncertainty

In conditions of uncertainty more evidence is needed of the existence of an asset than is needed for the existence of a liability.

This has been known in the past as the **concept of prudence**. Therefore, if there is any evidence of significant uncertainty about the receipt of cash from a receivable then it may be that this asset, the receivable, should not be recognised.

1.3 Aged receivable analysis

Definition – Aged receivable analysis

An aged receivable analysis shows when the elements of the total debt owed by each customer were incurred.

An aged receivable analysis should be produced on a regular basis and studied with care. If a customer has outstanding debts which are old or if there are regular occurrences of a customer not paying debts when due, there may be a problem with the receivable.

1.4 Other information about receivables

It is not uncommon for businesses to go into liquidation or receivership, in which case it is often likely that any outstanding credit supplier will not receive payment. This will often be reported in the local or national news or the information could be discovered informally from conversation with other parties in the same line of business.

If information is gathered about a receivable with potential problems which may lead to your organisation not receiving amounts due, this must be investigated.

Care should be taken as customers are very important to a business and any discussion or correspondence with the customer must be carried out with tact and courtesy.

2 Irrecoverable debts

2.1 What is an irrecoverable debt?

If information is reliably gathered that a credit customer is having problems paying the amount they owe, a decision has to be made about how to account for this uncertainty. This will normally take the form of deciding whether the debt is an irrecoverable debt or a doubtful receivable.

> **Definition – Irrecoverable debt**
>
> An irrecoverable debt is a debt that is not going to be received from the credit customer (receivable).

An irrecoverable debt is one that the organisation is reasonably certain will not be received at all from the credit customer. This may be decided after discussions with the credit customer (receivable), after legal advice (if the customer has gone into liquidation) or simply because the credit customer has disappeared.

2.2 Accounting treatment of an irrecoverable debt

An irrecoverable debt is one where it has been determined that the debt will never be recovered and therefore the receivable amount must not be recognised.

The double entry reflects:

(a) the business no longer has the debt, so this asset must be removed from the accounts

(b) the business must put an expense equal to the debt as a charge to its statement of profit or loss because it has 'lost' this money. It does this by putting the expense initially through an 'irrecoverable debt expense' account.

Irrecoverable and doubtful debts: Chapter 9

The double entry for the irrecoverable debt is:

Dr Irrecoverable debts expense account (SPL)

Cr Receivables ledger control account (RLCA) (SFP)

There is also a credit entry in the individual receivable's account in the memorandum (subsidiary) receivables ledger to match the entry in the RLCA.

Example 1

Aamir reviews his receivables (which total £10,000) and notices an amount due from Blake of £500. Aamir knows that this will never be recovered so he wants to write it off.

Solution

Receivables ledger control account

	£		£
Balance b/d	10,000	Irrecoverable debts expense	500
		Balance c/d	9,500
	10,000		10,000
Balance b/d	9,500		

Irrecoverable debts expense

	£		£
RLCA	500	SPL	500

In the memorandum (subsidiary) receivables ledger there will also be an entry in Blake's account:

Blake's account

	£		£
Balance b/d	500	Irrecoverable debts written off	500

FINANCIAL ACCOUNTING: PREPARING FINANCIAL STATEMENTS

Test your understanding 1

A business has total receivables of £117,489. One of these debts from J Casy totalling £2,448 is now considered to be irrecoverable and must be accounted for.

Record the accounting entries in the general ledger for the irrecoverable debt.

Receivables ledger control account

£	£

Irrecoverable debts expense

£	£

The accounting treatment of irrecoverable debts means that the debt is not recognised as a receivable in the accounting records and the statement of profit or loss is charged with an expense.

3 Doubtful receivables

3.1 What are doubtful receivables?

In the previous section we considered debts that we were reasonably certain would not be recovered. The recoverability position with some receivables is not so clear cut. The organisation may have doubts about whether the debt will be received but may not be certain that it will not.

Definition – Doubtful receivables

Doubtful receivables are those where the recovery of debt is in doubt.

The situation here is not as clear cut as when a debt is determined to be irrecoverable and the accounting treatment is therefore different. If there is doubt about the recoverability of this debt then according to the prudence concept this must be recognised in the accounting records but not to the extreme of writing the debt off.

Recording an allowance for doubtful receivables is an example of the application of the accruals concept; it is estimating future irrecoverable debts and therefore improves the accuracy of the financial statements.

3.2 Accounting treatment of doubtful receivables

As the debt is only doubtful rather than irrecoverable we do not need to write it off but the doubt has to be reflected another way. This is done by setting up an allowance for doubtful receivables.

Definition – Allowance for doubtful receivables

An allowance for doubtful receivables is an amount that is netted off against the receivables balance in the statement of financial position to show that there is some doubt about the recoverability of those amounts.

An allowance for doubtful receivables account is credited in order to net this off against the receivables balance and the debit entry is made to an allowance for doubtful receivables adjustment expense account recognised in the statement of profit or loss.

The double entry therefore is:

Dr Allowance for doubtful receivables adjustment account (SPL)

Cr Allowance for doubtful receivables account (SFP)

FINANCIAL ACCOUNTING: PREPARING FINANCIAL STATEMENTS

 Example 2

At the end of her first year of trading Beatriz has receivables of £120,000 and has decided that of these, there is some doubt as to the recoverability of £5,000 of this balance.

Set up the allowance for doubtful receivables in the ledger accounts and show how the net receivables would appear in the statement of financial position at the end of the year.

Solution

Allowance for doubtful receivables account

	£		£
		Allowance for doubtful receivables adjustments	5,000

Allowance for doubtful receivables adjustment account

	£		£
Allowance for doubtful receivables	5,000		

Statement of financial position extract

	£
Receivables	120,000
Less: Allowance for doubtful receivables	(5,000)
	———
Net receivables	115,000
	———

The accounting treatment of doubtful receivables ensures that the statement of financial position clearly shows that there is some doubt about the collectability of some of the debts and the statement of profit or loss is charged with the possible loss from not collecting these debts.

3.3 Changes in the allowance

As the allowance for doubtful receivables account is a statement of financial position balance, the balance on that account will remain in the ledger accounts until it is changed. When the allowance is altered, **only the increase or the decrease** is charged or credited to the allowance for doubtful receivables adjustment.

Increase in allowance:

Dr Allowance for doubtful receivables **adjustment** account (SPL)

Cr Allowance for doubtful receivables account (SFP)

Decrease in allowance:

Dr Allowance for doubtful receivables account (SFP)

Cr Allowance for doubtful receivables **adjustment** account (SPL)

Example 3

At the end of the second year of trading Beatriz feels that the allowance should be increased to £7,000. At the end of the third year of trading Beatriz wishes to decrease the allowance to £4,000.

Show the entries in the ledger accounts required at the end of year 2 and year 3 of trading.

Solution

Allowance for doubtful receivables account

	£		£
		Balance b/d	5,000
End of year 2 balance c/d	7,000	Year 2 – Allowance for doubtful receivables adjustment account	2,000
	7,000		7,000
Year 3 – Allowance for doubtful receivables adjustment account	3,000	Balance b/d	7,000
End of year 3 balance c/d	4,000		
	7,000		7,000
		Balance b/d	4,000

FINANCIAL ACCOUNTING: PREPARING FINANCIAL STATEMENTS

Allowance for doubtful receivables adjustment account

	£		£
Year 2 Allowance for doubtful receivables account	2,000	Statement of profit or loss year 2	2,000
	2,000		2,000
Statement of profit or loss year 3	3,000	Year 3 Allowance for doubtful receivables account	3,000
	3,000		3,000

Take care that the statement of profit or loss is only debited or credited with the increase or decrease in the allowance each year.

4 Types of allowances for doubtful receivables

4.1 Introduction

There are two main types of allowances for doubtful receivables:

- specific allowances
- general allowances.

This does not affect the accounting for allowance for doubtful receivables but it does affect the calculation of the allowance.

4.2 Specific allowances

Definition – Specific allowance

A specific allowance is an allowance against identified specific debts.

This will normally be determined by close scrutiny of the aged receivable analysis in order to determine whether there are specific debts that the organisation feels may not be paid.

4.3 General allowance

Definition – General allowance

A general allowance is an allowance against receivables as a whole normally expressed as a percentage of the receivable balance.

Most businesses will find that not all of their receivables pay their debts. Experience may indicate that generally a percentage of debts, say 3%, will not be paid.

The organisation may not know which debts these are going to be but they will maintain an allowance for 3% of the receivable balance at the year end.

Care should be taken with the calculation of this allowance as the percentage should be of the receivable balance after deducting any specific allowances as well as any irrecoverable debts written off.

Order of dealing with irrecoverable and doubtful receivables:

1 Write off irrecoverable debts
2 Create specific allowances
3 Calculate the net receivables figures after both irrecoverable debts and specific allowances
4 Calculate the general provision using the net receivables figure from point 3.

Example 4

A business has receivables of £356,000 of which £16,000 are to be written off as irrecoverable debts.

Of the remainder a specific allowance is to be made against a debt of £2,000 and a general allowance of 4% is required against the remaining receivables.

The opening balance on the allowance for doubtful receivables account is £12,000.

Show the entries in the allowance for doubtful receivables account, the allowance for doubtful receivables adjustment account and the irrecoverable debts expense account.

Solution

Calculation of allowance required:

		£
	Receivables	356,000
1	Less: irrecoverable debt to be written off	(16,000)
2	Less: specific allowances	(2,000)
3	Remaining receivables	338,000
4	General allowance 4% × £338,000	13,520
	Specific allowance	2,000
	Allowance at year end	15,520

Allowance for doubtful receivables (note 1)

	£		£
		Balance b/d	12,000
Balance c/d	15,520	Allowance for doubtful receivables adjustment – increase in allowance	3,520
	15,520		15,520
		Balance b/d	15,520

Receivables ledger control account (note 2)

	£		£
Balance b/d	356,000	Irrecoverable debt expense – written off	16,000
		Balance c/d	340,000
	356,000		356,000
Balance b/d	340,000		

Irrecoverable debt expense account

	£		£
Receivables (Note 2)	16,000	Statement of profit or loss	16,000
	16,000		16,000

Allowance for doubtful receivables adjustment account

	£		£
Allowance for doubtful receivables account (Note 1)	3,520	Statement of profit or loss	3,520
	3,520		3,520

Note 1

The balance on the allowance account is simply increased or decreased at each year end. In this case the required allowance has been calculated to be £15,520. The existing allowance is £12,000 so the increase is calculated as:

	£
Allowance at start of year b/f	12,000
Allowance required at year end	15,520
Increase in allowance	3,520

This is credited to the allowance account and debited to the allowance for doubtful receivables adjustment account.

Note 2

The £16,000 irrecoverable debt is written out of the books. The double entry for this is to credit the RLCA and debit the irrecoverable debt expense.

Note that the allowance does not affect the RLCA.

Any specific allowance must be deducted from the receivables balance before the general allowance percentage is applied.

Test your understanding 2

DD makes an allowance for doubtful receivables of 5% of receivables.

On 1 January 20X5 the balance on the allowance for doubtful receivables account was £1,680.

During the year the business incurred irrecoverable debts amounting to £1,950. On 31 December 20X5 receivables amounted to £32,000 after writing off the irrecoverable debts of £1,950.

Required:

Write up the relevant accounts for the year ended 31 December 20X5.

FINANCIAL ACCOUNTING: PREPARING FINANCIAL STATEMENTS

Test your understanding 3

Genaro had the following balances in his trial balance at 31 March 20X4:

	£
Total receivables	61,000
Allowance for doubtful receivables at 1 April 20X3	1,490

After the trial balance had been prepared it was decided to carry forward at 31 March 20X4 a specific allowance of £800 and a general allowance equal to 1% of remaining receivables. It was also decided to write off debts amounting to £1,000.

What is the total charge for irrecoverable and doubtful receivables which should appear in the business's statement of profit or loss for the year ended 31 March 20X4?

5 Writing off a debt already provided for

5.1 Introduction

It may occur that a doubtful receivables allowance is made at a year end, and then it is decided in a later year to write the debt off completely as an irrecoverable debt as it will not be received.

Example 5

At 31 December 20X2, Johan has a balance on the RLCA of £20,000 and a specific allowance for doubtful receivables of £1,000 which was created in 20X1.

This £1,000 relates to Ali whose debt was thought to be doubtful. There is no general allowance.

At 31 December 20X2, Ali has still not paid and Johan has decided to write the debt off as irrecoverable.

Make the related entries in the books.

Irrecoverable and doubtful debts: Chapter 9

Solution

Step 1

Open the RLCA and the allowance account.

RLCA

	£		£
Balance b/d	20,000		

Allowance for doubtful receivables

	£		£
		Balance b/d	1,000

Step 2

Remove Ali's debt from the accounts.

Ali's £1,000 is included in the £20,000 balance on the RLCA, and this has to be removed. Similarly, the £1,000 in the allowance account related to Ali.

The double entry is simply to:

Debit   Allowance account with £1,000
Credit   RLCA with £1,000

RLCA

	£		£
Balance b/d	20,000	Allowance	1,000

Allowance for doubtful receivables

	£		£
RLCA	1,000	Balance b/d	1,000

Note that there is no impact on the statement of profit or loss. The profits were charged with £1,000 when an allowance was made for Ali's debt, and there is no need to charge profits with another £1,000.

6 Money received from irrecoverable and doubtful receivables

6.1 Receipt of a debt previously written off as irrecoverable

Occasionally money may be received from a receivable whose balance has already been written off as an irrecoverable debt.

The full double entry for this receipt has two elements:

Dr   Receivables ledger control account (SFP)
Cr   Irrecoverable debt expense account (SPL)

FINANCIAL ACCOUNTING: PREPARING FINANCIAL STATEMENTS

In order to reinstate the receivable that has been previously written off.

Dr   Bank account (SFP)

Cr   Receivables ledger control account (SFP)

To account for the cash received from this receivable.

However, this double entry can be simplified to:

Dr   Bank account (SFP)

Cr   Irrecoverable debts expense account (SPL)

Note that the receivable is not reinstated as there is both a debit and credit to the receivables ledger control account which cancel each other out.

6.2   Receipt from a doubtful receivable

On occasion, money may be received from a receivable for whose balance a specific allowance was previously made.

The double entry for this receipt is:

Dr   Bank account (SFP)

Cr   Receivables ledger control account (SFP)

This is accounted for as a normal receipt from a receivable and at the year end, the requirement for an allowance against this debt will no longer be necessary.

Example 6

At the end of 20X6 Bjorn had made an allowance of £500 against doubtful receivables. This was made up as follows:

		£
Specific allowance	A	300
Specific allowance	50% × B	200
		500

At the end of 20X7 Bjorn's receivables total £18,450. After reviewing each debt, Bjorn discovers the following, none of which have been entered in the books: (1)   A has paid £50 of the debt outstanding at the beginning of the year. (2) B has paid his debt in full.

Show the ledger entries required to record the above.

Step 1

Calculate the new allowance required at the year end.

	£
A	250
B	Nil
	250

Step 2

Enter the cash on the RLCA.

Receivables ledger control account

	£		£
Balance b/d	18,450	Cash – A	50
		Cash – B	400
		Balance c/d	18,000
	18,450		18,450
Balance b/d	18,000		

Step 3

Bring down the new allowance required in the allowance account.

Allowance for doubtful receivables adjustment account

	£		£
		Allowance for doubtful receivables	250

Allowance for doubtful receivables account

	£		£
Allowance for doubtful receivables adjustment	250	Balance b/d	500
Balance c/d	250		
	500		500
		Balance b/d	250

Note: Because the allowance has been reduced from £500 to £250, there is a credit entry in the allowance for doubtful receivables adjustment account which will be taken to the statement of profit or loss.

6.3 Journal entries

The necessary journals must be entered into the relevant ledger accounts in the accounting system at the year end.

> **Test your understanding 4**
>
> Record the following journal entries needed in the general ledger to deal with the items below.
>
> (a) Entries need to be made for an irrecoverable debt of £240.
>
> | Journal | Dr £ | Cr £ |
> |---|---|---|
> | | | |
> | | | |
>
> (b) Entries need to be made for a doubtful receivables allowance. The receivable's balance at the year-end is £18,000 and an allowance is to be made against 2% of these.
>
> | Journal | Dr £ | Cr £ |
> |---|---|---|
> | | | |
> | | | |
>
> (c) A sole trader has an opening balance on the allowance for doubtful receivables account of £2,500. At the year end the sole trader wishes to make an allowance for 2% of the year end receivables of £100,000.
>
> | Journal | Dr £ | Cr £ |
> |---|---|---|
> | | | |
> | | | |
>
> (d) Entries need to be made for an amount of £200 that has been recovered, it was previously written off in the last accounting period.
>
> | Journal | Dr £ | Cr £ |
> |---|---|---|
> | | | |
> | | | |

Irrecoverable and doubtful debts: Chapter 9

 Test your understanding 5

John Stamp has opening balances at 1 January 20X6 on his receivables account and allowance for doubtful receivables account of £68,000 and £3,400 respectively.

During the year to 31 December 20X6 John Stamp makes credit sales of £354,000 and receives cash from his receivables of £340,000.

At 31 December 20X6 John Stamp reviews his receivables listing and acknowledges that he is unlikely ever to receive debts totalling £2,000. These are to be written off as irrecoverable.

John also wishes to provide an allowance against 5% of his remaining receivables after writing off the irrecoverable debts.

You are required to write up the:

- Receivables account
- Allowance for doubtful receivables account and the irrecoverable debts expense account for the year to 31 December 20X6
- Show the receivables and allowance for doubtful receivables extract from the statement of financial position at that date.

 Test your understanding 6

Angola

Angola started a business on 1 January 20X7 and during the first year of business it was necessary to write off the following debts as irrecoverable:

		£
10 April	Cuba	46
4 October	Kenya	29
6 November	Peru	106

On 31 December 20X7, after examination of the receivables ledger, it was decided to provide an allowance against two specific debts of £110 and £240 from Chad and Chile respectively and to make a general allowance of 4% against the remaining debts.

On 31 December 20X7, the total of the receivables balances stood at £5,031; Angola had not yet adjusted this total for the irrecoverable debts written off.

Required:

Show the accounts for irrecoverable debts expense and allowance for doubtful receivables.

 Test your understanding 7

Zambia

On 1 January 20X8 Angola sold their business, including the receivables, to Zambia. During the year ended 31 December 20X8 Zambia found it necessary to write off the following debts as irrecoverable:

		£
26 February	Fiji	125
8 August	Mexico	362

Zambia also received on 7 July an amount of £54 against the debt of Peru which had been written off during 20X7.

No specific allowance was required at 31 December 20X8 but it was decided to make a general allowance of 5% against outstanding receivables.

On 31 December 20X8 the total of the receivables balances stood at £12,500 (before making any adjustments for irrecoverable debts written off during the year) and the balance brought down on the allowance for doubtful receivables account stood at £530.

Required:

Show the accounts for irrecoverable debt expense and allowance for doubtful receivables, bringing forward any adjustments for Angola.

Irrecoverable and doubtful debts: **Chapter 9**

7 Summary

When sales are made on credit they are recognised as income when the invoice is sent out on the assumption that the money due will eventually be received from the receivable. According to the prudence concept if there is any doubt about the recoverability of any of the debts this must be recognised in the accounting records. The accounting treatment will depend upon whether the debt is considered to be an irrecoverable debt or a doubtful receivable.

Irrecoverable debts are written out of the receivables ledger control account, by crediting the receivables ledger control account, to decrease the asset and debiting the irrecoverable debt expense, increasing the expense in the statement of profit or loss.

For doubtful receivables, an allowance is set up which is netted off against the receivables figure in the statement of financial position. If the allowance for doubtful receivables is to be increased at the year end, there will be a debit to the statement of profit or loss, representing an increase to the expense. If the allowance for doubtful receivables is to be decreased at the year end, there will be a credit to the statement of profit or loss, representing a decrease to the expense.

FINANCIAL ACCOUNTING: PREPARING FINANCIAL STATEMENTS

Test your understanding answers

Test your understanding 1

Receivables ledger control account

	£		£
Balance b/d	117,489	Irrecoverable debts expense	2,448
		Balance c/d	115,041
	117,489		117,489
Balance b/d	115,041		

Irrecoverable debts expense account

	£		£
Receivables ledger control account	2,448	SPL	2,448

Test your understanding 2

Allowance for doubtful receivables accounts

	£		£
Allowance for doubtful receivables adjustment	80	Balance b/d	1,680
Balance c/d	1,600		
	1,680		1,680
		Balance b/d	1,600

Note: the allowance required at 31 December 20X5 is calculated by taking 5% of the total receivables at 31 December 20X5 (i.e. 5% × £32,000 = £1,600). As there is already an allowance of £1,680, there will be a release of the allowance (decrease) of £80.

Irrecoverable debts expense

	£		£
Irrecoverable debts written off	1,950	Statement of profit or loss	1,950
	1,950		1,950

Allowance for doubtful receivables adjustment

	£		£
		Allowance for doubtful receivables	80
Statement of profit or loss	80		
	80		80

Test your understanding 3

Allowance for doubtful receivables accounts

	£		£
Allowance for doubtful receivables adjustment	98	Balance b/d	1,490
Balance c/d	1,392		
	1,490		1,490
		Balance b/d (800 + 592)	1,392

Required allowance of £1,392 is made up of the specific allowance of £800 and a general allowance calculated as £592 ((£61,000 – £1,000 – £800) × 1%)

Irrecoverable debts expense

	£		£
Irrecoverable debts written off	1,000	Statement of profit or loss	1,000
	1,000		1,000

Allowance for doubtful receivables adjustment

	£		£
		Allowance for doubtful receivables	98
Statement of profit or loss	98		
	98		98

> **Test your understanding 4**
>
> (a) Entries need to be made for an irrecoverable debt of £240; main ledger accounts therefore will be as below.
>
> | Journal | Dr £ | Cr £ |
> |---|---|---|
> | Irrecoverable debts expense account | 240 | |
> | Receivables ledger control account | | 240 |
>
> (b) Allowance is calculated as £18,000 × 2%.
>
> | Journal | Dr £ | Cr £ |
> |---|---|---|
> | Allowance for doubtful receivables adjustment account | 360 | |
> | Allowance for doubtful receivables account | | 360 |

Irrecoverable and doubtful debts: Chapter 9

(c) Allowance for doubtful receivables are ((100,000 × 2%) – 2,500)

Journal	Dr £	Cr £
Allowance for doubtful receivables	500	
Allowance for doubtful receivables adjustment account		500

(d) Entries need to be made for an amount of £200 in the bank and irrecoverable debt expense account.

Journal	Dr £	Cr £
Bank account	200	
Irrecoverable debt expense account		200

Test your understanding 5

Step 1

Write up the receivables account showing the opening balance, the credit sales for the year and the cash received.

Receivables

20X6		£	20X6		£
1 Jan	Bal b/d	68,000	31 Dec	Cash	340,000
31 Dec	Revenue	354,000			

Step 2

Write off the irrecoverable debts for the period:

Dr   Irrecoverable debts expense account
Cr   Receivables account

Irrecoverable debts expense

20X6		£	20X6	£
31 Dec	Receivables	2,000		

Receivables

20X6		£	20X6		£
1 Jan	Balance b/d	68,000	31 Dec	Cash	340,000
			31 Dec	Irrecoverable	
31 Dec	Revenue	354,000		debts expense	2,000

Step 3

Balance off the receivables account to find the closing balance against which the allowance is required.

Receivables

20X6		£	20X6		£
1 Jan	Balance b/d	68,000	31 Dec	Cash	340,000
31 Dec	Revenue	354,000	31 Dec	Irrecoverable debts expense	2,000
			31 Dec	Balance c/d	80,000
		422,000			422,000
20X7					
1 Jan	Balance b/d	80,000			

Step 4

Set up the allowance required of 5% of £80,000 = £4,000. Remember that there is already an opening balance on the allowance for doubtful receivables account of £3,400 therefore only the increase in allowance required of £600 is credited to the allowance account and debited to the allowance for doubtful receivables adjustment account.

Allowance for doubtful receivables adjustment

20X6	£	20X6	£
Allowance for doubtful receivables	600	31 Dec SPL	600
	600		600

Allowance for doubtful receivables

20X6	£	20X6	£
		1 Jan Balance b/d	3,400
31 Dec Balance c/d	4,000	31 Dec Allowance for doubtful receivables adjustment	600
	4,000		4,000
		20X7	
		1 Jan Balance b/d	4,000

Irrecoverable and doubtful debts: **Chapter 9**

Step 5

The relevant extract from the statement of financial position at 31 December 20X6 would be as follows:

	£	£
Current assets		
Receivables	80,000	
Less: Allowance for doubtful receivables	(4,000)	
		76,000

Test your understanding 6

Angola

Allowance doubtful receivables

	£		£
Balance c/d	530	Allowance for doubtful receivables adjustment	530
	530		530
		Balance b/d	530

Irrecoverable debts expense

	£		£
Receivables written off		Statement of profit or loss	181
Cuba	46		
Kenya	29		
Peru	106		
	181		181

Allowance for doubtful receivables adjustment

	£		£
Allowance for doubtful receivables	530	Statement of profit or loss	530
	530		530

FINANCIAL ACCOUNTING: PREPARING FINANCIAL STATEMENTS

Working – Allowance carried down

Specific:	£110 + £240	£350
General:	4% × (£5,031 – £46 – £29 – £106 – £350)	£180
		530

Test your understanding 7

Zambia

Allowance for doubtful receivables

	£		£
		Balance b/d	530
Balance c/d (W1)	601	Allowance for doubtful receivables adjustment (W2)	71
	601		601
		Balance b/d	601

Working

1 Allowance carried down

		£
Specific:		
General:	5% × (£12,500 – £125 – £362)	601
		601

2 Extra charge required

	£
Allowance required at year end	601
Allowance brought down and available	530
Increase required in allowance	71

Irrecoverable debts expense			
	£		£
Receivables written off		Cash	54
Fiji	125	Statement of profit or loss	433
Mexico	362		
	487		487

Allowance for doubtful receivables adjustment			
	£		£
Allowance for doubtful receivables	71	Statement of profit or loss	71
	71		71

FINANCIAL ACCOUNTING: PREPARING FINANCIAL STATEMENTS

Control account reconciliations

Introduction

Before the preparation of a trial balance or extended trial balance, we should consider reconciling the receivables ledger control account and the payables ledger control account.

The purpose is to detect any errors made in accounting for sales and purchases and to ensure that the correct figure is used for receivables and payables in the statement of financial position.

ASSESSMENT CRITERIA	CONTENTS
Carry out financial period end routines (2.4)	1 Memorandum (subsidiary) ledgers 2 Contra entries 3 Receivables and payables ledger control accounts 4 Control account reconciliations

Control account reconciliations: Chapter 10

1 Memorandum (subsidiary) ledgers

1.1 Introduction

As you have seen in your earlier studies double-entry bookkeeping is performed in the ledger accounts in the general ledger. This means that when double entry is performed with regard to credit sales and purchases this takes place in the receivables ledger control account and payables ledger control account.

The details of each transaction with each customer and supplier are also recorded in the memorandum (subsidiary) ledgers. There will be a memorandum (subsidiary) ledger for receivables (called the receivables ledger) and a memorandum (subsidiary) ledger for payables (called the payables ledger).

Accounting software automates the transfer of data into the control accounts.

Note: The receivables ledger control account may also be called the sales ledger control account, while the payables ledger control account can also be called the purchases ledger control account.

1.2 Receivables ledger

Definition – Receivables ledger

The receivables ledger is a collection of records for each individual receivable of the organisation. It may alternatively be called the sales ledger.

The record for each receivable is normally in the form of a ledger account and each individual sales invoice, credit note and receipt from the receivable is recorded in the account. These accounts are known as memorandum (subsidiary) accounts as they are not part of the double-entry system.

This means that at any time it is possible to access the details of all the transactions with a particular receivable and the balance on that receivable's account.

1.3 Payables ledger

Definition – Payables ledger

The payables ledger is a collection of records for each individual payable of the organisation. It may alternatively be called the purchases ledger.

The record for each payable is normally in the form of a ledger account and each individual purchase invoice, credit note and payment to the payable is recorded in the account. These accounts are again known as memorandum (subsidiary) accounts as they are not part of the double-entry system.

This means that at any time it is possible to access the details of all of the transactions with a particular payable and the balance on that payable's account.

1.4 Credit sales

In the general ledger the double entry for credit sales (with VAT) is:

Dr Receivables ledger control account (gross amount)

Cr VAT (VAT amount)

Cr Sales account (net amount)

The figures that are used in the double entry are the totals taken from the sales day book for the period.

Each individual invoice (including VAT) from the sales day book is then debited to the individual receivable accounts in the receivables ledger to increase the amount owed by the receivable.

Example 1

Celia started business on 1 January 20X5 and made all of her sales on credit terms. No discount was offered for prompt payment. VAT should be ignored. During January 20X5, Celia made the following credit sales:

	£
To Shelagh	50
To John	30
To Shelagh	25
To Godfrey	40
To Shelagh	15
To Godfrey	10

Control account reconciliations: Chapter 10

Solution

By the end of January 20X5 the **sales day book (SDB)** will appear as follows:

Customer	Invoice no.	£
Shelagh	1	50
John	2	30
Shelagh	3	25
Godfrey	4	40
Shelagh	5	15
Godfrey	6	10
		170

At the end of the month, the following **double entry in the general ledger** will be made:

		£	£
Debit	Receivables ledger control account	170	
Credit	Sales account		170

Also, the following postings will be made to the **memorandum accounts in the receivables ledger**:

		£
Debit	Shelagh	50
Debit	John	30
Debit	Shelagh	25
Debit	Godfrey	40
Debit	Shelagh	15
Debit	Godfrey	10

The **receivables ledger** will now show:

John

	£		£
SDB	30		

Shelagh

	£		£
SDB	50		
SDB	25		
SDB	15		

Godfrey

	£		£
SDB	40		
SDB	10		

The **general ledger** will include:

Receivables ledger control account

	£		£
SDB	170		

Sales

	£		£
		SDB	170

1.5 Cash receipts from receivables

The cash receipts from receivables are initially recorded in the cash receipts book. The double entry in the general ledger is:

Dr Bank account

Cr Receivables ledger control account

The figure used for the posting is the total from the cash receipts book.

Each individual receipt is then credited to the individual receivable accounts in the receivables ledger to reduce the amount owed by the receivable.

Control account reconciliations: Chapter 10

 Example 2

Continuing with Celia's business. During January 20X5, the following amounts of cash were received:

	£
From John	30
From Godfrey	10
From Shelagh	50

Solution

By the end of the month the analysed cash book will show:

Debit side

Date	Narrative	Total	Receivables ledger	Cash sales	Other
		£	£	£	£
1/X5	John	30	30		
1/X5	Godfrey	10	10		
1/X5	Shelagh	50	50		
		90	90		

Now for the double entry. At the end of the month, the bank account in the general ledger will be debited and the receivables ledger control account in the general ledger will be credited with £90.

Memorandum entries will be made to the individual accounts in the receivables ledger as follows:

		£
Credit	John	30
Credit	Godfrey	10
Credit	Shelagh	50

The receivables ledger will now show:

John

	£		£
SDB	30	Analysed cash book	30

Shelagh

	£		£
SDB	50	Analysed cash book	50
SDB	25	Balance c/d	40
SDB	15		
	90		90
Balance b/d	40		

Godfrey

	£		£
SDB	40	Analysed cash book	10
SDB	10	Balance c/d	40
	50		50
Balance b/d	40		

The general ledger will include:

Receivables ledger control account

	£		£
SDB	170	Analysed cash book	90
		Balance c/d	80
	170		170
Balance b/d	80		

Sales account

	£		£
		SDB	170

Cash account

	£		£
Analysed cash book	90		

The trial balance will show:

	Dr £	Cr £
Receivables ledger control account	80	
Sales		170
Cash	90	
	170	170

Notes

- As the individual accounts in the receivables ledger are not part of the double entry, they will not appear in the trial balance.
- The total of the individual balances in the receivables ledger should agree to the balance on the receivables ledger control account. Normally, before the trial balance is prepared a reconciliation will be performed between the individual accounts and the receivables ledger control account:

	£
John	–
Shelagh	40
Godfrey	40
Total per individual accounts	80
Balance per receivables ledger control account	80

This reconciliation will help to ensure the accuracy of our postings. We shall look at this in more detail later in this chapter.

If all of the entries in the control account and the receivables ledger have been made correctly then the total of the individual balances in the receivables ledger should equal the balance on the receivables ledger control account in the general ledger.

1.6 Sales returns

The double entry for sales returns (with VAT) is:

Dr   Sales returns account (net amount)

Dr   VAT (VAT amount)

Cr   Receivables ledger control account (gross amount)

Each return (including VAT) is also credited to the individual receivable's account in the receivables ledger to reduce the amount owed by the receivable.

1.7 Discounts allowed

Discounts allowed to receivables are recorded in the discounts allowed book if a receivable takes advantage of a prompt payment discount. The double entry for these discounts (with VAT if VAT registered) is:

Dr   Discounts allowed account (net amount)

Dr   VAT (VAT amount)

Cr   Receivables ledger control account (gross amount)

The discount (including VAT) is also credited to the individual receivable's account in the receivables ledger to show a reduction to the amount owed by the receivable.

1.8 Accounting for purchases on credit

The accounting system for purchases on credit works in the same manner as for sales on credit and is summarised as follows.

The total of the purchases day book is used for the double entry in the general ledger:

Dr   Purchases account (net amount)

Dr   VAT (VAT amount)

Cr   Payables ledger control account (gross amount)

Each individual invoice (including VAT) is also credited to the individual payable accounts in the payables ledger to increase the amount owed to the payable.

The total of the cash payments book is used for the double entry in the general ledger:

Dr   Payables ledger control account

Cr   Bank account

Each individual payment is then debited to the payable's individual account in the payables ledger to decrease the amount owed to the payable.

1.9 Purchases returns

The double entry for purchases returns is:

Dr   Payables ledger control account (gross amount)

Cr   VAT (VAT amount)

Cr   Purchases returns account (net amount)

Each purchase return is also debited to the individual payable's account in the payables ledger to decrease the amount owed to the payable.

1.10 Discounts received

Discounts received from suppliers are recorded in the discounts received book when they are deducted from payments made to the supplier due to taking up an offer of a prompt payment discount. They are then posted in the general ledger as:

Dr   Payables ledger control account (gross amount)

Cr   VAT (VAT amount)

Cr   Discounts received account (net amount)

Each discount (including VAT) is also debited to the individual payable's account in the payables ledger to show a reduction to the amount owed.

2 Contra entries

2.1 Introduction

A business sometimes sells goods to, and purchases goods from, the same person, i.e. one of the receivables is also a payable. As it would seem pointless to pay the payable and then receive payment for the debt, a business will often offset as much as is possible of the receivable and the payable balances. The entry that results is called a contra entry and the double entry for this is:

Dr   Payables ledger control account

Cr   Receivables ledger control account

Example 3

Celia sells goods to Godfrey but also purchases some supplies from him. At the end of the period, Godfrey owes Celia £40 but Celia also owes Godfrey £50. The balances on the accounts in the memorandum receivables and payables ledgers in Celia's books will be:

Receivables ledger

Godfrey		
	£	£
Balance b/d	40	

Payables ledger

Godfrey

	£		£
		Balance b/d	50

The maximum amount which can be offset is £40 and after recording the contra entries the accounts will show:

Receivables ledger

Godfrey

	£		£
Balance b/d	40	Contra with payables ledger	40

Payables ledger

Godfrey

	£		£
Contra with receivables ledger	40	Balance b/d	50
Balance c/d	10		
	50		50
		Balance b/d	10

i.e. Celia still owes Godfrey £10.

We have so far considered only the individual receivables' and payables' accounts but we know that every entry which is put through an individual account must also be recorded in the control accounts in the general ledger. Assuming that the balances before the contras on the receivables ledger control account (RLCA) and the payables ledger control account (PLCA) were £15,460 and £12,575 respectively, they will now show:

RLCA

	£		£
Balance b/d	15,460	Contra with PLCA	40
		Balance c/d	15,420
	15,460		15,460
Balance b/d	15,420		

PLCA

	£		£
Contra with RLCA	40	Balance b/d	12,575
Balance c/d	12,535		
	12,575		12,575
		Balance b/d	12,535

i.e. receivables and payables have both been reduced by £40.

3 Receivables and payables ledger control accounts

3.1 Introduction

Now that you have been reminded of the entries to the receivables ledger and payables ledger control accounts we will summarise the typical entries in these accounts.

3.2 Pro forma receivables ledger control account

Receivables ledger control account

	£		£
Balance b/d	X	Returns per returns day book	X
Sales per sales day book	X	Cash from receivables *	X
		Discounts allowed *	X
		Irrecoverable debts written off	X
		Contra with purchases ledger control a/c	X
		Balance c/d	X
	X		X
Balance b/d	X		

3.3 Pro forma payables ledger control account

Payables ledger control account

	£		£
		Balance b/d	X
Cash to suppliers *	X	Purchases per purchase day book	X
Discounts received *	X		
Returns per returns day book	X		
Contra with receivables ledger control a/c	X		
Balance c/d	X		
	X		X
		Balance b/d	X

* Per cash book, discounts allowed and received books.

> ### Test your understanding 1
>
> The following information is available concerning Meads' receivables ledger:
>
> | | £ |
> |---|---|
> | Receivables 1.1.X7 | 3,752 |
> | Returns inwards | 449 |
> | Cheques received from customers, subsequently dishonoured | 25 |
> | Credit sales in year to 31.12.X7 | 24,918 |
> | Cheques from receivables | 21,037 |
> | Cash from receivables | 561 |
> | Payables ledger contra | 126 |
> | Cash sales | 3,009 |
>
> **Required:**
>
> Write up the receivables ledger control account for the year ended 31 December 20X7.

Receivables ledger control account		
	£	£

4 Control account reconciliations

4.1 Introduction

As we have seen earlier in the chapter the totals of the balances on the receivables or payables ledgers should agree with the balance on the receivables ledger control account and payables ledger control account respectively.

If the balances do not agree then there has been an error in the accounting which must be investigated and corrected.

Therefore, this reconciliation of the total of the memorandum ledger balances to the control account total should take place on a regular basis, usually monthly, and certainly should take place before the preparation of a trial balance.

4.2 Procedure

The steps involved in performing a control account reconciliation are as follows:

Step 1

Determine the balance on the control account.

Step 2

Total the individual balances in the memorandum (subsidiary) ledger.

Step 3

Compare the two totals as they should agree.

Step 4

If the totals do not agree then the difference must be investigated and corrected.

4.3 Possible reasons for differences

Errors could have taken place in the accounting in the control account or in the individual customer or supplier accounts in the memorandum (subsidiary) ledgers. Possible errors include:

- Errors in casting (i.e. adding up) of the day books – this means that the totals posted to the control accounts are incorrect but the individual entries to the memorandum ledgers are correct.

- A transposition error made in posting to either the control account or the individual accounts in the memorandum (subsidiary) ledger.

- A contra entry has not been recorded in all of the relevant accounts i.e. the control accounts and the memorandum (subsidiary) ledger accounts.

- A balance has been omitted from the list of subsidiary ledger balances.

- A balance in the memorandum (subsidiary) ledger has been included in the list of balances as a debit when it was a credit, or vice versa.

4.4 Treatment of the differences in the control account reconciliation

When the reasons for the difference have been discovered the following procedure takes place:

- the control account balance is adjusted for any errors affecting the control account

- the list of memorandum ledger balances is adjusted for any errors that affect the list of individual balances

- after these adjustments the balance on the control account should agree to the total of the list of individual balances.

The key to these reconciliations is to be able to determine which types of error affect the control account and which affect the list of balances.

Control account reconciliations: **Chapter 10**

 Test your understanding 2

A credit sale, made by The Pine Warehouse, was correctly entered into the general ledger but was then credited to the customer's memorandum account in the receivables ledger.

(a) Would the error be detected by drawing up a trial balance?

Yes / No

(b) Briefly explain the reason for your answer to (a).

 Example 4

The balance on Diana's receivables ledger control account at 31 December 20X6 was £15,450. The balances on the individual accounts in the receivables ledger have been extracted and total £15,705. Diana is not VAT registered. On investigation the following errors are discovered:

1. a debit balance of £65 has been omitted from the list of balances

2. a contra between the memorandum payables and receivables ledgers of £40 has not been recorded in the control accounts

3. discounts allowed totalling £70 have been recorded in the individual accounts but not in the control account

4. the sales day book was 'overcast' by £200 (this means the total was added up as £200 too high), and

5. an invoice for £180 was recorded correctly in the sales day book but was posted to the receivables' individual account as £810.

Solution

Step 1

We must first look for those errors which will mean that the control account is incorrectly stated: they will be points 2, 3 and 4 above.

The control account is then adjusted as follows.

Receivables ledger control account

	£		£
Balance b/d	15,450	Contra	40
		Discounts allowed	70
		Overcast of SDB	200
		Adjusted balance c/d	15,140
	15,450		15,450
Balance b/d	15,140		

Step 2

There will be errors in the total of the individual balances per the receivables ledger as a result of points 1 and 5. The extracted list of balances must be adjusted as follows:

	£
Original total of list of balances	15,705
Debit balance omitted	65
Transposition error (810 – 180)	(630)
	15,140

Step 3

As can be seen, the adjusted total of the list of balances now agrees with the adjusted balance per the receivables ledger control account.

Test your understanding 3

The balance on Mead's receivables ledger control account is £6,522. Mead extracts his list of receivables' balances at 31 December 20X7 and they total £6,617.

He discovers the following:

1. The sales day book has been under cast by £100.
2. A contra with the payables ledger of £20 with the account of Going has not been entered in the control account.
3. The account of Murdoch in the receivables ledger which shows a credit balance of £65 has been shown as a debit balance in the list of balances.
4. McCormack's account with a debit balance of £80 has been omitted from the list of balances.
5. Discounts allowed of £35 recorded in the receivables ledger were not shown in the receivables ledger control account.

Mead is not VAT registered.

Control account reconciliations: Chapter 10

Required:

Show the necessary adjustment to the receivables ledger control account and prepare a statement reconciling the list of balances with the balance on the receivables ledger control account.

Receivables ledger control account

£	£

List of balances per receivables ledger

£

Total per draft list
Less:

Add:

Total per receivables' control account

4.5 Payables ledger control account reconciliation

The procedure for a payables ledger control account reconciliation is just the same as for the receivables ledger control account reconciliation however you must remember that the entries are all the other way around.

Example 5

The balance on John's payables ledger control account at 31 May 20X5 was £14,667. However the total of the list of balances from the payables ledger totalled £14,512.

Upon investigation the following errors were noted:

1. an invoice from J Kilpin was credited to his account in the payables ledger as £210 whereas it was correctly entered into the purchases day book as £120.

2. the cash payments book was under cast by £100.

3. a transfer of £50 from a receivables' account in the receivables ledger to their account in the payables ledger has been correctly made in the memorandum ledgers but not in the control accounts (a contra entry).

FINANCIAL ACCOUNTING: PREPARING FINANCIAL

4   a debit balance of £40 on a payable's account in the memorandum ledger was included in the list of balances as a credit balance.

5   the discounts received total of £175 was not posted to the control account in the general ledger.

John is not VAT registered.

Required:

Reconcile the corrected balance on the payables ledger control account with the correct total of the list of payables' balances from the memorandum ledger.

Solution

Payables ledger control account

	£		£
Under cast of CPB (2)	100	Balance b/d	14,667
Contra (3)	50		
Discounts received (5)	175		
Adjusted balance c/d	14,342		
	14,667		14,667
		Balance b/d	14,342

List of balances per payables ledger

	£
Total per draft list	14,512
Transposition error (210 – 120) (1)	(90)
Debit balance included as a credit balance (2 × 40) (4)	(80)
	14,342

Control account reconciliations: Chapter 10

 Test your understanding 4

The total of the list of balances extracted from Morphy's payables ledger on 30 September 20X1 amounted to £5,676 which did not agree with the balance on the payables ledger control account of £6,124.

1   An item of £20 being purchases from R Fischer had been posted from the purchases day book to the credit of Lasker's account.

2   On 30 June 20X1 Spasskey had been debited for goods returned to him, £85, and no other entry had been made.

3   Credit balances in the payables ledger amounting to £562 and debit balances amounting to £12 (Golombek, £7, Alexander £5) had been omitted from the list of balances.

4   Morphy had correctly recorded returns outwards of £60. However, these returns were later disallowed. No record was made when the returns were disallowed.

5   A contra of £90 with the receivables ledger had been recorded twice in the control account.

6   The purchases day book has been undercast by £100.

7   A payment to Steinitz of £3 for a cash purchase of goods had been recorded in the petty cash book and posted to his account in the payables ledger, no other entry having been made.

Morphy is not VAT registered.

Required:

(a)   Prepare the payables ledger control account showing the necessary adjustments.

(b)   Prepare a statement reconciling the original balances extracted from the payables ledger with the corrected balance on the payables ledger control account.

Payables ledger control account

£	£

FINANCIAL ACCOUNTING: PREPARING FINANCIAL

List of balances per payables ledger

	£
Total per draft list	

Test your understanding 5

1. What is the double entry in the general ledger for sales returns?

2. What is the double entry in the general ledger for discounts received (ignore VAT)?

3. When preparing the receivables ledger control account reconciliation it was discovered that discounts allowed had been under cast in the discounts allowed book by £100. You should ignore VAT. What is the double entry required to correct this?

4. A credit note sent to a credit customer for £340 had been entered in the customer's account in the receivables ledger at £430. How would this be adjusted for in the receivables ledger control account reconciliation?

5. When preparing the payables ledger control account reconciliation it was discovered that the total of the purchases returns day book had been posted as £1,300 rather than £300. What is the double entry required to correct this?

6. A payment to a credit supplier was correctly recorded in the cash payments book at £185 but was posted to the payable's individual account in the payables ledger as £158. How would this be adjusted for in the payables ledger control account reconciliation?

7. A contra entry for £100 had only been entered in the general ledger accounts and not in the memorandum ledger accounts. How would this be adjusted for in the payables ledger control account reconciliation?

Control account reconciliations: Chapter 10

 Test your understanding 6

Mortimer Wheeler

Mortimer Wheeler is a general dealer and is not VAT registered. The following is an extract from the opening trial balance of his business at 1 January 20X6:

	Dr £	Cr £
Cash	1,066	
Trade receivables	5,783	
Trade payables		5,531
Allowance for doubtful receivables		950

Receivables and payables are listed below:

		£
Receivables	Pitt-Rivers	1,900
	Evans	1,941
	Petrie	1,942
		5,783
Payables	Cunliffe	1,827
	Atkinson	1,851
	Piggott	1,853
		5,531

In January the following purchases, sales and cash transactions were made:

		£			£
Purchases	Cunliffe	950	Payments	Cuncliffe	900
	Atkinson	685		Atkinson	50
	Piggott	1,120		Piggott	823
		2,755			1,773

		£			£
Sales	Pitt-Rivers	50	Receipts	Pitt-Rivers	–
	Evans	1,760		Evans	1,900
	Petrie	1,665		Petrie	1,942
		3,475			3,842

The £950 allowance was against 50% of Pitt-Rivers' debt. Pitt-Rivers was declared bankrupt half way through the year.

Evans denied knowledge of £41 of the balance outstanding at 1 January 20X6 and Mortimer felt that this amount should be provided for as a doubtful receivable.

Mortimer received £15 discount from Cunliffe for prompt payment.

Required:

Write up:

(a) Sales and purchases accounts, sales and payables ledger control accounts, the allowance for doubtful receivables account and the irrecoverable debts expense account, the sales and payables ledgers.

(b) Lists of receivables and payables balances at the end of January.

Test your understanding 7

Data

The individual balances of the accounts in the receivables ledger of a business were listed, totalled and compared with the £73,450 balance of the receivables ledger control account.

The total of the list came to £76,780 and after investigation the following errors were found:

(a) A customer account with a balance of £400 was omitted from the list.

(b) A £50 discount allowed had been debited to a customer's account.

(c) A customer's account with a balance of £2,410 was included twice in the list.

(d) A customer's balance of £320 was entered in the list as £230.

(e) A customer with a balance of £540 had been written off as an irrecoverable debt during the year but the balance was still included in the list.

(f) Sales returns totalling £770 (including VAT) had been omitted from the relevant customer accounts.

Control account reconciliations: Chapter 10

Task

Make appropriate adjustments to the total of the list using the table below. For each adjustment show clearly the amount involved and whether the amount is to be added or subtracted.

	£
Total from listing of balances	76,780
Adjustment for (a) add/(subtract)	....
Adjustment for (b) add/(subtract)	....
Adjustment for (c) add/(subtract)	....
Adjustment for (d) add/(subtract)	....
Adjustment for (e) add/(subtract)	....
Adjustment for (f) add/(subtract)	....
Revised total to agree with receivables ledger control account	....

✱ Test your understanding 8

On 30 November 20X3 the balances of the accounts in the payables ledger of a business were listed, totalled and then compared with the updated balance of the payables ledger control account. The total of the list of balances amounted to £76,670. After investigation the following errors were found:

(a) A credit purchase of £235 (inclusive of VAT) had been omitted from a supplier's account in the payables ledger.

(b) A payment of £1,600 to a supplier had been credited to the supplier's account in the payables ledger.

(c) A supplier's balance of £1,194 had been listed as £1,914.

Enter the appropriate adjustments in the table shown below. For each adjustment show clearly the amount involved and whether the amount is to be added or subtracted.

	£
Total from listing of balances	76,670
Adjustment for (a) add/subtract*	....
Adjustment for (b) add/subtract*	....
Adjustment for (c) add/subtract*	....
Revised total to agree with payables ledger control account	....

5 Summary

The chapter began with a revision of the entries from the books of prime entry to the receivables and payables ledger control accounts and to the receivables ledger and payables ledger.

If the entries are all correctly made the balance on the control account should agree to the total of the list of balances in the appropriate memorandum (subsidiary) ledger. This must however be checked on a regular basis by carrying out a reconciliation of the control account and the total of the list of balances.

The process of carrying out a control account reconciliation is to consider each error and determine whether it affects the control account, the individual receivable/payable accounts in the memorandum (subsidiary) ledger or both. The control account will then be adjusted to find a corrected balance and this should agree to the corrected total of the individual accounts from the memorandum ledger.

Test your understanding answers

Test your understanding 1

Receivables ledger control account

	£		£
Balance b/d	3,752	Returns inwards	449
Cheques dishonoured	25	Cheques	21,037
Credit sales	24,918	Cash	561
		Contra with payables ledger	126
		Balance c/d	6,522
	28,695		28,695
Balance b/d	6,522		

Note: cash sales do not affect the RLCA

Test your understanding 2

(a) No

(b) The trial balance is constructed by extracting the various balances from the general ledger. If no errors have been made then the total of the debit balances should be equal to the total of the credit balances. In this case the error was made in the receivables ledger and since the balances of the accounts in the receivables ledger are not included in the trial balance, the error would not be detected.

Test your understanding 3

Receivables ledger control account

	£		£
Balance b/d	6,522	Contra with payables ledger (2)	20
Sales day book (1)	100	Discounts (5)	35
		Balance c/d	6,567
	6,622		6,622
Balance b/d	6,567		

List of balances per receivables ledger

	£
Total per draft list	6,617
Less: Murdoch's balance included as a credit (3) (£65 × 2)	(130)
	6,487
Add: McCormack's balance (4)	80
Total per receivables' control account	6,567

Test your understanding 4

Payables ledger control account

	£		£
Returns allowed (2)	85	Balance b/d	6,124
Balance c/d	6,289	Returns disallowed (4)	60
		Correction of contra recorded twice (5)	90
		Under cast of purchases day book (6)	100
	6,374		6,374
		Balance b/d	6,289

List of balances per payables ledger

	£
Total per draft list	5,676
Credit balances omitted (3)	562
Debit balances omitted (3)	(12)
Returns disallowed (4)	60
Petty cash purchase (7) (used incorrectly to reduce amount owing for credit purchases)	3
	6,289

(**Note** point (1) in the question does not affect the overall balance of the accounts. It has been treated correctly but posted to the wrong suppliers account)

Test your understanding 5

1 Debit   Sales returns account
   Credit Receivables ledger control account

2 Debit   Payables ledger control account
   Credit Discounts received account

3 Debit   Discounts allowed account   £100
   Credit Receivables ledger control account   £100

4 The total of the list of receivable balances would be increased by £90 (£430 – £340).

5 Debit   Purchases returns account   £1,000
   Credit Payables ledger control account   £1,000

6 The total of the list of payable balances would be reduced by £27 (£185 – £158).

7 The total of the list of payable balances would be reduced by £100.

Test your understanding 6

Mortimer Wheeler

(a)

Revenue

	£		£
SPL	3,475	Receivables ledger control a/c	3,475

Purchases

	£		£
Payables ledger control a/c	2,755	SPL	2,755

Receivables ledger control account

	£		£
Balance b/d	5,783	Cash	3,842
Revenue	3,475	Irrecoverable debts – expense	1,950
		Balance c/d	3,466
	9,258		9,258
Balance b/d	3,466		

Payables ledger control account

	£		£
Cash	1,773	Balance b/d	5,531
Discount	15	Purchases	2,755
Balance c/d	6,498		
	8,286		8,286
		Balance b/d	6,498

Allowance for doubtful receivables

	£		£
Irrecoverable debt expense (bal figure)	909	Balance b/d	950
Balance c/d	41		
	950		950
		Balance b/d	41

Irrecoverable debt expense

	£		£
Receivables ledger control account (Pitt-Rivers)	1,950	Allowance for doubtful receivables	909
		SPL	1,041
	1,950		1,950

Receivables ledger

Pitt-Rivers

	£		£
Balance b/d	1,900	Irrecoverable debt	1,950
Revenue	50		
	1,950		1,950

Evans

	£		£
Balance b/d	1,941	Cash	1,900
Revenue	1,760	Balance c/d	1,801
	3,701		3,701
Balance b/d	1,801		

Petrie

	£		£
Balance b/d	1,942	Cash	1,942
Revenue	1,665	Balance c/d	1,665
	3,607		3,607
Balance b/d	1,665		

Payables ledger

Cunliffe

	£		£
Cash	900	Balance b/d	1,827
Discount	15	Purchases	950
Balance c/d	1,862		
	2,777		2,777
		Balance b/d	1,862

Atkinson

	£		£
Cash	50	Balance b/d	1,851
Balance c/d	2,486	Purchases	685
	2,536		2,536
		Balance b/d	2,486

Piggott

	£		£
Cash	823	Balance b/d	1,853
Balance c/d	2,150	Purchases	1,120
	2,973		2,973
		Balance b/d	2,150

(b) **List of receivables**

	£
Evans	1,801
Petrie	1,665
	3,466

List of payables

	£
Cunliffe	1,862
Atkinson	2,486
Piggott	2,150
	6,498

Test your understanding 7

		£
Total from listing of balances		76,780
Adjustment for (a)	**add**/subtract*	400
Adjustment for (b)	add/**subtract***	(100)
Adjustment for (c)	add/**subtract***	(2,410)
Adjustment for (d)	**add**/subtract*	90
Adjustment for (e)	add/**subtract***	(540)
Adjustment for (f)	add/**subtract***	(770)
Revised total		73,450

Test your understanding 8

	£
Total from listing of balances	76,670
Adjustment for (a) add/~~subtract~~	235
Adjustment for (b) ~~add~~/subtract	(3,200)
Adjustment for (c) ~~add~~/subtract	(720)
Revised total to agree with payables ledger control account	72,985

FINANCIAL ACCOUNTING: PREPARING FINANCIAL STATEMENTS

Bank reconciliations

Introduction

In addition to reconciling the receivables and payables ledger control accounts, before the preparation of a trial balance or extended trial balance, we must also perform a bank reconciliation. A bank reconciliation compares the bank statement (external document) and the cash book (internal document).

ASSESSMENT CRITERIA
Carry out financial period end routines (2.4)

CONTENTS	
1	Bank reconciliations

1 Bank reconciliations

1.1 Introduction

At regular intervals the accuracy of the cash book should be checked by comparing it with the bank statement.

Why might they not agree?

Uncleared lodgements

- Cheques we have paid into the bank have not yet cleared.
- The cash book is up to date.

Unpresented cheques

- Cheques we have written have not yet been taken to the bank or have not yet cleared.
- The cash book is up to date.

Unrecorded transactions

- The cash book may not be up to date if not all transactions have been recorded.
- Examples include direct credits into the bank account or transactions made using the direct payment facility – BACS, CHAPS or Faster Payments.
- Other examples of where there may be unrecorded transactions in the cash book include bank charges, standing orders or direct debits that appear in the bank statement which have not yet been updated in the cash book.

1.2 Bank reconciliation process

1. Tick off outstanding items from previous reconciliation and agree the opening balance between the cash book and bank statement.

2. Tick off items in the debit side of the cash book (cash received) to the bank statement.

FINANCIAL ACCOUNTING: PREPARING FINANCIAL STATEMENTS

3   Tick off items in the credit side of the cash book (cash payments) to the bank statement.

4   Update the cash book with any items not ticked in the bank statement – i.e. unrecorded transactions.

5   Any items that now remain unticked in the cash book should be included in the reconciliation – i.e. as uncleared lodgements or unpresented cheques.

1.3 Bank reconciliation pro forma

	£	£
Balance per bank statement		X
Add: Uncleared lodgements		
Details		X
Less: Unpresented cheques		
Details	X	
Details	X	(X)
Balance per cash book		X

Example 1

The balance showing on Pinkie's bank statement is a credit of £19,774 (in funds) and the balance on the cash book is a debit balance of £7,396.

The bank statement is compared to the cash book and the following differences were identified:

1   Bank charges paid of £52 were not entered in the cash book.

2   A cheque payment for £650 has been incorrectly recorded in the cash book as £560.

3   Cheque payments to suppliers totalling an amount of £7,400 have been written but are not yet showing in the bank statement.

4   A BACS receipt of £5,120 from a customer has not been entered in the cash book.

Required:

Identify the THREE adjustments you need to make to the cash book and record these adjustments in the cash book ledger. Reconcile the bank statement to the cash book.

The three adjustments to the cash book are:

1   Bank charges of £52 should be entered into the cash book on the credit side.

2   The cheque payment that was incorrectly recorded in the cash book should be corrected. The payment was understated by £90, this will be entered on the credit side of the cash book.

4   The BACS receipt of £5,120 should be entered into the cash book on the debit side.

Solution

Cash book

	£		£
Balance b/d	7,396	Bank charges (1)	52
BACS receipt (4)	5,120	Cheque (650 – 560) (2)	90
		Balance c/d	12,374
	12,516		12,516
Balance b/d	12,374		

Bank reconciliation

	£
Balance per bank statement	19,774
Less unpresented cheques (3)	(7,400)
Balance per cash book	12,374

FINANCIAL ACCOUNTING: PREPARING FINANCIAL STATEMENTS

 Test your understanding 1

Given below is the cash book of a business and the bank statement for the week ending 20 April 20X1.

Required:

Compare the cash book to the bank statement and note any differences that you find.

Cash book

		£			£
16/4	Donald & Co	225.47	16/4	Balance b/d	310.45
17/4	Harper Ltd	305.68	17/4	Cheque 03621	204.56
	Fisler Partners	104.67	18/4	Cheque 03622	150.46
18/4	Denver Ltd	279.57	19/4	Cheque 03623	100.80
19/4	Gerald Bros	310.45		Cheque 03624	158.67
20/4	Johnson & Co	97.68	20/4	Cheque 03625	224.67
			20/4	Balance c/d	173.91
		1,323.52			1,323.52

EXPRESS BANK   CONFIDENTIAL

High Street   Account   CURRENT   Sheet no. 0213
Fenbury
TL4 6JY   Account name P L DERBY LTD

Telephone: 0169 422130

Statement date 20 April 20X1   Account Number 40429107

Date	Details	Withdrawals (£)	Deposits (£)	Balance (£)
16/4	Balance from sheet 0212			310.45 OD
17/4	DD – District Council	183.60		494.05 OD
18/4	Credit		225.47	
19/4	Credit		104.67	
	Cheque 03621	240.56		
	Bank interest	3.64		408.11 OD
20/4	Credit		305.68	
	Credit		279.57	
	Cheque 03622	150.46		
	Cheque 03624	158.67		131.99 OD

DD	Standing order	DD	Direct debit	CP	Card purchase
AC	Automated cash	OD	Overdrawn	TR	Transfer

Test your understanding 2

Graham

The cash account of Graham showed a debit balance of £204 on 31 March 20X3. A comparison with the bank statements revealed the following:

		£
1	Cheques drawn but not presented	3,168
2	Amounts paid into the bank but not credited	723
3	Entries in the bank statements not recorded in the cash account	
	(i) Standing orders	35
	(ii) Interest on bank deposit account	18
	(iii) Bank charges	14
4	Balance on the bank statement at 31 March	2,618

Tasks

(a) Show the appropriate adjustments required in the cash account of Graham bringing down the correct balance at 31 March 20X3.

(b) Prepare a bank reconciliation statement at that date.

 Test your understanding 3

The following are the cash book and bank statements of KT Ltd.

Receipts June 20X1

CASH BOOK – JUNE 20X1				
Date	Details	Total	Receivables ledger control	Other
1 June	Balance b/d	7,100.45		
8 June	Cash and cheques	3,200.25	3,200.25	–
15 June	Cash and cheques	4,100.75	4,100.75	–
23 June	Cash and cheques	2,900.30	2,900.30	–
30 June	Cash and cheques	6,910.25	6,910.25	–
		£24,212.00	£17,111.55	

Payments June 20X1

Date	Payee	Cheque no	Total £	Payables ledger control £	Operating overhead £	Admin overhead £	Other £
1 June	Hawsker Chemical	116	6,212.00	6,212.00			
7 June	Wales Supplies	117	3,100.00	3,100.00			
15 June	Wages and salaries	118	2,500.00		1,250.00	1,250.00	
16 June	Drawings	119	1,500.00				1,500.00
18 June	Blyth Chemical	120	5,150.00	5,150.00			
25 June	Whitby Cleaning Machines	121	538.00	538.00			
28 June	York Chemicals	122	212.00	212.00			
			19,212.00	15,212.00	1,250.00	1,250.00	1,500.00

Bank statement

Crescent Bank plc
High Street
Sheffield
Account: Alison Robb t/a KT Ltd
Account no: 57246661

Statement no: 721
Page 1

Date	Details	Payments £	Receipts £	Balance £
20X1				
1 June	Balance b/d			8,456.45
1 June	113	115.00		8,341.45
1 June	114	591.00		7,750.45
1 June	115	650.00		7,100.45
4 June	116	6,212.00		888.45
8 June	CC		3,200.25	4,088.70
11 June	117	3,100.00		988.70
15 June	CC		4,100.75	5,089.45
15 June	118	2,500.00		2,589.45
16 June	119	1,500.00		1,089.45
23 June	120	5,150.00		4,060.55 O/D
23 June	CC		2,900.30	1,160.25 O/D

Key:	S/O	Standing Order	DD	Direct debit
	CC	Cash and cheques	CHGS	Charges
	BACS	Bankers automated clearing	O/D	Overdrawn

Bank reconciliations: Chapter 11

Task

Examine the business cash book and the business bank statement shown in the data provided above. Prepare a bank reconciliation statement as at 30 June 20X1. Set out your reconciliation in the pro forma below.

Pro forma

BANK RECONCILIATION STATEMENT AS AT 30 JUNE 20X1

£

Balance per bank statement
Add: Uncleared lodgements:

Less: Unpresented cheques:

‾‾‾‾‾‾

Balance per cash book   £

‾‾‾‾‾‾

2   Summary

The final bank reconciliation needs to be prepared prior to the final financial statements being drawn up. This is a comparison between the bank statement (external document) and the cash book (internal document). It is necessary to complete the reconciliation on a regular basis to ensure that the cash book is updated and any errors are identified.

Test your understanding answers

Test your understanding 1

Cash book

		£			£
16/4	Donald & Co	225.47✓	16/4	Balance b/d	310.45✓
17/4	Harper Ltd	305.68✓	17/4	Cheque 03621	204.56
	Fisler Partners	104.67✓	18/4	Cheque 03622	150.46✓
18/4	Denver Ltd	279.57✓	19/4	Cheque 03623	100.80
19/4	Gerald Bros	310.45		Cheque 03624	158.67✓
20/4	Johnson & Co	97.68	20/4	Cheque 03625	224.67
			20/4	Balance c/d	173.91
		1,323.52			1,323.52

There are three unticked items on the bank statement:

- direct debit £183.60 to the District Council

- cheque number 03621 £240.56 – this has been entered into the cash book as £204.56

- bank interest £3.64.

The unticked items on the bank statement would be updated to the cash book.

Cheques 03623 and 03625 are unticked items in the cash book but these are payments that have not yet cleared through the banking system. Also, the receipts from Gerald Bros and Johnson & Co have not yet cleared the banking system.

The payments of cheques 03623 and 03625 are known as unpresented cheques and would form part of the reconciliation between the bank statement balance and the cash book balance.

The receipts from Gerald Bros and Johnson & Co are known as uncleared lodgements and would form part of the reconciliation between the bank statement balance and the cash book balance.

Bank reconciliations: Chapter 11

EXPRESS BANK CONFIDENTIAL

High Street Account CURRENT Sheet no. 0213
Fenbury
TL4 6JY Account name P L DERBY LTD
Telephone: 0169 422130

Statement date 20 April 20X1 Account Number 40429107

Date	Details	Withdrawals (£)	Deposits (£)	Balance (£)
16/4	Balance from sheet 0212			310.45 OD
17/4	DD – District Council	183.60		494.05 OD
18/4	Credit		225.47 ✓	
19/4	Credit		104.67 ✓	
	Cheque 03621	240.56		
	Bank interest	3.64		408.11 OD
20/4	Credit		305.68 ✓	
	Credit		279.57 ✓	
	Cheque 03622	150.46 ✓		
	Cheque 03624	158.67 ✓		131.99 OD

DD	Standing order	DD	Direct debit	CP	Card purchase
AC	Automated cash	OD	Overdrawn	TR	Transfer

Test your understanding 2

Graham

(a)

Cash account

	£		£
Balance b/d	204	Standing orders (i)	35
Interest on deposit account (ii)	18	Bank charges (iii)	14
		Balance c/d	173
	222		222
Balance b/d	173		

(b)

BANK RECONCILIATION STATEMENT AT 31 MARCH 20X3

	£
Balance per bank statement	2,618
Add Uncleared lodgements	723
	3,341
Less Unpresented cheques	(3,168)
Balance per cash account	173

Test your understanding 3

BANK RECONCILIATION STATEMENT AS AT 30 JUNE 20X1

	£	£
Balance per bank statement		(1,160.25) O/D
Uncleared lodgements:		
Cash & cheques (cashbook 30 June)		6,910.25
		5,750.00
Unpresented cheques:		
121 Whitby Cleaning Machines	538.00	
122 York Chemicals	212.00	
		(750.00)
Balance per cash book (W1)		£5,000.00

(W1)

Balance as per cash book:	
Total receipts (incl. op. bal)	£24,212.00
Total payments	(£19,212.00)
	£5,000.00

FINANCIAL ACCOUNTING: PREPARING FINANCIAL STATEMENTS

Accruals and prepayments

Introduction

In this chapter we review the need to account for accruals and prepayments of income and expenses. It is important to note that accounting software may be used to automate recurring entries such as those involved when accounting for accruals and prepayments.

ASSESSMENT CRITERIA
Record accruals and prepayments of income and expenditure (5.1)

CONTENTS
1 Recording income and expenditure
2 Accounting for accrued expenses
3 Accounting for prepaid expenses
4 Accounting for accrued income
5 Accounting for prepaid income
6 Journal entries

Accruals and prepayments: **Chapter 12**

1 Recording income and expenditure

1.1 The accruals concept

> **Definition – The accruals concept**
>
> The accruals basis of accounting requires that transactions should be reflected in the financial statements for the period in which they occur. This means that the amount of income should be recognised as it is earned and expenses when they are incurred. This is not necessarily when cash is received or paid.

For example, consider credit sales. When a sale is made on credit it is still recorded even though it may be a considerable time before the cash is actually received from the customer.

1.2 Recording sales and purchases on credit

Sales on credit are recorded in the ledger accounts from the sales day book.

The double entry is:

- **debit the receivables ledger control account (receivables)**
- **credit the sales account**.

All sales made in the period are accounted for in that accounting period whether or not the money has yet been received from the customer.

Purchases on credit are recorded in ledger accounts from the purchases day book.

The double entry is:

- **debit the purchases account**
- **credit the payables ledger control account (payables)**.

All purchases are recorded at the date of the transaction whether or not the supplier has yet been paid.

1.3 Recording expenses of the business

Most business expenses such as rent, rates, telephone, power costs etc. tend to be entered into the ledger accounts from the cash payments book. This means that the amount recorded in the ledger accounts is only the cash payment.

In accordance with the accruals concept, the amount of the expense to be recognised in the statement of profit or loss may be different to the cash payments made during the accounting period.

Expenses should be charged to the statement of profit or loss at the amount incurred in the accounting period rather than the amount of cash that has been paid during the period.

2 Accounting for accrued expenses

2.1 Introduction

If an expense is to be adjusted, the adjustment may be an accrual or a prepayment.

Definition – Accrued expense

An accrued expense is an expense incurred during the accounting period but not paid by the period end, i.e. a liability.

A business may not know the exact amount of expense incurred until the invoice for payment is received; in this case they must make a prudent estimate of the accrued cost.

Example 1

A business has a year-end of 31 December. During the year 20X1 the following electricity bills were paid:

		£
15 May	4 months to 30 April	400
18 July	2 months to 30 June	180
14 Sept	2 months to 30 August	150
15 Nov	2 months to 31 October	210

The business estimated that the average monthly electricity bill is £100.

What was the total charge for electricity for the year-ended 31 December 20X1?

Solution

	£
Jan to April	400
May to June	180
July to August	150
Sept to Oct	210
Accrual for Nov/Dec (2 × 100)	200
Total charge	1,140

 Test your understanding 1

Olwen commenced business on 1 May 20X0 and is charged rent at the rate of £6,000 per annum. During the period to 31 December 20X0, he paid rent of £3,400.

What should his charge in the statement of profit or loss for the period to 31 December 20X0 be in respect of rent?

2.2 Accounting for accrued expenses

The method of accounting for an accrued expense is to:

- **debit the expense account**

  to increase the expense recognised in the statement of profit or loss, to reflect an expense has been incurred; and

- **credit an accrued expenses account**

  to reflect there is a liability for the expense recognised in the statement of financial position.

FINANCIAL ACCOUNTING: PREPARING FINANCIAL STATEMENTS

 Example 2

Using the electricity example from above, the accounting entries will now be made in the ledger accounts.

Solution

Electricity expenses (SPL)

	£		£
15 May Bank	400		
18 July Bank	180		
14 Sept Bank	150		
15 Nov Bank	210		
31 Dec Accrued expenses	200	SPL	1,140
	1,140		1,140

Accrued expenses (SFP)

£		£
	Electricity expenses	200

The statement of profit or loss is charged with the full amount of electricity used in the period and there is an accrual shown in the statement of financial position of £200.

The amount owed for the accrued expense would appear in the statement of financial position as a current liability.

Test your understanding 2

Olwen commenced business on 1 May 20X0 and is charged rent at the rate of £6,000 per annum. During the period to 31 December 20X0, he actually paid £3,400.

Write up the ledger account for rent for the period to 31 December 20X0. Clearly state whether the year-end adjustment is an accrual or prepayment.

Rent expenses (SPL)

£	£

2.3 Reversal of accrued expenses

At the start of the next accounting period, the closing liability from the prior year's accrued expense will remain as a credit balance in the accrued expense liability account. The amount due will be paid within this next accounting period.

The payment of the relating invoice would be recorded as

- **debit the expense account (SPL)**
- **credit the bank account (SFP)**.

However, this expense was already recognised at the time it was accrued for in the last accounting period. To avoid double counting the expense, we reverse the opening liability from the accrued expense account.

The required accounting entry is

- **debit accrued expenses account (SFP)**
- **credit the expense account (SPL)**.

Example 3

Continuing with our earlier electricity expense example the closing accrual at the end of 20X0 was £200. During 20X1 £950 of electricity bills were paid and a further accrual of £220 was estimated at the end of 20X1.

Write up the ledger account for electricity for 20X1 clearly showing the charge to the statement of profit or loss and any accrued balance.

Solution

Electricity expenses (SPL)

	£		£
Bank	950	Reversal of accrued expenses	200
Accrued expenses	220	SPL	970
	1,170		1,170

The reversal of accrued expenses of £200 relates to expenses incurred in the prior year which we accrued for in the prior year. Therefore of the £950 paid from the bank, £200 relates to the prior year (which has already been recognised as an expense) and £750 to the current year. The reversal of the prior period's closing accrual ensures duplication of expense recognition does not occur.

The business owes a further £220 for the current year that it has not yet paid and so this is recognised as a closing accrued expense.

Accruals and prepayments: Chapter 12

 Test your understanding 3

The insurance account of a business had an opening accrual of £340 at 1 July 20X0. During the year insurance payments of £3,700 were made and it has been calculated that a closing accrual of £400 was required.

Prepare the insurance expense account for the year-ended 30th June 20X1 and close it off by showing the transfer to the statement of profit or loss.

Insurance expenses (SPL)

£	£

3 Accounting for prepaid expenses

3.1 Introduction

Another type of adjustment that might need to be made to an expense account is to adjust for a prepayment.

 Definition – Prepaid expense

A prepaid expense is a payment made during the accounting period (and therefore debited to the expense account) for an expense that relates to the following accounting period.

FINANCIAL ACCOUNTING: PREPARING FINANCIAL STATEMENTS

 Example 4

The rent of a business is £3,000 per quarter payable in advance. During 20X0 the rent ledger account shows that £15,000 of rent was paid during the year.

What was the correct charge to the statement of profit or loss for the year and what was the amount of any prepayment at 31st December 20X0?

Solution

The statement of profit or loss charge should be £12,000 for the year, four quarterly charges of £3,000 each. The prepaid expense is £3,000 (£15,000 – £12,000), rent paid in advance for next year.

 Test your understanding 4

Julie paid £1,300 insurance during the year to 31 March 20X6. The charge in the statement of profit or loss for the year to 31 March 20X6 was £1,200.

What was the amount of the prepayment at 31 March 20X6?

3.2 Accounting for prepaid expenses

Accounting for prepayments is the mirror image of accounting for accruals, except we use a separate prepayments account.

(a) **credit the expense account**

to reduce the expense in the statement of profit or loss by the amount of the prepayment; and

(b) **debit a prepaid expense account**

to show that the business has an asset (the prepayment) in the statement of financial position at the period end.

Example 5

A business paid rent of £3,000 per quarter payable in advance. During 20X0 the rent ledger account shows that £15,000 of rent has been paid during the year.

Show how these entries would be made in the ledger accounts.

Solution

Rent expenses (SPL)

	£		£
Bank	15,000	Prepaid expenses	3,000
		SPL	12,000
	15,000		15,000

Prepaid expenses (SFP)

	£		£
Rent expenses	3,000		

The charge to the statement of profit or loss is now the correct figure of £12,000 and there is a debit balance on the prepayments account.

This balance on the prepayments account will appear as a prepayment within current assets in the statement of financial position at the period end date.

3.3 Reversal of prepaid expenses

At the start of the next accounting period, the closing asset from the prior year's prepaid expense will remain as a debit balance in the prepaid expense asset account. The amount of the expense prepaid relates to this accounting period.

As we must prepare accounts in accordance with the accruals concept, where expenses are recognised as incurred, the prepaid expense should be recognised in the period it relates, even though it has been paid for in a prior accounting period.

To reverse the opening prepayment, the required accounting entry is:

- **debit expenses account (SPL)**
- **credit the prepaid expenses account (SFP).**

FINANCIAL ACCOUNTING: PREPARING FINANCIAL STATEMENTS

 Example 6

Continuing with the previous rent example the prepayment at the end of 20X0 was £3,000. The payments for rent during 20X1 were £15,000 and the charge for the year was £14,000.

Write up the ledger account for rent clearly showing the charge to the statement of profit or loss and the closing prepaid expense at 31 December 20X1.

Solution

Rent expenses (SPL)

	£		£
Reversal of prepaid expenses	3,000	SPL	14,000
Bank	15,000	Prepaid expenses	4,000
	18,000		18,000

Note that you were given the charge for the year in the question and therefore the prepayment figure is the missing or balancing amount.

The reversal of prepaid expense relates to £3,000 of cash paid in the prior year which should be recognised as an expense in this year in which it relates.

 Test your understanding 5

The following information relates to the rent and rates account of a business:

Balances as at:	1 April 20X0 £	31 March 20X1 £
Prepaid rates expenses	20	30
Accrued rent expenses	100	120

The bank summary for the year shows payments for rent and rates of £840.

Prepare the rent and rates account for the year-ended 31st March 20X1 and close it off by showing the transfer to the statement of profit or loss.

KAPLAN PUBLISHING

Rent and rates expenses (SPL)	
£	£
———	———
———	———

4 Accounting for accrued income

4.1 Introduction

Businesses may have sundry forms of income. The cash received may not always match the income earned in the accounting period and therefore similar adjustments to those for accrued and prepaid expenses will be required.

4.2 Accrued income

  Definition – Accrued income

Accrued income is income that has been earned but has not yet been received.

If the amount of income received in cash is less than the income earned for the period then this additional income must be accrued for. The required accounting entry is:

- **credit the income account**

  to increase income recognised in the statement of profit or loss and

- **debit accrued income** (within current assets in the statement of financial position)

  to recognise the current asset in the statement of financial position of the cash due to be received.

4.3 Reversal of accrued income

At the start of the next accounting period, the closing asset from the prior year's accrued income will remain as a debit balance in the accrued income asset account. The amount of income due will be received within this next accounting period.

The receipt of this income would be recorded as

- **debit the bank account (SFP)**
- **credit the income account (SPL)**.

However, this income was already recognised at the time it was accrued for in the last accounting period. To avoid double counting the income, we reverse the opening asset from the accrued income account and the duplicating entry in the income account. The accounting entry required is:

- **debit the income account (SPL)**
- **credit the accrued income (SFP)**.

5 Accounting for prepaid income

5.1 Introduction

Another type of adjustment that might need to be made to an income account is to adjust for a prepayment of income.

5.2 Prepaid income

Definition – Prepaid income

Prepaid income is payment received in advance of it being earned. It may also be referred to as 'deferred income'.

If the amount of cash received is greater than the income earned in the accounting period then this income has been prepaid. The required accounting entry is:

- **debit the income account**

  to reduce income recognised in the statement of profit or loss and

- **credit prepaid income**

  to recognise the current liability in the statement of financial position for the amount of income that has been prepaid and not yet earned.

5.3 Reversal of prepaid income

At the start of the next accounting period, the closing liability from the prior year's prepaid income will remain as a credit balance in the prepaid income liability account. The amount of the income prepaid relates to this accounting period.

As we must prepare accounts in accordance with the accruals concept, where income is recognised as earned, the prepaid income should be recognised in the period it relates, even though it has been received in a prior accounting period.

To reverse the opening prepaid income, the required accounting entry is:

- **debit the prepaid income (SFP)**
- **credit the income account (SPL)**.

Example 7

Minnie's business has two properties, A and B that are rented out to other parties. The rental on property A for the year is £12,000 but only £10,000 has been received. The rental on property B is £15,000 and the client has paid £16,000 this year.

Write up separate rent accounts for properties A and B showing the income credited to the statement of profit or loss and any closing balances on the income accounts.

Explain what each balance means.

Solution

Rent account – A

	£		£
SPL	12,000	Bank	10,000
		Accrued income	2,000
	12,000		12,000

The bank amount of £10,000 is the amount received by the client. The income for the year earned on this property is £12,000 which is shown as the amount to be recognised in the SPL. The difference of £2,000 is the amount of the accrued income; income earned but not yet received. Accrued income is an asset in the statement of financial position showing that Minnie is owed £2,000 for rent on property A.

FINANCIAL ACCOUNTING: PREPARING FINANCIAL STATEMENTS

	Rent account – B		
	£		£
SPL	15,000	Bank	16,000
Prepaid income	1,000		
	16,000		16,000

The bank amount of £16,000 is the amount received by the client. The income for the year earned on this property is £15,000 which is shown as the amount to be recognised in the SPL. The difference of £1,000 is the amount of the prepaid income; Minnie has received £1,000 in excess of the income earned. Prepaid income is a liability on the statement of financial position showing that Minnie has an obligation in relation to income not yet earned.

Test your understanding 6

Hyde wishes to use your shop to display and sell framed photographs. He will pay £40 per month for this service in cash.

(a) How would you account for this transaction each month?

(b) If, at the end of the year, Hyde owed one month's rental, how would this be treated in the accounts?

(c) Which accounting concept is being applied?

6 Journal entries

6.1 Recurring journal entries

As with accounting for depreciation expenses, accruals and prepayments are adjustments to the accounts which do not appear in the accounting records from the primary records. Therefore, adjustments for accruals and prepayments must be entered into the accounting records by means of a journal entry.

Recurring journal entries are associated with particular expenses or transactions that are repeated every accounting period. When setting up recurring journal entries, the accountant needs to define the total amount and the schedule for allocating and posting the entry. Manually performing this process can take a considerable amount of time, accounting software can automate the process for creating recurring journal entries.

Accruals and prepayments: **Chapter 12**

 Example 8

An accrual for electricity is to be made at the year-end of £200. Show the journal entry required for this adjustment.

Solution

Journal entry			No:
Date			
Prepared by			
Authorised by			
Account	Code	Debit £	Credit £
Electricity expenses (SPL)	0442	200	
Accrued expenses (SFP)	1155		200
Totals		200	200

 Test your understanding 7

A prepayment adjustment is to be made at the year-end of £1,250 for insurance expense.

Record the journal entry required for this adjustment.

The following account codes and account names should be used.

0445 Insurance expenses (SPL)

1000 Prepaid expenses (SFP)

Journal entry			No:
Date			
Prepared by			
Authorised by			
Account	Code	Debit £	Credit £
Totals			

FINANCIAL ACCOUNTING: PREPARING FINANCIAL STATEMENTS

 Test your understanding 8

Siobhan

Siobhan, the proprietor of a sweet shop, provides you with the following information relating to sundry expenditure and income of her business for the year-ended 31 December 20X4:

1 **Rent payable**

   £15,000 was paid during 20X4 to cover the 15 months ending 31 March 20X5.

2 **Gas**

   £840 was paid during 20X4 to cover gas charges from 1 January 20X4 to 31 July 20X4. Gas charges can be assumed to accrue evenly over the year. There was no outstanding balance at 1 January 20X4.

3 **Advertising**

   Included in the payments totalling £3,850 made during 20X4 was an amount of £500 payable in respect of a planned advertising campaign for 20X5.

4 **Bank interest**

   The bank statements of the business show that the following interest was charged to the account.

   For period up to 31 May 20X4   Nil (no overdraft)
   For 1 June – 31 August 20X4   £28
   1 September – 30 November 20X4   £45

   The bank statements for 20X5 show that £69 was charged to the account on 28 February 20X5.

5 **Rates**

   Towards the end of 20X3 £4,800 was paid to cover the six months ended 31 March 20X4.

   In May 20X4 £5,600 was paid to cover the six months ended 30 September 20X4.

   In early 20X5 £6,600 was paid for the six months ending 31 March 20X5.

6   Rent receivable

During 20X4, Siobhan received £250 rent from Joe Soap for the use of a lock-up garage attached to the shop, for the six months ended 31 March 20X4.

She increased the rent to £600 pa from 1 April 20X4, and during 20X4 Joe Soap paid her rent for the full year-ending 31 March 20X5.

Required:

Write up ledger accounts for each of the above items, showing:

(a)   the reversal of opening accrued or prepaid amounts at 1 January 20X4, if any

(b)   any bank amounts paid or received

(c)   the closing accrued or prepaid amounts at 31 December 20X4

(d)   the charge or credit for the year to the statement of profit or loss.

 Test your understanding 9

A Metro

A Metro owns a number of antique shops and, in connection with this business, he runs a small fleet of motor vans. He prepares his accounts to 31 December each year.

On 1 January 20X0 the amount prepaid for motor tax and insurance was £570.

On 1 April 20X0 he paid £420 which represented motor tax on six of the vans for the year-ended 31 March 20X1.

On 1 May 20X0 he paid £1,770 insurance for all ten vans for the year-ended 30 April 20X1.

On 1 July 20X0 he paid £280 which represented motor tax for the other four vans for the year-ended 30 June 20X1.

Required:

Write up the account for 'motor tax and insurance' for the year-ended 31 December 20X0.

7 Summary

In order for the final accounts to accord with the accruals concept, the cash receipts and payments for income and expenses must be adjusted to ensure that they include all of the income earned during the year and expenses incurred during the year.

The sales and purchases are automatically dealt with through the receivables ledger control account and payables ledger control account.

However the expenses and sundry income of a business are recorded in the ledger accounts on cash paid and received basis and therefore adjustments for accruals and prepayments must be made by journal entries.

Accruals and prepayments: Chapter 12

Test your understanding answers

Test your understanding 1

$(\frac{8}{12} \times £6,000) = £4,000$ The expense should reflect the proportion of the year's £6,000 charge consumed, not what has been paid.

Test your understanding 2

Rent expenses (SPL)

	£		£
Bank	3,400	Statement of profit or loss $(6,000 \times \frac{8}{12})$	4,000
Accrued expenses	600		
	4,000		4,000

Test your understanding 3

Insurance expenses (SPL)

	£		£
Bank	3,700	Reversal of accrued expenses	340
Accrued expenses	400	SPL	3,760
	4,100		4,100

FINANCIAL ACCOUNTING: PREPARING FINANCIAL STATEMENTS

Test your understanding 4

The prepayment was £1,300 – 1,200 = £100

Test your understanding 5

Rent and rates expenses (SPL)

	£		£
Reversal of prepaid rates expenses	20	Reversal of accrued rent expenses	100
Bank	840	SPL (bal fig)	850
Accrued rent expenses	120	Prepaid rates expenses	30
	980		980

Test your understanding 6

(a) Dr   Cash account
     Cr   Sundry income account

(b) A sundry receivable
     Dr   Sundry receivable (SFP)
     Cr   Sundry income (SPL)

(c) The accruals concept

Test your understanding 7

Journal entry			No:
Date			
Prepared by			
Authorised by			
Account	**Code**	**Debit £**	**Credit £**
Prepaid expenses (SFP)	1000	1,250	
Insurance expenses (SPL)	0445		1,250
Totals		1,250	1,250

Test your understanding 8

Rental expenses

	£		£
Bank	15,000	SPL	12,000
		Prepaid expenses	3,000
	15,000		15,000

Gas expenses

	£		£
Bank	840	SPL	1,440
Accrued expenses	600		
	1,440		1,440

Advertising expenses

	£		£
Bank	3,850	SPL	3,350
		Prepaid expenses	500
	3,850		3,850

Bank interest

	£		£
Bank	28	SPL	96
Bank	45		
Accrued expenses	23		
	96		96

Rates

	£		£
Reversal of prepaid expense ($^3/_6$ × 4,800)	2,400	SPL	11,300
Bank	5,600		
Accrued expenses ($^3/_6$ × 6,600)	3,300		
	11,300		11,300

Rental income

	£		£
Reversal of accrued income (250 × 3/6)	125	Bank	250
SPL (W)	575	Bank	600
Prepaid income (3/12 × 600)	150		
	850		850

Working – Statement of profit or loss – rental income

	£
1 January 20X4 – 31 March 20X4 ($^3/_6$ × 250)	125
1 April 20X4 – 31 December 20X4 ($^9/_{12}$ × 600)	450
	575

Accruals and prepayments: Chapter 12

Test your understanding 9

A Metro

Motor tax and insurance

	£		£
Reversal of prepaid expenses	570	SPL (W2)	2,205
Bank		Prepaid expenses	835
1 April	420		
1 May	1,770		
1 July	280		
	3,040		3,040

Workings

(W1) Prepayment at the end of the year

	£
Motor tax on six vans paid 1 April 20X0 ($\frac{3}{12} \times 420$)	105
Insurance on ten vans paid 1 May 20X0 ($\frac{4}{12} \times 1{,}770$)	590
Motor tax on four vans paid 1 July 20X0 ($\frac{6}{12} \times 280$)	140
Total prepayment	835

(W2) SPL charge for the year

There is no need to calculate this as it is the balancing figure, but it could be calculated as follows.

	£
Opening prepayment (reversal)	570
Motor tax ($\frac{9}{12} \times 420$)	315
Insurance ($\frac{8}{12} \times 1{,}770$)	1,180
Motor tax ($\frac{6}{12} \times 280$)	140
SPL charge	2,205

FINANCIAL ACCOUNTING: PREPARING FINANCIAL STATEMENTS

Suspense accounts and errors

Introduction

When preparing a trial balance or an extended trial balance it is likely that a suspense account will have to be opened and then any errors and omissions adjusted for and the suspense account cleared.

There are a variety of different types of errors that you need to be aware of. Some of the errors are detected by a trial balance and some are not.

Before the final accounts are prepared the suspense account must be cleared by correcting each of the errors that have caused the trial balance not to balance.

ASSESSMENT CRITERIA
Prepare an initial trial balance (6.1)
Prepare an adjusted trial balance (6.2)

CONTENTS
1 The trial balance
2 Opening a suspense account
3 Clearing the suspense account

1 The trial balance

1.1 Introduction

We saw in an earlier Chapter that one of the purposes of the trial balance is to provide a check on the accuracy of the double-entry bookkeeping performed and it is important that this is done regularly.

Although accounting software may be used to automate bookkeeping processes including the transfer of ledger accounting balances into the trial balance, it may also be performed manually. Once all ledger balances have been extracted and the trial balance has been prepared, it might be that the trial balance does not balance – i.e. total debits do not equal total credits. If the trial balance does not balance then an error or a number of errors have occurred and this must be investigated and the errors corrected.

If the trial balance does balance, this does not necessarily mean that all of the entries are correct. There are some types of errors that are not detected by the trial balance. The benefit of using accounting software is that after adjustments are made, the software automatically recalculates balances.

1.2 Errors where the trial balance does not balance

The following types of error will cause a difference in the trial balance and therefore will be detected by the trial balance and can be investigated and corrected:

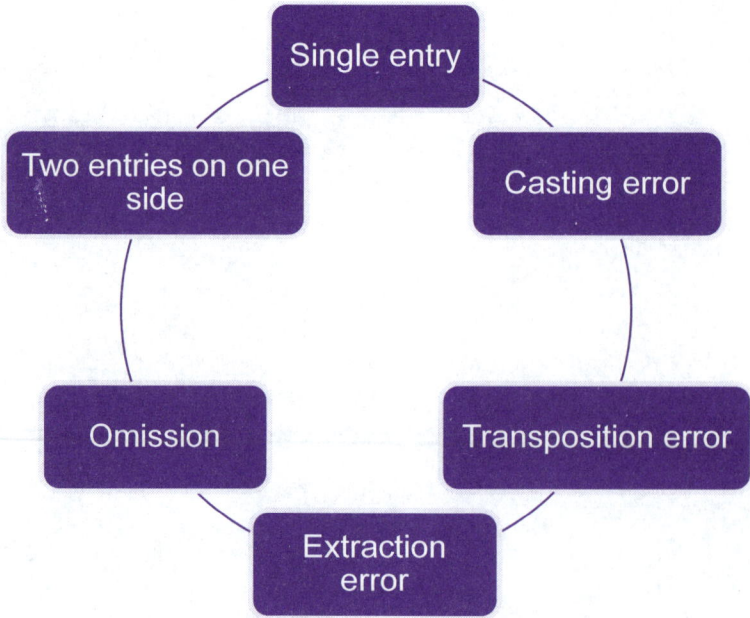

FINANCIAL ACCOUNTING: PREPARING FINANCIAL STATEMENTS

Definition – Single entry error

If only one side of a double entry has been made then this means that the trial balance will not balance e.g. if only the debit entry for receipts from receivables has been made then the debit total on the trial balance will exceed the credit balance.

Definition – Casting error

If a ledger account has not been balanced correctly due to a casting error then this will mean that the trial balance will not balance.

Definition – Transposition error

If an amount in a ledger account or a balance on a ledger account has been transposed and incorrectly recorded then the trial balance will not balance e.g. a debit entry was recorded correctly as £5,276, but the related credit entry was entered as £5,726.

Definition – Extraction error

If a ledger account balance is incorrectly recorded on the trial balance, either by recording the wrong figure or putting the balance on the wrong side of the trial balance, then the trial balance will not balance.

Definition – Omission error

If a ledger account balance is inadvertently omitted from the trial balance then the trial balance will not balance.

Definition – Two entries on one side

If a transaction is entered as a debit in two accounts, or as a credit in two accounts, instead of the normal debit and credit entry, then the trial balance will not balance.

1.3 Errors where the trial balance still balances

Certain other errors cannot be detected by preparing a trial balance, as these errors will not cause a difference between the total debits and total credits in that trial balance.

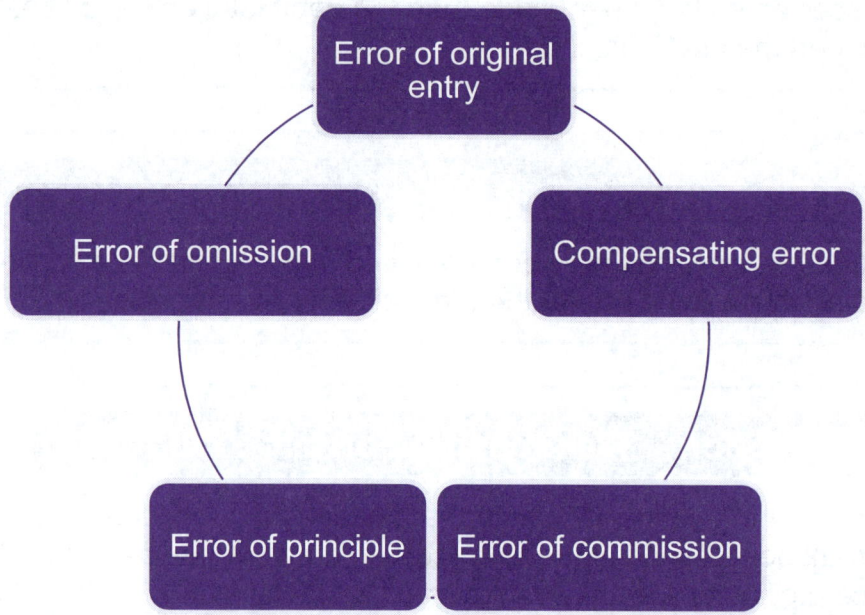

Definition – Error of original entry

This is where the wrong figure is entered as both the debit and credit entry e.g. a payment of the electricity expense was correctly recorded as a debit in the electricity account and a credit to the bank account but it was recorded as £300 instead of £330.

Definition – Compensating error

This is where two separate errors are made, one on the debit side of a particular ledger account and the other on the credit side of a different ledger account. By coincidence the two errors are of the same amount and therefore cancel each other out when the trial balance is prepared.

Definition – Error of commission

With this type of error, a debit entry and an equal credit entry have been made. However, one of the entries has been to the wrong account e.g. if the electricity expense was debited to the rent account but the credit entry was correctly made in the bank account – here both the electricity account and rent account will be incorrect but the trial balance will still balance.

Definition – Error of principle

This is similar to an error of commission in that part of an entry has been posted to the wrong account. However, the error is one of principle. For example, instead of capitalising the cost of a non-current asset on the statement of financial position (by debiting non-current assets) the cost has been debited to a statement of profit or loss expense account. This is fundamentally incorrect but the trial balance will still balance.

Definition – Error of omission

This is where an entire double entry is omitted from the ledger accounts. As both the debit and credit have been omitted the trial balance will still balance.

1.4 Correction of errors

Whatever type of error is discovered, either by producing the trial balance or by other checks on the ledger accounts, it will need to be corrected. Errors will normally be corrected by putting through a double-entry journal for the correction. If using accounting software, the recalculation of balances is performed automatically.

Suspense accounts and errors: Chapter 13

The procedure for identifying what journal is required to correct those errors is as follows:

Step 1 – What did you do?
- Determine the precise nature of the incorrect double entry that has been made.

Step 2 – What should you have done?
- Determine the correct entries that should have been made.

Step 3 – What is the correction?
- Produce a journal entry that cancels the incorrect part and puts through the correct entries.

Example 1

The electricity expense of £450 has been correctly credited to the bank account but has been debited to the rent account.

Step 1 – What did they do?

Dr	Rent account	£450
Cr	Bank account	£450

Step 2 – What should they have done?

Dr	Electricity account	£450
Cr	Bank account	£450

Step 3 – What is the correction?

The journal entry required is:

Dr	Electricity account	£450
Cr	Rent account	£450

Note that this removes the incorrect debit from the rent account and puts the correct debit into the electricity account.

FINANCIAL ACCOUNTING: PREPARING FINANCIAL STATEMENTS

 Test your understanding 1

Colin returned some goods to a supplier because they were faulty. The original purchase price of these goods was £8,260.

The ledger clerk has correctly accounted for the transaction but has used the figure £8,620 in error.

Required:

What is the correcting entry which needs to be made?

2 Opening a suspense account

2.1 Introduction

A suspense account is a temporary account that can be created to deal with any errors or omissions arising in our general ledger accounting. It means that it is possible to continue with the production of financial accounts whilst the reasons for any errors are investigated and then corrected.

2.2 Reasons for opening a suspense account

A suspense account will be opened in two main circumstances:

(a) an unknown entry – i.e. the bookkeeper does not know how to deal with one side of a transaction

(b) the trial balance does not balance.

2.3 Unknown entry

In some circumstances the bookkeeper may come across a transaction for which there is some uncertainty of the correct double entry and therefore, rather than making an error, one side of the entry will be posted to a suspense account until the correct entry can be determined.

Example 2

A new bookkeeper is dealing with a cheque received from a garage for £800 for the sale of an old car. The bookkeeper correctly debits the bank account with the amount of the cheque but does not know what to do with the credit entry.

Solution

It will be entered into the suspense account:

Suspense account

£		£
	Bank account – receipt from sale of car	800

2.4 Trial balance does not balance

If the total of the debits on the trial balance does not equal the total of the credits, then an error or a number of errors have been made. These must be investigated, identified and eventually corrected.

In the meantime, the difference between the debit total and the credit total is inserted as a suspense account balance in order to make the two totals agree.

Example 3

The totals of the trial balance are as follows:

	Debits £	Credits £
Totals as initially extracted	108,367	109,444
Suspense account, to make the TB balance	1,077	
	109,444	109,444

Suspense account

	£		£
Opening balance	1,077		

FINANCIAL ACCOUNTING: PREPARING FINANCIAL STATEMENTS

> **Test your understanding 2**
>
> The debit balances on a trial balance exceed the credit balances by £2,600.
>
> **Required:**
>
> Open up a suspense account to record this difference.

3 Clearing the suspense account

3.1 Introduction

Whatever the reason for the suspense account being opened, it is only ever a temporary account. The reasons for the difference must be identified and then correcting entries should be put through the ledger accounts, via the journal, in order to correct the accounts and clear the suspense account balance to zero.

3.2 Procedure for clearing the suspense account

Step 1

Determine the incorrect entry that has been made or the omission from the ledger accounts – i.e. the reason for the creation of the suspense account balance.

Step 2

Determine the double-entry journal required to correct the error or omission – this will not always require an entry to the suspense account e.g. when the electricity expense was debited to the rent account the journal entry did not require any entry to be made in the suspense account.

Step 3

Post the correcting journals through the ledger accounts and calculate any revised balances carried down. When all the corrections have been made the suspense account should normally have no remaining balance on it.

Example 4

Some purchases for cash of £100 have been correctly entered into the cash account but no entry has been made in the purchases account. An entry of £100 was debited to the suspense account.

Draft a journal entry to correct this error.

Solution

Step 1 – Reason for suspense account

The cash account has been credited with £100 but no other entry was made. In this case the Dr would have been posted to the suspense account.

Did do:

Dr   Suspense   £100
Cr   Cash account   £100

Should have done:

Dr   Purchases   £100
Cr   Cash account   £100

Step 2 – Correction journal

A debit entry is required in the purchases account and the credit is to the suspense account to cancel the original debit and to clear the balance to nil.

		£	£
Dr	Purchases account	100	
Cr	Suspense account		100

Being correction of double entry for cash purchases.

Remember that normally a journal entry needs a narrative to explain what it is for – however in most examinations you are told not to provide the narratives so always read the requirements carefully.

Example 5

On 31 December 20X0 the trial balance of John Jones, a small manufacturer who is not VAT registered, failed to agree and the difference of £967 was entered as a debit balance on a suspense account. After the final accounts had been prepared, the following errors were discovered and the balance on the suspense account was eliminated.

1. A purchase of goods from A Smith for £170 had been credited in error to the account of H Smith.
2. The purchase day book was under cast by £200.
3. Machinery purchased for £150 had been debited to the purchases account.
4. Discounts received of £130 had been debited to the discounts received account.
5. Rates paid by a cheque for £46 had been debited to the rates account as £64.
6. Cash drawings by the owner of £45 had been posted to the cash account correctly but not posted to the drawings account.
7. A non-current asset balance of £1,200 had been omitted from the trial balance.

Note: The control accounts are part of the double entry.

Required:

(a) Show the journal entries necessary to correct the above errors.

(b) Show the entries in the suspense account to eliminate the differences entered in the suspense account.

Solution

Tuition note: Not all the errors relate to the suspense account. Part of the way of dealing with these questions is to identify which entries do not relate to the suspense account. Do not assume that they all do just because this is a question about suspense accounts.

(a) **Journal – John Jones**

	Dr £	Cr £
31 December 20X0		
1 H Smith	170	
A Smith		170

Being adjustment of incorrect entry for purchases from A Smith – this correction takes place in the payables ledger (no effect on suspense account).

2	Purchases	200	
	Payables ledger control account		200

Being the correction of undercast purchases day book (no effect on suspense account as control account is the double entry, however the error should have been found during the reconciliation of the control account).

3	Machinery	150	
	Purchases		150

Being adjustment for wrong entry for machinery purchased (no effect on suspense account).

4	Suspense account	260	
	Discount received		260

Being correction of discounts received entered on wrong side of account.

5	Suspense account	18	
	Rates		18

Being correction of transposition error to rates account.

6	Drawings	45	
	Suspense account		45

Being completion of double entry for drawings.

7	Non-current asset	1,200	
	Suspense account		1,200

Being inclusion of non-current asset balance. There is no double entry for this error in the ledger as the mistake was to omit the item from the trial balance.

(b)

Suspense account

	£		£
Difference in trial balance	967	Drawings	45
Discounts received	260	Non-current asset per trial balance	1,200
Rates	18		
	1,245		1,245

FINANCIAL ACCOUNTING: PREPARING FINANCIAL STATEMENTS

Test your understanding 3

The following questions are about errors and suspense accounts.

1. A telephone expense is debited to the rent expense account. This is an example of (tick the correct answer):

    A casting error ☐

    An error of commission ☐

    A compensating error ☐

    A single entry ☐

2. A repair expense is debited to a non-current asset account. This is an example of (tick the correct answer):

    A casting error ☐

    An error of commission ☐

    A compensating error ☐

    An error of principle ☐

3. Discounts received of £400 have been entered as a credit into the discount allowed account. What is the journal entry required to correct this?

Debit	**Credit**	
Discounts received	Discounts allowed	☐
Discounts allowed	Discounts received	☐

4. The total of the debit balances on a trial balance are £312,563 whilst the credit balances total to £313,682. Will the suspense account balance be a debit or a credit balance?

    Debit of £1,119 ☐

    Credit of £1,119 ☐

5   Purchases returns of £210 had been correctly posted to the payables ledger control account but had been debited to the purchases returns account. What is the journal entry required to correct this?

Debit	Credit	
Purchase returns account	Payables ledger control account	☐
Suspense account	Purchase returns account	☐

6   An invoice from a supplier for £485 had been entered in the purchases day book as £458. What journal entry is required to correct this?

Debit	Credit	
Purchase account	Payables ledger control account	☐
Purchases account	Suspense account	☐

7   When producing the trial balance the telephone account expense of £300 was omitted from the trial balance. What journal entry is required to correct this?

Debit	Credit	
Suspense account	Telephone account	☐
Telephone account	Suspense account	☐

8   Motor expenses of £500 were correctly dealt with in the bank account but were debited to the motor vehicles non-current asset account. What journal entry is required to correct this?

Debit	Credit	
Bank account	Motor vehicles at cost account	☐
Motor expenses account	Motor vehicles at cost account	☐

Test your understanding 4

On extracting a trial balance, the accountant of ETT discovered a suspense account with a debit balance of £1,075 included; it was also found that the debits (including the suspense account) exceeded the credits by £957.

The difference was posted to the suspense account, for the situation to be investigated.

It was discovered:

(a) A debit balance of £75 on the postages account had been incorrectly extracted on the trial balance as £750 debit.

(b) A payment of £500 to a payable, X, had been correctly entered in the bank account, but no entry had been made in the payables control account.

(c) When a motor vehicle had been purchased during the year the bookkeeper did not know what to do with the debit entry so the entry was made Dr Suspense, Cr bank £1,575.

(d) A credit balance of £81 in the sundry income account had been incorrectly extracted on the trial balance as a debit balance.

(e) A receipt of £5 from a receivable had been correctly posted to the receivables control account but had been entered in the cash account as £625.

(f) The bookkeeper was not able to deal with the receipt of £500 from the proprietor of ETT's own bank account, and the bookkeeper made the entry Dr Bank and Cr Suspense.

(g) No entry has been made for a cheque of £120 received from a receivable.

(h) A receipt of £50 from a receivable had been entered into the receivables control account as £5 and into the cash at bank account as £5.

Task

Show how the suspense account balance is cleared by means of a ledger account.

Test your understanding 5

Julia

The difference on the trial balance of Julia's business whereby the credit column exceeded the debit by £144 has been transferred to a suspense account.

The following errors had been made:

1. Purchase of goods from A Myers for £120 had been credited to the account of H Myers.
2. A total from the sales day book of £27 had been credited to the control account.
3. Sale of plant for £190 had been credited to sales.
4. One total of £120 from the sales day book had been debited to the receivables ledger control account as £12.
5. Sales day book undercast by £200.
6. Rent payable accrued as £30 in the previous period had not been entered as an opening balance in the current period.
7. Petty cash balance of £12 omitted from the trial balance.

Required:

Prepare the necessary journal entries, and the entries in the suspense account to clear it.

FINANCIAL ACCOUNTING: PREPARING FINANCIAL STATEMENTS

 Test your understanding 6

GA (not VAT registered) extracted the following trial balance from the ledgers at 31 May 20X4.

	£	£
Petty cash	20	
Capital		1,596
Drawings	1,400	
Sales		20,607
Purchases	15,486	
Purchases returns		210
Inventory (1 January 20X4)	2,107	
Fixtures and fittings	710	
Receivables ledger control	1,819	
Payables ledger control		2,078
Carriage on purchases	109	
Carriage on sales	184	
Rent and rates	460	
Light and heat	75	
Postage and telephone	91	
Sundry expenses	190	
Cash at bank	1,804	
	24,455	24,491

The trial balance did not agree. On investigation, GA discovered the following errors which had occurred during the month of May.

(a) **Record the journal entries to correct the errors below.**

1 In extracting the receivables balance the credit side of the receivables ledger control account had been overcast by £10.

Journal	Dr £	Cr £

2 An amount of £4 for carriage on sales had been posted in error to the carriage on purchases account.

Journal	Dr £	Cr £

3   A credit note for £17 received from a payable had been entered in the purchase returns account but no entry had been made in the payables ledger control account.

Journal	Dr £	Cr £

4   £35 charged by Builders Ltd for repairs to GA's private residence had been charged, in error, to the sundry expenses account.

Journal	Dr £	Cr £

5   A payment of a telephone bill of £21 had been entered correctly in the cash book but had been posted, in error, to the postage and telephone account as £12.

Journal	Dr £	Cr £

(b)   **Show how the suspense account is cleared**

Suspense account

(c) **Re-write the trial balance as it would appear after all the above corrections have been made.**

Trial balance for GA at 31 May 20X4

	£	£
Petty cash		
Capital		
Drawings		
Sales		
Purchases		
Purchases returns		
Inventory (1 January 20X4)		
Fixtures and fittings		
Receivables ledger control		
Payables ledger control		
Carriage on purchases		
Carriage on sales		
Rent and rates		
Light and heat		
Postage and telephone		
Sundry expenses		
Cash at bank		

4 Summary

Preparation of the trial balance is an important element of control over the double-entry system but it will not detect all errors. The use of accounting software can automate part of the process.

The trial balance will still balance if a number of types of error are made. If the trial balance does not balance then a suspense account will be opened temporarily to make the debits equal the credits in the trial balance.

The errors or omissions that have caused the difference on the trial balance must be discovered and then corrected using journal entries.

Not all errors will require an entry to the suspense account. However, any that do should be put through the suspense account in order to try to eliminate the balance on the account.

Test your understanding answers

Test your understanding 1

Step 1 – What did they do?

The payables ledger control account has been debited and the purchases returns account credited but with £8,620 rather than £8,260.

| Dr | Payables ledger control account | £8,620 |
| Cr | Purchases returns account | £8,620 |

Step 2 – What should they have done?

| Dr | Payables ledger control account | £8,260 |
| Cr | Purchases returns account | £8,260 |

Step 3 – What is the correction?

Both of the entries need to be reduced by the difference between the amount used and the correct amount (8,620 – 8,260) = £360

Journal entry:

		£	£
Dr	Purchases returns account	360	
Cr	Payables ledger control account		360

Being correction of misposting of purchase returns

Test your understanding 2

As the debit balances exceed the credit balances the balance needed is a credit balance to make the two totals equal.

Suspense account

	£		£
		Opening balance	2,600

Suspense accounts and errors: Chapter 13

> **Test your understanding 3**

1 An error of commission.

2 An error of principle.

3 Debit   Discount allowed account   £400
   Credit Discount received account   £400

4 £1,119 debit balance

5 Debit   Suspense account   £420
   Credit Purchases returns account   £420

6 Debit   Purchases account   £27
   Credit Payables ledger control account   £27

7 Debit   Telephone account (TB)   £300
   Credit Suspense account   £300

8 Debit   Motor expenses account   £500
   Credit Motor vehicles at cost account   £500

> **Test your understanding 4**

Suspense account

	£		£
Balance b/d	1,075	Trial balance – difference	957
Postage (trial balance only) (a)	675	Payables control (b)	500
Sundry income (trial balance only) (d)	162	Non-current asset – cost (c)	1,575
Cash (e)	620		
Capital account – ETT (f)	500		
	3,032		3,032

Explanatory notes:

The £1,075 debit balance is already included in the books, whilst the £957 is entered on the credit side of the suspense account because the trial balance, as extracted, shows debits exceeding credits by £957. Although the two amounts arose in different ways they are both removed from suspense by the application of double entry.

(a) The incorrect extraction is corrected by amending the balance on the trial balance and debiting the suspense account with £675. In this case the 'credit' entry is only on the trial balance, as the postages account itself shows the correct balance, the error coming in putting that balance on the trial balance.

(b) The non-entry of the £500 to the debit of X's account causes the account to be incorrectly stated and the trial balance to be unbalanced. To correct matters Dr Payables control Cr Suspense.

(c) The suspense entry here arose from adherence to double-entry procedures, rather than a numerical error. In this case the bookkeeper should have Dr Non-current asset – cost, Cr Bank instead of Dr Suspense, Cr Bank, so to correct matters the entry Dr Non-current asset – cost, Cr Suspense is made.

(d) Is similar to (a), but note that the incorrect extraction of a credit balance as a debit balance means that twice the amount involved has to be amended on the trial balance and debited to suspense account.

(e) Is similar to (b) – on this occasion Dr Suspense, Cr Cash, and amend the cash account balance on the trial balance.

(f) Is similar to (c). The bookkeeper should have Dr Bank, Cr ETT – capital, but has instead Dr Bank, Cr Suspense, so to correct matters Dr Suspense, Cr Capital.

(g) Item (g) does not appear in the suspense account as the error does not affect the imbalance of the trial balance. As no entry has been made for the cheque, the correcting entry is

	£	£
Dr Cash at bank account	120	
Cr Receivables control account		120

(h) item (h) also does not appear in the suspense account. Although an entry has been made in the books which was wrong, the entry was incorrect for both the debit and credit entry. The correcting entry is

	£	£
Dr Cash at bank account	45	
Cr Receivables control account		45

Test your understanding 5

Julia

Suspense account

	£		£
Difference on trial balance	144	RLCA (£27 × 2) (2)	54
Rent payable account (6)	30	RLCA (120 – 12) (4)	108
		Petty cash account (7)	12
	174		174

Journal entries

	£	£
Dr H Myers' account	120	
Cr A Myers' account		120

Correction of posting to incorrect personal account (1).

	£	£
Dr Receivables ledger control account	54	
Cr Suspense account		54

Correction of posting to wrong side of RLCA (2).

	£	£
Dr Revenue account	190	
Cr Disposal account		190

Correction of error of principle – sales proceeds of plant previously posted to revenue account (3).

	£	£
Dr RLCA	108	
Cr Suspense account		108

Correction of posting £12 rather than £120 (4).

	£	£
Dr Receivables ledger control account	200	
Cr Revenue account		200

Correction of under casting of sales day book (5).

30

Dr   Suspense account
    Cr   Rent payable account   30
Amount of accrual not Balance b/d on the account (6).

     12

Dr   Petty cash account (not posted)
    Cr   Suspense account   12
Balance omitted from trial balance (7).

Test your understanding 6

			Dr £	Cr £
1	Debit	Receivables ledger control account	10	
	Credit	Suspense account		10
	being correction of overcast in receivables' control account			
2	Debit	Carriage on sales	4	
	Credit	Carriage on purchases		4
	being correction of posting to the wrong account			
3	Debit	Payables ledger control account	17	
	Credit	Suspense account		17
	being correction of omitted credit note entry			
4	Debit	Drawings	35	
	Credit	Sundry expenses		35
	being correction to posting of payment for private expenses			
5	Debit	Postage and telephone	9	
	Credit	Suspense account		9
	being correction of transposition error			

Suspense account

	£		£
Difference per trial balance (24,455 – 24,491)	36	RLCA	10
		PLCA	17
		Postage and telephone	9
	36		36

Trial balance after adjustments

	Dr £	Cr £
Petty cash	20	
Capital		1,596
Drawings	1,435	
Sales		20,607
Purchases	15,486	
Purchases returns		210
Inventory (1 January 20X4)	2,107	
Fixtures and fittings	710	
Receivables ledger control	1,829	
Payables ledger control		2,061
Carriage on purchases	105	
Carriage on sales	188	
Rent and rates	460	
Light and heat	75	
Postage and telephone	100	
Sundry expenses	155	
Cash at bank	1,804	
	24,474	24,474

FINANCIAL ACCOUNTING: PREPARING FINANCIAL STATEMENTS

The extended trial balance – in action

Introduction

As discussed in Chapter 6 'The extended trial balance – an introduction', the examination will contain an exercise involving the preparation or the completion of an extended trial balance. You need to be familiar with the technique for entering adjustments to the initial trial balance and extending the figures into the statement of financial position and statement of profit or loss columns.

The relevant adjustments (accruals, prepayments, depreciation charges, irrecoverable and doubtful receivables, errors and closing inventory), have all been covered in previous Chapters.

In this chapter we will bring all of this knowledge together in preparation of an extended trial balance.

ASSESSMENT CRITERIA	CONTENTS
Considerations for recording period end adjustments (5.4)	1 Procedure for preparing an extended trial balance
Prepare an initial trial balance (6.1)	
Prepare an adjusted trial balance (6.2)	
Complete the extended trial balance (ETB) (6.3)	

KAPLAN PUBLISHING

The extended trial balance – in action: Chapter 14

1 Procedure for preparing an extended trial balance

1.1 Procedure for preparing an extended trial balance

Step 1

Each ledger account name and its balance are initially entered in the trial balance columns.

Total the debit and credit columns to ensure they equal; i.e. that all balances have been transferred across. Any difference should be put to a suspense account.

Step 2

The adjustments required are then entered into the adjustments columns. The typical adjustments required are:

- Correction of any errors
- Depreciation charges for the period
- Irrecoverable debt write offs
- Allowance for doubtful receivables adjustments
- Accruals or prepayments of income and expense
- Closing inventory

Note: it is always important to ensure that all adjustments have an equal and opposite debit and credit. Never enter a one-sided journal.

Step 3

Total the adjustments columns to ensure that the double entry has been correctly made in these columns.

Step 4

All the entries on the line of each account are then cross-cast and the total is entered into the correct column in either the statement of profit or loss columns or statement of financial position columns.

FINANCIAL ACCOUNTING: PREPARING FINANCIAL STATEMENTS

> **Step 5**
>
> The statement of profit or loss column totals are totalled in order to determine the profit (or loss) for the period. This profit (or loss) is entered in the statement of profit or loss columns as the balancing figure. See Example 1 for further clarification on the adjustment required.
>
> **Step 6**
>
> The profit (or loss) for the period calculated in step 5 is entered in the statement of financial position columns and the statement of financial position columns are then totalled.

When entering period end adjustments, the results of the business may be changed quite significantly. It is essential to ensure that policies and procedures are followed correctly, regulations are adhered to and timescales are observed.

Within the accounting environment there are likely to be time pressures at the period end. There may also be pressure from owners and/or managers of the business to report favourable financial results. It is good practice to ensure that adjustments are checked by an appropriate person, to mitigate the risk of errors occurring. Any period end pressures i.e. time pressure or pressure to report favourable results should be discussed with an appropriate person. Remember it is just as important that accuracy is ensured for a manual bookkeeping system as it is for a digital system, not just in the accounting entries and amounts but also the dates of transactions!

Example 1

Set out below is the trial balance of Lyttleton, a sole trader, extracted at 31 December 20X5.

	Dr £	Cr £
Capital account		7,830
Cash at bank	2,010	
Non-current assets at cost	9,420	
Accumulated depreciation at 31.12.X4		3,470
Receivables ledger control account	1,830	
Inventory at 31.12.X4	1,680	
Payables ledger control account		390
Revenue		14,420
Purchases	8,180	
Rent	1,100	
Electricity	940	
Rates	950	
	26,110	26,110

On examination of the accounts, the following points are noted:

1. Depreciation for the year of £942 is to be charged.

2. An allowance for doubtful receivables of 3% of total debts is to be set up.

3. Purchases include £1,500 of goods which were bought for the proprietor's personal use.

4. The rent account shows the monthly payments of £100 made from 1 January to 1 November 20X5 inclusive. Due to an oversight, the payment due on 1 December 20X5 was not made.

5. The rates account shows the prepayment of £150 brought forward at the beginning of 20X5 (and representing rates from 1 January 20X5 to 31 March 20X5) together with the £800 payment made on 1 April 20X5 and relating to the period from 1 April 20X5 to 31 March 20X6.

6. The electricity charge for the last three months of 20X5 is outstanding and is estimated to be £400.

7. Inventory at 31.12.X5 was valued at £1,140.

Solution

Step 1

The balances from the trial balance are entered into the trial balance columns.

Account name	Trial balance		Adjustments		Statement of profit or loss		Statement of fin. pos.	
	Dr £	Cr £	Dr £	Cr £	Dr £	Cr £	Dr £	Cr £
Capital		7,830						
Cash	2,010							
Non-current asset cost	9,420							
Accumulated depreciation		3,470						
RLCA	1,830							
Inventory	1,680							
PLCA		390						
Revenue		14,420						
Purchases	8,180							
Rent	1,100							
Electricity	940							
Rates	950							
Total	26,110	26,110						

There are a number of points to note here:

- the accumulated depreciation is the balance at the end of the previous year as this year's depreciation charge has not yet been accounted for

- the figure for inventory is the inventory at the start of the year – the opening inventory. The inventory at the end of the year, the closing inventory, will be dealt with later.

Make sure you total each column at this stage to ensure that you have entered the figures correctly, and nothing has been missed.

The extended trial balance – in action: Chapter 14

Step 2

Deal with all of the adjustments required from the additional information given.

Adjustment 1 – Depreciation charge

The double entry for the annual depreciation charge is:

    Dr Depreciation charges account   £942

    Cr Accumulated depreciation account   £942

You will need to open up a new account line for the depreciation expense account at the bottom of the extended trial balance.

Account name	Trial balance		Adjustments		Statement of profit or loss		Statement of fin. pos.	
	Dr £	Cr £	Dr £	Cr £	Dr £	Cr £	Dr £	Cr £
Capital		7,830						
Cash	2,010							
Non-current asset cost	9,420							
Accumulated depreciation		3,470		942				
RLCA	1,830							
Inventory	1,680							
PLCA		390						
Revenue		14,420						
Purchases	8,180							
Rent	1,100							
Electricity	940							
Rates	950							
Depreciation charges			942					

FINANCIAL ACCOUNTING: PREPARING FINANCIAL STATEMENTS

Adjustment 2 – Allowance for doubtful receivables

There is no allowance in the accounts yet so this will need to be set up. The amount of the allowance is 3% of receivables therefore £1,830 × 3% = £55

The double entry for this is:

Dr Allowance for doubtful receivables adjustment £55

Cr Allowance for doubtful receivables £55

As neither of these accounts yet exists they will be added in at the bottom of the ETB.

Revision point: If an allowance for doubtful receivables account already exists then only the increase or decrease is accounted for as the adjustment.

Account name	Trial balance		Adjustments		Statement of profit or loss		Statement of fin. pos.	
	Dr £	Cr £	Dr £	Cr £	Dr £	Cr £	Dr £	Cr £
Capital		7,830						
Cash	2,010							
Non-current asset cost	9,420							
Accumulated depreciation		3,470		942				
RLCA	1,830							
Inventory	1,680							
PLCA		390						
Revenue		14,420						
Purchases	8,180							
Rent	1,100							
Electricity	940							
Rates	950							
Depreciation charges			942					
Allowance for doubtful receivables adjustment			55					
Allowance for doubtful receivables				55				

The extended trial balance – in action: Chapter 14

Adjustment 3 – Owner taking goods for own use

If the owner of a business takes either cash or goods out of the business these are known as drawings. Where goods have been taken by the owner then they are not available for resale and must be taken out of the purchases figure and recorded as drawings.

The double entry is:

    Dr Drawings account   £1,500

    Cr Purchases account   £1,500

A drawings account must be added to the list of balances:

Account name	Trial balance		Adjustments		Statement of profit or loss		Statement of fin. pos.	
	Dr £	Cr £	Dr £	Cr £	Dr £	Cr £	Dr £	Cr £
Capital		7,830						
Cash	2,010							
Non-current asset cost	9,420							
Accumulated depreciation		3,470		942				
RLCA	1,830							
Inventory	1,680							
PLCA		390						
Revenue		14,420						
Purchases	8,180			1,500				
Rent	1,100							
Electricity	940							
Rates	950							
Depreciation charges			942					
Allowance for doubtful receivables adjustment				55				
Allowance doubtful receivables				55				
Drawings			1,500					

FINANCIAL ACCOUNTING: PREPARING FINANCIAL STATEMENTS

Adjustment 4 – Rent

The rent charges for the year should be £1,200 (£100 per month) therefore an accrual is required for the December rent of £100.

The double entry is:

　Dr Rent account　　　　　£100

　Cr Accruals account　　　£100

An accruals account must be added at the bottom of the extended trial balance.

Revision note: The treatment for an accrued expense is to increase the charge to the statement of profit or loss. This ensures that the cost for all goods/services used in the period is captured. We must also recognise a liability known as an accrual.

Account name	Trial balance Dr £	Trial balance Cr £	Adjustments Dr £	Adjustments Cr £	Statement of profit or loss Dr £	Statement of profit or loss Cr £	Statement of fin. pos. Dr £	Statement of fin. pos. Cr £
Capital		7,830						
Cash	2,010							
Non-current asset cost	9,420							
Accumulated depreciation		3,470		942				
RLCA	1,830							
Inventory	1,680							
PLCA		390						
Revenue		14,420						
Purchases	8,180			1,500				
Rent	1,100		100					
Electricity	940							
Rates	950							
Depreciation charges			942					
Allowance for doubtful receivables adjustments			55					
Allowance for doubtful receivables				55				
Drawings			1,500					
Accruals				100				

KAPLAN PUBLISHING

Adjustment 5 – Rates

The charge for rates for the year should be:

	£
1 Jan to 31 March	150
1 April to 31 Dec (800 × 9/12)	600
	750

As the invoice of £800 covers 1 April 20X5 to 31 March 20X6, a prepayment should be recognised for the period 1 Jan X6 to 31 March X6 as this relates to costs incurred outside of the accounting period. (£800 × 3/12 = £200).

This is accounted for by the following double entry:

Dr Prepayments account   £200

Cr Rates account   £200

A prepayment account must be set up at the bottom of the extended trial balance.

Revision note: The accounting treatment for a prepayment is to reduce the charge to the statement of profit or loss, as the expense is too high because it includes a payment for another period's costs; and to set up a receivable account in the statement of financial position known as a prepayment.

Account name	Trial balance		Adjustments		Statement of profit or loss		Statement of fin. pos.	
	Dr £	Cr £	Dr £	Cr £	Dr £	Cr £	Dr £	Cr £
Capital		7,830						
Cash	2,010							
Non-current asset cost	9,420							
Accumulated depreciation		3,470		942				
RLCA	1,830							
Inventory	1,680							
PLCA		390						
Revenue		14,420						
Purchases	8,180			1,500				
Rent	1,100		100					
Electricity	940							
Rates	950			200				
Depreciation charges			942					
Allowance for doubtful receivables adjustment			55					
Allowance for doubtful receivables				55				
Drawings			1,500					
Accruals				100				
Prepayments			200					

The extended trial balance – in action: Chapter 14

Adjustment 6 – Electricity

There needs to be a further accrual of £400 for electricity.

The double entry for this is:

    Dr Electricity account   £400

    Cr Accruals account   £400

Therefore £400 needs to be added to the accruals account balance of £100 to bring it up to £500.

Account name	Trial balance		Adjustments		Statement of profit or loss		Statement of fin. pos.	
	Dr £	Cr £	Dr £	Cr £	Dr £	Cr £	Dr £	Cr £
Capital		7,830						
Cash	2,010							
Non-current asset cost	9,420							
Accumulated depreciation		3,470		942				
RLCA	1,830							
Inventory	1,680							
PLCA		390						
Revenue		14,420						
Purchases	8,180			1,500				
Rent	1,100		100					
Electricity	940		400					
Rates	950			200				
Depreciation charges			942					
Allowance for doubtful receivables adjustments				55				
Allowance for doubtful receivables				55				
Drawings			1,500					
Accruals				500				
Prepayments			200					

Adjustment 7 – Closing inventory

We saw in a previous Chapter on inventory that the closing inventory appears in both the statement of financial position (SFP) as a debit (as a current asset), and in the statement of profit or loss (SPL) as a credit (a reduction to cost of sales). Therefore, two entries will be made in the ETB:

> Dr Inventory – statement of financial position   £1,140
>
> Cr Inventory – statement of profit or loss   £1,140

The closing inventory adjustment shown in the ETB below, has separate rows for the debit to the SFP and the credit to the SPL. However, the debit and credit entries for closing inventory may alternatively be recorded on the same row.

The extended trial balance – in action: Chapter 14

Account name	Trial balance		Adjustments		Statement of profit or loss		Statement of fin. pos.	
	Dr £	Cr £	Dr £	Cr £	Dr £	Cr £	Dr £	Cr £
Capital		7,830						
Cash	2,010							
Non-current asset cost	9,420							
Accumulated depreciation		3,470		942				
RLCA	1,830							
Inventory	1,680							
PLCA		390						
Revenue		14,420						
Purchases	8,180			1,500				
Rent	1,100		100					
Electricity	940		400					
Rates	950			200				
Depreciation charges			942					
Allowance for doubtful receivables adjustment			55					
Allowance for doubtful receivables				55				
Drawings			1,500					
Accruals				500				
Prepayments			200					
Closing inventory SFP			1,140					
Closing inventory SPL				1,140				

FINANCIAL ACCOUNTING: PREPARING FINANCIAL STATEMENTS

Step 3

The adjustments columns must now be totalled. Each adjustment was made in double-entry form and therefore the total of the debit column should equal the total of the credit column. Leave a spare line before putting in the total as there will be a further balance to enter, the profit or loss for the period.

Account name	Trial balance		Adjustments		Statement of profit or loss		Statement of fin. pos.	
	Dr £	Cr £	Dr £	Cr £	Dr £	Cr £	Dr £	Cr £
Capital		7,830						
Cash	2,010							
Non-current asset cost	9,420							
Accumulated depreciation		3,470		942				
RLCA	1,830							
Opening inventory	1,680							
PLCA		390						
Revenue		14,420						
Purchases	8,180			1,500				
Rent	1,100		100					
Electricity	940		400					
Rates	950			200				
Depreciation charges			942					
Allowance for doubtful receivables adjustments			55					
Allowance for doubtful receivables				55				
Drawings			1,500					
Accruals				500				
Prepayments			200					
Closing inventory SFP			1,140					
Closing inventory SPL				1,140				
	26,110	26,110	4,337	4,337				

The extended trial balance – in action: **Chapter 14**

Step 4

Each of the account balances must now be cross-cast (added across) and then entered as a debit or credit in either the statement of profit or loss columns or the statement of financial position columns.

Income and expenses are entered in the statement of profit or loss columns and assets and liabilities are entered in the statement of financial position columns.

This is how it works taking each account balance in turn:

- capital account: there are no adjustments to this therefore the balance is entered in the credit column of the statement of financial position – the liability of the business owed back to the owner

- cash account: again no adjustments here therefore this is entered into the debit column of the statement of financial position – an asset

- non-current asset cost account: no adjustments therefore entered in the debit column of the statement of financial position – an asset

- accumulated depreciation: (£3,470 + 942 = £4,412) this is the amount that has to be deducted from the non-current asset cost total in the statement of financial position, as it is the accumulated depreciation, and therefore the credit entry is to the statement of financial position – part of non-current asset net book value

- RLCA: no adjustments therefore entered in the debit column of the statement of financial position – an asset

- opening inventory account: entered as a debit in the statement of profit or loss as it increases expenses – part of cost of sales

- PLCA: no adjustment and so is entered as a credit in the statement of financial position – a liability

- sales account: no adjustments therefore a credit in the statement of profit or loss – income

- purchases account: (£8,180 – 1,500 = £6,680) note that the £1,500 is deducted from the initial balance, as the £8,180 is a debit and the £1,500 a credit. The total is then entered as a debit in the statement of profit or loss – part of cost of sales

- rent account: (£1,100 + 100 = £1,200) these two amounts are added together as they are both debits and the total is entered in the debit column of the statement of profit or loss – an expense

- electricity account: (£940 + 400 = £1,340) again two debits so added together and the total entered in the debit column of the statement of profit or loss – an expense
- rates account: (£950 – 200 = £750) the balance of £950 is a debit therefore the credit of £200 must be deducted and the final total is entered in the debit column of the statement of profit or loss – an expense
- depreciation charges account: adjustment is entered in the statement of profit or loss debit column – an expense
- allowance for doubtful receivables adjustment – another expense account to the statement of profit or loss debit column
- allowance for doubtful receivables account: this is the amount that is deducted from receivables in the statement of financial position and is therefore entered in the credit column of the statement of financial position
- drawings account – this is a reduction of the amount the business owes to the owner and is therefore a debit in the statement of financial position, it is a reduction of the amount of overall capital
- accruals account: this balance is a liability in the statement of financial position therefore is entered into the credit column in the statement of financial position
- prepayments account: this balance is an asset in the statement of financial position and is therefore a debit in the statement of financial position columns.

The extended trial balance – in action: Chapter 14

Account name	Trial balance Dr £	Trial balance Cr £	Adjustments Dr £	Adjustments Cr £	Statement of profit or loss Dr £	Statement of profit or loss Cr £	Statement of fin. pos. Dr £	Statement of fin. pos. Cr £
Capital		7,830						7,830
Cash	2,010						2,010	
Non-current asset cost	9,420						9,420	
Accumulated depreciation		3,470		942				4,412
RLCA	1,830						1,830	
Opening inventory	1,680				1,680			
PLCA		390						390
Revenue		14,420				14,420		
Purchases	8,180			1,500	6,680			
Rent	1,100		100		1,200			
Electricity	940		400		1,340			
Rates	950			200	750			
Depreciation charges			942		942			
Allowance for doubtful receivables adjustment			55		55			
Allowance doubtful receivables				55				55
Drawings			1,500				1,500	
Accruals				500				500
Prepayments			200				200	
Closing inventory SFP			1,140				1,140	
Closing inventory SPL				1,140		1,140		
	26,110	26,110	4,337	4,337	12,647	15,560	16,100	13,187

Steps 5 and 6

- Total the debit and credit columns of the statement of profit or loss – they will not be equal as the difference between them is any profit or loss.

- If the credit total exceeds the debits the difference is a profit which must be entered in the last line of the ETB and put into the debit column of the statement of profit or loss columns in order to make them equal.

FINANCIAL ACCOUNTING: PREPARING FINANCIAL STATEMENTS

- To complete the double entry the same figure is also entered as a credit in the statement of financial position columns – the profit owed back to the owner.
- If the debit total of the statement of profit or loss columns exceeds the credit total then a loss has been made – this is entered as a credit in the statement of profit or loss and a debit in the statement of financial position columns. Finally total the statement of financial position debit and credit columns, these should now be equal.

Account name	Trial balance Dr £	Trial balance Cr £	Adjustments Dr £	Adjustments Cr £	Statement of profit or loss Dr £	Statement of profit or loss Cr £	Statement of fin. pos. Dr £	Statement of fin. pos. Cr £
Capital		7,830						7,830
Cash	2,010						2,010	
NCA cost	9,420						9,420	
Accumulated depreciation		3,470		942				4,412
RLCA	1,830						1,830	
Open. inventory	1,680				1,680			
PLCA		390						390
Revenue		14,420				14,420		
Purchases	8,180			1,500	6,680			
Rent	1,100		100		1,200			
Electricity	940		400		1,340			
Rates	950			200	750			
Depreciation charges			942		942			
Allowance for doubtful receivables adjustment			55		55			
Allowance for doubtful receivables				55				55
Drawings			1,500				1,500	
Accruals				500				500
Prepayments			200				200	
Closing inventory SFP			1,140				1,140	
Closing inventory SPL				1,140		1,140		
Profit (15,560 – 12,647)					2,913			2,913
	26,110	26,110	4,337	4,337	15,560	15,560	16,100	16,100

The extended trial balance – in action: Chapter 14

> **Test your understanding 1**
>
> 1 What is the double entry for a depreciation charge for the year of £640? (record the account name and amount)
>
> | Account name | £ | £ |
> |---|---|---|
> | Debit | | |
> | Credit | | |
>
> 2 The owner of a business takes goods costing £1,000 out of the business for personal use. What is the double entry for this? (record the account name and amount)
>
> | Account name | £ | £ |
> |---|---|---|
> | Debit | | |
> | Credit | | |
>
> 3 What is the double entry required to put closing inventory into the adjustment columns of the extended trial balance? (record the account names)
>
> | Account name | £ | £ |
> |---|---|---|
> | Debit | | |
> | Credit | | |
>
> 4 Does the accumulated depreciation appear in the statement of profit or loss or statement of financial position columns of the ETB?
>
> Statement of profit or loss ☐
>
> Statement of financial position ☐
>
> 5 Does opening inventory appear in the statement of profit or loss or statement of financial position columns of the ETB?
>
> Statement of profit or loss ☐
>
> Statement of financial position ☐

FINANCIAL ACCOUNTING: PREPARING FINANCIAL STATEMENTS

Test your understanding 2

The following is the trial balance of Hick at 31 December 20X6

	Dr £	Cr £
Shop fittings at cost	7,300	
Accumulated shop fitting depreciation at 1 January 20X6		2,500
Leasehold premises at cost	30,000	
Accumulated leasehold depreciation at 1 January 20X6		6,000
Inventory at 1 January 20X6	15,000	
Receivables ledger control account at 31 December 20X6	10,000	
Allowance for doubtful receivables at 1 January 20X6		800
Cash in hand	50	
Cash in bank	1,250	
Payables ledger control account at 31 Dec 20X6		18,000
Proprietor's capital at 1 January 20X6		19,050
Drawings to 31 December 20X6	4,750	
Purchases	80,000	
Revenue		120,000
Wages	12,000	
Advertising	4,000	
Rates for 15 months	1,800	
Bank charges	200	
	166,350	166,350

Complete the journal entries for the adjustments below.

Depreciation of shop fittings: £400; depreciation of leasehold: £1,000.

Journal	Dr £	Cr £

Journal	Dr £	Cr £

A debt of £500 is irrecoverable and is to be written off; the doubtful receivables allowance is to be 3% of the remaining receivables.

Journal	Dr £	Cr £

Journal	Dr £	Cr £

Advertising fees of £200 have been treated incorrectly as wages.

Journal	Dr £	Cr £

The proprietor has withdrawn goods costing £1,200 for personal use, these have not been recorded as drawings.

Journal	Dr £	Cr £

The inventory at 31 December 20X6 is valued at £21,000.

Journal	Dr £	Cr £

The rates included in the trial balance relate to the 15-month period to 31 March 20X7.

Journal	Dr £	Cr £

Prepare an extended trial balance at 31 December 20X6.

FINANCIAL ACCOUNTING: PREPARING FINANCIAL STATEMENTS

Extended trial balance at 31 December 20X6

Account name	Trial balance		Adjustments		Statement of profit or loss		Statement of fin. pos.	
	Dr	Cr	Dr	Cr	Dr	Cr	Dr	Cr
	£	£	£	£	£	£	£	£
Shop fittings cost								
Accumulated shop fitting dep'n								
Leasehold								
Accumulated leasehold dep'n								
Open. inventory								
RLCA								
Allowance for doubtful receivables 1.1.X6								
Cash in hand								
Cash at bank								
PLCA								
Capital								
Drawings								
Purchases								
Revenue								
Wages								
Advertising								
Rates								
Bank charges								
Dep'n charges								
– Fittings								
– Lease								
Irrecoverable debts expense								
Allowance for doubtful receivables adjustment								
Prepayments								
Closing Inventory SFP								
Closing Inventory SPL								
Net profit								
TOTAL								

The extended trial balance – in action: Chapter 14

Test your understanding 3

Michael carries on business as a clothing manufacturer. The trial balance of the business at 31 December 20X6:

	Dr £	Cr £
Capital account		30,000
Freehold factory at cost (including land £4,000)	20,000	
Factory plant and machinery at cost	4,800	
Motor vehicles at cost	2,600	
Accumulated depreciation, 1 January 20X6		
Freehold factory		1,920
Factory plant and machinery		1,600
Motor vehicles		1,200
Inventories, 1 January 20X6	8,900	
Trade receivables and payables	3,600	4,200
Allowance for doubtful receivables		280
Purchases	36,600	
Wages & salaries	19,800	
Rates & insurance	1,510	
Sundry expenses	1,500	
Motor expenses	400	
Revenue		72,000
Balance at bank	11,490	
	111,200	111,200

Complete the journal entries for the adjustments below.

Inventories at 31 December were valued at £10,800.

Journal	Dr £	Cr £

Wages and salaries include drawings by Michael of £2,400 and motor expenses of £600.

Journal	Dr £	Cr £

Journal	Dr £	Cr £

Depreciation on the freehold factory, plant and machinery and sales reps' cars is 2%, 10% and 25% respectively on a straight-line basis.

Journal	Dr £	Cr £

Journal	Dr £	Cr £

Journal	Dr £	Cr £

On 31 December 20X6 £120 was owed for sundry expenses and rates paid in advance amounted to £260. Neither of these had been adjusted for in the trial balance.

Journal	Dr £	Cr £

Journal	Dr £	Cr £

A trade receivables balance of £60, had previously had an allowance made against it. This balance is now to be written off. The original allowance accounted for should be reversed before accounting for the irrecoverable debt. Any movements in the allowance for doubtful receivables are accounted for within an allowance for doubtful receivables adjustment account.

Journal	Dr £	Cr £

The extended trial balance – in action: Chapter 14

Prepare an extended trial balance at 31 December 20X6 dealing with the above information.

Extended trial balance at 31 December 20X6

Account name	Trial balance		Adjustments		Statement of profit or loss		Statement of financial position	
	Dr £	Cr £	Dr £	Cr £	Dr £	Cr £	Dr £	Cr £
Capital account								
Freehold factory cost								
Plant cost								
Motor vehicles cost								
Accum dep'n								
– factory								
– plant								
– motor vehicles								
Op. inventory								
Receivables ledger control								
Payables ledger control								
Allowance for doubtful receivables								
Purchases								
Wages & salaries								
Rates & insurance								
Sundry expenses								
Motor expenses								
Revenue								
Cash at bank								
Cl. inventory SFP								
Cl. inventory SPL								
Drawings								
Depreciation								
– factory								
– plant								
– motor vehicles								
Accruals								
Prepayments								
Allowance for doubtful receivables adjustment								
Irrecoverable debt expense								
Net profit								
TOTAL								

1.2 Treatment of goods taken by the owner

In the earlier example we saw how goods taken for use by the owner must be taken out of purchases and transferred to drawings. The double entry was:

Dr   Drawings account
Cr   Purchases account

with the cost of the goods taken.

There is however an alternative method which may be required by some examinations:

Dr   Drawings account with the selling price plus VAT (Gross)
Cr   Sales account with the net of VAT selling price (Net)
Cr   VAT account with the VAT

As a general guide, use the first method when the goods are stated at cost price and the second method when the goods are stated at selling price. If both methods are possible from the information given use the first method as it is simpler.

Test your understanding 4

You have been asked to prepare the 20X0 accounts of Rugg, a retail merchant. Rugg has balanced the books at 31 December 20X0 and gives you the following list of balances:

	£
Capital account at 1 January 20X0	2,377
Rent	500
Inventory as at 1 January 20X0	510
Rates	240
Insurance	120
Wages	1,634
Receivables	672
Revenue	15,542
Repairs	635
Purchases	9,876
Discounts received	129
Drawings	1,200
Petty cash in hand 31 December 20X0	5
Bank balance 31 December 20X0	763
Motor vehicles, at cost	1,740
Fixtures and fittings at cost	829
Accumulated depreciation at 1 January 20X0	
– Motor vehicles	435
– Fixtures and fittings	166
Travel and entertaining	192
Payables	700
Sundry expenses	433

Complete the journal entries for the adjustments below.

Closing inventory, valued at cost, amounts to £647.

Journal	Dr £	Cr £

Rugg has drawn £10 a month and these drawings have been charged to wages.

Journal	Dr £	Cr £

Depreciation is to be provided at 25% straight line on motor vehicles and 20% straight line on fixtures and fittings.

Journal	Dr £	Cr £

Journal	Dr £	Cr £

Irrecoverable debts totalling £37 are to be written off.

Journal	Dr £	Cr £

Sundry expenses include £27 spent on electrical repairs and cash purchases of goods for resale of £72.

Journal	Dr £	Cr £

Journal	Dr £	Cr £

Rugg has taken goods from inventory for his own use. When purchased by his business, these goods cost £63 and would have been sold for £91.

Journal	Dr £	Cr £

The annual rental of the business premises is £600; in addition £180 of rates charges paid in August 20X0 covers the year ending 30 June 20X1.

Journal	Dr £	Cr £

Journal	Dr £	Cr £

Prepare an extended trial balance reflecting the above information

Extended trial balance at 31 December 20X0

Account name	Trial balance Dr £	Trial balance Cr £	Adjustments Dr £	Adjustments Cr £	Statement of profit or loss Dr £	Statement of profit or loss Cr £	Statement of fin. pos. Dr £	Statement of fin. pos. Cr £
Capital 1.1.X0								
Rent								
Open. inventory								
Rates								
Insurance								
Wages								
Receivables								
Revenue								
Repairs								
Purchases								
Discounts received								
Drawings								
Petty cash								
Cash at bank								
Vehicles cost								
Fixtures cost								
Accum'd dep'n								
– Vehicles								
– Fixtures								
Travel								
Payables								
Sundry expenses								
Closing Inventory SFP								
Closing Inventory SPL								
Dep'n charges								
– Vehicles								
– Fixtures								
Irrecoverable debts								
Accruals								
Prepayments								
Net profit								
TOTAL								

Test your understanding 5

Randall

Trial balance at 31 December 20X6

	Dr £	Cr £
Shop fittings at cost	2,000	
Depreciation accumulated at 1 January 20X6		100
Leasehold premises at cost	12,500	
Depreciation accumulated at 1 January 20X6		625
Inventory in trade at 1 January 20X6	26,000	
Receivables at 31 December 20X6	53,000	
Allowance for doubtful receivables at 1 January 20X6		960
Cash in hand	50	
Cash at bank	4,050	
Payables for supplies		65,000
Proprietor's capital at 1 January 20X6		28,115
Drawings to 31 December 20X6	2,000	
Purchases	102,000	
Revenue		129,000
Wages	18,200	
Advertising	2,300	
Rates for 15 months to 31 March 20X7	1,500	
Bank charges	200	
	223,800	223,800

The following adjustments are to be made:

1. Depreciation of shop fittings £100

   Depreciation of leasehold £625

2. A debt of £500 is irrecoverable and is to be written off; the doubtful receivables allowance is to be increased to 2% of the receivables.

3. Advertising fees of £200 have been treated incorrectly as wages.

4. The proprietor has withdrawn goods costing £1,000 for personal use; these have not been recorded as drawings.

5. The inventory in trade at 31 December 20X6 is valued at £30,000.

Required:

Prepare an extended trial balance at 31 December 20X6.

FINANCIAL ACCOUNTING: PREPARING FINANCIAL STATEMENTS

Test your understanding 6

Data

Amanda Carver is the proprietor of Automania, a business which supplies car parts to garages to use in servicing and repair work.

- You are employed by Amanda Carver to assist with the bookkeeping.

- The business currently operates a manual system consisting of a general ledger, a receivables ledger and a payables ledger.

- Double entry takes place in the general ledger and the individual accounts of receivables and payables are therefore regarded as memoranda accounts.

- Day books including a purchases day book, a sales day book, a purchases returns day book and a sales returns day book are used. Totals from the various columns of the day books are transferred into the general ledger.

At the end of the financial year, on 30 April 20X3, the balances were extracted from the general ledger and entered into an extended trial balance as shown below.

Task

Make appropriate entries in the adjustments columns of the extended trial balance to take account of the following:

(a) Rent payable by the business is as follows:

    For period to 31 July 20X2   – £1,500 per month
    From 1 August 20X2   – £1,600 per month

(b) The insurance balance includes £100 paid for the period of 1 May 20X3 to 31 May 20X3.

(c) Depreciation is to be calculated as follows:

    Motor vehicles   – 20% per annum straight line method
    Fixtures and fittings   – 10% per annum reducing balance method

(d) The allowance for doubtful receivables is to be adjusted to a figure representing 2% of receivables.

(e) Inventory has been valued at cost on 30 April 20X3 at £119,360. However, this figure includes old inventory, the details of which are as follows:

Cost price of old inventory – £3,660
Net realisable value of old inventory – £2,060

Also included is a badly damaged car door which was to have been sold for £80 but will now have to be scrapped. The cost price of the door was £60.

(f) A credit note received from a supplier on 5 April 20X3 for goods returned was filed away with no entries having been made. The credit note has now been discovered and is for £200 net plus £35 VAT.

Extended trial balance at 30 April 20X3

Description	Ledger balances Dr £	Ledger balances Cr £	Adjustments Dr £	Adjustments Cr £
Capital		135,000		
Drawings	42,150			
Rent	17,300			
Purchases	606,600			
Revenue		857,300		
Sales returns	2,400			
Purchases returns		1,260		
Salaries and wages	136,970			
Motor vehicles (MV) at cost	60,800			
Accumulated depreciation (MV)		16,740		
Office equipment (F&F) at cost	40,380			
Accumulated depreciation (F&F)		21,600		
Bank		3,170		
Cash	2,100			
Lighting and heating	4,700			
VAT		9,200		
Inventory at 1 May 20X2	116,100			
Irrecoverable debts	1,410			
Allowance for doubtful receivables		1,050		
Receivables ledger control account	56,850			
Payables ledger control account		50,550		
Sundry expenses	6,810			
Insurance	1,300			
Accruals				
Prepayments				
Depreciation				
Allowance for doubtful receivables adjustments				
Closing inventory – SPL				
Closing inventory – SFP				
Totals	**1,095,870**	**1,095,870**		

Note: Only the above columns of the extended trial balance are required for this question.

Test your understanding 7

Willis

Willis extracts the following trial balance at 31 December 20X6.

	Dr £	Cr £
Capital		3,112
Cash at bank		2,240
Petty cash	25	
Plant and machinery at cost	2,750	
Accumulated depreciation at 1 January 20X6		1,360
Motor vehicles at cost	2,400	
Accumulated depreciation at 1 January 20X6		600
Fixtures and fittings at cost	840	
Accumulated depreciation at 1 January 20X6		510
Inventory at 1 January 20X6	1,090	
Receivables	1,750	
Allowance for doubtful receivables		50
Payables		1,184
Purchases	18,586	
Revenue		25,795
Selling and distribution expenses	330	
Establishment and administration expenses	520	
Financial expenses	60	
	28,351	34,851

You discover the following:

1. Closing inventory is valued at £1,480.

2. The difference on the trial balance is a result of Willis' omission of the balance on his deposit account of £6,500. Willis transferred this amount on 30 September 20X6 by 31 December 20X6 the account had earned £50 interest, which has not yet been reflected in the ledgers.

3. All non-current assets are to be depreciated at 25% per annum on carrying amount.

4. The allowance for doubtful receivables has been carried forward from last year. It is felt that receivables of £30 should be written off and the allowance increased to 5% of receivables.

FINANCIAL ACCOUNTING: PREPARING FINANCIAL STATEMENTS

5   Included in the selling and distribution expenses are £20 of payments which are better described as 'purchases'.

6   In establishment expenses are prepaid rent and rates of £30.

7   Also in establishment expenses are amounts paid for electricity. At 31 December 20X6 £28 was due for electricity.

8   An accrual of £50 should be made to cover accountancy fees.

9   The cash book does not reconcile with the bank statement since bank charges and interest have been omitted from the former, totalling £18.

10 On enquiring into Willis' drawings, you discover that £4,000 of the amount transferred to a deposit account on 30 September 20X6 was then immediately switched to Willis' private bank account.

Required:

Prepare an extended trial balance at 31 December 20X6.

2 Summary

Once the initial trial balance has been prepared, it may be necessary to correct any errors in the ledger accounts, in addition to putting through the various year-end adjustments that we have considered. These adjustments may include closing inventory, depreciation, irrecoverable and doubtful receivables or accruals and prepayments. These can all be conveniently put through on the extended trial balance.

The ETB is then extended and the totals shown in the appropriate statement of profit or loss and statement of financial position columns. Finally, the profit or loss is calculated and it is entered into the relevant SPL and SFP columns.

Test your understanding answers

Test your understanding 1

1	Debit	Depreciation expense account	£640
	Credit	Accumulated depreciation account	£640
2	Debit	Drawings account	£1,000
	Credit	Purchases account	£1,000
3	Debit	Closing inventory – statement of financial position	
	Credit	Closing inventory – statement of profit or loss	
4	Statement of financial position		
5	Statement of profit or loss		

Test your understanding 2

Extended trial balance at 31 December 20X6

Account name	Trial balance Dr £	Trial balance Cr £	Adjustments Dr £	Adjustments Cr £	Statement of profit or loss Dr £	Statement of profit or loss Cr £	Statement of fin. pos. Dr £	Statement of fin. pos. Cr £
Shop fittings cost	7,300						7,300	
Accumulated shop fitting dep'n		2,500		400				2,900
Leasehold	30,000						30,000	
Accumulated leasehold dep'n		6,000		1,000				7,000
Opening Inventory	15,000				15,000			
RLCA	10,000			500			9,500	
Allowance for doubtful receivables 1.1.X6		800	515					285
Cash in hand	50						50	
Cash at bank	1,250						1,250	
PLCA		18,000						18,000
Capital		19,050						19,050
Drawings	4,750		1,200				5,950	
Purchases	80,000			1,200	78,800			
Revenue		120,000				120,000		
Wages	12,000			200	11,800			
Advertising	4,000		200		4,200			
Rates	1,800			360	1,440			
Bank charges	200				200			
Dep'n charges								
– Fittings			400		400			
– Lease			1,000		1,000			

Irrecoverable debts			500		500			
Allowance for doubtful receivables adjustment				515		515		
Prepayments			360				360	
Closing Inventory SFP			21,000				21,000	
Closing Inventory SPL				21,000		21,000		
Sub total					113,340	141,515		
Net profit					28,175			28,175
TOTAL	166,350	166,350	25,175	25,175	141,515	141,515	75,410	75,410

Revision point: Take care with the doubtful receivables allowance.

Allowance required is 3% of receivables after writing off the irrecoverable debt.

	£
Allowance 3% × (10,000 – 500)	285
Allowance in trial balance	800
Decrease in allowance	515

Test your understanding 3

Extended trial balance at 31 December 20X6

Account name	Trial balance Dr £	Trial balance Cr £	Adjustments Dr £	Adjustments Cr £	Statement of profit or loss Dr £	Statement of profit or loss Cr £	Statement of fin. pos. Dr £	Statement of fin. pos. Cr £
Capital account		30,000						30,000
Freehold factory cost	20,000						20,000	
Plant cost	4,800						4,800	
Motor vehicles cost	2,600						2,600	
Accum dep'n								
– factory *1		1,920		320				2,240
– plant		1,600		480				2,080
– motor vehicles		1,200		650				1,850
Op. inventory	8,900				8,900			
RLCA	3,600			60			3,540	
PLCA		4,200						4,200
Allowance for doubtful receivables		280	60					220
Purchases	36,600				36,600			
Wages & salaries	19,800			3,000	16,800			
Rates & insurance	1,510			260	1,250			
Sundry expenses	1,500		120		1,620			
Motor expenses	400		600		1,000			
Revenue		72,000				72,000		
Cash at bank	11,490						11,490	
Cl. inventory SFP			10,800				10,800	
Cl. inventory SPL				10,800		10,800		

Drawings			2,400			2,400	
Depreciation							
– factory			320		320		
– plant			480		480		
– motor vehicles			650		650		
Accruals				120			120
Prepayments			260			260	
Allowance for doubtful receivables adjustment				60		60	
Irrecoverable debt expense			60		60		
Sub total					67,680	82,860	55,890	40,710
Net profit					15,180			15,180
TOTAL	111,200	111,200	15,750	15,750	82,860	82,860	55,890	55,890

NOTE:

*1 – as the factory also includes land, the depreciation charge is $(20{,}000 - 4{,}000) \times 2\% = 320$

The extended trial balance – in action: Chapter 14

 Test your understanding 4

Extended trial balance at 31 December 20X0

Account name	Trial balance Dr £	Trial balance Cr £	Adjustments Dr £	Adjustments Cr £	Statement of profit or loss Dr £	Statement of profit or loss Cr £	Statement of fin. pos. Dr £	Statement of fin. pos. Cr £
Capital 1.1.X0		2,377						2,377
Rent	500		100		600			
Open. inventory	510				510			
Rates	240			90	150			
Insurance	120				120			
Wages	1,634			120	1,514			
Receivables	672			37			635	
Revenue		15,542				15,542		
Repairs	635		27		662			
Purchases	9,876		72	63	9,885			
Discounts Received		129				129		
Drawings	1,200		63				1,383	
			120					
Petty cash	5						5	
Bank	763						763	
MV cost	1,740						1,740	
F&F cost	829						829	
Accumulated dep'n								
– MV		435		435				870
– F&F		166		166				332
Travel	192				192			
Payables		700						700
Sundry expenses	433			27	334			
				72				
Closing Inventory SFP			647				647	
Closing Inventory SPL				647		647		
Dep'n charges								
– Vehicles			435		435			
– Fixtures			166		166			
Irrecoverable debts			37		37			
Accruals				100				100
Prepayments			90				90	
Sub total					14,605			
Net profit					1,713			1,713
TOTAL	**19,349**	**19,349**	**1,757**	**1,757**	**16,318**	**16,318**	**6,092**	**6,092**

Test your understanding 5

Extended trial balance of Randall at 31 Dec 20X6

Account	Trial balance Dr £	Trial balance Cr £	Adjustments Dr £	Adjustments Cr £	Statement of profit or loss Dr £	Statement of profit or loss Cr £	Statement of fin. pos. Dr £	Statement of fin. pos. Cr £
Fittings	2,000						2,000	
Accumulated depn 1 Jan 20X6		100		100				200
Leasehold	12,500						12,500	
Accumulated depn 1 Jan 20X6		625		625				1,250
Inventory 1 Jan 20X6	26,000				26,000			
Receivables	53,000			500			52,500	
Allowance doubtful receivables 1 Jan 20X6		960		90				1,050
Cash in hand	50						50	
Cash at bank	4,050						4,050	
Payables		65,000						65,000
Capital		28,115						28,115
Drawings	2,000		1,000				3,000	
Purchases	102,000			1,000	101,000			
Revenue		129,000				129,000		
Wages	18,200			200	18,000			
Advertising	2,300		200		2,500			
Rates	1,500			300	1,200			
Bank charges	200				200			
Prepayments			300				300	
Depreciation Fittings			100		100			
Lease			625		625			
Irrecoverable debts			500		500			
Allowance for doubtful receivables adjustment			90		90			
Closing inventory SFP			30,000				30,000	
Closing inventory SPL				30,000		30,000		
Sub totals					150,215	159,000		
Net profit					8,785			8,785
Totals	223,800	223,800	32,815	32,815	159,000	159,000	104,400	104,400

The extended trial balance – in action: Chapter 14

 Test your understanding 6

Extended trial balance at 30 April 20X3

Description	Ledger balances		Adjustments	
	Dr	Cr	Dr	Cr
	£	£	£	£
Capital		135,000		
Drawings	42,150			
Rent	17,300		1,600	
Purchases	606,600			
Revenue		857,300		
Sales returns	2,400			
Purchases returns		1,260		200
Salaries and wages	136,970			
Motor vehicles (MV) at cost	60,800			
Accumulated depreciation (MV)		16,740		12,160
Office equipment (F&F) at cost	40,380			
Accumulated depreciation (F&F)		21,600		1,878
Bank		3,170		
Cash	2,100			
Lighting and heating	4,700			
VAT		9,200		35
Inventory at 1 May 20X2	116,100			
Irrecoverable debts	1,410			
Allowance for doubtful receivables		1,050		87
Receivables ledger control account	56,850			
Payables ledger control account		50,550	235	
Sundry expenses	6,810			
Insurance	1,300			100
Accruals				1,600
Prepayments			100	
Depreciation			14,038	
Allowance for doubtful receivables – adjustments			87	
Closing inventory – SPL				117,700
Closing inventory – SFP			117,700	
TOTALS	**1,095,870**	**1,095,870**	**133,760**	**133,760**

FINANCIAL ACCOUNTING: PREPARING FINANCIAL STATEMENTS

 Test your understanding 7

Willis
Extended trial balance at 31 December 20X6

Account	Trial balance Dr £	Trial balance Cr £	Adjustments Dr £	Adjustments Cr £	Statement of profit or loss Dr £	Statement of profit or loss Cr £	Statement of fin. pos. Dr £	Statement of fin. pos. Cr £
Capital		3,112						3,112
Cash at bank		2,240		18				2,258
Petty cash	25						25	
Plant and machinery	2,750						2,750	
Accumulated depreciation		1,360		348				1,708
Motor vehicles	2,400						2,400	
Accumulated depreciation		600		450				1,050
Fixtures and fittings	840						840	
Accumulated depreciation		510		83				593
Inventory 1 Jan 20X6	1,090				1,090			
Receivables	1,750			30			1,720	
Allowance for doubtful receivables		50		36				86
Payables		1,184						1,184
Purchases	18,586		20		18,606			
Revenue		25,795				25,795		
Selling and distribution	330			20	310			
Establishment and admin	520		28	30	518			
Financial expenses	60		18 50		128			
Deposit account	6,500		50	4,000			2,550	
Inventory at 31 Dec 20X6								
SFP			1,480				1,480	
SPL				1,480		1,480		
Deposit interest				50		50		
Depreciation								
Plant and mach			348		348			
Motor vehicles			450		450			
F&F			83		83			
Irrecoverable debts expense			30		30			
Allowance for doubtful receivables adjustment			36		36			
Drawings			4,000				4,000	
Accruals				28 50				78
Prepayments			30				30	
Profit					5,726			5,726
	34,851	34,851	6,623	6,623	27,325	27,325	15,795	15,795

FINANCIAL ACCOUNTING: PREPARING FINANCIAL STATEMENTS

Preparation of accounts for a sole trader

Introduction

You need to be able to prepare the financial statements; a statement of profit or loss and a statement of financial position for a sole trader. These financial statements may be prepared directly from the extended trial balance or from a trial balance plus various adjustments.

In this chapter we will consider the step by step approach to the financial statements preparation, firstly from an extended trial balance and then directly from an initial trial balance. You will be expected to apply the skills learned earlier in the study text to complete the financial statements.

ASSESSMENT CRITERIA	CONTENTS
Prepare financial statements for sole traders (7.1)	1 Statement of profit or loss for a sole trader
Opening and closing capital for sole traders (7.2)	2 The statement of financial position for a sole trader
	3 Preparing financial statements from the trial balance

1 Statement of profit or loss for a sole trader

1.1 Introduction

Earlier in this study text, we were introduced to the purpose of a statement of profit or loss. Now we will consider it in more detail.

1.2 Statement of profit or loss

The statement of profit or loss is split into two elements:

- the trading account to determine gross profit;
- the statement of profit or loss to determine net profit.

Generally, the whole statement is referred to as the statement of profit or loss. The statement of profit or loss shows business performance over a specific period of time, the accounting period.

1.3 Trading account

The trading account calculates the gross profit or loss that has been made from the trading activities of the sole trader – the buying and selling of goods.

> **Definition**
>
> The gross profit (or loss) is the profit (or loss) from the trading activities of the sole trader.

The trading account looks like this:

		£	£
Sales revenue			X
Less:	Cost of goods sold		
	Opening inventory	X	
	Purchases	X	
		X	
	Less: Closing inventory	(X)	
			(X)
	Gross profit (loss)		X

If there are sales returns (returns inwards) this amount would be deducted from sales revenue.

Net purchases are calculated by adding the cost of carriage inwards and deducting any purchases returns.

1.4 Profit or loss

The remaining content of the statement of profit or loss is a list of any sundry income and the expenses of the business. These are deducted from the gross profit to give the profit for the year (or the net profit).

Definition

The net profit or loss is the profit or loss after deduction of all of the expenses of the business.

Preparation of accounts for a sole trader: Chapter 15

Test your understanding 1

Statement of profit or loss for the year ended 31 December 20X2.

Calculate the sales revenue and the cost of goods sold (complete the boxes).

	£	£
Sales revenue		☐
Less: Cost of goods sold		
Opening inventory	37,500	
Purchases	158,700	
	196,200	☐
Less: Closing inventory	(15,000)	
Gross profit		111,300

A typical statement of profit or loss is shown below.

Statement of profit or loss of Stanley for the year-ended 31 December 20X2

	£	£
Sales revenue		X
Less: Cost of goods sold		
Inventory on 1 January (opening inventory)	X	
Add: Purchases of goods	X	
	X	
Less: Inventory on 31 December (closing inventory)	(X)	
		(X)
Gross profit		X
Sundry income:		
Discounts received	X	
Commission received	X	
Rent received	X	
Interest received	X	
		X
		X

Less: Expenses:		
Rent	X	
Rates	X	
Lighting and heating	X	
Telephone	X	
Postage	X	
Insurance	X	
Stationery	X	
Payroll expenses	X	
Depreciation	X	
Accountancy and audit fees	X	
Bank charges and interest	X	
Irrecoverable debts	X	
Allowance for doubtful receivables adjustment	X	
Delivery costs	X	
Van running expenses	X	
Selling expenses	X	
Discounts allowed	X	
		(X)
Profit/(loss) for the year		X/(X)

1.5 Preparation of the statement of profit or loss

The statement of profit or loss is prepared by listing all of the entries from the ETB that are in the profit or loss columns.

Example 1

Given below is the final ETB for Lyttleton

Account name	Trial balance Dr £	Trial balance Cr £	Adjustments Dr £	Adjustments Cr £	Statement of profit or loss Dr £	Statement of profit or loss Cr £	Statement of financial position Dr £	Statement of financial position Cr £
Capital		7,830						7,830
Cash	2,010						2,010	
Non-current assets	9,420						9,420	
Accumulated depreciation		3,470		942				4,412
RLCA	1,830						1,830	
Opening inventory	1,680				1,680			
PLCA		390						390
Sales		14,420				14,420		
Purchases	8,180			1,500	6,680			
Rent	1,100		100		1,200			
Electricity	940		400		1,340			
Rates	950			200	750			
Depreciation expense			942		942			
Allowance for doubtful receivables adjustments			55		55			
Allowance for doubtful receivables				55				55
Drawings			1,500				1,500	
Accruals				500				500
Prepayments			200				200	
Closing inventory SFP			1,140				1,140	
Closing inventory SPL				1,140		1,140		
Profit					2,913			2,913
	26,110	26,110	4,337	4,337	15,560	15,560	16,100	16,100

We will now show how the final statement of profit or loss for Lyttleton would look.

FINANCIAL ACCOUNTING: PREPARING FINANCIAL STATEMENTS

Solution

Statement of profit or loss of Lyttleton for the year-ended 31 December 20X5

		£	£
Sales revenue			14,420
Less:	Cost of goods sold		
	Opening inventory	1,680	
	Purchases	6,680	
		8,360	
Less:	Closing inventory	(1,140)	
			(7,220)
Gross profit			7,200
Less: Expenses			
	Rent	1,200	
	Electricity	1,340	
	Rates	750	
	Depreciation	942	
	Allowance for doubtful receivables increase	55	
Total expenses			(4,287)
Net profit for the year			2,913

All of the figures in the statement of profit or loss columns in the ETB have been used to prepare this statement of profit or loss.

The final net profit is the profit figure calculated as a balancing figure in the ETB.

2 The statement of financial position for a sole trader

2.1 Introduction

 Definition

A statement of financial position is a list of the assets and liabilities of the sole trader at the end of the accounting period.

The assets are split into non-current assets and current assets.

Definition

Non-current assets are assets that will be used within the business over a long period (usually greater than one year), e.g. land and buildings

Definition

Current assets are assets that are expected to be realised within the business in the normal course of trading (usually a period less than one year) e.g. inventory.

The liabilities are split into current liabilities and non-current liabilities.

Definition

Current liabilities are the short-term payables of a business. This generally means payables that are due to be paid within twelve months of the statement of financial position date e.g. trade payables.

Definition

Non-current liabilities are payables that will be paid over a longer period, which is normally in excess of one year, e.g. loans.

FINANCIAL ACCOUNTING: PREPARING FINANCIAL STATEMENTS

An example of a typical sole trader's statement of financial position is given below:

Statement of financial position of Stanley at 31 December 20X2

	Cost £	Accumulated Depreciation £	Carrying amount £
Non-current assets			
Freehold factory	X	X	X
Machinery	X	X	X
Motor vehicles	X	X	X
	───	───	───
	X	X	X
	───	───	
Current assets			
Inventory		X	
Trade receivables	X		
Less: Allowance for doubtful receivables	(X)		
	───		
		X	
Prepayments		X	
Cash at bank		X	
Cash in hand		X	
		───	
		X	
Current liabilities			
Trade payables	X		
Accruals	X		
	───		
		(X)	
Net current assets			X
			───
Total assets less current liabilities			X
Non-current liabilities			
12% loan			(X)
			───
Net assets			X
			───
Capital at 1 January			X
Net profit for the year			X
			───
			X
Less: Drawings			(X)
			───
Closing capital (proprietor's funds)			X
			───

Preparation of accounts for a sole trader: **Chapter 15**

2.2 Assets and liabilities

The assets and liabilities in a formal statement of financial position are listed in a particular order:

- Firstly, the non-current assets less the accumulated depreciation (remember that this net total is known as the carrying amount).
- Next the current assets in the following order – inventory, receivables, prepayments then bank and cash balances.
- Next the current liabilities – payables and accruals that are payable within 12 months.
- Finally, the long-term payables such as loan accounts.

The assets are all added together and the liabilities are then deducted. This gives the statement of financial position total.

2.3 Capital balances

The total of the assets less liabilities of the sole trader should be equal to the capital of the sole trader.

The capital is shown in the statement of financial position as follows:

	£
Opening capital at the start of the year	X
Add: Capital invested during the year	X
Add: Net profit/(loss) for the year	X
	X
Less: Drawings	(X)
Closing capital	X

This closing capital should equal the total of all of the assets less all liabilities, as shown in the accounting equation assets – liabilities = capital. (NB: this formula can be rearranged as assets = capital + liabilities).

The capital balance represents the owner's (proprietor's) funds, i.e. what the owner will be left with if the business is wound up and all the assets are sold and all the liabilities paid off.

Example 2

Given below is the completed ETB for Lyttleton. This time the statement of financial position will be prepared.

Account name	Trial balance		Adjustments		Statement of profit or loss		Statement of financial position	
	Dr £	Cr £	Dr £	Cr £	Dr £	Cr £	Dr £	Cr £
Capital		7,830						7,830
Cash	2,010						2,010	
Non-current assets	9,420						9,420	
Accumulated depreciation		3,470		942				4,412
RLCA	1,830						1,830	
Inventory	1,680				1,680			
PLCA		390						390
Revenue		14,420				14,420		
Purchases	8,180			1,500	6,680			
Rent	1,100		100		1,200			
Electricity	940		400		1,340			
Rates	950			200	750			
Depreciation expense			942		942			
Allowance for doubtful receivables adjustments			55		55			
Allowance for doubtful receivables				55				55
Drawings			1,500				1,500	
Accruals				500				500
Prepayments			200				200	
Closing inventory: SPL				1,140		1,140		
Closing inventory: SFP			1,140				1,140	
Profit (15,560 – 12,647)					2,913			2,913
	26,110	26,110	4,337	4,337	15,560	15,560	16,100	16,100

Each of the assets and liabilities that appear in the statement of financial position columns will appear in the statement of financial position.

Preparation of accounts for a sole trader: Chapter 15

Solution

Statement of financial position of Lyttleton at 31 December 20X5

	Cost £	Accumulated depreciation £	Carrying amount £
Non-current assets	9,420	4,412	5,008
Current assets			
Inventory			1,140
Trade receivables		1,830	
Less: Allowance for doubtful receivables		(55)	
			1,775
Prepayments			200
Cash			2,010
			5,125
Less:			
Current liabilities			
Payables		390	
Accruals		500	
		(890)	
Net current assets			4,235
Net assets			9,243
Capital 1 January			7,830
Net profit for the year			2,913
			10,743
Less: Drawings			(1,500)
Closing capital			9,243

Note:

- the non-current assets are shown at their carrying amounts

- the current assets are sub-totalled as are the current liabilities – the current liabilities are then deducted from the current assets to give net current assets

- the net current assets are added to the non-current asset carrying amount to reach the statement of financial position total, net assets.

FINANCIAL ACCOUNTING: PREPARING FINANCIAL STATEMENTS

The statement of financial position total of net assets should be equal to the closing capital; the statement of financial position balances (it used to be referred to as a 'balance sheet'). If the statement of financial position does not balance check the arithmetic and that there are no omissions.

Test your understanding 2

Given below is a completed extended trial balance.

Extended trial balance at 31 December 20X6

Account name	Trial balance		Adjustments		Statement of profit or loss		Statement of financial position	
	Dr £	Cr £	Dr £	Cr £	Dr £	Cr £	Dr £	Cr £
Fittings	7,300						7,300	
Accumulated depreciation 1.1.X6		2,500		400				2,900
Leasehold	30,000						30,000	
Accumulated depreciation 1.1.X6		6,000		1,000				7,000
Inventory 1 January 20X6	15,000				15,000			
Receivables ledger control account	10,000			500			9,500	
Allowance for doubtful receivables 1.1.X6		800	515					285
Cash in hand	50						50	
Cash at bank	1,250						1,250	
Payables ledger control account		18,000						18,000
Capital		19,050						19,050
Drawings	4,750		1,200				5,950	
Purchases	80,000			1,200	78,800			
Sales		120,000				120,000		
Wages	12,000			200	11,800			
Advertising	4,000		200		4,200			
Rates	1,800			360	1,440			
Bank charges	200				200			
Depreciation charge			1,400		1,400			

KAPLAN PUBLISHING

Allowance for doubtful receivables adjustments				515		515		
Irrecoverable debts			500		500			
Prepayments			360				360	
Closing inventory SFP			21,000				21,000	
Closing inventory SPL				21,000		21,000		
					113,340	141,515		
Net profit					28,175			28,175
	166,350	166,350	25,175	25,175	141,515	141,515	75,410	75,410

Prepare the statement of profit or loss for the business.

Select the appropriate account headings from the options below.

Statement of profit or loss for the year-ended 31 December 20X6

£ £

Sales revenue

Less: Cost of goods sold

    Opening inventory/Closing inventory/Purchases

    Purchases/Opening inventory/Closing inventory

    Opening inventory/Closing inventory/Purchases

Gross profit

Less: Expenses

    Trade receivables/Wages
    Advertising/Prepayments
    Drawings/Rates
    Bank charges/Capital
    Depreciation charge
    Allowance for doubtful receivables adjustment
    Irrecoverable debts

Total expenses

Profit for the year

Prepare the statement of financial position for the business.

Select the appropriate account headings from the options below.

Statement of financial position as at 31 December 20X6

	£	£	£

Non-current assets:
Fittings/Closing inventory
Trade receivables/Leasehold

_____ _____ _____

_____ _____

Current assets:
Closing inventory/Opening inventory
Trade payables/Trade receivables
Less: Allowance for doubtful receivables

_____

Accruals/Prepayments
Cash at bank/Drawings
Capital/Cash in hand

_____

Current liabilities:
Trade receivables/Trade payables

_____

_____

_____

Owner's capital
Capital at 1.1.X6
Drawings/Net profit for the year
Less: Capital/Drawings

_____

_____

Preparation of accounts for a sole trader: **Chapter 15**

3 Preparing financial statements from the trial balance

3.1 Introduction

The extended trial balance is a useful working paper for the eventual preparation of the financial statements of a sole trader. However, in the examination you may be required to prepare a set of financial statements directly from the initial trial balance.

In this section we will work through a comprehensive example which will include the extraction of the initial trial balance, correction of errors and clearing a suspense account, accounting for year-end adjustments and finally the preparation of the financial statements.

> **Example 3**
>
> Given below are the balances taken from a sole trader's ledger accounts on 31 March 20X4
>
> | | £ |
> |---|---:|
> | Receivables ledger control account | 30,700 |
> | Telephone | 1,440 |
> | Payables ledger control account | 25,680 |
> | Heat and light | 2,480 |
> | Motor vehicles at cost | 53,900 |
> | Computer equipment at cost | 4,500 |
> | Carriage inwards | 1,840 |
> | Carriage outwards | 3,280 |
> | Wages | 67,440 |
> | Loan interest | 300 |
> | Capital | 48,000 |
> | Drawings | 26,000 |
> | Allowance for doubtful receivables | 450 |
> | Bank overdraft | 2,880 |
> | Purchases | 126,800 |
> | Petty cash | 50 |
> | Sales | 256,400 |
> | Insurance | 3,360 |
> | Accumulated depreciation – motor vehicles | 15,000 |
> | Accumulated depreciation – computer equipment | 2,640 |
> | Inventory at 1 April 20X3 | 13,200 |
> | Loan | 8,000 |
> | Rent | 23,760 |

The following information is also available:

(i) The value of inventory at 31 March 20X4 was £14,400.

(ii) Motor vehicles are to be depreciated at 30% on a diminishing balance basis and computer equipment at 20% on cost.

(iii) A telephone bill for £180 for the three months to 31 March 20X4 did not arrive until after the trial balance had been drawn up.

(iv) Of the insurance payments, £640 is for the year-ending 31 March 20X5.

(v) An irrecoverable debt of £700 is to be written off and an allowance of 2% is required against the remaining receivables.

Solution

Step 1

The first stage is to draw up the initial trial balance. Remember that assets and expenses are debit balances and liabilities and income are credit balances.

	£	£
Receivables ledger control account	30,700	
Telephone	1,440	
Payables ledger control account		25,680
Heat and light	2,480	
Motor vehicles at cost	53,900	
Computer equipment at cost	4,500	
Carriage inwards	1,840	
Carriage outwards	3,280	
Wages	67,440	
Loan interest	300	
Capital		48,000
Drawings	26,000	
Allowance for doubtful receivables		450
Bank overdraft		2,880
Purchases	126,800	
Petty cash	50	
Sales		256,400
Insurance	3,360	
Accumulated depreciation – motor vehicles		15,000
Accumulated depreciation – computer equipment		2,640
Inventory at 1 April 20X3	13,200	
Loan		8,000
Rent	23,760	
	359,050	359,050

Step 2

Now to deal with the year-end adjustments:

(a) The value of inventory at 31 March 20X4 was £14,400.

Closing inventory – statement of profit or loss

	£		£
		Closing inventory – statement of financial position	14,400

Closing inventory – statement of financial position

	£		£
Closing inventory – statement of profit or loss	14,400		

- We now have the closing inventory for the statement of profit or loss.

(b) The motor vehicles and computer equipment have yet to be depreciated for the year. Motor vehicles are depreciated at 30% on a diminishing balance basis and computer equipment at 20% on cost.

Motor vehicles depreciation (53,900 – 15,000) × 30% = £11,670

Computer equipment depreciation 4,500 × 20% = £900

Depreciation charges

	£		£
Accumulated depreciation – motor vehicles	11,670	Balance c/d	12,570
Accumulated depreciation – computer equipment	900		
	12,570		12,570
Balance b/d	12,570		

Accumulated depreciation account – motor vehicles

	£		£
		Balance b/d	15,000
Balance c/d	26,670	Depreciation charges	11,670
	26,670		26,670
		Balance b/d	26,670

Accumulated depreciation account – computer equipment

	£		£
		Balance b/d	2,640
Balance c/d	3,540	Depreciation charges	900
	─────		─────
	3,540		3,540
	─────		─────
		Balance b/d	3,540

(c) A telephone bill for £180 for the three months to 31 March 20X4 did not arrive until after the trial balance had been drawn up.

This needs to be accrued for:

Debit	Telephone	£180
Credit	Accruals	£180

Telephone expenses

	£		£
Balance b/d	1,440		
Accrual	180	Balance c/d	1,620
	─────		─────
	1,620		1,620
	─────		─────
Balance b/d	1,620		

Accruals

	£		£
		Telephone expenses	180

(d) Of the insurance payments £640 is for the year-ending 31 March 20X5.

This must be adjusted for as a prepayment:

Debit	Prepayment	£640
Credit	Insurance	£640

Prepayments

	£		£
Insurance expenses	640		

Insurance expenses

	£		£
Balance b/d	3,360	Prepayment	640
		Balance c/d	2,720
	-----		-----
	3,360		3,360
	-----		-----
Balance b/d	2,720		

(e) An irrecoverable debt of £700 is to be written off and an allowance of 2% is required against the remaining receivables.

Firstly, the irrecoverable debt must be written off in order to find the amended balance on the receivables ledger control account.

Debit   Irrecoverable debts expense   £700
Credit   Receivables ledger control account £700

Irrecoverable debts expense

	£		£
Receivables ledger control account	700		

Receivables ledger control account

	£		£
Balance b/d	30,700	Irrecoverable debts expense	700
		Balance c/d	30,000
	-----		-----
	30,700		30,700
	-----		-----
Balance b/d	30,000		

Now we can determine the allowance for doubtful receivables required at £30,000 × 2% = £600. The balance on the allowance account in the trial balance is £450, therefore an increase of £150 is required.

Debit   Allowance for doubtful receivables adjustment (SPL) £150
Credit   Allowance for doubtful receivables account (SFP) £150

Allowance for doubtful receivables adjustment account

	£		£
Allowance for doubtful receivables	150	Balance c/d	150
	150		150
Balance b/d	150		

Allowance for doubtful receivables account

	£		£
		Balance b/d	450
Balance c/d	600	Allowance for doubtful receivables adjustment	150
	600		600
		Balance b/d	600

Step 5

Now that all of the adjustments have been put through the ledger accounts, an amended trial balance can be drawn up as a check and as a starting point for preparing the financial statements.

Remember to consider the adjustments just identified as required when preparing the trial balance.

Trial balance at 31 March 20X4

	£	£
Receivables ledger control account	30,000	
Telephone	1,620	
Payables ledger control account		25,680
Heat and light	2,480	
Motor vehicles at cost	53,900	
Computer equipment at cost	4,500	
Carriage inwards	1,840	
Carriage outwards	3,280	
Wages	67,440	
Loan interest	300	
Capital		48,000
Drawings	26,000	
Allowance for doubtful receivables		600
Bank overdraft		2,880
Purchases	126,800	
Petty cash	50	
Sales		256,400
Insurance	2,720	
Accumulated depreciation – motor vehicles		26,670
Accumulated depreciation – computer equipment		3,540
Inventory at 1 April 20X3	13,200	
Loan		8,000
Rent	23,760	
Inventory at 31 March 20X4	14,400	14,400
Depreciation charges	12,570	
Accruals		180
Prepayments	640	
Allowance for doubtful receivables adjustment	150	
Irrecoverable debts expense	700	
	386,350	386,350

Step 6

We are now in a position to prepare the financial statements for the sole trader. Take care with the carriage inwards and carriage outwards which are expenses of the business. Carriage inwards is treated as part of cost of goods sold, whereas carriage outwards is one of the list of expenses.

FINANCIAL ACCOUNTING: PREPARING FINANCIAL STATEMENTS

Statement of profit or loss for the year-ended 31 March 20X4

	£	£
Sales revenue		256,400
Less: Cost of goods sold		
Opening inventory	13,200	
Carriage inwards	1,840	
Purchases	126,800	
	141,840	
Less: Closing inventory	(14,400)	
		127,440
Gross profit		128,960
Less: Expenses		
Telephone	1,620	
Heat and light	2,480	
Carriage outwards	3,280	
Wages	67,440	
Loan interest	300	
Insurance	2,720	
Rent	23,760	
Depreciation charge	12,570	
Irrecoverable debts	700	
Allowance for doubtful receivables adjustment	150	
Total expenses		115,020
Profit for the year		13,940

Statement of financial position as at 31 March 20X4

	Cost £	Accumulated depreciation £	Carrying amount £
Non-current assets			
Motor vehicles	53,900	26,670	27,230
Computer equipment	4,500	3,540	960
	58,400	30,210	28,190
Current assets			
Inventory		14,400	
Trade receivables	30,000		
Less: Allowance for doubtful receivables	(600)		
		29,400	
Prepayment		640	
Petty cash		50	
		44,490	
Current liabilities			
Bank overdraft	2,880		
Trade Payables	25,680		
Accruals	180		
		28,740	
Net current assets			15,750
Total assets less current liabilities			43,940
Non-current liability:			
Loan			(8,000)
Net assets			35,940
Capital			
Opening capital			48,000
Net profit for the year			13,940
			61,940
Less: Drawings			26,000
Closing capital (proprietor's funds)			35,940

FINANCIAL ACCOUNTING: PREPARING FINANCIAL STATEMENTS

Test your understanding 3

Given below is the list of ledger balances for a sole trader at 30 June 20X4 after all year-end adjustments have been put through.

	£
Sales	165,400
Receivables ledger control account	41,350
Wages	10,950
Bank	1,200
Rent	8,200
Capital	35,830
Payables ledger control account	15,100
Purchases	88,900
Electricity	1,940
Telephone	980
Drawings	40,000
Inventory at 1 July 20X3	9,800
Motor vehicles at cost	14,800
Accumulated depreciation – motor vehicles	7,800
Fixtures at cost	3,200
Accumulated depreciation – fittings	1,800
Accruals	100
Prepayments	210
Inventory at 30 June 20X4 – statement of financial position	8,300
Inventory at 30 June 20X4 – statement of profit or loss	8,300
Depreciation charges	4,500

You are required to:

(i) Draw up a trial balance to check that it balances (you should find that the trial balance does balance).

(ii) Prepare the financial statements for the sole trader for the year-ending 30 June 20X4.

(i) Trial balance as at 30 June 20X4

	£	£
Sales		
Receivables ledger control account		
Wages		
Bank		
Rent		
Capital		
Payables ledger control account		
Purchases		
Electricity		
Telephone		
Drawings		
Inventory at 1 July 20X3		
Motor vehicles at cost		
Accumulated depreciation – motor vehicles		
Fixtures at cost		
Accumulated depreciation – fittings		
Accruals		
Prepayments		
Inventory at 30 June 20X4 – SFP		
Inventory at 30 June 20X4 – SPL		
Depreciation charges		

FINANCIAL ACCOUNTING: PREPARING FINANCIAL STATEMENTS

(ii) Statement of profit or loss for the year-ending 30 June 20X4

	£	£
Sales revenue		
Less: Cost of goods sold		
	———	
Less:		
	———	
		———
Gross profit		
Less: Expenses		
	———	
Total expenses		———
Net profit		———

Statement of financial position as at 30 June 20X4

	Cost £	Accumulated Depreciation £	Carrying amount £
Non-current assets			
	———	———	———
	———	———	———
Current assets			
		———	
Current liabilities			
	———		
		———	
Net current assets			———
Net assets			———
Capital			
Net profit for the year			
			———
Drawings			
			———
Closing capital (proprietor's funds)			
			———

FINANCIAL ACCOUNTING: PREPARING FINANCIAL STATEMENTS

> **Test your understanding 4**

Tick as appropriate.

1 Opening inventory is recorded in the statement of profit or loss as

    An expense ☐

    Cost of goods sold ☐

2 Indicate where the drawings should be shown in the financial statements

    Statement of profit or loss expenses ☐

    Statement of financial position as a deduction to capital ☐

3 Payroll expenses are recorded as

    A liability in the statement of financial position ☐

    An expense in the statement of profit or loss ☐

4 Does the allowance for doubtful receivables adjustment appear in the statement of profit or loss or the statement of financial position?

    Statement of profit or loss ☐

    Statement of financial position ☐

5 Irrecoverable debt expenses are recorded in the statement of financial position as an increase in the allowance for doubtful receivables

    True ☐

    False ☐

Test your understanding 5

David Pedley

The following information is available for David Pedley's business for the year-ended 31 December 20X8. He started his business on 1 January 20X8.

	£
Payables	6,400
Receivables	5,060
Purchases	16,100
Sales	28,400
Motor van	1,700
Drawings	5,100
Insurance	174
General expenses	1,596
Rent and rates	2,130
Salaries	4,162
Inventory at 31 December 20X8	2,050
Sales returns	200
Cash at bank	2,628
Cash in hand	50
Capital introduced	4,100

Required:

Prepare a statement of profit or loss for the year-ended 31 December 20X8 and a statement of financial position at that date.

FINANCIAL ACCOUNTING: PREPARING FINANCIAL STATEMENTS

 Test your understanding 6

Karen Finch

On 1 April 20X7 Karen Finch started a business with capital of £10,000 which she paid into a business bank account.

The following is a summary of the cash transactions for the first year.

	£
Amounts received from customers	17,314
Salary of assistant	2,000
Cash paid to suppliers for purchases	10,350
Purchase of motor van on 31 March 20X8	4,000
Drawings during the year	2,400
Amounts paid for electricity	560
Rent and rates for one year	1,100
Postage and stationery	350

At the end of the year, Karen was owed £4,256 by her customers and owed £5,672 to her suppliers. She has promised her assistant a bonus for the year of £400. At 31 March 20X8 this had not been paid.

At 31 March 20X8 there was closing inventory of £4,257 and the business owed £170 for electricity for the last quarter of the year. A year's depreciation is to be charged on the motor van at 25% on cost.

Required:

Prepare a statement of profit or loss for the year-ended 31 March 20X8 and a statement of financial position at that date.

Test your understanding 7

The trial balance of Elmdale at 31 December 20X8 is as follows

	Dr £	Cr £
Capital		8,602
Inventory	2,700	
Sales		21,417
Purchases	9,856	
Rates	1,490	
Drawings	4,206	
Electricity	379	
Freehold shop	7,605	
Receivables	2,742	
Payables		3,617
Cash at bank		1,212
Cash in hand	66	
Sundry expenses	2,100	
Wages and salaries	3,704	
	34,848	34,848

In addition, Elmdale provides the following information:

(i) Closing inventory has been valued for accounts purposes at £3,060.

(ii) An electricity bill amounting to £132 in respect of the quarter to 28 February 20X9 was paid on 7 March 20X9.

(iii) Rates include a payment of £1,260 made on 10 April 20X8 in respect of the year to 31 March 20X9.

Tasks

(a) Show the adjustments to the ledger accounts for the end-of-period adjustments (i) to (iii).

(b) Prepare a statement of profit or loss for the year-ended 31 December 20X8.

FINANCIAL ACCOUNTING: PREPARING FINANCIAL STATEMENTS

4 Summary

This unit requires the preparation of the financial statements for a sole trader. The statement of profit or loss summarises the transactions during the period and leads to a net profit or loss. The statement of financial position lists the assets and liabilities of the business on the last day of the accounting period in a particular order.

If you have to prepare the financial statements from an extended trial balance each balance will have been categorised as either a profit or loss item or a statement of financial position item.

If you are preparing the financial statements from an initial trial balance, you will have to recognise whether the balances should appear in the statement of profit or loss or in the statement of financial position.

Test your understanding answers

Test your understanding 1

Statement of profit or loss extract for the year-ended 31 December 20X2

Calculate the sales revenue and the cost of goods sold.

	£	£
Sales revenue		292,500
Less: Cost of goods sold		
Opening inventory	37,500	
Purchases	158,700	
	196,200	
Less: Closing inventory	(15,000)	
		(181,200)
Gross profit		111,300

Test your understanding 2

Statement of profit or loss for the year-ended 31 December 20X6

	£	£
Sales revenue		120,000
Less: Cost of goods sold		
Opening inventory	15,000	
Purchases	78,800	
	93,800	
Less: Closing inventory	(21,000)	
		(72,800)
Gross profit		47,200

Less: Expenses

Wages	11,800	
Advertising	4,200	
Rates	1,440	
Bank charges	200	
Depreciation charges	1,400	
Allowance for doubtful receivables adjustment	(515)	
Irrecoverable debts	500	
Total expenses		(19,025)
Profit for the year		28,175

Statement of financial position at 31 December 20X6

	£	£	£
Non-current assets			
Fittings	7,300	2,900	4,400
Leasehold	30,000	7,000	23,000
	37,300	9,900	27,400
Current assets			
Inventory		21,000	
Trade receivables	9,500		
Less: Allowance for doubtful receivables	(285)		
		9,215	
Prepayments		360	
Cash at bank		1,250	
Cash in hand		50	
		31,875	
Current liabilities			
Trade payables		(18,000)	
Net current assets			13,875
Net assets			41,275
Owner's capital			
Capital at 1.1.X6			19,050
Net profit for the year			28,175
Less: Drawings			(5,950)
Closing capital (proprietor's funds)			41,275

Preparation of accounts for a sole trader: Chapter 15

Test your understanding 3

(i) Trial balance as at 30 June 20X4

	£	£
Sales		165,400
Receivables ledger control account	41,350	
Wages	10,950	
Bank	1,200	
Rent	8,200	
Capital		35,830
Payables ledger control account		15,100
Purchases	88,900	
Electricity	1,940	
Telephone	980	
Drawings	40,000	
Inventory at 1 July 20X3	9,800	
Motor vehicles at cost	14,800	
Accumulated depreciation – motor vehicles		7,800
Fixtures at cost	3,200	
Accumulated depreciation – fittings		1,800
Accruals		100
Prepayments	210	
Inventory at 30 June 20X4 – SPL		8,300
Inventory at 30 June 20X4 – SFP	8,300	
Depreciation charges	4,500	
	234,330	234,330

(ii) **Statement of profit or loss for the year-ending 30 June 20X4**

	£	£
Sales revenue		165,400
Less: Cost of goods sold		
Opening inventory	9,800	
Purchases	88,900	
	98,700	
Less: Closing inventory	(8,300)	
		(90,400)
Gross profit		75,000
Less: Expenses		
Wages	10,950	
Rent	8,200	
Electricity	1,940	
Telephone	980	
Depreciation charges	4,500	
Total expenses		(26,570)
Net profit		48,430

Statement of financial position as at 30 June 20X4

	Cost £	Accumulated Depreciation £	Carrying amount £
Non-current assets			
Motor vehicles	14,800	7,800	7,000
Fittings	3,200	1,800	1,400
	18,000	9,600	8,400
Current assets			
Inventory		8,300	
Trade receivables		41,350	
Prepayments		210	
Bank		1,200	
		51,060	
Current liabilities			
Trade payables	15,100		
Accruals	100		
		(15,200)	
Net current assets			35,860
Net assets			44,260
Capital			35,830
Net profit for the year			48,430
			84,260
Drawings			(40,000)
Closing capital (proprietor's funds)			44,260

FINANCIAL ACCOUNTING: PREPARING FINANCIAL STATEMENTS

> **Test your understanding 4**
>
> 1. Opening inventory is recorded in the statement of profit or loss as
>
>   Cost of goods sold
>
> 2. Indicate where the drawings should be shown in the financial statements
>
>   Statement of financial position
>
> 3. Payroll expenses are recorded as
>
>   An expense in the statement of profit or loss
>
> 4. Does the allowance for doubtful receivables adjustment appear in the statement of profit or loss or statement of financial position?
>
>   Statement of profit or loss
>
> 5. Irrecoverable debt expenses are recorded in the statement of financial position as an increase in the allowance for doubtful receivables
>
>   False

Test your understanding 5

David Pedley

Statement of profit or loss for the year ended 31 December 20X8

	£	£
Sales revenue		28,400
Less: Returns		(200)
		28,200
Opening inventory	–	
Purchases	16,100	
Less: Closing inventory	(2,050)	
Cost of goods sold		(14,050)
Gross profit		14,150
Salaries	4,162	
Rent and rates	2,130	
Insurance	174	
General expenses	1,596	
Total expenses		(8,062)
Profit for the year		6,088

Statement of financial position as at 31 December 20X8

	£	£
Non-current assets		
Motor van		1,700
Current assets		
Closing inventory	2,050	
Trade receivables	5,060	
Cash at bank	2,628	
Cash in hand	50	
	9,788	
Trade payables	(6,400)	
Net current assets		3,388
Net assets		5,088

Capital account	
Capital introduced	4,100
Profit for the year (per income statement)	6,088
Less: Drawings	(5,100)
Closing capital (proprietor's funds)	**5,088**

Test your understanding 6

Karen Finch

Statement of profit or loss for the year ended 31 March 20X8

	£	£
Sales revenue (£17,314 + £4,256)		21,570
Purchases (£10,350 + £5,672)	16,022	
Closing inventory	(4,257)	
		(11,765)
Gross profit		9,805
Assistant's salary plus bonus (£2,000 + £400)	2,400	
Electricity (£560 + £170)	730	
Rent and rates	1,100	
Postage and stationery	350	
Depreciation charge	1,000	
Total expenses		(5,580)
Profit for the year		4,225

Statement of financial position at 31 March 20X8

	£	£
Non-current assets		
Motor van at cost		4,000
Accumulated depreciation		(1,000)
Carrying amount		3,000
Current assets		
Inventory	4,257	
Trade receivables	4,256	
Cash (W1)	6,554	
	15,067	
Current liabilities		
Trade payables	5,672	
Accruals (400 + 170)	570	
	6,242	
Net current assets		8,825
Net assets		11,825
Capital		10,000
Capital introduced at 1 April 20X7		
Profit for the year	4,225	
Less Drawings	(2,400)	
Retained profit for the year		1,825
Closing capital (proprietor's funds)		11,825

(W1)

Cash

	£		£
Capital	10,000	Salary	2,000
RLCA	17,314	PLCA	10,350
		Motor van	4,000
		Drawings	2,400
		Electricity	560
		Rent and rates	1,100
		Postage and stationery	350
		Balance c/d	6,554
	27,314		27,314

Test your understanding 7

(a) Ledger accounts

(i)

Closing inventory (SPL)

	£		£
Statement of profit or loss	3,060	Closing inventory SFP	3,060

Closing inventory (SFP)

	£		£
Closing inventory SPL	3,060	Balance c/d	3,060
	3,060		3,060
Balance b/d	3,060		

(ii)

Electricity

	£		£
Per trial balance	379	Statement of profit or loss	423
Accrual	44		
	423		423

Rates

	£		£
Per trial balance	1,490	Statement of profit or loss	1,175
		Prepayment	315
	1,490		1,490

Points to note:

- As regards electricity the accrual of £44 is shown on the statement of financial position as a current liability and increases the charge to the statement of profit or loss for electricity for expenses incurred but not yet paid.

- The rates prepayment of £315 is shown on the statement of financial position as a current asset and reduces the charge to the statement of profit or loss. This reflects the fact that some of the expense recorded relates to the next accounting year.

(b)

Elmdale
Statement of profit or loss for the year ended 31 December 20X8

	£	£
Sales revenue		21,417
Opening inventory	2,700	
Purchases	9,856	
	12,556	
Closing inventory	(3,060)	
Cost of goods sold		9,496
Gross profit		11,921
Rates	1,175	
Electricity	423	
Wages and salaries	3,704	
Sundry expenses	2,100	
Total expenses		7,402
Profit for the year		4,519

FINANCIAL ACCOUNTING: PREPARING FINANCIAL STATEMENTS

Partnership accounts

Introduction

You need to apply acquired knowledge and skills to prepare a set of partnership accounts. This involves preparing a statement of profit or loss for a partnership, a partnership appropriation account, a current account, a capital account and a statement of financial position for the partnership.

ASSESSMENT CRITERIA

Produce the SPL for partnerships (7.3)

Produce the SFP for partnerships (7.4)

CONTENTS

1. The nature of a partnership
2. Appropriation of profit
3. Accounting for partnerships

1 The nature of a partnership

1.1 What is a partnership?

Definition

A partnership is where two or more people carry on business together with a view to making a profit and sharing that profit.

In a partnership each of the partners will invest capital into the business and each partner will have a share in the profits of the business. Either a profit or a loss may require allocation to the partners.

1.2 Partnership capital

Each of the partners in a partnership will invest capital into the business in the same way a sole trader does. In order to keep a record of the capital invested by each partner a separate capital account for each partner is kept in the general ledger. This is a record of how much the business owes back to each of the partners.

Definition

A capital account in a partnership is an account for each partner which records the capital that they have invested into the business.

When a partner invests capital into the business the double entry is:

Dr   Bank account

Cr   Partner's capital account

FINANCIAL ACCOUNTING: PREPARING FINANCIAL STATEMENTS

Example 1

Alberto and Brielle set up in partnership on 1 January 20X1. They each paid in £15,000 of capital.

Show the accounting entries for this capital in the ledger accounts.

Solution

Bank account

	£		£
Alberto – capital	15,000		
Brielle – capital	15,000		

Alberto – capital account

	£		£
		Bank	15,000

Brielle – capital account

	£		£
		Bank	15,000

2 Appropriation of profit

2.1 Types of profit appropriation

When a partnership makes a profit or a loss for an accounting period this is shared between the partners. This is known as 'appropriation'. This is the difference between drawing up a partnership SPL and a sole trader SPL, a sole trader's profit does not need to be apportioned.

The split of profit may include agreements of salaries, commissions, interest on capital and drawings as well as residual profit sharing.

2.2 Salaries

A partnership agreement may specify that one or more partners will receive a salary as a form of profit appropriation, reflecting the level of work in the partnership. It is important to ensure you understand this is an appropriation of profit and not an expense of the business. Appropriating the profit as a salary will take place before a residual profit share calculation.

2.3 Sales commission

Some partnership agreements may specify the partners will receive commission on their sales during the year. This is part of the appropriation of profit and takes place before the calculation of the residual profit share.

2.4 Interest on capital

Partners will often have invested different amounts of capital into the partnership. The partnership agreement may specify a rate of interest is due to each partner on their capital balances. This is part of the appropriation of the profit for the period and must take place before the residual profit share.

AAT have confirmed amounts of interest on capital will be stated in the assessment – you will not have to calculate these. However, this study text contains some examples where you are required to do calculations to aid your understanding.

2.5 Interest on drawings

Interest on drawings is a penalty charge to partners who make drawings from the business. Interest may be based on all drawings or those above a certain level, depending on the partnership's own policies.

Interest on drawings are included in the appropriation account, reducing the amount of profit that a partner is allocated and therefore increasing the profit available for the residual profit share calculation.

AAT have confirmed amounts of interest on drawings will be stated in the assessment. Although you will not have to calculate these amounts in your exam, some study text examples review the calculations for your understanding.

2.6 Residual profit share

The residual profit share may be referred to as the profit share ratio (PSR). This is the ratio in which any remaining profits should be shared amongst the partners after they have been allocated salaries, interest on capital and interest on drawings.

2.7 Partnership agreement

Usually there will be a partnership agreement which sets out what percentage of the profit each partner is to receive. If there is no written partnership agreement, profits should be shared equally between all of the partners.

2.8 Partnership losses

If a partnership makes a loss, the appropriation works in the same way as if a profit were made. Firstly, the salaries, interest on capital etc. are accounted for and the remaining balance is then divided according to the profit share agreement.

3 Accounting for partnerships

3.1 Statement of profit or loss

The first stage in preparing a partnership's financial statements from either a trial balance or an extended trial balance is to prepare the statement of profit or loss. This will be exactly the same as the preparation of a statement of profit or loss for a sole trader with the same types of adjustments such as depreciation expenses, closing inventory, irrecoverable and doubtful receivables and accruals and prepayments

3.2 Appropriation account

Definition

A partnership appropriation account shows how profit for the year has been split between the partners.

The profit appropriation account can take the form of a ledger account or it can be presented as a vertical calculation, shown in the pro forma below, with figures selected for illustration purposes.

	Year ended 31 Dec 20X7 £	Total £
Net profit (SPL)		100,000
Salaries:		
A	–	
B	(12,000)	(12,000)
Sales commission:		
A	(1,000)	
B	(2,000)	(3,000)
Interest on capital:		
A	(5,000)	
B	(7,000)	(12,000)
Interest on drawings:		
A	5,000	
B	–	5,000
Profit available for distribution:		78,000
Profit share:		
A	(39,000)	
B	(39,000)	(78,000)
Balance		Nil

Test your understanding 1

Ella, Krish and Amelie are in partnership sharing profits in the ratio 3:2:1

The profits for the year to 30 June 20X7 were £100,000.

Amelie receives a salary of £12,000 per annum.

The partners' capital accounts have brought down balances of £50,000, £30,000 and £10,000 respectively. Interest on capital amounts for the year for each partner are £2,500, £1,500 and £500 respectively.

Produce the appropriation account for the year.

FINANCIAL ACCOUNTING: PREPARING FINANCIAL STATEMENTS

Solution

	Year ended 30 June 20X7 £	Total £
Net profit		
Salaries:		
Ella		
Krish		
Amelie		
	————	
Interest on capital		
Ella		
Krish		
Amelie		
	————	
Profit available for distribution		
Profit share		
Ella		
Krish		
Amelie		
		————
Balance		
		————

3.3 Current account

Once the profit has been appropriated this can be transferred to the current accounts of the partners.

Definition

A current account records the amount of profit that is due to each partner from the business. This is not to be confused with a bank account of the same name.

If a ledger appropriation account has been used, the profit would appear as a credit balance which would then be transferred to the current accounts by:

Dr Appropriation account

Cr Current account(s)

Both the capital accounts and current accounts are usually credit balances as these are amounts owed back to the partners by the business, i.e. special payables of the business.

A credit balance in a partner's current account is the same as a credit balance for 'net profit for the year' on the bottom half of the sole trader statement of financial position. It represents the amount due to the owners (proprietors).

Example 2

Alberto and Brielle made a profit of £20,000, to be shared equally for the year 20X1.

We will show how the partnership profit is appropriated in a ledger appropriation account.

Solution

Ledger appropriation account

The net profit of the partnership is shown as a credit balance, amount owing to the partners, in the appropriation account.

Appropriation account

	£		£
		Balance b/d	20,000

A journal entry will be put through for the split of the profit.

Debit Appropriation account	£20,000
Credit Current account – Alberto	£10,000
Credit Current account – Brielle	£10,000

The appropriation account and the current accounts are written up as:

Appropriation account

	£		£
Current account – Alberto	10,000	Balance b/d	20,000
Current account – Brielle	10,000		
	20,000		20,000

Current account – Alberto

	£		£
		Appropriation account (profit)	10,000

FINANCIAL ACCOUNTING: PREPARING FINANCIAL STATEMENTS

Current account – Brielle

£		£
	Appropriation account (profit)	10,000

Test your understanding 2

Kareela and Ora earn £20,000 of profit for the 20X9. The partnership agreement is to share this profit equally. Show their current accounts and an extract of the trial balance for the year 20X9.

Solution

Kareela – current account

£		£

Ora – current account

£		£

Trial balance extract

	Dr	Cr
Current accounts – Kareela		
– Ora		

In some partnerships the ledger accounts for capital and current accounts are produced in columnar form which means that each partner has a column in a joint capital and current account.

Example 3

Using the previous examples of Alberto and Brielle we will see how their capital and current accounts would look if the ledger accounts were in columnar form.

Solution

Capital accounts

	Alberto £	Brielle £		Alberto £	Brielle £
			Bank	15,000	15,000

Current accounts

	Alberto £	Brielle £		Alberto £	Brielle £
			Appropriation account (profit)	10,000	10,000

3.4 Drawings

Just as a sole trader withdraws money and/or goods out of the business, partners may also. For a sole trader we have seen that a drawing is account for as:

Dr Drawings

Cr Bank account / Purchases

(the credit entry depends upon whether the drawing is of cash or inventory)

When a partner makes a drawing, the amount may be recorded directly in their current account as shown in the double entries below.

If a partner withdraws cash the double entry is:

Dr Partner's current account

Cr Bank account

If a partner withdraws inventory the double entry is:

Dr Partner's current account

Cr Purchases

FINANCIAL ACCOUNTING: PREPARING FINANCIAL STATEMENTS

Example 4

During 20X1 Alberto had drawings of £6,000 and Brielle had drawings of £8,000. Show how these transactions would appear in the current accounts of the partners and what balances would be shown in the trial balance.

Solution

Current account – Alberto

	£		£
Drawings	6,000	Appropriation account (profit)	10,000
Balance c/d	4,000		
	10,000		10,000
		Balance b/d	4,000

Current account – Brielle

	£		£
Drawings	8,000	Appropriation account (profit)	10,000
Balance c/d	2,000		
	10,000		10,000
		Balance b/d	2,000

Trial balance extract

		Dr	Cr
Capital accounts	– Alberto		15,000
	– Brielle		15,000
Current accounts	– Alberto		4,000
	– Brielle		2,000

However, it may be that during the year, drawings are recorded in separate drawings accounts for each partner with a transfer being made to their current accounts at the end of the year. This alternative approach is demonstrated in the example that follows:

Example 5

Alberto and Brielle each have current account balances of £10,000.

During 20X1 Alberto had drawings of £6,000 and Brielle had drawings of £8,000 which had been posted to individual drawings accounts.

Show how the drawings account balances are transferred to the partners' current accounts.

Solution

At the year end the drawings accumulated in the drawings accounts are transferred by a journal entry to the current accounts of the partners as follows:

Debit Current account – Alberto £6,000
Debit Current account – Brielle £8,000
Credit Drawings account – Alberto £6,000
Credit Drawings account – Brielle £8,000

Drawings account – Alberto

	£		£
Cash	6,000	Current account	6,000

Drawings account – Brielle

	£		£
Cash	8,000	Current account	8,000

Current account – Alberto

	£		£
Drawings – Alberto	6,000	Appropriation account (profit)	10,000
Balance c/d	4,000		
	10,000		10,000
		Balance b/d	4,000

FINANCIAL ACCOUNTING: PREPARING FINANCIAL STATEMENTS

Current account – Brielle

	£		£
Drawings – Brielle	8,000	Appropriation account (profit)	10,000
Balance c/d	2,000		
	─────		─────
	10,000		10,000
	─────		─────
		Balance b/d	2,000

Example 6

Ciara and Drew are in partnership and their capital balances are £100,000 and £60,000 respectively.

During 20X4 the profit made by the partnership totalled £80,000.

The partnership agreement specifies the following:

- Drew receives a salary of £15,000 per annum.

- Both partners receive interest on their capital balances at the rate of 5%. Although this example shows the calculations being made you are not required to calculate interest on capital balances as part of the assessment.

- The profit sharing ratio is 2:1.

We will now appropriate the profit and write up the partners' current accounts.

Ciara made £37,000 of drawings during the year and Drew made £33,500 of drawings during the year.

The brought down balances on their current accounts were both £1,000 credit balances.

Solution

The salary and the interest on capital must be deducted first from the available profits.

The remainder is then split in the profit share ratio of 2:1.

This means that Ciara gets two thirds of the remaining profit whilst Drew gets one third of the remaining profit.

Appropriation account

	£	£
Profit for the year		80,000
Salary – D	15,000	
Interest on capital – C (100,000 × 5%)	5,000	
D (60,000 × 5%)	3,000	
		(23,000)
Profit available for the profit share		57,000
Profit share – C (57,000 × 2/3)		38,000
– D (57,000 × 1/3)		19,000
		57,000

The current accounts can now be written up to reflect the profit share and the drawings for the year.

Current accounts

	Ciara £	Drew £		Ciara £	Drew £
Drawings	37,000	33,500	Balance b/d	1,000	1,000
			Salary		15,000
			Interest on capital	5,000	3,000
Balance c/d	7,000	4,500	Profit share	38,000	19,000
	44,000	38,000		44,000	38,000
			Balance b/d	7,000	4,500

FINANCIAL ACCOUNTING: PREPARING FINANCIAL STATEMENTS

 Test your understanding 3

Christophe and Niamh are in partnership. The opening balances on their capital and current account are provided in the ledger accounts that follow.

During the current year of 20X2, Christophe paid a further £5,000 of capital into the business.

The profit of the business for the year was £28,000 and this is to be shared equally between Christophe and Niamh.

During the year Christophe had cash drawings of £12,000 and Niamh had cash drawings of £13,000.

Record these transactions in the capital and current accounts of Christophe and Niamh. Show the balances on these accounts that would appear in the trial balance at the end of 20X2.

Capital account – Christophe

	£		£
		Balance b/d	15,000

Capital account – Niamh

	£		£
		Balance b/d	15,000

Current account – Christophe

	£		£
		Balance b/d	4,000
	———		———
	———		———

Current account – Niamh

	£		£
		Balance b/d	2,000
	———		———
	———		———

Trial balance extract

	Dr £	Cr £
Capital account – Christophe		
Capital account – Niamh		
Current account – Christophe		
Current account – Niamh		

3.5 Debit balances on current accounts

In some instances, a partner may withdraw more in cash drawings than is owed out of accumulated profits. In this case the partner's current account will show a debit balance.

FINANCIAL ACCOUNTING: PREPARING FINANCIAL STATEMENTS

 Example 7

Suppose that the balance on a partner's current account at the start of the year is a credit balance of £3,000.

The partner's share of profit for the year is £17,000 and the partner has £22,000 of drawings.

Show the partner's current account for the year.

Solution

Current account

	£		£
Drawings	22,000	Balance b/d	3,000
		Profit share	17,000
		Balance c/d	2,000
	———		———
	22,000		22,000
	———		———
Balance b/d	2,000		

The balance on the current account is a debit balance and would be shown in the trial balance as such.

Always assume that any balances given for partners' current accounts are credit balances unless you are specifically told otherwise.

 Test your understanding 4

Hamish and Campbell started a business on 1 January 20X6, investing £20,000 and £14,000 respectively.

In the first year of trade, the business made £25,000 profit.

They have set up the following partnership agreement:

- Neither partner receives a salary.
- Interest on capital has been calculated as £800 for Hamish and £560 for Campbell
- Interest on drawings has been calculated as £50 each.
- The balance of profit is to be split in the ratio 3:2.

Both Hamish and Campbell withdrew £5,000 from the business on 1 July 20X6.

Show how this information appears in the partners' capital and current accounts and in the statement of financial position.

Solution

	Year ended 31 Dec X6 £	Total £
Net profit		
Interest on capital:		
Hamish		
Campbell	_____	
Interest on drawings:		
Hamish		
Campbell	_____	_____
Profit available for distribution		
Profit share:		
Hamish		
Campbell	_____	_____
Balance		_____

Capital accounts

Hamish £	Campbell £	Hamish £	Campbell £

Current account

Hamish £	Campbell £	Hamish £	Campbell £

FINANCIAL ACCOUNTING: PREPARING FINANCIAL STATEMENTS

Statement of financial position extract:

		£	£
Capital accounts:	Hamish		
	Campbell		
Current accounts:	Hamish		
	Campbell		
			_____
			_____

Test your understanding 5

Nico and Tia are in partnership sharing profits in the ratio of 3:2. During the year ended 30 June 20X4 the partnership made a profit of £120,000.

The partnership agreement states that Tia is to receive a salary of £20,000. Interest on capital has been calculated for the year as £6,000 to be received by Tia and £9,000 to be received by Nico. Both Nico and Tia are entitled to 2.5% commission on their sales for the year, provided that their sales exceed £45,000.

The balances on the current accounts, capital accounts and drawings accounts at the year-end before the appropriation of profit were as follows:

		£
Capital	– Nico	150,000
	Tia	100,000
Current	– Nico	3,000 (credit)
	Tia	1,000 (debit)
Drawings	– Nico	56,000
	Tia	59,000
Sales	– Nico	82,400
	Tia	48,600

Complete the appropriation account and the partners' current accounts after appropriation of profit and transfer of drawings at 30 June 20X4.

Appropriation account

	£	£
Net profit		
Salary — Tia		
Sales commission — Nico		
Tia		
		___
		___
Interest on capital — Nico		
Tia		
	___	
		___
Profit available		___
Profit share — Nico		
Tia		
		___
		___

Current accounts

	Nico £	Tia £		Nico £	Tia £
Balance b/d			Balance b/d		
Drawings			Salary		
			Sales commission		
			Interest on capital		
Balance c/d			Profit share		
	___	___		___	___
	___	___		___	___
			Balance b/d		

3.6 Partnership losses in the current account

Any salaries and interest on capital must be appropriated first to the partners even if the partnership makes a loss or if this appropriation turns a profit into a loss.

A loss is split between the partners in the profit share ratio by debiting their current accounts. The partners suffer the loss in the same proportion they share the profits.

Example 8

The partnership of Ed and Flo made a profit of £10,000 for the year ended 31 March 20X5.

The partnership agreement states that each partner receives interest on their capital balances of 10% per annum with Ed receiving £5,000 and Flo receiving £4,000. Ed receives a salary of £8,000.

Any remaining profits or losses are split in the ratio of 3:1.

The balances on their capital accounts were £50,000 and £40,000 respectively and neither partner had a balance brought down on their current accounts.

Neither partner made any drawings during the year.

Write up the partnership profit appropriation account and the partners' current accounts for the year.

Appropriation account

		£	£
Partnership profit			10,000
Salary — Ed		8,000	
Interest — Ed		5,000	
Flo		4,000	
			(17,000)
Loss to be shared			(7,000)
Loss share — Ed (7,000 × 3/4)			(5,250)
Flo (7,000 × 1/4)			(1,750)
			(7,000)

Current accounts

	Ed	Flo		Ed	Flo
	£	£		£	£
Loss share	5,250	1,750	Salary	8,000	
Balance c/d	7,750	2,250	Interest on capital	5,000	4,000
	13,000	4,000		13,000	4,000
			Balance b/d	7,750	2,250

3.7 Loans from partners

A partner may loan the business some money and may then receive interest on this loan.

The double entry when the loan is made is:

Dr   Cash

Cr   Loan (liability)

The interest arising is treated as a business expense which is charged to profits before the profits are shared between the partners.

The double entry for the loan interest is:

Dr   Interest expense (P&L)

Cr   Bank (if paid) or

Cr   Current account (if outstanding)

3.8 Partnerships in the extended trial balance

The extended trial balance may be used in the preparation of partnership accounts. The process is largely as for a sole trader, although the following entries will also be required in the adjustments columns:

Account for interest accrued on a loan from a partner:

Dr   Interest expense

Cr   Current accounts

Transfer drawings to the current account:

Dr   Current accounts

Cr   Drawings

Divide profits as calculated in the appropriation statement:

Dr   Statement of profit or loss

Cr   Current accounts

3.9 Statement of financial position

The final stage is to prepare the statement of financial position of the partnership. The top part of the statement of financial position will be exactly the same as that for a sole trader. Only the capital section of the statement of financial position is different. Here the capital account balances and the current account balances for each partner are listed and totalled, and this total should agree with the net assets total of the top part of the statement of financial position.

FINANCIAL ACCOUNTING: PREPARING FINANCIAL STATEMENTS

 Example 9

Ami, Bao and Cam are in partnership with a partnership agreement that Bao receives a salary of £8,000 per annum and Cam a salary of £12,000 per annum.

Interest on capital is allowed at 4% per annum and the profits are shared in the ratio of 2:1:1.

The list of ledger balances at the year end of 31 March 20X4 are given below:

		£
Drawings	Ami	43,200
	Bao	26,000
	Cam	30,200
Payables ledger control account		56,000
Bank balance		2,800
Current accounts at 1 April 20X3	Ami	3,500
	Bao	7,000
	Cam	4,200
Purchases		422,800
Inventory at 1 April 20X3		63,000
Capital accounts	Ami	42,000
	Bao	32,200
	Cam	14,000
Receivables ledger control account		75,600
Sales		651,000
Non-current assets at cost		112,000
Accumulated depreciation at 1 April 20X3		58,900
Allowance for doubtful receivables at 1 April 20X3		2,000
Expenses		95,200

You are also given the following information:

(i) Inventory at 31 March 20X4 has been valued at £70,000.

(ii) Depreciation for the year has yet to be provided at 20% on cost.

(iii) An irrecoverable debt of £5,600 is to be written off and an allowance for doubtful receivables is to be 2% of the remaining receivables.

(iv) Expenses of £7,000 are to be accrued.

Task 1

Draw up an initial trial balance at 31 March 20X4

Trial balance at 31 March 20X4

		£	£
Drawings	Ami	43,200	
	Bao	26,000	
	Cam	30,200	
Payables ledger control account			56,000
Bank balance		2,800	
Current accounts at 1 April 20X3	Ami		3,500
	Bao		7,000
	Cam		4,200
Purchases		422,800	
Capital accounts	Ami		42,000
	Bao		32,200
	Cam		14,000
Inventory at 1 April 20X3		63,000	
Receivables ledger control account		75,600	
Sales			651,000
Non-current assets at cost		112,000	
Accumulated depreciation at 1 April 20X3			58,900
Allowance for doubtful receivables at 1 April 20X3			2,000
Expenses		95,200	
		870,800	870,800

Task 2

Prepare the statement of profit or loss for the year ended 31 March 20X4.

Statement of profit or loss for the year ending 31 March 20X4

		£	£
Sales revenue			651,000
Less:	Cost of goods sold		
	Opening inventory	63,000	
	Purchases	422,800	
		485,800	
Less:	Closing inventory	(70,000)	
			415,800
Gross profit			235,200
Less:	Expenses (95,200 + 7,000)	102,200	
	Depreciation (20% × 112,000)	22,400	
	Irrecoverable debts	5,600	
	Allowance in doubtful receivables adjustment		
	(2% × (75,600 – 5,600) – 2,000)	(600)	
Total expenses			129,600
Net profit			105,600

Partnership accounts: Chapter 16

Task 3

Prepare the appropriation account.

Appropriation account

			£	£
Net profit				105,600
Salaries	–	Bao	8,000	
		Cam	12,000	
				(20,000)
Interest on capital	–	Ami (42,000 × 4%)	1,680	
		Bao (32,200 × 4%)	1,288	
		Cam (14,000 × 4%)	560	
				(3,528)
Profit for profit share				82,072
Ami (82,072 × 2/4)			41,036	
Bao (82,072 × 1/4)			20,518	
Cam (82,072 × 1/4)			20,518	
				82,072

Task 4

Prepare the partners current account to include salaries, interest, profit share and drawings.

Current accounts

	Ami £	Bao £	Cam £		Ami £	Bao £	Cam £
Drawings	43,200	26,000	30,200	Balance b/d	3,500	7,000	4,200
				Salaries		8,000	12,000
				Interest on cap	1,680	1,288	560
Balance c/d	3,016	10,806	7,078	Profit share	41,036	20,518	20,518
	46,216	36,806	37,278		46,216	36,806	37,278
				Balance b/d	3,016	10,806	7,078

Task 5

Prepare the statement of financial position for the partnership at 31 March 20X4

Statement of financial position as at 31 March 20X4

	£	£	£
Non-current assets at cost			112,000
Accumulated depreciation (58,900 + 22,400)			(81,300)
Carrying amount			30,700
Current assets			
Inventory		70,000	
Trade receivables	70,000		
Less: Allowance for doubtful receivables	(1,400)		
		68,600	
Bank		2,800	
		141,400	
Current liabilities:			
Trade payables	56,000		
Accruals	7,000		
		(63,000)	
Net current assets			78,400
Net assets			109,100

		£	£
Capital accounts –	Ami	42,000	
	Bao	32,200	
	Cam	14,000	
			88,200
Current accounts –	Ami	3,016	
	Bao	10,806	
	Cam	7,078	
			20,900
			109,100

Test your understanding 6

The partnership of Li and Tayo has made a net profit of £58,000 for the year ended 30 June 20X3.

The partnership agreement is that Tayo receives a salary of £8,000 per annum and that the profits are split in the ratio of 3:2.

The list of statement of financial position balances at 30 June 20X3 are given below:

			£
Capital accounts	–	Li	75,000
		Tayo	50,000
Current accounts at 1 July 20X2	–	Li	3,000
		Tayo	2,000
Drawings	–	Li	28,000
		Tayo	24,000
Non-current assets at cost			100,000
Accumulated depreciation at 30 June 20X3			30,000
Inventory at 30 June 20X3			44,000
Trade receivables			38,000
Bank			10,000
Trade payables			26,000

Prepare the appropriation account

Appropriation account

	£	£
Net profit		
Salary – Tayo		
		_____
Profit available		
		_____
Profit share – Li		
Tayo		
		_____
		_____

FINANCIAL ACCOUNTING: PREPARING FINANCIAL STATEMENTS

Write up and balance the partners' current accounts.

Current accounts

	Li £	Tayo £		Li £	Tayo £
Drawings			Balance b/d		
Balance c/d			Appropriation a/c		
	___	___		___	___
	___	___		___	___
			Balance b/d		

Prepare the statement of financial position as at 30 June 20X3.

Statement of financial position as at 30 June 20X3

	£	£
Non-current assets at cost		
Accumulated depreciation		___
Current assets		
Inventory		
Trade Receivables		
Bank	___	
Less: Trade payables		
Net current assets		___
Net assets		___
Capital accounts Li		
Tayo		___
Current accounts Li		
Tayo		___
		___

Test your understanding 7

1. What is the double entry when a partner withdraws goods from the partnership?

   Debit [   ]

   Credit [   ]

2. What is the double entry required to transfer a partner's drawings from the drawings account to the current account? (complete the account name in the box)

   Debit [   ]

   Credit [   ]

3. What is the double entry for interest on a partner's capital?

   Debit [   ]

   Credit [   ]

Test your understanding 8

Low, High and Broad are in partnership sharing profits and losses in the ratio 2:2:1 respectively. Interest is credited on partners' capital account balances at the rate of 5% per annum.

High is the firm's sales manager and for his specialised services he is to receive a salary of £800 per annum.

During the year ended 30 April 20X1 the profit for the year of the firm was £6,200 and the partners' drawings were as follows:

	£
Low	1,200
High	800
Broad	800

On 31 October 20X0 the firm agreed that Low and Broad should subscribe £1,000 each to their capital accounts.

The credit balances on the partners' accounts at 1 May 20X0 were as follows:

	Capital accounts £	Current accounts £
Low	8,000	640
High	7,000	560
Broad	6,000	480

Required:

(a) Prepare a profit appropriation statement for the year ended 30 April 20X1.

(b) Prepare the partners' capital and current accounts for the year ended 30 April 20X1.

Test your understanding 9

Curran and Edgar are in partnership as motor engineers.

The following figures were available after the preparation of the trial balance at 31 December 20X3.

Capital account (C)	£26,000
Capital account (E)	£20,000
Current account (C)	£6,100
Current account (E)	£5,200

Both current accounts showed credit balances

Drawings (C)	£16,250
Drawings (E)	£14,750

After the preparation of the statement of profit or loss, profit was determined as £42,100.

Profits are shared equally by the partners.

Task 1

Show the capital account for each partner updated to 1 January 20X4.

Task 2

Prepare the current account for each partner, balancing these off at the year end.

Test your understanding 10

Wilson and Bridget are in partnership running a toyshop. They have not had a successful year and have reported a loss of £56,000 in the year ended 30 September 20X8.

Their partnership agreement states the following:

- A salary of £9,000 for Wilson and £12,000 for Bridget.
- Interest on drawings above £10,000 in the year at 5%.
- Interest on capital at 10%.
- The balance of the profits to be shared equally.

Wilson has invested £30,000 in the business and Bridget £15,000. Wilson and Bridget took £14,000 and £8,000 respectively as drawings on 1 July 20X8.

What is Wilson's share of the loss?

4 Summary

In this chapter we have dealt with all aspects of partnership accounts which are required for the exam. In terms of preparing financial statements for a partnership, the preparation of the statement of profit or loss is exactly the same as that for a sole trader; therefore, in this chapter we have concentrated on the areas of difference between a sole trader and a partnership.

When partners pay capital into the partnership this is recorded in the partner's individual capital account. The profit of the partnership must then be shared between the partners according to the partnership agreement. This may include salaries for some partners, interest on capital as well as the final profit share ratio. All aspects of sharing out the profit take place in the appropriation account which can take the form of a ledger account or a vertical statement. The appropriated profit is credited to the partners' current accounts and their current accounts are debited with their drawings for the period. The balances on the partners' capital accounts and current accounts are listed in the bottom part of the statement of financial position and should be equal in total to the net assets total of the top part of the statement of financial position.

Test your understanding answers

Test your understanding 1

Ella, Krish and Amelie are in partnership sharing profits in the ratio 3:2:1

The profits for the year to 30 June 20X7 were £100,000.

Amelie receives a salary of £12,000 per annum.

The partners' capital accounts have brought down balances of £50,000, £30,000 and £10,000 respectively. Interest on capital amounts for the year for each partner are £2,500, £1,500 and £500 respectively.

Produce the appropriation account for the year.

Solution

	Year ended 30 June 20X7 £	Total £
Net profit		100,000
Salaries:		
Ella		
Krish		
Amelie	(12,000)	(12,000)
Interest on capital		
Ella	(2,500)	
Krish	(1,500)	
Amelie	(500)	(4,500)
Profit available for distribution		83,500
Profit share		
Ella (83,500 × 3/6)	(41,750)	
Krish (83,500 × 2/6)	(27,833)	
Amelie (83,500 × 1/6)	(13,917)	(83,500)
Balance		Nil

FINANCIAL ACCOUNTING: PREPARING FINANCIAL STATEMENTS

> **Test your understanding 2**
>
> Kareela and Ora earn £20,000 of profit for the 20X9. The partnership agreement is to share this profit equally. Show their current accounts and an extract of the trial balance for the year 20X9.
>
> **Solution**
>
> **Kareela – current account**
>
> | | £ | | £ |
> |---|---|---|---|
> | | | Profit for year | 10,000 |
>
> **Ora – current account**
>
> | | £ | | £ |
> |---|---|---|---|
> | | | Profit for year | 10,000 |
>
> **Trial balance extract**
>
> | | | Dr | Cr |
> |---|---|---|---|
> | Current accounts | – Kareela | | 10,000 |
> | | – Ora | | 10,000 |

> **Test your understanding 3**
>
> **Capital account – Christophe**
>
> | | £ | | £ |
> |---|---|---|---|
> | Balance c/d | 20,000 | Balance b/d | 15,000 |
> | | | Bank | 5,000 |
> | | 20,000 | | 20,000 |
> | | | Balance b/d | 20,000 |
>
> **Capital account – Niamh**
>
> | | £ | | £ |
> |---|---|---|---|
> | Balance c/d | 15,000 | Balance b/d | 15,000 |
> | | 15,000 | | 15,000 |
> | | | Balance b/d | 15,000 |

Current account – Christophe

	£		£
Drawings	12,000	Balance b/d	4,000
Balance c/d	6,000	Profit	14,000
	18,000		18,000
		Balance b/d	6,000

Current account – Niamh

	£		£
Drawings	13,000	Balance b/d	2,000
Balance c/d	3,000	Profit	14,000
	16,000		16,000
		Balance b/d	3,000

Trial balance extract

	Dr	Cr
	£	£
Capital account – Christophe		20,000
Capital account – Niamh		15,000
Current account – Christophe		6,000
Current account – Niamh		3,000

Test your understanding 4

	Year ended 31 Dec X6 £	Total £
Net profit		25,000
Interest on capital:		
Hamish	(800)	
Campbell	(560)	(1,360)
Interest on drawings:		
Hamish	50	
Campbell	50	100
Profit available for distribution		23,740
Profit share:		
Hamish	(14,244)	
Campbell	(9,496)	(23,740)
Balance		Nil

Workings

Hamish total: £800 – £50 + £14,244 = £14,994

Campbell total: £560 – £50 + £9,496 = £10,006

Capital accounts

	Hamish £	Campbell £		Hamish £	Campbell £
Bal c/d	20,000	14,000	Bal b/d	20,000	14,000
	20,000	14,000		20,000	14,000
			Bal b/d	20,000	14,000

Current account

	Hamish £	Campbell £		Hamish £	Campbell £
Drawings	5,000	5,000	Profit share	14,994	10,006
Bal c/d	9,994	5,006			
	14,994	10,006		14,994	10,006
			Bal b/d	9,994	5,006

Statement of financial position extract:

		£	£
Capital accounts:	Hamish	20,000	
	Campbell	14,000	
			34,000
Current accounts:	Hamish	9,994	
	Campbell	5,006	
			15,000
			49,000

Test your understanding 5

Appropriation account

			£	£
Net profit				120,000
Salary – Tia			20,000	
Sales commission	–	Nico (2.5% × 82,400)	2,060	
		Tia (2.5% × 48,600)	1,215	
Interest on capital	–	Nico	9,000	
		Tia	6,000	
				(38,275)
Profit available				81,725
Profit share	–	Nico (81,725 × 3/5)		49,035
		Tia (81,725 × 2/5)		32,690
				81,725

Current accounts

	Nico £	Tia £		Nico £	Tia £
Balance b/d		1,000	Balance b/d	3,000	
Drawings	56,000	59,000	Salary		20,000
			Sales commission	2,060	1,215
			Interest on capital	9,000	6,000
			Profit share	49,035	32,690
Balance c/d	7,095		Balance c/d		95
	63,095	60,000		63,095	60,000
Balance b/d		95	Balance b/d	7,095	

Test your understanding 6

Appropriation account

	£	£
Net profit		58,000
Salary — Tayo		(8,000)
Profit available		50,000
Profit share — Li (50,000 × 3/5)	30,000	
Tayo (50,000 × 2/5)	20,000	
		50,000

Current accounts

	Li £	Tayo £		Li £	Tayo £
Drawings	28,000	24,000	Balance b/d	3,000	2,000
Balance c/d	5,000	6,000	Appropriation a/c	30,000	28,000
	33,000	30,000		33,000	30,000
			Balance b/d	5,000	6,000

Statement of financial position as at 30 June 20X3

	£	£
Non-current assets at cost		100,000
Accumulated depreciation		(30,000)
		70,000
Current assets:		
Inventory	44,000	
Trade receivables	38,000	
Bank	10,000	
	92,000	
Less: Trade payables	(26,000)	
Net current assets		66,000
Net assets		136,000
Capital accounts – Li		75,000
Tayo		50,000
		125,000
Current accounts – Li	5,000	
Tayo	6,000	
		11,000
		136,000

FINANCIAL ACCOUNTING: PREPARING FINANCIAL STATEMENTS

Test your understanding 7

1. Debit   Partner's current account
   Credit   Purchases
2. Debit   Partner's current account
   Credit   Partner's drawings account
3. Debit   Appropriation account
   Credit   Partners' current accounts

Test your understanding 8

(a) Profit appropriation statement – year ended 30 April 20X1:

	Year ended 30 Apr 20X1 £	Total £
Profit for the year		6,200
Salaries		
Low	–	
High	(800)	
Broad	–	(800)
Interest on capital		
Six months to 31 Oct 20X0		
Low	(200)	
High	(175)	
Broad	(150)	(525)
Six months to 30 Apr 20X1		
Low	(225)	
High	(175)	
Broad	(175)	(575)
Profit available for distribution		4,300
Profit share		
Low	(1,720)	
High	(1,720)	
Broad	(860)	(4,300)
Balance		Nil

Partnership accounts: Chapter 16

Summary of profit share for the year:

Low: £200 + £225 + £1,720 = £2,145

High: £800 + £175 + £175 + £1,720 = £2,870

Broad: £150 + £175 + £860 = £1,185

(b)

Capital accounts

	Low £	High £	Broad £		Low £	High £	Broad £
				Balance b/d	8,000	7,000	6,000
Balance c/d	9,000	7,000	7,000	Cash	1,000		1,000
	8,000	7,000	7,000		9,000	7,000	7,000
				Balance b/d	9,000	7,000	7,000

Current accounts

	Low £	High £	Broad £		Low £	High £	Broad £
Drawings	1,200	800	800	Balance b/d	640	560	480
Balance c/d	1,585	2,630	865	Profit apportionment	2,145	2,870	1,185
	2,785	3,430	1,665		2,785	3,430	1,665
				Balance b/d	1,585	2,630	865

Test your understanding 9

Capital accounts

	(C) £	(E) £		(C) £	(E) £
31 Dec Balance c/d	26,000	20,000	31 Dec Balance b/d	26,000	20,000
	26,000	20,000		26,000	20,000
			01 Jan Balance b/d	26,000	20,000

Current accounts

	(C) £	(E) £		(C) £	(E) £
31 Dec Drawings	16,250	14,750	Balance b/d	6,100	5,200
31 Dec Balance c/d	10,900	11,500	31 Dec Share of profit	21,050	21,050
	27,150	26,250		27,150	26,250
			01 Jan Balance b/d	10,900	11,500

FINANCIAL ACCOUNTING: PREPARING FINANCIAL STATEMENTS

Test your understanding 10

	Year ended 30 Sep 20X8 £	Total £
Loss for the year		(56,000)
Salaries		
Wilson	(9,000)	
Bridget	(12,000)	(21,000)
Interest on capital		
Wilson	(3,000)	
Bridget	(1,500)	(4,500)
Interest on drawings		
Wilson (£4,000 × 5% × 3/12)	50	
Bridget	–	50
Loss available for distribution		(81,450)
Loss share		
A	40,725	
B	40,725	81,450
Balance		Nil

Wilson's total share = £9,000 + £3,000 − £50 − £40,725 = **£28,775 loss.**

FINANCIAL ACCOUNTING: PREPARING FINANCIAL STATEMENTS

Incomplete records

Introduction

The reconstruction of financial information from incomplete evidence is a key element of this unit when preparing accounts for a business.

There are a variety of techniques that can be used to reconstruct financial information when full accounting records are not available.

These include reconstruction of net asset totals, reconstruction of cash, bank, receivables and payables accounts and the use of mark-ups or margins in order to calculate missing accounting figures.

Each of these techniques will be considered in this chapter.

ASSESSMENT CRITERIA

Identify missing figures (9.1)

Mark-up and margin (9.2)

Reasonableness of figures when information is incomplete (9.3)

CONTENTS

1. What are incomplete records?
2. The net assets approach
3. Cash and bank account
4. Receivables ledger control account and payables ledger control account
5. Margins and mark-ups
6. Assessing the reasonableness of figures
7. Examination style questions

Incomplete records: **Chapter 17**

1 What are incomplete records?

1.1 Introduction

We have been considering the accounting systems of sole traders and partnerships. They have all kept full accounting records consisting of primary records and a full set of ledger accounts, leading to a trial balance from which final accounts can be prepared.

In this chapter we will be considering businesses that do not keep full accounting records – incomplete records.

1.2 Limited records

Many businesses especially those of small sole traders or partnerships will only keep the bare minimum of accounting records. These may typically consist of:

- bank statements
- files of invoices sent to customers probably marked off when paid
- files of invoices received from suppliers marked off when paid
- files of bills marked off when paid
- till rolls
- a record of non-current assets owned.

From these records it will normally be possible to piece together the information required to prepare a statement of profit or loss and a statement of financial position but a number of techniques are required. These will all be covered in this chapter.

1.3 Destroyed records

In some situations, particularly in examinations, either the whole, or part of, the accounting records have been destroyed by fire, flood, thieves or computer failure. It will then be necessary to try to piece together the picture of the business from the information that is available.

1.4 Missing figures

A further element of incomplete records is that a particular figure or balance may be missing. Typically, inventory will be destroyed in accidents and drawings will be unknown. Incomplete records techniques can be used to find the missing amount or value as a balancing figure.

1.5 Techniques

In order to deal with these situations a number of specific accounting techniques are required and these will be dealt with, in this chapter. They are:

- the net assets approach (based on the accounting equation)
- the cash and bank account
- receivables and payables control accounts
- mark-ups and margins.

It is important to note that an actual balance may differ from a calculated balance, as with incomplete records you are piecing information together.

2 The net assets approach

2.1 Introduction

The net assets approach is used in a particular type of incomplete records situation. This is where there are no detailed records of the transactions of the business during the accounting period. This may be due to the fact that they have been destroyed or that they were never kept in the first place. The only facts that can be determined are the net assets at the start of the year, the net assets at the end of the year and some details about the capital of the business.

2.2 The accounting equation

We have come across the accounting equation in earlier Chapters when dealing with the statement of financial position.

The basic accounting equation is that:

Net assets = Capital

Remember that net assets = assets – liabilities

This can be expanded to:

Increase in net assets = Capital introduced + profit – drawings

This is important: any increase in the net assets of the business must be due to the introduction of new capital and/or the making of profit less drawings.

Incomplete records: Chapter 17

2.3 Using the accounting equation

The increase in net assets is the difference between the opening and closing net assets figures.

If capital introduced is known together with drawings made by the owner, the profit for the period can be deduced.

Alternatively, if the profit and capital introduced are known, the drawings can be found as the balancing figure.

Example 1

Archibald started a business on 1 January 20X1 with £2,000. On 31 December 20X1 the position of the business was as follows:

	£
The business owned:	
Freehold lock–up shop, at cost	4,000
Shop fixtures and equipment, at cost	500
Inventory of goods bought for resale, at cost	10,300
Debts owing by customers	500
Cash in till	10
Cash at bank	150
The business owed:	
Mortgage on shop premises	3,000
Payables for goods	7,000
Accrued mortgage interest	100

Archibald had drawn £500 for personal living expenses.

The shop fixtures are to be depreciated by £50 and certain goods in inventory which had cost £300 can be sold for only £50.

No records had been maintained throughout the year.

You are required to calculate the profit earned by Archibald's business in the year ended 31 December 20X1.

Solution

This type of question is answered by calculating the net assets at the year-end as follows:

Net assets at 31 December 20X1

	Cost £	Accumulated depreciation £	Carrying amount £
Non-current assets			
Freehold shop	4,000	–	4,000
Fixtures and fittings	500	50	450
	4,500	50	4,450

480

Current assets

Inventory at lower of cost and net realisable value (10,300 – 300 + 50)		10,050
Trade receivables		500
Cash and bank balances (150 + 10)		160
		10,710
Current liabilities		
Trade payables	7,000	
Mortgage interest	100	
		(7,100)
		3,610
		8,060
Mortgage		(3,000)
Net assets		5,060

The profit is now calculated from the accounting equation.

The opening net assets will be the cash paid into the bank when the business was started on 1 January 20X1.

Change in net assets during the year = Profit plus capital introduced in year less drawings

£5,060 – 2,000 = Profit + Nil – 500

£3,060 = Profit – 500

Therefore, profit equals £3,560.

Archibald's statement of financial position is made up of the above together with the bottom half which can be established after calculating the profit, i.e.

	£
Opening capital	2,000
Profit (balancing figure)	3,560
	5,560
Drawings	(500)
Closing capital	5,060

The 'incomplete records' part of the question is concerned with just one figure. After calculating the incomplete information, the financial statements can be prepared.

Incomplete records: Chapter 17

Test your understanding 1

The net assets of a business at the start of the year were £14,600. At the end of the year the net assets were £17,300. During the year the owner had paid in £2,000 of additional capital and withdrew £10,000 from the business for living expenses.

What is the profit of the business?

3 Cash and bank account

3.1 Introduction

In this section we must be clear about the distinction between cash and bank accounts.

Definition

Cash is the amount of notes and coins in a till or in the petty cash box.

Definition

The bank account is the amount held in the current account or cheque account of the business.

If the opening and closing balances of cash and bank are known together with most of the movements in and out, then, if there is only one missing figure this can be found as the balancing figure.

3.2 Cash account

When dealing with incomplete records a cash account deals with cash either from the petty cash box or more usually from the till in a small retail business. If the opening balance and the closing balance of cash is known, provided there is only one missing figure this can be determined from the summarised cash account.

FINANCIAL ACCOUNTING: PREPARING FINANCIAL STATEMENTS

 Example 2

Henry's sales are all for cash. During the year Henry:

- banked £50,000
- paid wages of £5,000 out of the till, and
- paid expenses by cash of £10,000.

There were no opening or closing cash balances.

What were Henry's sales?

Solution

Cash

	£		£
Cash sales (bal fig)	65,000	Bankings	50,000
		Wages	5,000
		Expenses	10,000
	65,000		65,000

The rationale is that if £65,000 of cash was taken out of the till for various purposes, £65,000 must have been received.

 Test your understanding 2

Henrietta runs a milliner's shop making all her sales for cash. You ascertain the following information:

	£
Cash in the till at the beginning of the year	50
Cash in the till at the end of the year	75
Bingo winnings put into the till	500
Bankings	15,000
Cash wages	1,000
Cash expenses	5,000

Complete the ledger account below to establish Henrietta's sales during the year.

Cash

	£		£

3.3 Bank account

The same ideas can be applied to the bank account – if the opening and closing balances and all of the transactions except one are known, a missing figure can be found. In practice this may not be required, as bank statements should show all the necessary details.

Note that the double entry for a banking of cash is:

Dr   Bank account

Cr   Cash account

Example 3

Henry writes cheques only for his own use. Henry knows the bankings were £50,000.

The opening and closing bank balances were £10,000 and £40,000 respectively. What were Henry's drawings?

Solution

Bank

	£		£
Balance b/d	10,000	Drawings (bal fig)	20,000
Bankings	50,000	Balance c/d	40,000
	60,000		60,000
Balance b/d	40,000		

The bankings are the amounts paid out of the till, reducing cash, and paid into the bank account. Therefore a debit entry is made in the bank account.

FINANCIAL ACCOUNTING: PREPARING FINANCIAL STATEMENTS

3.4 Combined cash and bank account

In examinations it is often easier to combine the cash and bank accounts into one ledger account with a column for cash and a column for bank.

In the case of Henry this would be written as:

Cash and bank

	Cash £	Bank £		Cash £	Bank £
Balance b/d		10,000	Drawings (bal fig)		20,000
Bankings		50,000	Bankings	50,000	
Cash sales (bal fig)	65,000		Wages	5,000	
			Expenses	10,000	
			Balance c/d		40,000
	65,000	60,000		65,000	60,000

The key figure here is how much has been banked. If the bankings were paid into the bank account, they must have come out of cash.

In examinations you may only be given the bankings figure from the bank statement – this will show the amount paid into the bank account. You must ensure that you make this entry not only as a debit in the bank column but also as a credit in the cash column.

4 Receivables ledger control account and payables ledger control account

4.1 Introduction

In many incomplete records situations you will find that figures for sales and purchases are missing.

A technique for finding these missing figures is to recreate the receivables and payables accounts in order to find the missing figures as balancing figures.

The receivables ledger control account and the payables ledger control account are used to find the missing figures.

4.2 Receivables ledger control account

Firstly, a reminder of what is likely to be in a receivables ledger control account is detailed below:

Receivables ledger control account

	£		£
Opening balance (bal b/d)	X	Receipts from customers	X
Sales (per sales day book)	X	Sales returns	X
		Irrecoverable debts	X
		Discounts allowed	X
		Contra with PLCA	X
		Closing balance (bal c/d)	X
	X		X

If the opening and closing receivables are known, together with the receipts from customers, sales returns, details of any irrecoverable debts, discounts allowed and contras, the sales figure can be found as the balancing figure.

Example 4

A business has receivables at the start of the year of £4,220 and at the end of the year receivables of £4,870, after accounting for the contra with the PLCA as noted below.

During the year customers paid a total of £156,350 and one debt of £1,000 was irrecoverable. In addition, an agreed amount of £2,000 due from a credit customer was offset against the PLCA amount due to that same customer who also makes supplies to the business on credit.

What were the sales for the year?

Solution

Receivables ledger control account

	£		£
Balance b/d	4,220	Receipts from customers	156,350
		Irrecoverable debt written off	1,000
		Contra with PLCA	2,000
Sales (bal fig)	160,000	Balance c/d	4,870
	164,220		164,220

The sales figure of £160,000 can be deduced from this account as the balancing figure.

FINANCIAL ACCOUNTING: PREPARING FINANCIAL STATEMENTS

4.3 Payables ledger control account

The payables ledger control account works in the same way as a potential working for finding the purchases figure.

Payables ledger control account

	£		£
Payments to suppliers	X	Opening balance (bal b/d)	X
Discount received	X	Purchases	X
Purchase returns	X		
Contra with RLCA	X		
Closing balance (bal c/d)	X		
	——		——
	X		X
	——		——

Example 5

Dominic paid his payables £5,000 during a period.

At the beginning of the period he owed £1,500 and at the end he owed £750, after accounting for the contra account entry as explained below. Dominic also agreed to contra an amount of £250 which was owed to a supplier who is also a credit customer of Dominic. What were his purchases for the period?

Solution

Payables ledger control account

	£		£
Cash	5,000	Balance b/d	1,500
Contra with RLCA	250	Purchases (bal fig)	4,500
Balance c/d	750		
	——		——
	6,000		6,000
	——		——
		Balance b/d	750

4.4 Cash, bank, receivables and payables

In many incomplete records questions you will need to combine the techniques reviewed so far.

You may need to use the cash and bank account in order to determine the receipts from customers and then transfer this amount to the receivables ledger control account in order to find the sales figure.

Incomplete records: Chapter 17

 Example 6

Andrea does not keep a full set of accounting records but she has been able to provide you with some information about her opening and closing balances for the year ended 31 December 20X1.

	1 January 20X1 £	31 December 20X1 £
Inventory	5,227	4,892
Trade receivables	6,387	7,221
Trade payables	3,859	4,209
Bank	1,448	1,382
Cash	450	300

Andrea tells you that the trade receivables balances and the trade payables balances at 31 December 20X1 are stated after accounting for a contra entry of £400 to offset an agreed amount due from another business which also supplies goods to her.

You have also been provided with a summary of Andrea's payments out of her bank account:

	£
Payments to trade payables	48,906
Purchase of new car	12,000
Payment of expenses	14,559

Andrea also tells you that she has taken £100 per week out of the till in cash in order to meet her own expenses.

Calculate sales, purchases, cost of goods sold and gross profit for Andrea for the year ended 31 December 20X1.

Solution

Step 1

Open up ledger accounts for cash and bank, receivables and payables and enter the opening and closing balances given.

Cash and bank

	Cash £	Bank £		Cash £	Bank £
Opening balance	450	1,448	Closing balance	300	1,382

488   KAPLAN PUBLISHING

FINANCIAL ACCOUNTING: PREPARING FINANCIAL STATEMENTS

Receivables ledger control account

	£		£
Opening balance	6,387	Closing balance	7,221

Payables ledger control account

	£		£
Closing balance	4,209	Opening balance	3,859

Step 2

Enter the payments from the bank account in the credit column of the bank account and complete the double entry for the payable's payment.

Cash and bank

	Cash £	Bank £		Cash £	Bank £
Opening balance	450	1,448	Payables		48,906
			Car		12,000
			Expenses		14,559
			Closing balance	300	1,382

Payables ledger control account

	£		£
Bank	48,906	Opening balance	3,859
Closing balance	4,209		

Step 3

Find the balancing figure in the bank account as this is the amount of money paid into the bank in the period. If it was paid into the bank it must have come out of the till therefore enter the same figure as a credit in the cash account.

Cash and bank

	Cash	Bank		Cash	Bank
Opening balance	450	1,448	Payables		48,906
Bankings (bal fig)		75,399	Car		12,000
			Expenses		14,559
			Bankings	75,399	
			Closing balance	300	1,382
		76,847			76,847

Step 4

Enter the drawings into the cash account (assume a 52-week year unless told otherwise).

Cash and bank

	Cash £	Bank £		Cash £	Bank £
Opening balance	450	1,448	Payables		48,906
Bankings (bal fig)		75,399	Car		12,000
			Expenses		14,559
			Bankings	75,399	
			Drawings	5,200	
			Closing balance	300	1,382
		76,847			76,847

Step 5

Balance the cash account – the missing figure is the amount of receipts from customers – this is a debit in the cash account and a credit in the receivables ledger control account.

Cash and bank

	Cash £	Bank £		Cash £	Bank £
Opening balance	450	1,448	Payables		48,906
Bankings (bal fig)		75,399	Car		12,000
			Expenses		14,559
			Bankings	75,399	
			Drawings	5,200	
Receipts – receivables (bal fig)	80,449		Closing balance	300	1,382
	80,899	76,847		80,899	76,847

Receivables ledger control account

	£		£
Opening balance	6,387	Receipts from customers	80,449
		Closing balance	7,221

The receipts figure of £80,449 is not technically all from receivables since some may be for cash sales; however as the receivables ledger control account is only a working account designed to find the total sales this distinction is unimportant.

Step 6

Find the sales and purchases figures as the missing figures in the receivables and payables account.

Receivables ledger control account

	£		£
Opening balance	6,387	Receipts from customers	80,449
		Contra with PLCA	400
Sales (bal fig)	81,683	Closing balance	7,221
	88,070		88,070

Payables ledger control account

	£		£
Bank	48,906	Opening balance	3,859
Contra with RLCA	400		
Closing balance	4,209	Purchases (bal fig)	49,656
	53,515		53,515

Step 7

Prepare the trading account.

	£	£
Sales revenue		81,683
Less: cost of goods sold		
Opening inventory	5,227	
Purchases	49,656	
	54,883	
Less: closing inventory	(4,892)	
		(49,991)
Gross profit		31,692

In this example we dealt with all four accounts – cash, bank, receivables and payables – simultaneously in order to show how the double entry works between the four working accounts.

However, in examinations you will be prompted to work through the situation step by step. So, this same example might be approached in the examination as follows:

Task 1

Calculate the amount of cash received from customers from sales.

This will come from the cash and bank account workings

Cash and bank

	Cash £	Bank £		Cash £	Bank £
Opening balance	450	1,448	Payables		48,906
Bankings (bal fig)		75,399	Car		12,000
			Expenses		14,559
			Bankings	75,399	
			Drawings	5,200	
Receipts – receivables (bal fig)	80,449		Closing balance	300	1,382
	80,899	76,847		80,899	76,847

Cash from customers for sales = £80,449

Task 2

Determine the sales for the period.

This will come from the receivables ledger control account.

Receivables ledger control account

	£		£
Opening balance	6,387	Receipts from customers	80,449
		Contra with PLCA	400
Sales (bal fig)	81,683	Closing balance	7,221
	88,070		88,070

Sales = £81,683

Task 3

Determine the purchases for the period.

This will come from the payables ledger control account.

Payables ledger control account

	£		£
Bank	48,906	Opening balance	3,859
Contra with RLCA	400		
Closing balance	4,209	Purchases (bal fig)	49,656
	53,515		53,515

Purchases = £49,656

FINANCIAL ACCOUNTING: PREPARING FINANCIAL STATEMENTS

Task 4

Calculate the gross profit for the period.

This will come from the statement of profit or loss.

	£	£
Sales revenue		81,683
Less: cost of goods sold		
Opening inventory	5,227	
Purchases	49,656	
	54,883	
Less: closing inventory	(4,892)	
		(49,991)
Gross profit		31,692

Gross profit = £31,692

5 Margins and mark-ups

5.1 Introduction

The final technique that you may be required to use is that of dealing with margins and mark-ups. This is often useful when dealing with the records of a retailer and is a useful method of reconstructing missing figures.

5.2 Cost structure

The key to dealing with mark-ups and margins is in setting up the cost structure of the sales of an organisation from the information given in the question.

> **Definition**
>
> A cost structure is the relationship between the selling price of goods, their cost and the gross profit earned in percentage terms.

Example 7

An item is sold for £150 and it originally cost £100. We need to set up the cost structure for this sale.

Solution

	£
Sales revenue	150
Cost of goods sold	100
Gross profit	50

The cost structure, in percentage terms, can be set up in one of two ways.

(i) Assume that cost of goods sold represents 100% therefore the cost structure would be:

	£	%
Sales revenue	150	150
Cost of goods sold	100	100
Gross profit	50	50

We can now say that this sale gives a gross profit percentage of 50% on cost of goods sold.

(ii) Assume that sales revenue represents 100% therefore the cost structure would be:

	£	%
Sales revenue	150	100
Cost of goods sold	100	$66^{2}/_{3}$
Gross profit	50	$33^{1}/_{3}$

We can now say that this sale gives a gross profit percentage of $33^{1}/_{3}$% on sales.

FINANCIAL ACCOUNTING: PREPARING FINANCIAL STATEMENTS

5.3 The difference between a mark-up and a margin

If it is cost of goods sold that is 100% this is known as a mark-up on cost. Therefore in the previous example the sale would be described as having a mark-up on cost of 50%.

If it is sales revenue that is 100% this is known as a sales margin. In the previous example the sale would be described as having a gross profit margin of $33^{1}/_{3}$%.

Example 8

Calculate the cost of goods which have been sold for £1,200 on which a gross profit margin of 25% has been achieved.

Solution

Step 1

Work out the cost structure.

The phrase 'gross profit margin' means 'gross profit on sales'. Following the rule above we therefore make sales revenue equal to 100%. We know the gross profit is 25%; therefore the cost of goods sold must be 75%.

	%
Sales revenue	100
Less: cost of goods sold	75
Gross profit	25

Step 2

Work out the missing figure, in this case 'cost of goods sold'.

	£	%
Sales revenue	1,200	100
Cost of goods sold	?	75
Gross profit	?	25

Cost of goods sold = 75% of revenue

= $\frac{75}{100} \times 1,200 = £900$

Therefore gross profit = £300 (£1,200 − £900)

Example 9

Calculate the cost of goods which have been sold for £1,200 on which a mark-up on cost of goods sold of 25% has been achieved.

Solution

Step 1

The cost structure.

The gross profit here is on cost of goods sold rather than sales, as above makes all the difference. When we construct the 'cost structure', cost of goods sold will be 100%; gross profit will be 25%, and sales revenue must be 125%.

In other words:

	%
Sales revenue	125
Less: cost of goods sold	100
Gross profit	25

Step 2

Calculate the missing figure, again the cost of goods sold

	£	%
Sales revenue	1,200	125
Cost of goods sold	?	100
Gross profit	?	25

Cost of goods sold = $\frac{100}{125}$ of sales revenue

= $\frac{100}{125}$ × 1,200 = £960

Remember the rule – whatever the margin or mark-up is 'on' or 'of' must be 100%.

- If there is a margin on the sales price, the sales revenue is 100%.
- If there is a mark-up on the cost, the cost of goods sold is 100%.

FINANCIAL ACCOUNTING: PREPARING FINANCIAL STATEMENTS

> **Test your understanding 3**
>
> (a) Mark-up on cost of goods sold = 10%
>
>   Sales revenues were £6,160
>
>   Cost of goods sold =
>
> (b) Gross profit on sales revenues = 20%
>
>   Cost of goods sold was £20,000
>
>   Sales revenues =
>
> (c) Mark-up on cost of goods sold = 33%
>
>   Cost of goods sold was £15,000
>
>   Sales revenues =
>
> (d) Gross profit on sales revenues = 25%
>
>   Cost of goods sold was £13,200
>
>   Sales revenues =
>
> (e) Sales revenues were £20,000
>
>   Cost of goods sold was £16,000
>
>   Gross profit on sales revenues as a % =
>
>   Gross profit on cost of goods sold as a % =

5.4 Margins and mark-ups and incomplete records

We will now look at how mark-ups and margins can be used when dealing with incomplete records. They can be a great help in finding missing revenue and cost of goods sold figures but a little practice is required in using them.

5.5 Calculating revenues

In a question if you have enough information to calculate cost of goods sold and you are given some information about the cost structure of the sales revenues you will be able to calculate the sales figure.

Incomplete records: Chapter 17

 Example 10

A business has purchases of £18,000 and opening and closing inventory of £2,000 and £4,000 respectively. The gross profit margin is always 25%.

What are the revenues for the period?

Solution

Step 1

Cost structure

As it is a gross profit margin this is a margin 'on' revenue and therefore revenues are 100%

	%
Sales revenue	100
Cost of goods sold	75
Gross profit	25

Step 2

Calculate cost of goods sold

	£
Opening inventory	2,000
Purchases	18,000
	20,000
Less: closing inventory	(4,000)
	16,000

Step 3

Determine the sales revenue figure

$£16,000 \times \dfrac{100}{75} = £21,333$

FINANCIAL ACCOUNTING: PREPARING FINANCIAL STATEMENTS

 Test your understanding 4

You are given the following information relating to Clarence's business for the year ended 31 December 20X3.

Cash paid to trade payables was £9,000. Other assets and liabilities were:

	1 January £	31 December £
Payables	2,100	2,600
Inventory	1,800	1,600

Mark-up on cost of goods sold 20%

Task 1

Calculate the purchases for the year.

Task 2

Calculate the cost of goods sold for the year.

Task 3

Calculate the revenues for the year.

5.6 Calculating cost of goods sold, purchases or closing inventory

If you know the figure for sales revenue and you know about the cost structure then it is possible to find the total for cost of goods sold and then deduce any missing figures such as purchases or closing inventory.

Example 11

A business had made sales in the month of £25,000. The business sells its goods at a mark-up of 20%. The opening inventory was £2,000 and the closing inventory was £3,000.

What were the purchases for the period?

Solution

Step 1

Cost structure

	%
Revenue	120
Cost of goods sold	100
Gross profit	20

Step 2

Determine cost of goods sold using the cost structure.

Cost of goods sold = £25,000 × $\frac{100}{120}$

= £20,833

Step 3

Reconstruct cost of goods sold to find purchases.

	£
Opening inventory	2,000
Purchases (bal fig)	21,833
	23,833
Less: closing inventory	(3,000)
Cost of goods sold	20,833

6 Assessing the reasonableness of figures

6.1 Introduction

Accountants should ensure they are applying professional scepticism, when assessing the reasonableness of figures provided in a given context.

6.2 Professional scepticism

Definition

Professional scepticism is an attitude that includes a questioning mind, being alert to conditions which may indicate possible misstatement due to error or fraud.

Professional scepticism should be considered when estimating figures using the incomplete record methods, outlined in this chapter. It is important to take a step back and consider 'does this amount seem reasonable?' For example, if the gross profit as a percentage of sales was calculated to be 80% for the current year, compared to the prior year's gross profit representing 25% of sales, this rather significant difference from one year to the next, would indicate the calculation should be double checked to ensure accuracy.

It is important that information is checked for accuracy regardless of whether the information is from a manual bookkeeping system or the information is produced by accounting software. Examiners like questions on incomplete records as not only do they test a variety of bookkeeping and accounting techniques, the application of professional scepticism is also tested.

Incomplete records: Chapter 17

7 Examination style questions

7.1 Introduction

So far, we have studied the techniques that you have to use to deal with incomplete records questions in the exam. Although the examiner may ask any style of question, the examiner tends to ask questions in a particular way – leading you through the question a bit at a time and telling you what you have to calculate next. We shall now see how these questions might appear in the exam.

Example 12

John is a sole trader and prepares his accounts to 30 September 20X8. The summary of his bank account is as follows.

	£		£
Balance b/d 1 Oct 20X7	15,000	Stationery	2,400
Receipts from receivables	74,865	General expenses	4,300
		Rent	4,500
		Payments to suppliers	27,000
		Drawings	24,000
		Balance at 30 Sept 20X8	27,665
	89,865		89,865

Receivables at 1 October 20X7 were 24,000 and at 30 September 20X8 were 30,000.

Payables at 1 October 20X7 were 17,500 and at 30 September 20X8 were 23,000.

Rent was paid at £1,500 per quarter, and the rent had not been paid for the final quarter to 30 September 20X8.

During September 20X8 a payment of £300 was made for electricity which covered the period 1 August 20X8 to 31 October 20X8. Electricity is included in general expenses.

Task 1

Calculate the capital at 1 October 20X7.

Task 2

Prepare the receivables ledger control account for the year ended 30 September 20X8, showing credit sales as the balancing figure.

Receivables ledger control account

	£		£

Task 3

Prepare the payables ledger control account for the year ended 30 September 20X8, showing credit purchases as the balancing figure.

Payables ledger control account

	£		£

Task 4

Prepare the rent account for the year ended 30 September 20X8.

Rent account

	£		£

Task 5

Prepare the general expenses account for the year ended 30 September 20X8.

General expenses account

	£		£

Task 6

Prepare a trial balance at 30 September 20X8

FINANCIAL ACCOUNTING: PREPARING FINANCIAL STATEMENTS

Solution

Task 1

Capital at 1 October 20X7 = net assets at 1 October 20X7

Net assets at 1 October 20X7:	£
Bank	15,000
Receivables	24,000
Payables	(17,500)
Net assets	21,500 = capital at 1 October 20X7

Tutorial note. Remember that capital equals net assets. You therefore have to list all the assets and liabilities at the start of the year to find the net assets and therefore the capital.

Task 2

Receivables ledger control account

	£		£
Balance b/d 1 Oct 20X7	24,000	Cash from receivables	74,865
Credit sales (bal fig)	80,865	Balance c/d 30 Sept 20X8	30,000
	104,865		104,865

Task 3

Payables ledger control account

	£		£
Paid to payables	27,000	Balance b/d 1 Oct 20X7	17,500
Balance c/d 30 Sept 20X8	23,000	Purchases (bal fig)	32,500
	50,000		50,000

Task 4

Rent account

	£		£
Cash paid	4,500	SPL	6,000
Balance c/d	1,500		
	6,000		6,000

Tutorial note. The £1,500 rent that has not been paid for the final quarter is an accrual – it is brought down into the next period as a credit balance as it is money owed by the business.

Task 5

General expenses account

	£		£
Cash paid	4,300	SPL	4,200
		Balance c/d (1/3 × £300)	100
	4,300		4,300

Tutorial note. Of the £300 paid in September 20X8, £100 is for the month of October 20X8 – it is therefore a prepayment and is carried forward as an asset – a debit balance

Task 6

Trial balance as at 30 September 20X8

	£	£
Capital at 1 October 20X7		21,500
Bank	27,665	
Sales		80,865
Receivables ledger control a/c	30,000	
Purchases	32,500	
Payables ledger control a/c		23,000
Accrual – rent		1,500
Prepayment – general expenses	100	
Stationery	2,400	
Rent (SPL)	6,000	
General expenses (SPL)	4,200	
Drawings	24,000	
	126,865	126,865

7.2 Another example

In many examination questions you will be required to use the incomplete records techniques to determine missing figures. We have already looked at finding sales revenue, cost of goods sold, purchases and closing or opening inventory. The final common missing figure is that of the owner's drawings.

Often the owner of a business will not keep a record of exactly how much has been taken out of the business especially if money tends to be taken directly from the till.

In examination questions if you are told that the owner's drawings were, for example, approximately £35 each week, this figure can be used as the actual drawings figure.

However, if the question states that drawings were between £25 and £45 per week you cannot take an average figure; you must use incomplete records techniques to find the drawings figure as the balancing figure.

Example 13

Simone runs a television and video shop.

All purchases are made on credit.

Sales are a mixture of cash and credit.

For the year ended 31 December 20X8, the opening and closing payables, receivables and inventory were:

	1.1.X8	21.12.X8
	£	£
Payables	11,000	11,500
Receivables	12,000	11,800
Inventory	7,000	10,000

Her mark-up is 20% on cost.

The payments for purchases are posted to the bank account and the payables ledger control account.

All cash and cheques are posted to the cash account and receivables ledger control account. Surplus cash and cheques are paid into the bank.

A summary of her business bank account for the year ended 31 December 20X8 is as follows.

Bank account

	£		£
Balance b/d 1/1/X8	12,500	Payments to suppliers	114,000
Cash banked	121,000	Rent and rates	10,000
		Other expenses	4,000
		Balance c/d 31.12.X8	5,500
	133,500		133,500

The opening and closing cash balances were:

1/1/X8	31/12/X8
£120	£150

Cash was used to pay for petrol costing £400 and stationery costing £200. She also drew money out of the till for her personal use, but she has not kept a record of the amounts drawn.

Task 1

Prepare the payables ledger control account.

Payables ledger control account

	£		£

Task 2

Calculate the cost of goods sold using the following pro forma.

	£
Opening inventory	
Purchases	
	_____
Closing inventory	
	_____
Cost of goods sold	
	_____

Task 3

Calculate the sales revenue for the year using the following pro forma and the details of the mark-up given in the question.

	£	%
Sales revenue		
Cost of goods sold	_____	
Gross profit	_____	

Task 4

Prepare the receivables ledger control account to find the cash received from receivables during the year.

Receivables ledger control account

	£		£

Incomplete records: Chapter 17

Task 5

Complete the cash account given below where drawings will be the balancing figure.

Cash account

	£		£
Balance b/d		Petrol	
Receipts – receivables		Stationery	
		Bankings – to bank a/c	
		Drawings	
		Balance c/d	

Solution

Task 1

Calculation of purchases.

Payables ledger control account

	£		£
Bank account	114,000	Balance b/d	11,000
Balance c/d	11,500	Purchases (bal fig)	114,500
	125,500		125,500

Task 2

Calculation of cost of goods sold.

	£
Opening inventory	7,000
Purchases (Task 1)	114,500
	121,500
Closing inventory	(10,000)
	111,500

Task 3

Calculation of sales revenue.

	£	%
Sales ($\frac{120}{100}$ × 111,500)	133,800	120
Cost of goods sold (Task 2)	111,500	100
Gross profit	22,300	20

Task 4

Receivables ledger control account

	£		£
Balance b/d	12,000	Receipts (bal fig)	134,000
Sales (Task 3)	133,800	Balance c/d	11,800
	145,800		145,800

Task 5

Calculation of drawings.

Cash account

	£		£
Balance b/d	120	Petrol	400
Receipts – receivables	134,000	Stationery	200
		Bankings	121,000
		Drawings (bal fig)	12,370
		Balance c/d	150
	134,120		134,120

Take care with the order in which you work.

- As a mark-up is given you will need to use it – you have enough information to determine purchases and cost of goods sold therefore use the mark-up to calculate sales revenue.

- Make sure that you enter these sales into the receivables ledger control account on the debit side – even though some are for cash rather than on credit they should all be entered into the receivables account as you are only using it as a vehicle for calculating the total sales revenue.

- Once sales have been entered into the receivables account the only missing figure is the cash received – this should be then entered into the cash account as a debit.

- Finally once all of the cash payments are entered as credits the balancing figure on the credit side of the cash account will be the drawings.

Test your understanding 5

Ignatius owns a small wholesale business and has come to you for assistance in the preparation of his accounts for the year ended 31 December 20X4.

For the year ended 31 December 20X4 no proper accounting records have been kept, but you establish the following information:

1 A summary of Ignatius's bank statements for the year to 31 December 20X4 is as follows:

	£		£
Opening balance	1,870	Payments to suppliers	59,660
Receipts from credit customers	12,525	Rent – one year	4,000
Cash banked	59,000	Rates – year beginning 1.4.X4	2,000
		Other administration costs	1,335
		Selling costs	1,940
		Equipment – bought 1.1.X4	800
			69,735
		Closing balance	3,660
	73,395		73,395

2   Credit sales for the year, as shown by a summary of copy invoices, totalled £12,760.

3   No record has been kept by Ignatius of cash sales or his personal drawings, in cash. It is apparent, however, that all sales are on the basis of a 33$\frac{1}{3}$% mark-up on cost.

4   Apart from drawings, cash payments during the year have been:

	£
Payments to suppliers	755
Sundry expenses	155
Wages	3,055

The balance of cash in hand at 31 December 20X4 is estimated at £20, and it is known that £12 was in hand at the beginning of the year.

5   At the year-end, closing inventory, valued at cost, was £5,375 (31 December 20X3 £4,570) and payables for goods bought for resale amounted to £4,655.

6   At 31 December 20X3 payables for goods bought for resale amounted to 3,845.

Task 1

Calculate the purchases for the year.

Payables ledger control account

	£		£
	___		___
	___		___

Task 2

Calculate the cost of goods sold for the year.

	£
Opening inventory 1.1.X4	
Purchases	
	___
Inventory 31.12.X4	
	___
Cost of goods sold	
	___

Task 3

Calculate total sales revenue for the year

Sales revenue = (workings)

Cost structure

Cost of goods sold =

Mark-up =

Therefore sales =

Task 4

Calculate the cash sales for the year.

£

Cash sales

Task 5

Prepare calculations to determine the owner's drawings for the year.

Enter the cash sales in the cash account. This will give drawings as a balancing figure. The cash account is reproduced here.

Cash account

	£		£

Test your understanding 6

1. According to the accounting equation, what is an increase in net assets equal to? (Write your answer below.)

2. What is the double entry for bankings from the cash till to the bank account? (Circle as appropriate.)

   Debit   **Revenue account / Bank account**

   Credit   **Cash account / Takings account**

3. The opening and closing receivables for a business were £1,000 and £1,500 and receipts from customers totalled £17,500. What were revenues? (Circle as appropriate.)

   Revenues are: **£17,500 / £17,000 / £18,000**

4. The opening and closing payables for a business were £800 and £1,200 with payments to suppliers totalling £12,200. What is the purchases figure? (Circle as appropriate.)

   Purchases are: **£12,600 / £12,200 / £11,800**

5. Goods costing £2,000 were sold at a mark-up of 20%. What was the selling price? (Circle as appropriate.)

   Selling price is: **£2,500 / £2,400**

6. Goods costing £2,000 were sold with a margin of 20%. What was the selling price? (Circle as appropriate.)

   Selling price is: **£2,500 / £2,400**

7. Revenues were £24,000 and were at a margin of 25%. What is the figure for cost of goods sold? (Circle as appropriate.)

   Cost of goods sold is: **£18,000 / £6,000**

Incomplete records: Chapter 17

8   Revenues were £24,000 and were at a mark-up of 25%. What is the figure for cost of goods sold? (Circle as appropriate.)

Cost of goods sold is   £18,000 / £19,200

9   Revenues for a business were £100,000 achieved at a margin of 40%. Opening inventory was £7,000 and purchases were £58,000. What is the figure for closing inventory? (Complete the pro forma.)

	£	£
Revenues		
Less cost of goods sold		
Opening inventory		
Purchases		
Less closing inventory		
Gross profit		

10 Revenues for a business were £80,000 and they were sold at a mark-up of 25%. Opening and closing inventory was £10,000 and £8,000 respectively. What is the purchase total? (Complete the pro forma.)

	£	£
Revenues		
Less cost of goods sold		
Opening inventory		
Purchases		
Less closing inventory		
Gross profit		

Test your understanding 7

You work as a senior for a self-employed 'Licensed Accounting Technician' and Peter Ryan, the proprietor of a local shop trading in 'home brew products', is one of your clients.

The business trades under the name of Brew-By-Us.

You have been provided with the following information:

Balances as at:	31 May X0 £	31 May X1 £
Trade receivables	2,000	1,800
Trade payables	1,200	1,500
Inventory	6,000	8,000

All the business's sales and purchases are on a credit basis.

All payments for expenses have been made by cheque.

A summary of the bank transactions for the year ended 31 May 20X1 is as follows:

	£
Balance b/d	(1,015) overdrawn
Receipts	
Loan receipt	4,000
Receipts from receivables	45,000
	49,000
Wages	3,850
Advertising	750
Payments to payables	36,200
Heat and light	1,060
Shop fixtures	2,000
Insurance	400
Rent and rates	5,200
Drawings	200
Bank charges	55
Stationery	200
	49,915
Balance 31 May 20X1	(1,930) overdrawn

Additional information for the year ended 31 May 20X1 is provided below:

- Discounts allowed to customers totalled £2,750 for the year.
- The business returned £1,280 of goods to their suppliers during the year.
- Capital at 31st May 20X0 was £5,785 and Peter did not invest any further capital during the year.
- Depreciation is to be charged on the shop fixtures purchased during the year. Fixtures are depreciated at 15% using the straight line method. A full year's depreciation is to be charged in the year of acquisition.

Required:

(a) Prepare the receivables ledger control account to determine the sales for the period.

(b) Prepare the payables ledger control account to determine the purchases for the period.

(c) Prepare a statement of profit or loss for the year ended 31 May 20X1, and a statement of financial position at that date.

Test your understanding 8

Diane Kelly has been employed for several years supplying cleaning materials to schools, restaurants, public houses and industrial units.

She operates an incomplete system of accounting records for her business, from which the following information is available.

1   **Assets and liabilities**

	1 June 20X0 £	31 May 20X1 £
Warehouse fittings (CA)	8,000	?
Van (at cost)	–	6,500
Inventory	10,000	16,000
Trade receivables	16,000	19,000
Trade payables	15,000	20,000
Rates prepaid	1,200	1,600
Accruals		
Telephone	400	500
Heat and light	300	500

2   Bank account summary for the year

	£	£
Balance at 1 June 20X0		9,800
Receipts		
Receivables	79,000	
Cash sales banked	7,700	
Proceeds of sale of caravan	2,500	89,200
Payments		
Payables	70,000	
Purchase of van	6,500	
Heat and light	1,800	
Office expenses	2,600	
Rent and rates	4,200	
Telephone	1,200	
Wages	9,800	
Van expenses	1,200	
Insurance	800	98,100
Balance at 31 May X1		900

Notes

- The caravan was Diane's own personal property.
- All non-current assets are depreciated on the diminishing balance basis; a rate of 20% should be applied.
- The van was acquired on 1 June 20X0.
- During the year cash discounts of £1,100 had been allowed and £1,800 had been received.
- Diane paid sundry office expenses of £420 and used £15,600 for personal reasons – both amounts had been taken from the proceeds of cash sales.
- All the remaining cash had been banked.

Required:

(a) Determine the sales for the year.

(b) Determine the purchases for the year.

(c) Show accounts for rates, telephone and heat and light to determine the charge for the year.

(d) Prepare the statement of profit or loss for the year ended 31 May 20X1 and a statement of financial position at that date.

Test your understanding 9

(a) A business marks up its goods by 60%. Revenues are £200,000 for the year. What is the gross profit?

(b) A business makes a 30% margin on its sales. Opening inventory is £40,000, closing inventory is £10,000 and purchases are £180,000. What is the amount for revenue?

Test your understanding 10

Data

A friend of Donald Johnson, Sheena Gordon, has been trading for just over 12 months as a dressmaker.

She has kept no accounting records at all, and she is worried that she may need professional help to sort out her financial position.

Knowing that Donald Johnson runs a successful business, Sheena Gordon approached him for advice. He recommended that you, his bookkeeper, should help Sheena Gordon.

You meet with Sheena Gordon and discuss the information that you require her to give you.

Sometime later, you receive a letter from Sheena Gordon providing you with the information that you requested, as follows:

(a) She started her business on 1 October 20X2. She opened a business bank account and paid in £5,000 of her savings.

(b) During October she bought the equipment and the inventory that she needed. The equipment cost £4,000 and the inventory of materials cost £1,800. All of this was paid for out of the business bank account.

(c) A summary of the business bank account for the 12 months ended 30 September 20X3 showed the following:

Bank

	£		£
Capital	5,000	Equipment	4,000
Cash banked	27,000	Purchases	1,800
		Purchases of materials	18,450
		General expenses	870
		Drawings	6,200
		Balance c/d	680
	32,000		32,000

(d) All of the sales are on a cash basis. Some of the cash is paid into the bank account while the rest is used for cash expenses. She has no idea what the total value of her sales is for the year, but she knows that from her cash received she has spent £3,800 on materials and £490 on general expenses. She took the rest of the cash not banked for her private drawings. She also keeps a cash float of £100.

(e) The gross profit margin on all sales is 50%.

(f) She estimates that all the equipment should last for five years. You therefore agree to depreciate it using the straight-line method.

(g) On 30 September 20X3, the payables for materials amounted to £1,400.

(h) She estimates that the cost of inventory of materials that she had left at the end of the year was £2,200.

Task 10.1

Calculate the total purchases for the year ended 30 September 20X3.

Task 10.2

Calculate the total cost of goods sold for the year ended 30 September 20X3.

Task 10.3

Calculate revenue for the year ended 30 September 20X3.

Task 10.4

Show the entries that would appear in Sheena Gordon's cash account.

Task 10.5

Calculate the total drawings made by Sheena Gordon throughout the year.

Task 10.6

Calculate the figure for net profit for the year ended 30 September 20X3.

Test your understanding 11

Fariah is a sole trader running an IT support business and prepares accounts to 31 December 20X8. The summary of her bank account is as follows.

	£		£
Balance b/d 1 Jan 20X8	25,000	Advertising	10,000
Receipts from receivables	80,000	General expenses	8,000
		Rent	9,000
		Payments to suppliers	10,000
		Drawings	36,000
		Balance at 31 Dec 20X8	32,000
	105,000		**105,000**

Receivables at 1 January 20X8 were £20,000 and at 31 December 20X8 were £30,000, after accounting for the contra transaction explained below.

Payables at 1 January 20X8 were £13,000 and at 31 December 20X8 were £15,000, after accounting for the contra transaction explained below.

All Fariah's sales are on credit. One of Fariah's receivables has been made bankrupt owing her £3,400. She wrote this debt off in November 20X8.

Fariah offset an agreed amount of £300 with another business which makes both purchases and sales on credit to her.

During December 20X8 a payment of £3,000 was made for insurance which covered the period 1 November 20X8 to 31 October 20X9. Insurance is included in general expenses.

Fariah depreciated her computers at 40% reducing balance. The carrying amount of the computers at 1 January 20X8 was £4,600.

FINANCIAL ACCOUNTING: PREPARING FINANCIAL STATEMENTS

Task 11.1

Calculate the capital at 1 January 20X8.

Task 11.2

Prepare the journal that Fariah would have made in November 20X8 to record the write off of the irrecoverable debt.

Journal

Account name	Dr (£)	Cr (£)
Narrative		

Task 11.3

Prepare the receivables ledger control account for the year ended 31 December 20X8, showing credit sales as the balancing figure.

Receivables ledger control account

	£		£

Task 11.4

Prepare the payables ledger control account for the year ended 31 December 20X8, showing credit purchases as the balancing figure.

Payables ledger control account

	£		£

Task 11.5

Prepare the general expenses account for the year ended 31 December 20X8.

General expenses account

	£		£

Task 11.6

Calculate the depreciation that Fariah will provide for the year ended 31 December 20X8.

Task 11.7

Prepare the journal that Fariah will make at the year end to record depreciation.

Account name	Dr (£)	Cr (£)
Narrative		

Task 11.8

Prepare a trial balance at 31 December 20X8. The trial balance should show the computers at their carrying amount (not cost less accumulated depreciation).

8 Summary

This chapter has covered all of the varying techniques that might be required to deal with an incomplete records problem in an examination.

The techniques are the net assets approach, cash and bank accounts, receivables ledger control account and payables ledger control account, plus use of mark-ups and margins.

Many of these questions will look formidable in an examination but they are all answerable if you think about all of these techniques that you have learnt and apply them to the particular circumstances of the question.

You will also find that the AAT style is to lead you through a question with small tasks prompting you to carry out the calculations in a particular order which makes the process more manageable.

Test your understanding answers

Test your understanding 1

Increase in net assets	=	capital introduced	+ profit – drawings
(17,300 – 14,600)	=	2,000	+ profit – 10,000
2,700	=	2,000	+ profit – 10,000
Profit	=	£10,700	

Test your understanding 2

Cash

	£		£
Balance b/d	50	Bankings	15,000
Capital (Bingo)	500	Wages	1,000
Cash sales (bal fig)	20,525	Expenses	5,000
		Balance c/d	75
	21,075		21,075

The rationale is that £21,075 has been 'used' for bankings, expenses and providing a float to start the next period therefore £21,075 must have been received.

Of this 'receipt':

- £50 is from last period; and
- £500 is an injection of capital.

Therefore £20,525 must have been sales.

Test your understanding 3

		%	£
(a)	Cost of goods sold	100	
	Add: mark-up	10	
	Therefore sales revenue	110	
	Therefore cost of goods sold	$^{100}/_{110} \times £6,160$	£5,600
(b)	Sales revenue	100	
	Less: gross profit	20	
	Therefore cost of goods sold	80	
	Therefore sales revenue	$^{100}/_{80} \times £20,000$	£25,000
(c)	Cost of goods sold	100	
	Add: mark-up	33	
	Therefore sales revenue	133	
	Therefore sales revenue	$^{133}/_{100} \times £15,000$	£19,950
(d)	Sales revenue	100	
	Less: gross profit	25	
	Therefore cost of goods sold	75	
	Therefore sales revenue	$^{100}/_{75} \times £13,200$	£17,600
(e)	Sales revenue	20,000	
	Less: cost of goods sold	16,000	
	Therefore gross profit	4,000	

Gross profit on sales revenue $\dfrac{4,000}{20,000} \times \dfrac{100}{1} = 20\%$

Gross profit on cost of goods sold $\dfrac{4,000}{16,000} \times \dfrac{100}{1} = 25\%$

Test your understanding 4

Task 1

Calculate the figure for purchases.

Payables ledger control account

	£		£
Cash	9,000	Balance b/d	2,100
Balance c/d	2,600	Purchases (bal fig)	9,500
	11,600		11,600

Note that we are constructing the total account, and producing the balancing figure which represents the purchases made during the year.

Remember the double entry involved here. The cash of £9,000 will be a credit in the cash account. The purchases (£9,500) will be debited to the purchases account and transferred to the statement of profit or loss at the year-end:

Purchases account

	£		£
Payables ledger control account	9,500	SPL	9,500

Task 2

Now complete the cost of goods sold

	£
Opening inventory	1,800
Purchases	9,500
	11,300
Less: closing inventory	(1,600)
Cost of goods sold	9,700

FINANCIAL ACCOUNTING: PREPARING FINANCIAL STATEMENTS

Task 3

Now you can work out the cost structure and sales revenue.

(a) Work out the cost structure.

The mark-up is arrived at by reference to the cost of goods sold. Thus, cost of goods sold is 100%, the mark-up is 20% and therefore the sales revenues are 120%:

	%
Sales revenue (balancing figure)	120
Less: Gross profit	20
Cost of goods sold	100

(b) Sales $= \dfrac{120}{100} \times$ cost of goods sold

$= \dfrac{120}{100} \times £9,700$

$= £11,640$

❋ Test your understanding 5

Task 1

Calculate purchases.

Payables ledger control account

	£		£
Cash – payments to suppliers	755	Payables 1/1/X4	3,845
Bank – payments to suppliers	59,660	Purchases (balancing figure)	61,225
Payables 31.12.X4	4,655		
	65,070		65,070

Task 2

Calculate the cost of goods sold.

	£
Opening inventory 1.1.X4	4,570
Purchases	61,225
	65,795
Inventory 31.12.X4	(5,375)
Cost of goods sold	60,420

Task 3

Calculate total sales.

Cost of structure

Cost of goods sold = 100%

Mark-up = $33^{1}/_{3}\%$

Therefore sales = $133^{1}/_{3}\%$

$$\text{Sales} = \frac{\text{Cost of goods sold}}{100} \times 133^{1}/_{3} = \frac{60{,}420}{100} \times 133^{1}/_{3} = £80{,}560$$

Task 4

Calculate cash sales.

	£
Total revenue	80,560
Less: credit sales (per question)	(12,760)
Therefore, cash sales	67,800

Task 5

Calculate drawings.

Enter the cash sales in the cash account. This will give drawings as a balancing figure.

The cash account is reproduced here:

Cash account

	£		£
Balance 1.1.X4	12	Payments to suppliers	755
Receipts from cash sales	67,800	Other costs	155
		Wages	3,055
		Cash banked	59,000
		Drawings (balancing figure)	4,827
		Balance c/d	20
	67,812		67,812

Test your understanding 6

1. Increase in net assets = capital introduced + profit – drawings

2. Debit   Bank account
   Credit   Cash account

3. £17,500 + 1,500 – £1,000   =   £18,000

4. £12,200 + £1,200 – £800   =   £12,600

5. £2,000 × 120/100   =   £2,400

6. £2,000 × 100/80   =   £2,500

7. £24,000 × 75/100   =   £18,000

8. £24,000 × 100/125   =   £19,200

9. Cost of goods sold = £100,000 × 60/100   =   £60,000
   Opening inventory + purchases   =   £65,000
   Closing inventory   =   £5,000

10. Cost of goods sold = £80,000 × 100/125   =   £64,000
    Purchases = £64,000 + £8,000 – £10,000   =   £62,000

Test your understanding 7

(a) Sales for the year

Receivables ledger control account

	£		£
01/6/X0 Balance b/d	2,000	31/5/X1 Discount allowed	2,750
31/5/X1 Sales (bal fig)	47,550	31/5/X1 Receipts (bank)	45,000
		31/5/X1 Balance c/d	1,800
	49,550		49,550

(b) Purchases for the year

Payables ledger control account

	£		£
31/5/X1 Payments (bank)	36,200	01/6/X0 Balance b/d	1,200
31/5/X1 Purchase returns	1,280	31/5/X1 Purchases (bal fig)	37,780
31/5/X1 Balance c/d	1,500		
	38,980		38,980

(c) **Statement of profit or loss of Peter Ryan trading as 'Brew-By Us' for the year ended 31 May 20X1**

	£	£
Sales revenue		47,550
Inventory at 1 June 20X0	6,000	
Add Purchases	37,780	
Less Purchase returns	(1,280)	
	42,500	
Less Inventory 31 May 20X1	(8,000)	
Cost of goods sold		(34,500)
Gross profit		13,050
Expenses		
Wages	3,850	
Advertising	750	
Heat and light	1,060	
Insurance	400	
Rent and rates	5,200	
Bank charges	55	
Discount allowed	2,750	
Stationery	200	
Depreciation charges		
Fixtures (15% × £2,000)	300	
Total expenses		(14,565)
Loss for the year		(1,515)

Statement of financial position as at 31 May 20X1

	Cost £	Accumulated depreciation £	Carrying amount £
Non-current assets			
Fixtures and fittings	2,000	300	1,700
	2,000	300	1,700
Current assets			
Inventory		8,000	
Receivables		1,800	
		9,800	
Current liabilities			
Payables		1,500	
Bank overdraft		1,930	
		3,430	
Net current assets			6,370
Non-current liabilities			
Loan			4,000
Net assets			4,070
Capital		5,785	
Less Loss for year		(1,515)	
		4,270	
Less Drawings		(200)	
Closing capital (proprietor's funds)			4,070

Test your understanding 8

(a) Revenue for the year

Receivables ledger control account

	£		£
01/6/X0 Balance b/d	16,000	31/5/X1 Bank	79,000
31/5/X1 Sales (bal fig)	83,100	31/5/X1 Discounts	1,100
		31/5/X1 Balance c/d	19,000
	99,100		99,100
01/6/X1 Balance b/d	19,000		

	£
Credit sales	83,100
Cash sales banked	7,700
Expenses paid by cash	420
Cash for personal use	15,600
Total revenue	106,820

(b) Purchases for the year

Payables ledger control account

	£		£
31/5/X1 Payments	70,000	01/6/X0 Balance b/d	15,000
31/5/X1 Discounts	1,800	31/5/X1 (Purchases) bal fig	76,800
31/5/X1 Balance c/d	20,000		
	91,800		91,800

(c)

Rates account

	£		£
01/6/X0 Balance b/d	1,200	31/5/X1 SPL	3,800
31/5/X1 Payments	4,200	31/5/X1 Balance c/d	1,600
	5,400		5,400
01/6/X1 Balance b/d	1,600		

Telephone account

	£		£
31/5/X1 Payments	1,200	01/6/X0 Balance b/d	400
31/5/X1 Balance c/d	500	31/5/X1 SPL	1,300
	1,700		1,700
		01/6/X1 Balance b/d	500

Heat and light

	£		£
31/5/X1 Payments	1,800	01/6/X0 Balance b/d	300
31/5/X1 Balance c/d	500	31/5/X1 SPL	2,000
	2,300		2,300
		01/6/X1 Balance b/d	500

(d) Statement of profit or loss for year ended 31 May 20X1

	£	£
Sales revenue		106,820
Inventory – 1/6/X0	10,000	
Add: purchases	76,800	
	86,800	
Less: Inventory 31/5/X1	16,000	
Cost of goods sold		70,800
Gross profit		36,020
Discounts received		1,800
Expenses		
Heat and light	2,000	
Office expenses (2,600 + 420)	3,020	
Rent and rates	3,800	
Telephone	1,300	
Wages	9,800	
Vehicle expenses	1,200	
Insurance	800	
Depreciation charge		
Warehouse fittings	1,600	
Van	1,300	
Discounts allowed	1,100	
Total expenses		25,920
Profit for the year for year		11,900

Statement of financial position as at 31 May 20X1

	£	£
Non-current assets		
Warehouse fittings (8,000 – 1,600)		6,400
Van (6,500 – 1,300)		5,200
		11,600
Current assets		
Inventory	16,000	
Trade receivables	19,000	
Prepayment (rates)	1,600	
Cash at bank	900	
	37,500	
Current liabilities		
Trade payables	20,000	
Accruals (500 + 500)	1,000	
	21,000	
Net current assets		16,500
Net assets		28,100
Capital (W)		29,300
Add: capital introduced (caravan sale)		2,500
Add: profit for year		11,900
		43,700
Less: drawings		15,600
Closing capital (proprietor's funds)		28,100

FINANCIAL ACCOUNTING: PREPARING FINANCIAL STATEMENTS

Working

The opening capital can be entered as the balancing figure on the statement of financial position. Alternatively, it can be proved as follows:

	£
Fittings	8,000
Inventory	10,000
Receivables	16,000
Payables	(15,000)
Prepayments	1,200
Accruals	(700)
Bank	9,800
	29,300

Test your understanding 9

(a)

	£	%
Sales revenue	200,000	160
Cost of goods sold		100
Gross profit ($\frac{60}{160} \times 200{,}000$)	75,000	60

(b)

	£	%
Sales = $((\frac{100}{70}) \times 210{,}000)$	300,000	100
Cost of goods sold (see below)	210,000	70
Gross profit	90,000	30

Cost of goods sold	
Opening inventory	40,000
Purchases	180,000
Closing inventory	(10,000)
	210,000

Test your understanding 10

Task 10.1

Total purchases

	£
Purchase of inventory bought in October	1,800
Purchases (bank)	18,450
Cash payments	3,800
Closing payables	1,400
	25,450

Task 10.2

Cost of goods sold

	£
Purchases	25,450
Less closing inventory	2,200
	23,250

Task 10.3

Sales for the year

If GP margin on sales is 50% then sales are £23,250 × $\dfrac{100}{50}$ = £46,500

Task 10.4

Cash account

	£		£
Cash sales	46,500	Bankings	27,000
		Materials	3,800
		General expenses	490
		Drawings (bal fig)	15,110
		Float balance c/d	100
	46,500		**46,500**

Task 10.5

	£
Cash drawings (from Task 4)	15,110
Bank	6,200
	21,310

Task 10.6

	£
Gross profit	23,250
Less expenses:	
General expenses (870 + 490)	(1,360)
Depreciation (4,000 × 1/5)	(800)
Profit for the year	21,090

Test your understanding 11

Task 11.1

Capital at 1 January 20X8

	£
Bank	25,000
Trade receivables	20,000
Computers	4,600
Trade payables	(13,000)
Capital	36,600

Tutorial note. Remember that capital equals net assets. You therefore have to list all the assets and liabilities at the start of the year to find the net assets and therefore the capital.

Task 11.2
Journal

Account name	Dr (£)	Cr (£)
Irrecoverable debt expense	3,400	
Receivables ledger control account		3,400
Narrative	Being the irrecoverable debt	

Task 11.3
Receivables ledger control account

	£		£
Balance b/d 1 Jan 20X8	20,000	Cash from receivables	80,000
		Irrecoverable debt	3,400
		Contra with PLCA	300
Credit sales (bal fig)	93,700	Balance c/d 31 Dec 20X8	30,000
	113,700		113,700

Task 11.4
Payables ledger control account

	£		£
Paid to payables	10,000	Balance b/d 1 Jan 20X8	13,000
Contra with RLCA	300		
Balance c/d 31 Dec 20X8	15,000	Purchases (bal fig)	12,300
	25,300		25,300

Task 11.5
General expenses account

	£		£
Cash paid	8,000	SPL	5,500
		Balance c/d	2,500
	8,000		8,000

Tutorial note: The insurance payment of £3,000 includes a prepayment of £3,000 × 10/12 = £2,500.

Task 11.6

Depreciation for the year ended 31 December 20X8

	£
Carrying amount at 1 January 20X8	4,600
Depreciation for the year at 40%	1,840
	2,760

Task 11.7

Journal

Account name	Dr (£)	Cr (£)
Depreciation expense	1,840	
Accumulated dep'n – computers		1,840
Narrative	Being the depreciation for the non-current assets for the year	

Task 11.8

Trial balance as at 31 December 20X8

	£	£
Capital at 1 October 20X7		36,600
Bank	32,000	
Sales		93,700
Receivables ledger control a/c	30,000	
Purchases	12,300	
Payables ledger control a/c		15,000
Advertising	10,000	
General expenses	5,500	
Prepayment – general expenses	2,500	
Rent	9,000	
Drawings	36,000	
Depreciation charge	1,840	
Irrecoverable debt expense	3,400	
Computers	2,760	
	145,300	145,300

FINANCIAL ACCOUNTING: PREPARING FINANCIAL STATEMENTS

The interpretation of profitability ratios

Introduction

This chapter considers how financial statements can be interpreted using profitability ratios. With each of these ratios you need to understand not only how to calculate the ratio, but how to interpret it. You should understand what changes to the ratio could indicate and whether they reflect positive or negative results for the business.

Ratios can aid planning, decision making and the control of businesses. Learners should be able to determine whether a ratio is better or worse than a comparative. Those comparatives may be another organisation, another time period i.e. the prior year, or an industry standard. It is essential that learners know the importance of professional scepticism.

ASSESSMENT CRITERIA	CONTENTS
Calculate profitability ratios (8.1)	1 Profitability ratios
The interpretation of profitability ratios (8.2)	2 The interpretation of profitability ratios

The interpretation of profitability ratios: Chapter 18

1 Profitability ratios

1.1 Introduction

 Definition – Profitability

Profitability is the ability of a business to earn a profit based on the use of resources.

Performing an analysis of profitability is crucial to identify new growth opportunities that can help drive a business forward. It can improve visibility for future performance. Having the right insight and strategy can enable management to change its direction as required to be as effective as possible in operations.

1.2 Using ratios

Ratios use simple calculations based upon the interactions in sets of data, for various users to analyse and interpret financial accounts. For Financial Accounting: Preparing Financial Statements we focus upon the use of profitability ratios, which may also be known as performance ratios. They compare the profit figures from the statement of profit or loss with other figures, and are often presented as percentages.

Calculating the ratios is only one step in the analysis process. When that is done, the results are analysed against comparisons. Comparisons are commonly made between:

- previous accounting periods
- industry averages
- budgets and expectations
- government statistics
- other ratios.

When analysing data, the following points should serve as a useful checklist:

- What does the ratio mean?
- What does a change in the ratio mean?
- What is the expectation or the norm?
- What are the limitations of the ratio?

FINANCIAL ACCOUNTING: PREPARING FINANCIAL STATEMENTS

 Test your understanding 1

Identify whether the following statements are true or false.

Statement 1

Only internal management are interested in the results of ratio analysis.

Statement 2

In order to be useful, ratio analysis should be performed in comparison to either previous results, an industry benchmark or with different organisations.

We will now consider the profitability ratios learners are required to understand:

- Gross profit margin
- Net profit margin
- Return on capital employed
- Expense over revenue percentage

1.3 Gross profit margin

The gross profit margin is calculated as:

$$\frac{\text{Gross profit}}{\text{Sales revenue}} \times 100$$

Gross profit represents the difference between sales revenue and cost of sales. The gross profit margin works out the proportion of sales revenue that becomes gross profit. The margin works this out in percentage terms on an average basis across all sales for the year.

Different industries will have different expectations of margins. Some businesses have a high volume of sales, with low margins, whereas others will have a lower volume of sales but with higher margins.

 Test your understanding 2

Leo had sales of £15,000 and a gross profit of £5,000.

What is Leo's gross profit margin?

Test your understanding 3

Bennu had sales of £20,000 and cost of sales of £15,400.

What is Bennu's gross profit margin?

1.4 Gross profit margin versus gross profit mark-up

Profit margin and mark-up are different accounting terms that use the same components, yet show a slightly different perspective. Both gross profit margin and gross profit mark-up use sales revenue and costs as part of their calculation.

Profit margin refers to sales minus the cost of goods sold. Mark-up refers to the amount by which the cost of a good is increased in order to get to the final selling price.

As seen in the earlier Chapter reviewing incomplete records, the cost structures under 'margin' and 'mark-up' are detailed below:

Gross profit margin structure:

	%	Illustrative %	Illustrative £
Sales revenue	100	100	800
Cost of goods sold	100 – margin	75	600
Gross profit	Margin	25	200

Gross profit mark-up structure:

	%	Illustrative %	Illustrative £
Sales revenue	100 + mark-up	125	750
Cost of goods sold	100	100	600
Gross profit	mark-up	25	150

 Test your understanding 4

If the selling price of a product was £700, and gross profit mark-up was 40%, what was the cost of the product?

1.5 Net profit margin

The net profit margin is calculated as:

$$\frac{\text{Profit for the year}}{\text{Sales revenue}} \times 100$$

Net profit represents the difference between sales revenue and all costs i.e. the overall profit made for the year. The net profit margin is an expansion of the gross profit margin and includes all of the expenses and other items that come after gross profit.

The net profit margin works out the proportion of sales revenue that becomes net profit. The margin works this out in percentage terms on an average basis across all sales for the year.

> **Test your understanding 5**
>
> The following extract relates to X Co for the years ended 30 June 20X5 and 20X6.
>
> | | 20X5 £ | 20X6 £ |
> |---|---|---|
> | Revenue | 20,000 | 26,000 |
> | Cost of sales | (15,400) | (21,050) |
> | Gross profit | 4,600 | 4,950 |
> | Less expenses | (2,460) | (2,770) |
> | Net profit | 2,140 | 2,180 |
>
> What was the net profit margin for 20X5 and 20X6?

> **Test your understanding 6**
>
> The statement of profit or loss for Rudi and Alex, for the year ended 31 December 20X1 are presented below:
>
> | | Rudi £ | Alex £ |
> |---|---|---|
> | Revenue | 987,000 | 567,000 |
> | Cost of sales | (564,000) | (336,000) |
> | Gross profit | 423,000 | 231,000 |
> | Less expenses | (240,560) | (120,090) |
> | Net profit | 182,440 | 110,910 |
>
> Using the individual financial statements for Rudi and Alex, calculate the gross profit margins and net profit margins for the year ended 31 December 20X1. Answers should be stated to one decimal place.
>
> Gross profit margin
>
> Rudi
>
> Alex
>
> Net profit margin
>
> Rudi
>
> Alex

1.6 Return on capital employed (ROCE)

People who invest their money in a business are interested in the return that business is earning on that capital. Expressing this return in the form of a ratio enables comparison with other possible investment opportunities.

ROCE measures how much net profit is generated for every £1 capital invested in the business.

$$\text{ROCE} = \frac{\text{Profit for the year}}{\text{Capital employed}} \times 100$$

Where capital employed = capital + non-current liabilities.

Test your understanding 7

GHI Ltd has a net profit for the year of £9,100. The capital balance is £15,000 and long term loans total £3,925 at the year end. Calculate the return on capital employed and state your answer to two decimal places.

1.7 Expense over revenue percentage

The expense over revenue percentage is calculated to show the relationship between an individual expense or a group of expenses and sales revenue.

It is calculated as:

$$\frac{\text{Expense}}{\text{Sales revenue}} \times 100$$

Test your understanding 8

Admin expenses are £15,000 and sales are £750,000.

In percentage terms, what are admin expenses as a proportion of sales?

Test your understanding 9

You have already calculated the selling expenses / sales revenue percentage of a business for the current year to be 20%. The same ratio was calculated for the prior year at 25%.

Does this decrease in selling expenses / sales revenue percentage show an improvement or a deterioration?

1.8 Relationship between the SPL and SFP

The statement of profit or loss and the statement of financial position are interrelated. The net profit figure in the statement of profit or loss is added to the capital section in the statement of financial position, to alter the overall total. In the case of a net loss figure, this would be deducted from the capital section in the statement of financial position, to alter the overall total.

2 The interpretation of profitability ratios

2.1 Planning, decision making and control for businesses

Definition – Planning

Planning is the detailed formulation of activities to achieve defined objectives.

Planning takes into consideration where a business is, where it wants to be and therefore how it will get there.

Definition – Decision making

Decision making is the process of deciding upon a solution based upon a number of alternatives.

Definition – Control

Control is monitoring the performance of a business in comparison to its objectives, in order to know if the objectives are being met and if not, what corrective action should be taken.

2.2 Factors that may cause changes in a business's ratios and differences between businesses' ratios

When performing ratio analysis, you will be required to consider what factors impact the result of ratios. We will consider each of the profitability ratios in turn, in order to identify factors that cause variations.

Gross profit margin

Changes in this ratio may be attributable to changes in:

- selling prices
- product mix i.e. range and quantities of products being sold
- purchase costs
- production costs for a manufacturing business
- inventory valuations.

Comparing gross profit margin over time

If gross profit has not increased in line with sales revenue, you need to establish why not. The discrepancy could be due to a number of factors, such as:

- increased 'purchase' costs: if so, are the costs under the control of the business (i.e. does the business manufacture the goods sold)?
- inventory write-offs (this could be likely where the business operates in a volatile marketplace where things quickly become undesirable, such as fashion retail)? or
- other costs allocated to cost of sales

Comparison of margins can be very useful, it is especially important to compare businesses within the same sector. For example, food retailing is able to support low margins because of the high volume of sales. Jewellers would usually need higher margins to offset lower sales volumes.

Low margins usually suggest poor performance but may be due to expansion costs (launching a new product) or trying to increase market share. Lower margins than usual suggest scope for improvement. Some businesses choose to adopt a pricing strategy where a product is sold at a price below its market cost, the product is known as a 'loss leader'. The aim is to stimulate interest and sales of other more profitable goods or services.

Above-average margins are usually a sign of good management although unusually high margins may make the competition keen to join in and enjoy the 'rich pickings'.

Test your understanding 10

Review the statements below and state whether each of the four scenarios would increase or decrease the gross profit margin.

Statement 1

Sales revenue over the years has remained stable, but costs have increased.

Statement 2

Sales revenue and costs have both decreased but costs by a greater proportion.

Statement 3

There was a change in the sales mix which resulted in a higher proportion of more profitable products being sold in the current year.

Statement 4

The business earned new trade discounts from key suppliers.

Net profit margin

If the gross profit margin is a measure of how profitably a business can produce and sell its products and services, the net profit margin also measures how effectively the business manages and administers that process.

Therefore, if the gross profit margin has remained consistent but the net profit margin has changed consider the following possibilities (these represent suggestions; it is not a comprehensive list):

- changes in employment patterns (recruitment, redundancy etc.)
- changes to depreciation due to large investment in or disposals of non-current assets
- significant write-offs of irrecoverable debts
- changes in rental agreements
- significant advertising costs incurred
- rapidly changing fuel costs.

This ratio is affected by more factors than the gross profit margin but it is equally useful to users and if the business does not disclose cost of sales, it may be used on its own in lieu of the gross profit percentage.

In arriving at net profit in the statement of profit or loss, there are many more factors to consider. If you are provided with a breakdown of expenses you can use this for further line-by-line comparisons. Bear in mind that:

- some costs are fixed or semi-fixed (e.g. property costs) and therefore not expected to change in line with revenue
- other costs are variable (e.g. packing and distribution, and commission).

Return on capital employed (ROCE)

This is an important analysis tool as it allows us to assess how much profit the business generates from the capital invested in it. Profit margins of different businesses are not necessarily comparable due to different sizes and business structures. You could have one business that makes high profits but based on huge levels of investment. Investors may decide that they can make similar returns in different businesses without such a high initial investment required.

When calculated, ROCE should be compared with:

- previous years' figures – provided there have been no changes in accounting policies, or suitable adjustments have been made to enable comparison. The effect of not replacing non-current assets is that their value will decrease and ROCE will increase.

- the target ROCE of the business
- other businesses in the same industry – care is required in interpretation, because of the possibility, noted above, of different accounting policies, ages of non-current assets, etc.

The ratio also shows how efficiently a business is using its resources. If the return on capital employed is very low, the business may be better off selling its assets and investing the proceeds in a high interest bank account. This may seem extreme, but should be considered particularly for a small, unprofitable business with valuable assets such as property. Furthermore, a low return can easily become a loss if the business suffers a downturn.

In principle, a higher ROCE indicates that a business has made better use of its resources to generate operating profit. However, this may be affected by the choice of accounting policies and business practices applied by an individual business as follows:

- if a business revalued its land and buildings, the value of capital employed will increase, with no increase in productive or operational activity to increase profit for the year. In this situation, ROCE is likely to fall.

- if a business has property, plant and equipment which is coming to the end of its expected useful lives, it will have a relatively low net carrying amount. This will reduce capital employed, with the consequence that it will increase ROCE.

- if a business invests in new property, plant and equipment, this will increase capital employed immediately (therefore reduce ROCE in the short-term), and it may be some time before this is reflected by an increase in profits in future years.

Test your understanding 11

Choose the appropriate words from the available options to complete the following two statements relating to the return on capital employed ratio.

Statement 1
If a business has property, plant and equipment which is coming to the end of its expected useful life, this will result in an *increase/decrease* to ROCE.

Statement 2
If a business invests in new property, plant and equipment, this will *increase/decrease* ROCE in the short term.

The interpretation of profitability ratios: Chapter 18

 Test your understanding 12

Would each of the following statements show an increase or decrease in the return on capital employed percentage?

Statement 1
The business reduced long-term borrowings during 20X8.

Statement 2
The business managed to increase profit margin during 20X8.

2.3 Advantages of ratio analysis

- Ratio analysis can validate or disprove business decisions. This is achieved by ratios providing summarised information for managers to focus upon.

- It simplifies more complex accounting statements and financial data.

- Drawing management's attention towards issues that need addressing but also highlights positives.

- Allows the business to conduct comparisons with others and industry standards.

2.4 Limitations of ratio analysis

- A business can make some year-end changes to their financial statements, to improve their ratios i.e. window dressing which will distort ratios.

- Ratios ignore changes caused by inflation as they are calculated using historical costs and overlook any changes in price level between the periods.

- Accounting ratios don't consider the qualitative aspects of a business, such as business reputation.

- There are no standard definitions of the ratios. Different business may use slightly different formulas.

- Accounting ratios do not resolve the financial problems of a business.

2.5 The importance of professional scepticism when interpreting financial information

Accountants should ensure they are applying professional scepticism, when assessing the reasonableness of results based upon interpretation of financial information.

> **Definition**
>
> Professional scepticism is an attitude that includes a questioning mind, being alert to conditions which may indicate possible misstatement.

It is important to take a step back and consider if the result of a ratio seems reasonable. We may reflect upon previous year's results or against expectations. Exercising scepticism is considering whether there are any factors which may distort the findings of a ratio. There should be a degree of caution exercised in interpretation which avoids drawing simplistic or dogmatic conclusions. Ratios rarely answer questions but can highlight areas where questions can be asked.

The ROCE ratio involves the use of statement of financial position figures i.e. capital employed. Ratios using statement of financial position figures should be interpreted with caution since the statement of financial position shows the position at a specific date only and this may not be typical of the average position. This point is particularly important when considering a ratio, such as ROCE, which is based on a statement of financial position figure as well as a figure from the statement of profit or loss. This is because one figure, the capital employed, relates to a specific date whereas profit for the year is a total for a period of time.

The main point of consideration is to ensure ratio analysis is used in combination with other analysis such as simple year on year comparisons in movement.

3 Summary

This chapter has introduced profitability ratios – how they are calculated and what information they can provide. Once ratios are calculated, comparisons can be drawn. These comparisons can be in relation to previous years, a competitor's or expected performance. Caution should be exercised and professional scepticism applied. In doing so, awareness will be raised of factors that may distort the results of that analysis.

Test your understanding answers

Test your understanding 1

Identify whether the following statements are true or false.

Statement 1

Only internal management are interested in the results of ratio analysis.

FALSE – there are many different users of accounts that would be interested in the results of ratio analysis.

Statement 2

In order to be useful, ratio analysis should be performed in comparison to either previous results, an industry benchmark or with different organisations.

TRUE – ratio analysis is useful when there are comparisons.

Test your understanding 2

To calculate Leo's gross profit margin, the gross profit is divided by sales.

The gross profit margin is calculated as £5,000 / £15,000 × 100 = 33%.

Test your understanding 3

To calculate Bennu's gross profit margin, the gross profit is divided by sales.

Gross profit has not been provided and so needs to be calculated by deducting cost of sales from sales.

Sales £20,000 less cost of sales £15,400 equals a gross profit of £4,600.

The gross profit margin is calculated as £4,600 / £20,000 × 100 = 23%.

Test your understanding 4

Cost of the product £500.

Selling price 140% £700
Cost of sales 100% £500   £700 × 100/140
Gross profit   40%?

Sales price of £700 represents 140%, therefore 1% can be calculated as £700/140 = £5. When using mark-up, cost represents 100%.
£5 × 100% = £500

Test your understanding 5

20X5 (£2,140 / £20,000) × 100 = 10.7%
20X6 (£2,180 / £26,000) × 100 = 8.4%

Test your understanding 6

Gross profit margin

Rudi £423,000 / £987,000 × 100 = 42.9%

Alex £231,000 / £567,000 × 100 = 40.7%

Net profit margin

Rudi £182,440 / £987,000 × 100 = 18.5%

Alex £110,910 / £567,000 × 100 = 19.6%

Test your understanding 7

Return on capital employed is calculated as:

(Profit for the year / capital employed) × 100

(£9,100 / £18,925*) × 100 = 48.08%.

*Capital employed is capital of £15,000 plus non-current liabilities of £3,925 = £18,925.

 Test your understanding 8

Admin expenses as a proportion of sales is calculated as:

£15,000 / £750,000 × 100 = 2%

 Test your understanding 9

If the selling expenses / sales revenue percentage has decreased by 5%, this shows that selling expenses are not as significant a proportion as they were in comparison to sales revenue. This is therefore an improvement in this percentage.

FINANCIAL ACCOUNTING: PREPARING FINANCIAL STATEMENTS

Test your understanding 10

Statement 1

Sales revenue over the years has remained stable, but costs have increased. **DECREASE to the gross profit margin.**

Statement 2

Sales revenue and costs have both decreased but costs by a greater proportion. **INCREASE to the gross profit margin.**

Statement 3

There was a change in the sales mix which resulted in a higher proportion of more profitable products being sold in the current year. **INCREASE to the gross profit margin.**

Statement 4

The business earned new trade discounts from key suppliers. **INCREASE to the gross profit margin.**

Test your understanding 11

Statement 1

If a business has property, plant and equipment which is coming to the end of its expected useful life, this will result in an *increase* to ROCE.

Statement 2

If a business invests in new property, plant and equipment, this will *decrease* ROCE in the short term.

Test your understanding 12

Statement 1

A reduction in long term borrowing would reduce capital employed which in turn would increase the return on capital employed percentage.

Statement 2

Similarly, an improved profit margin would increase profit, and therefore lead to an increase in the ratio.

FINANCIAL ACCOUNTING: PREPARING FINANCIAL STATEMENTS

Appendix 1 - International accounting terminology and the alternatives

AAT Q2022

Accounting terminology used in Kaplan learning materials

The Kaplan AAT Q2022 publications and related learning materials employ a range of terminology, in addition to the international accounting terminology used by AAT in its final unit specifications.

The mocks within our Study Texts and Exam Kits use terminology consistent with that in the AAT unit specifications.

This approach is adopted for the following reasons:

1. it aids and supports understanding of terminology and principles relevant to learners not only in their AAT studies but also throughout their practical training and employment

2. it aids and supports understanding by learners of their workplace activities where a range of terminology is used, or may be used, as and when they join the workforce

3. it aids learners throughout their studies, particularly those who commenced their studies under AQ2016 and are continuing under Q2022, or have transferred their studies from another training provider

4. our learning materials are written by expert tutors whose experience it is that learners do value this approach as it helps to provide clarification and understanding

5. it is also important for learners to know what they will encounter in their live assessments.

Many AAT learners will also be training as apprentices. Apprenticeship programmes require learners to develop appropriate technical knowledge, alongside work-relevant skills such as effective communication. Exposure to a range of terminology will help to support learners to develop this understanding of the different terminology used in their studies, their workplaces and in their everyday life, including in the press and media.

Examples

Examples of alternative terminology used in the news media include a BBC website item on the balance sheets of Irish banks on 18 January 2022, and, on 21 January 2022, it had an item on surplus Amazon stock being given away. The Times reported on a business collapse on 10 January 2022 with reference to its creditors and many other similar uses of alternative terminology in the news could be highlighted.

Alternative terminology is regularly used in recruitment adverts for job opportunities. Here are some recent examples:

'……are currently recruiting for the position of a Purchase Ledger Supervisor who will be based at our office in ….. The role is responsible for supervising a Purchase ledger team of 5….'

'We are looking for a Finance Administrator to assist with processing & inputting information in payroll and maintaining the purchase ledger. Finance Administrator responsibilities include….'

'An excellent opportunity to join a multibillion turnover, Global Leader in the automotive sector as a Purchase Ledger Clerk. You will utilise your skills in Accounting and Finance to work alongside this high performing accounts team. As you continue to enhance your skills development to senior and lead positions within the department will be available….You will be an integral part of the accounts team leading the way on multicurrency ERP systems.'

Within the Kaplan UK finance function, there are further examples of occupied posts. There is, for example, a 'Sales Ledger Assistant' and a 'Sales Ledger Manager'.

During your working life you will encounter a range of accounting terminology, and this will continue to evolve. A transfer to another department in the workplace, or a move to a new employer may well expose you to different terminology. Communicating with non-accountants in the workplace may also mean that you have to understand the alternatives that others are familiar with.

Activities

We have prepared a glossary of terms which maps this alternative terminology that is used on occasion in Kaplan's learning materials[1].

In many cases, the relevant study text includes a statement highlighting both the international accounting standards terminology used by AAT in its assessments and the equivalent alternatives.

Why not add the definitions of these terms to the glossary below as a reminder when you come across the alternative terminology in the workplace or in your everyday life that it has exactly the same meaning.

Then test your knowledge of accounting terminology with our crossword and "match the terms" activities.

International accounting terminology and the alternatives: **Chapter 19**

Glossary of terms

International accounting standards terminology	Alternative terminology	Complete the table by adding a definition
Inventory	Stock	
Non-current assets	Fixed assets	
Payable	Creditor	
Payables ledger	Purchases ledger Creditors ledger	
Payables ledger control account (PLCA)	Purchases ledger control account (PLCA) Creditors ledger control account (CLCA)	

Receivable	Debtor	
Receivables ledger	Sales ledger Debtors ledger	
Receivables ledger control account (RLCA)	Sales ledger control account (SLCA) Debtors ledger control account (DLCA)	
Allowance for doubtful receivables Allowance for doubtful debts	Doubtful debt provision	
Statement of financial position	Balance sheet	
Statement of profit or loss	Income statement	

Accounting Crossword

Test your knowledge of accounting terminology with the following crossword. The answers contain a mixture of international accounting standards terminology and some alternatives.

Across:

3   An international accounting standards word used to describe an amount due to the business from a customer. (10)

6   How would amounts held in a bank current account be presented in the statement of financial position? (7,5)

8   A bank loan due for repayment in five years is an example of this type of liability. (3-7)

10 An example of a non-current asset. (4)

12 If a business owes money to a supplier, it is often referred to as 'a _____ of the business'. (8)

13 'Early _____' discount is another term used for prompt payment discount. (10)

FINANCIAL ACCOUNTING: PREPARING FINANCIAL STATEMENTS

Down:

1 A word traditionally used to describe an amount due to the business from a customer. (6)

2 An amount introduced into the business by the owner. (7)

4 An estimate of an expense incurred but not yet paid. (7)

5 Another word for goods held for resale. (9)

7 Double entry bookkeeping consists of 'debits and _____'. (7)

9 The document produced by a business when it has sold goods to a customer on credit which is then recorded in a daybook. (7)

11 '_____ discount' is a term used to describe a reduction in the unit price of goods sold due to the quantity purchased by the customer. (5)

Match the terms

Test your knowledge of accounting terminology by finding a matching term for each item in the first column. Make your selection from the available options in the final column. The activity contains a mixture of international accounting standards terminology and some alternatives.

Term	Match	Options
Bad debt		Long-term liability
Doubtful debt provision		Value added tax
Equity		Sole proprietor
Fixed asset		Early settlement discount
Non-current liability		Capital
Prompt payment discount		Irrecoverable debt
Sales tax		Allowance for receivables
Sole trader		Non-current asset

International accounting terminology and the alternatives: Chapter 19

Solutions

Accounting crossword

			¹D					²C				
		³R	E	C	E	I	V	A	B	L	E	
			B					P				
			T					I				
⁴A			O			⁵I		T				
⁶C	U	R	R	E	N	T	A	S	S	E	T	
C						V		L				
R						E			⁷C			
U				⁸N	O	N-	C	U	R	R	E	N	T
A		⁹I				T			E			
¹⁰L	A	N	D			O			D			¹¹T
		V		¹²C	R	E	D	I	T	O	R
		O			Y			T			A
		I						S			D
		C									E
	¹³S	E	T	T	L	E	M	E	N	T	

Match the terms

Term	Match
Bad debt	Irrecoverable debt
Doubtful debt provision	Allowance for receivables
Equity	Capital
Fixed asset	Non-current asset
Non-current liability	Long-term liability
Prompt payment discount	Early settlement discount
Sales tax	Value added tax
Sole trader	Sole proprietor

Add your own notes below as you encounter uses of international accounting standards terminology and their alternatives

MOCK ASSESSMENT

FINANCIAL ACCOUNTING: PREPARING FINANCIAL STATEMENTS

1. Mock Assessment Questions – AQ2022

The assessment is 2.5 hours long and consists of 6 tasks. You should attempt all of the tasks.

- Each task is independent. You will not need to refer to your answers to previous tasks.
- The total number of marks for this assessment is 120.
- Read every task carefully to make sure you understand what is required.
- Where the date is relevant, it is given in the task data.
- Both minus signs and brackets can be used to indicate negative numbers **unless** task instructions state otherwise.
- You must use a full stop to indicate a decimal point. For example, write 100.57 **not** 100,57 or 10057.
- You may use a comma to indicate a number in the thousands, but you don't have to. For example, 10000 and 10,000 are both acceptable.
- The VAT rate is 20%.

Mock Assessment Questions

Task 1 (28 marks)

This task is about using daybooks, and accounting for and monitoring non-current assets.

(a) Identify whether the statements below are true or false (4 marks)

Statement	True	False
Digital bookkeeping systems can produce automated calculations for items such as depreciation		
The non-current asset register is one of the books of prime entry		
Recording capital expenditure within non-current assets is an application of the going concern principle		
Including items incorrectly within capital expenditure rather than revenue expenditure results in an overstatement of profit		

(b) Match each of the following descriptions to the correct definition (4 marks)

Description	Definition
The estimated value at the end of an asset's useful life	
The length of time the company expects to use the asset	
The cost of an asset less its residual value	
The cost of an asset less accumulated depreciation	

Definition picklist: Carrying amount, depreciable amount, useful life, residual value

FINANCIAL ACCOUNTING: PREPARING FINANCIAL STATEMENTS

You are working for Paul Futcher, a sole trader. Paul would like you to update his non-current asset register to reflect the following transactions which occurred during the year ended 31 December 20X3.

- On 1 January 20X3 Paul acquired some new computer equipment (serial no DL45G) for £6,000. In addition to this, Paul acquired a year's subscription to anti-virus software for £200.

- On 1 July 20X3, Paul sold a motor vehicle (licence JT14 TGF) for £4,000. This vehicle had cost Paul £9,000 on 1 January 20X1.

- Paul applies all depreciation on a pro-rata basis for the number of months the item has been owned. Computer equipment is depreciated on a 25% diminishing balance basis. Motor vehicles are depreciated on a straight-line basis over 5 years, assuming no residual value.

(c) (i) Enter the acquisition, disposal and current year depreciation charges into the non-current asset register

(10 marks)

Description	Acq'n date	Cost £	Dep'n charges £	Carrying amount £	Disposal proceeds £	Disposal date £
Computer:						
DL24F	1/1/X1	11,000				
Y/E 31/12/X1			2,750	8,250		
Y/E 31/12/X2			2,062.5	6,187.5		
Y/E 31/12/X3						
DL45G						
Y/E 31/12/X3						
Vehicles:						
JT14 TGF	1/1/X1	9,000				
Y/E 31/12/X1			1,800	7,200		
Y/E 31/12/X2			1,800	6,400		
Y/E 31/12/X3						

Mock Assessment Questions

(c) (ii) Complete the disposals account for the disposal of the vehicle, showing clearly any amount to be transferred to the statement of profit or loss. Ensure any balancing figure is shown on the bottom row. **(8 marks)**

Disposals			
	£		£
Total		Total	

Picklist: Vehicles cost, vehicles accumulated depreciation, depreciation expense, statement of profit or loss, Cash book, balance b/d, balance c/d

(d) Which TWO of the following could lead to the total on the non-current asset register exceeding the total on the general ledger? **(2 marks)**

	✓
Disposal proceeds have been omitted from the register	
A disposal has been omitted from the register	
An addition of a new asset has been omitted from the register	
Depreciation charges have been omitted from the register	

FINANCIAL ACCOUNTING: PREPARING FINANCIAL STATEMENTS

Task 2 (14 marks)

This task is about recording period end adjustments.

You have the following information regarding Paul's rental income during the year ended 31 December 20X3.

On 31 December 20X2 an entry was made into the rental income account for £1,200 in relation to prepaid income. This entry needs to be reversed from the prepaid income account in the current year.

Cash book entries for the year relating to rental income are £15,000. In January 20X4 Paul invoiced the customer £4,500 in respect of the three months to 31 January 20X4.

(a) Complete the rental income account for the year ended 31 December 20X3, ensuring the account is balanced off appropriately. Any balancing value should be shown on the bottom row of the account on the appropriate side. (8 marks)

Rental income

Details	Amount £	Details	Amount £
Total		Total	

Picklist: Balance b/d, balance c/d, accrued income, prepaid income, statement of profit or loss, cash book

Paul's allowance for doubtful receivables at 1 January 20X3 was £1,240.

At 31 December 20X3 Paul would like you to write off a balance of £850 from a customer who has gone into liquidation. Following that, Paul would like you to adjust the general allowance for doubtful receivables in line with the company policy.

The policy is to make a general allowance of 2% of the total receivables balance. The total of the receivables ledger control account before any adjustments at 31 December 20X3 is £58,400.

Mock Assessment Questions

(b) (i) Produce the journal entry to adjust for the write-off of the receivables balance. **(2 marks)**

Account	Debit £	Credit £

Picklist: Allowance for doubtful receivables, receivables ledger control account, irrecoverable debts, sales

(b) (ii) Produce the journal entry to adjust the allowance for doubtful receivables. **(2 marks)**

Account	Debit £	Credit £

Picklist: Allowance for doubtful receivables, receivables ledger control account, allowance for doubtful receivables adjustment, sales

(c) Identify whether an increase in the following items would be shown as a debit or credit in the statement of financial position. **(2 marks)**

Account	Debit ✓	Credit ✓
Prepayments		
Closing inventory: Statement of financial position		

FINANCIAL ACCOUNTING: PREPARING FINANCIAL STATEMENTS

Task 3 (24 marks)

This task is about producing, adjusting, checking and extending the trial balance.

You are working for Nish Mortimer, a sole trader that needs help finalising his financial statements for the year ended 31 December 20X3.

(a) **Identify the impact the following transactions will have on the accounting equation for Nish.** (5 marks)

Transaction	Assets	Liabilities	Capital
Recording a year-end accrual for electricity costs owed			
Receiving cash from a credit customer			
Recording depreciation expense for the year			
Writing off an irrecoverable receivable balance			
Recording closing inventory			

Picklist: Increase, decrease, no effect

Nish has asked you to complete his bank reconciliation for the year. The balance on Nish's bank statement is £1,430 but the balance on the cashbook shows a credit balance of £350.

Nish has identified the following items on the bank statement that have not been recorded in the cashbook:

- Interest earned of £14
- A direct debit for broadband of £68

Nish has also recorded a few year-end items in the cashbook that are yet to clear the bank. These are:

- Cheques for £2,040 sent out on 30 December 20X3
- Deposit of £206 paid into the bank on 31 December 20X3

(a) (i) What should the corrected cashbook balance be recorded as in Nish's financial statements? (1 Mark)

£ ⬜

Mock Assessment Questions

(b) (ii) Using the corrected cashbook total, produce the bank reconciliation statement for Nish at 31 December 20X3.

(5 marks)

Bank reconciliation statement	
Balance per bank statement	
Add:	
Less:	
Balance per cash book	

Picklist: Unpresented cheques, uncleared lodgements, direct debit

Nish is also looking at the trade payables by comparing the payables ledger control account to the payables ledger. He has found a number of differences between them and is unsure what to do for the financial statements for the year ended 31 December 20X3.

(c) Identify the correct action for Nish to take in the following situations to correct trade payables at 31 December 20X3.

(3 marks)

Transaction	Action to take
Invoice 456 from Reeves Ltd, a regular supplier. A check at the warehouse show the goods were received on 30 December 20X3.	
Invoice 457 from Reeves Ltd. You do not recognise the description of the goods detailed on the invoice and the warehouse is unsure what the invoice relates to	
Invoice 458 from Reeves Ltd. A check at the warehouse show the goods were received on 6 January 20X4.	

Picklist: Omit item from financial statements, include item within trade payables, query with supplier

FINANCIAL ACCOUNTING: PREPARING FINANCIAL STATEMENTS

Nish has now drafted a trial balance, but there are still a few errors to correct, which are:

- Closing inventory of £17,400 has been omitted
- A credit purchase of £400 was credited to trade payables and purchases
- Depreciation of £450 was recorded correctly in depreciation expense but credited to the cost account of non-current assets
- Capital introduced of £3,000 was debited to the bank but no other entry made
- A credit sale was incorrectly recorded at £540 rather than £450

(d) **Correct the following errors by entering adjustments in the extended trial balance.** (10 marks)

	Dr £	Cr £	Adj Dr £	Adj Cr £
Capital		28,400		
Non-current assets – Cost	44,500			
NC assets – Acc dep'n		21,400		
Closing inventory – SFP				
Closing inventory – SPL				
Prepayments	2,560			
Accruals		740		
Trade payables		10,430		
Sales revenue		154,760		
Bank	21,100			
Rent	45,320			
Wages	34,540			
Trade receivables	4,500			
VAT		3,840		
Purchases	48,720			
Advertising expenses	6,420			
Depreciation expense	3,900			
Opening inventory	10,210			
Suspense		2,200		
Total	221,770	221,770		

Mock Assessment Questions

Task 4 (24 marks)

This task is about producing financial statements for sole traders and partnerships.

You have the following trial balance for a partnership known as Toure Trading. All the necessary year-end adjustments have been made. The partners are Yaya and Kolo; they share profits 70:30 with Yaya taking the larger share.

Use a minus sign to indicate the following ONLY:

- a net loss for the year
- the closing inventory figure.

(a) **Prepare a statement of profit or loss for the business for the year ended 31 December 20X3.** (10 marks)

Toure Trading Trial balance as at 31 December 20X3		
	Dr £	Cr £
Accruals		7,175
Bank	6,125	
Closing inventory	34,125	34,125
Capital – Yaya		8,900
Capital – Kolo		8,900
Current– Yaya		1,610
Current – Kolo	1,300	
Depreciation charge	12,425	
Discounts allowed	2,360	
Drawings – Yaya	10,500	
Drawings – Kolo	8,750	
General expenses	45,675	
Machinery at cost	45,800	
Machinery accumulated depreciation		26,260
Opening inventory	30,975	
Prepayments	8,050	
Purchases	175,500	
Trade payables		56,000
Rent	12,775	
Revenue		302,840
Trade receivables	46,200	
VAT		9,625
Wages	14,875	
	455,435	455,435

FINANCIAL ACCOUNTING: PREPARING FINANCIAL STATEMENTS

Toure Trading

Statement of profit or loss for the year ended 31 December 20X3

	£	£
Revenue		
Cost of goods sold		
Gross profit		
Less:		
Total expenses		
Profit for the year		

(b) Calculate Kolo's share of the profit or loss and his final current account balance. **(3 marks)**

	£
Kolo's share of the profit or loss	
Kolo's final current account balance	

Mock Assessment Questions

(c) Identify whether the following statements are true or false.

(4 marks)

Statement	True	False
In partnership accounting, the capital account shows the long-term investment in the partnership.		
In partnership accounting, interest on capital is recorded in the capital account.		
In partnership accounting, the profit share must be split in the same ratio as any salaries		
In partnership accounting, both the capital and current accounts are shown in the statement of financial position		

One of your sole practitioner clients has asked you about transactions and how they would be recorded in the capital section of the statement of financial position.

(d) Identify whether the following transactions would be recorded as a debit or credit to the capital section of the statement of financial position.

(4 marks)

Transaction	Debit	Credit
A loss made in the year		
Goods taken by the owner for personal use		
A vehicle belonging to the owner put into the business		
The owner purchasing some inventory from the company for cash at below cost price		

(e) Select the correct equation for how each of the following items would be calculated. **(3 marks)**

Item	Equation
Net current assets	
Gross profit	
Net assets	

Picklist: Total income minus total expenses, total assets minus total liabilities, total assets minus current liabilities, current assets minus current liabilities, sales revenue minus cost of sales

Task 5 (18 marks)

This task is about accounting principles, qualities of useful information, and interpreting financial statements using profitability ratios.

(a) Identify which accounting principles are illustrated below.

(4 marks)

Description	Principle
Ensuring all long-term items are included as non-current assets or liabilities	
Writing down assets if they are damaged and expected to be sold at a loss	
Recording transactions with the owner separately from other transactions in the business	
Ensuring sales are recognised when goods are delivered, not when goods are ordered	

Picklist: accruals, going concern, business entity, materiality, consistency, prudence, money measurement

Mock Assessment Questions

(b) Identify which characteristics of useful financial information are described below. **(2 marks)**

Description	Characteristic
The information provided can affect the decisions made by the user	
Information provided ensures that the financial statements accurately reflect the substance of transactions during the period	

Picklist: relevance, faithful representation, understandability, timeliness, comparability

(c) Identify whether the following statements are true or false.

(4 marks)

Statement	True	False
Immaterial items refer to items that should not be included in the financial statements		
Investors are identified as one of the primary users of financial statements		
Accountants preparing financial statements are subject to codes of ethics		
Accounting for depreciation is an example of applying the accruals principle		

A company has made sales revenue of £106,300 in the year and has the following items relevant to its profitability:

Expenses	£
Opening inventory	22,300
Purchases	61,200
Closing inventory	12,400
Wages	15,200
Rent	2,500
Advertising	1,300

FINANCIAL ACCOUNTING: PREPARING FINANCIAL STATEMENTS

(d) Calculate the following profitability ratios. (4 marks)

Ratio	%
Gross profit margin	
Net profit margin	

(e) Identify whether the following situations would increase or decrease the Return on Capital Employed calculation. Treat each item separately, assuming all other items remained the same. (4 marks)

Situation	Increase	Decrease
The owner injects a large amount of capital		
A successful marketing campaign costing £10,000 led to an increase in sales of £80,000		
A receivable balance needs to be written off. The balance was not included in an allowance for doubtful receivables		
A long-term loan is repaid		

Task 6 (12 marks)

This task is about preparing accounting records from incomplete information.

Boulding Co makes a 25% mark-up on cost for all of its products. During the year ended 31 December 20X3, Boulding Co made total sales revenue of £146,000.

(a) Calculate Boulding Co's cost of sales and gross profit for the year ended 31 December 20X3. (2 marks)

	£
Cost of sales	
Gross profit	

Mock Assessment Questions

During the year, Boulding Co made purchases of £110,400. Of this, Boulding had £4,500 in inventory at 31 December 20X3.

(b) Using your answer from (a), what was Boulding Co's opening inventory at 1 January 20X3? **(2 marks)**

£ [   ]

You are working on the financial statements of Jobling Co for the year ended 31 December 20X3. You have the following information:

Day book summaries:	Goods £	VAT £	Total £
Sales	162,500	32,500	195,000
Purchases	92,500	18,500	111,000

Further information:	Net £	VAT £	Total £
Admin expenses	29,000	5,800	34,800
Office expenses	7,100	1,420	8,520

Bank summary (extract)	Dr £		Cr £
		HMRC for VAT	7,300

(c) Using the figures above find the closing balance for VAT by preparing the VAT control account for the year ended 31 December 20X3. **(6 marks)**

VAT Control			
		Balance b/d	4,500

Picklist: Balance c/d, sales daybook, purchases daybook, bank, admin expenses, office expenses

(d) Identify whether the following statements are true or false.

(2 marks)

Statement	True	False
If opening inventory is overstated, then the overall profit for the year will be overstated		
An automated inventory system will always be more accurate than a physical inventory count		

Mock Assessment Questions

FINANCIAL ACCOUNTING: PREPARING FINANCIAL STATEMENTS

2 Mock Assessment Answers – AQ2022

Task 1 (28 marks)

(a) Identify whether the statements below are true or false.

Statement	True	False
Digital bookkeeping systems can produce automated calculations for items such as depreciation	✓	
The non-current asset register is one of the books of prime entry		✓
Recording capital expenditure within non-current assets is an application of the going concern principle	✓	
Including items incorrectly within capital expenditure rather than revenue expenditure results in an overstatement of profit	✓	

(4 marks)

(b) Match each of the following descriptions to the correct definition.

Description	Definition
The estimated value at the end of an asset's useful life	Residual value
The length of time the company expects to use the asset	Useful life
The cost of an asset less its residual value	Depreciable amount
The cost of an asset less accumulated depreciation	Carrying amount

(4 marks)

Mock Assessment Answers

(c) (i) Enter the acquisition, disposal and current year depreciation charges into the non-current asset register

Description	Acq'n date	Cost £	Dep'n charges £	Carrying amount £	Disposal proceeds £	Disposal date £
Computer:						
DL24F	1/1/X1	11,000				
Y/E 31/12/X1			2,750	8,250		
Y/E 31/12/X2			2,062.5	6,187.5		
Y/E 31/12/X3			**1,546.88**	**4,640.62**		
DL45G	**1/1/X3**	**6,000**				
Y/E 31/12/X3			**1,500**	**4,500**		
Vehicles:						
JT14 TGF	1/1/X1	9,000				
Y/E 31/12/X1			1,800	7,200		
Y/E 31/12/X2			1,800	6,400		
Y/E 31/12/X3			**900**	**0**	**4,000**	**1/1/X3**

(10 marks)

Feedback:

The software is a revenue expense having a useful life of only 1 year

Depreciation on DL45G = £6,000 × 25% = £1,500

The MV (JT14 TGF) was held for 6 months before disposal resulting in depreciation of £9,000/5yrs × 6/12 = £900

The depreciation on the computer equipment is calculated on carrying amount (as DB basis is used) = £6,187.50 × 25% = £1,546.88

(c) (ii) Complete the disposals account for the disposal of the vehicle, showing clearly any amount to be transferred to the statement of profit or loss. Ensure any balancing figure is shown on the bottom row.

Disposals			
	£		£
Vehicles cost	9,000	Vehicles accumulated depreciation	4,500
		Cash book	4,000
		Statement of profit or loss	500
Total	9,000	Total	9,000

Picklist: Machinery cost, machinery accumulated depreciation, depreciation expense, statement of profit or loss, cash book, balance b/d, balance c/d

(8 marks)

Feedback:

Accumulated depreciation = £1,800 + £1,800 + £900 = £4,500

(d) **Which TWO of the following could lead to the total on the non-current asset register exceeding the total on the general ledger?**

	✓
Disposal proceeds have been omitted from the register	
A disposal has been omitted from the register	✓
An addition of a new asset has been omitted from the register	
Depreciation charges have been omitted from the register	✓

(2 marks)

Feedback:

Disposal proceeds do not affect the cost or accumulated depreciation.

An addition of a new asset omitted from the register would result in the general ledger balance exceeding the non-current asset register balance.

Mock Assessment Answers

Task 2 (14 marks)

(a)

Rental income

Details	Amount £	Details	Amount £
		Prepaid income	1,200
		Cash book	15,000
Statement of profit or loss	19,200	Accrued income	3,000
Total	19,200	Total	19,200

(8 marks)

Feedback:

Prepaid income represents a liability (it is deferred income) so the reversal is to Dr Prepaid income, Cr Rental income

Accrued income is an asset so the entry at the period end is Dr Accrued income, Cr Rental income

(b) (i) **Produce the journal entry to adjust for the write-off of the receivables balance.**

Account	Debit £	Credit £
Irrecoverable debts	850	
Receivables ledger control account		850

(2 marks)

(b) (ii) **Produce the journal entry to adjust the allowance for doubtful receivables.**

Account	Debit	Credit
Allowance for doubtful receivables	89	
Allowance for doubtful receivables adjustment		89

(2 marks)

Feedback:

Total allowance = 2% × (£58,400 – £850) = £1,151. Opening allowance is £1,240 so decreased by 89)

(c) Identify whether an increase in the following items would be shown as a debit or credit in the statement of financial position

Account	Debit ✓	Credit ✓
Prepayments	✓	
Closing inventory: Statement of financial position	✓	

(2 marks)

Task 3 (24 marks)

(a) Identify the impact the following transactions will have on the accounting equation for Nish.

Transaction	Assets	Liabilities	Capital
Recording a year-end accrual for electricity costs owed	No effect	Increase	Decrease
Receiving cash from a credit customer	No effect	No effect	No effect
Recording depreciation expense for the year	Decrease	No effect	Decrease
Writing off an irrecoverable receivable balance	Decrease	No effect	Decrease
Recording closing inventory	Increase	No effect	Increase

(5 marks)

Feedback:

Accruals are liabilities. The related expense will reduce profits and hence capital

Cash from a credit customer has no net effect as it increases one asset (cash) and reduces another (trade receivables)

Depreciation expense reduces profits and hence capital and reduces the carrying amount of non-current assets

Writing off an irrecoverable receivable reduces trade receivables and creates an expense against profit which reduces capital

Mock Assessment Answers

Closing inventory is recognised as an asset in the SFP and reduces cost of sales, resulting in increased profits and hence capital

(b) (i) What should the corrected cash book balance be recorded as in Nish's financial statements?

£-404 (overdrawn, credit balance)

(1 mark)

Cash book

Interest earned	14	B/F	350
C/F	**404**	Direct debit	68
	418		418

(b) (ii) Using the corrected cash book total, produce the bank reconciliation statement for Nish at 31 December 20X3

Bank reconciliation statement	
Balance per bank statement	£1,430
Add:	
Uncleared lodgements	£206
Less:	
Unpresented cheques	(£2,040)
Balance per cash book	(£404)

(5 marks)

(c) Identify the correct action for Nish to take in the following situations to correct trade payables at 31 December 20X3.

Transaction	Action to take
Invoice 456 from Reeves Ltd, a regular supplier. A check at the warehouse show the goods were received on 30 December 20X3.	Include item within trade payables
Invoice 457 from Reeves Ltd. You do not recognise the description of the goods detailed on the invoice and the warehouse is unsure what the invoice relates to	Query with supplier
Invoice 458 from Reeves Ltd. A check at the warehouse show the goods were received on 6 January 20X4.	Omit item from financial statements

(3 marks)

FINANCIAL ACCOUNTING: PREPARING FINANCIAL STATEMENTS

Feedback:

Invoice 456 – As the goods were accepted into inventory pre-y/e, a liability must be recognised

Invoice 457 – Due to the uncertainty surrounding this invoice it must be queried with the supplier

Invoice 458 – As the goods were accepted into inventory post-y/e, there is no liability or inventory to recognise this year

(d) Correct the following errors by entering adjustments in the extended trial balance

	Dr £	Cr £	Adj Dr £	Adj Cr £
Capital		28,400		3,000
Non-current assets – Cost	44,500		450	
NC assets – Acc dep'n		21,400		450
Closing inventory – SFP			17,400	
Closing inventory – SPL				17,400
Prepayments	2,560			
Accruals		740		
Trade payables		10,430		
Sales revenue		154,760	90	
Bank	21,100			
Rent	45,320			
Wages	34,540			
Trade receivables	4,500			90
VAT		3,840		
Purchases	48,720		800	
Advertising expenses	6,420			
Depreciation expense	3,900			
Opening inventory	10,210			
Suspense		2,200	3,000	800
Total	**221,770**	**221,770**	**21,740**	**21,740**

(10 marks)

Mock Assessment Answers

Feedback:

The suspense account only arises where there has been a mismatch between the debit and credit entries. This is true of items 2 and 4.

The corrections are:

Dr Purchases £800, Cr Suspense £800
Dr Suspense £3,000, Cr Capital £3,000

Task 4 (24 marks)

(a) Prepare a statement of profit or loss for the business for the year ended 31 December 20X3

(10 marks)

Toure Trading		
Statement of profit or loss for the year ended 31 December 20X3		
	£	£
Revenue		302,840
Opening inventory	30,975	
Purchases	175,500	
Closing inventory	-34,125	
Cost of goods sold		172,350
Gross profit		130,490
Less:		
Depreciation charge	12,425	
Discounts allowed	2,360	
General expenses	45,675	
Rent	12,775	
Wages	14,875	
Total expenses		88,110
Profit for the year		42,380

FINANCIAL ACCOUNTING: PREPARING FINANCIAL STATEMENTS

(b) Calculate Kolo's share of the profit or loss and his final current account balance.

	£
Kolo's share of the profit or loss	12,714
Kolo's final current account balance	2,664

(3 marks)

Feedback:

Kolo's share of profit = £42,380 × 30/100 = £12,714

Kolo's final current account balance =

£12,714 profit share – £1,300 B/f debit balance – £8,750 drawings = £2,664

(c) Identify whether the following statements are true or false

Statement	True	False
In partnership accounting, the capital account shows the long-term investment in the partnership.	✓	
In partnership accounting, interest on capital is recorded in the capital account.		✓
In partnership accounting, the profit share must be split in the same ratio as any salaries		✓
In partnership accounting, both the capital and current accounts are shown in the statement of financial position	✓	

(4 marks)

Feedback:

Interest on capital is an appropriation of profit

(d) Identify whether the following transactions would be recorded as a debit or credit to the capital section of the statement of financial position

Transaction	Debit	Credit
A loss made in the year	✓	
Goods taken by the owner for personal use	✓	
A vehicle belonging to the owner put into the business		✓
The owner purchasing some inventory from the company for cash at below cost price	✓	

(4 marks)

Mock Assessment Answers

Feedback:

Item 1 – losses reduce capital

Items 2 and 4 – these are drawings

Item 3 – this is capital introduced

(e) Select the correct equation for how each of the following items would be calculated

Item	Equation
Net current assets	current assets minus current liabilities
Gross profit	sales revenue minus cost of sales
Net assets	total assets minus total liabilities

(3 marks)

Task 5 (18 marks)

(a) Identify which accounting principles are illustrated below

Description	Principle
Ensuring all long-term items are included as non-current assets or liabilities	Going concern
Writing down assets if they are damaged and expected to be sold at a loss	Prudence
Recording transactions with the owner separately from other transactions in the business	Business entity
Ensuring sales are recognised when goods are delivered, not when goods are ordered	Accruals

(4 marks)

(b) Identify which characteristics of useful financial information are described below

Description	Characteristic
The information provided can affect the decisions made by the user	Relevance
Information provided ensures that the financial statements accurately reflect the substance of transactions during the period	Faithful representation

(2 marks)

FINANCIAL ACCOUNTING: PREPARING FINANCIAL STATEMENTS

(c) Identify whether the following statements are true or false

Statement	True	False
Immaterial items refer to items that should not be included in the financial statements		✓
Investors are identified as one of the primary users of financial statements	✓	
Accountants preparing financial statements are subject to codes of ethics	✓	
Accounting for depreciation is an example of applying the accruals principle	✓	

(4 marks)

(d) Calculate the following profitability ratios:

Ratio	%
Gross profit margin £35,200 / £106,300	33.1
Net profit margin £16,200 / £106,300	15.2

(4 marks)

Feedback:

Cost of sales = £22,300 + £61,200 – £12,400 = £71,100

Gross profit = £106,300 – £71,100 = £35,200

Net profit = £35,200 – £15,200 – £2,500 – £1,300 = £16,200

Mock Assessment Answers

(e) Identify whether the following situations would increase or decrease the Return on Capital Employed calculation. Treat each item separately, assuming all other items remained the same.

Situation	Increase	Decrease
The owner injects a large amount of capital		✓
A successful marketing campaign costing £10,000 led to an increase in sales of £80,000	✓	
A receivable balance needs to be written off. The balance was not included in an allowance for doubtful receivables		✓
A long-term loan is repaid	✓	

(4 marks)

Feedback

ROCE = Profit for the year/capital employed where capital employed = capital + non-current liabilities

Item 1 – Capital increases

Item 2 – Net profit increases

Item 3 – Net profit decreases

Item 4 – Non-current liabilities decrease

Task 6 (12 marks)

(a) Calculate Boulding Co's cost of sales and gross profit for the year ended 31 December 20X3.

	£
Cost of sales	116,800
Gross profit	29,200

(2 marks)

Feedback:

Cost of sales = £146,000 × 100/125 = £116,800

Gross profit = £146,000 × 25/125 = £29,200

FINANCIAL ACCOUNTING: PREPARING FINANCIAL STATEMENTS

(b) **Using your answer from (a), what was Boulding Co's opening inventory at 1 January 20X3?**

£10,900

(2 marks)

Feedback:

	£
Opening inventory (ß)	**10,900**
Purchases	110,400
Closing inventory	(4,500)
Cost of sales	116,800

(c) **Using the figures above find the closing balance for VAT by preparing the VAT control account for the year ended 31 December 20X3**

VAT Control			
Purchases day book	18,500	Balance b/d	4,500
Admin	5,800	Sales day book	32,500
Office	1,420		
Bank	7,300		
Balance c/d	3,980		
	37,000		37,000

(6 marks)

(d) **Identify whether the following statements are true or false**

Statement	True	False
If opening inventory is overstated, then the overall profit for the year will be overstated		✓
An automated inventory system will always be more accurate than a physical inventory count		✓

(2 marks)

Feedback:

Opening inventory is added in arriving at cost of sales, so if overstated will result in cost of sales being overstated and hence profit understated

Mock Assessment Answers

REFERENCES

The Board (2023) IAS 2 *Inventories*. London: IFRS Foundation.

The Board (2023) IAS 16 *Property, Plant and Equipment*. London: IFRS Foundation.

References

INDEX

A

Accounting equation, 3, 479, 481, 515

Accrual(s), 291, 292, 293, 296, 304, 392, 395, 397, 398, 401, 405, 408, 410, 411, 412, 422, 424
  concept, 100

Accumulated depreciation, 117, 121, 392, 399, 402, 403, 404, 408, 410, 411, 412, 422

Aged receivable analysis, 218

Allowance, 222, 223, 224, 225, 226, 228, 229, 230, 231, 232, 233
  doubtful debts, 346, 356
  for doubtful debts increase, 393
  for doubtful debts, 345, 347, 349, 350, 352, 353, 357, 359, 362

Appropriation, 446, 452, 453, 458, 460, 461
  account, 437

Assets, 3, 392, 393, 395, 396, 397, 398, 401, 403, 410, 414, 419, 421, 424

Authorisation, 148, 153

B

Balancing off a ledger account, 25

Bank, 11, 12, 13, 14, 15, 16, 17, 18, 20, 22, 23, 24, 45, 46, 47, 48, 49
  account, 484, 508, 510, 515, 531
  reconciliation, 277
  reconciliation process, 278
  reconciliation proforma, 279

Books of prime entry, 8

Bulk discount, 71

C

Capital, 3, 396, 435, 436, 445, 452, 453, 454, 458, 470
  expenditure, 82, 83, 97

Carrying amount, 101, 113

Cash, 1, 2, 10, 12, 13, 14, 15, 26
  account, 482, 484, 510, 511, 514, 515, 531
  book, 9
  discount, 71

Closing inventory, 196, 197, 200, 209, 214

Comparability, 177

Confidence, 188

Confidentiality, 184

Contras, 254

Control, 552
  account reconciliations, 245, 258

Cost, 85
  of goods sold, 389, 390, 393, 400, 409, 413, 415, 420, 423, 425
  structure, 493, 498, 500, 514

Credibility, 188

Credit, 1, 2, 10, 12, 13, 14, 15, 16, 17, 18, 19, 25, 26, 50
  sales, 247
  transactions, 15

CSV file, 36

Current, 461
  account(s), 439, 446, 448, 449, 452, 453, 458, 462
  assets, 3, 394, 395, 398, 401, 410, 414, 421, 424, 459
  liabilities, 4, 394

D

DEAD CLIC, 11

Debit, 25

Decision making, 552

Depreciable amount, 100

Index

Depreciation, 99, 100, 102, 104, 105, 107, 108, 110, 111, 112, 114, 115, 117, 121, 122, 123, 125, 344, 391, 392, 393, 395, 397, 399, 400, 404, 408, 409, 411, 412, 414, 421, 422
 accounting for, 109
 diminishing (reducing) balance, 104, 105, 106, 113, 122
 straight line, 104

Digital bookkeeping, 35, 36
 systems benefits of, 37

Discounts allowed, 253
 day book, 9
 received day book, 9
 received, 254

Disposal, 133, 136, 137, 138, 144, 146, 148, 149, 153, 155, 159

Double entry, 1, 11, 19, 21, 40
 bookkeeping, 10
 bookkeeping – the principles of, 2

Doubtful debts, 217, 221

Drawings, 22, 38, 392, 396, 397, 398, 399, 400, 401, 402, 403, 408, 410, 411, 412, 414, 421, 422, 424, 442, 444, 449, 451, 455, 458, 460, 461, 468

Dual effect, 2

E

Equity, 5

Errors, 314, 316, 317

Estimated residual value, 126

Exempt activities, 68

Expense(s), 5, 389, 391, 393, 400, 403, 408, 409, 413, 415, 421, 423, 425
 over revenue percentage, 551

Expertise, 189

Extended trial balance, 165, 166, 168, 339, 340, 344, 347, 348, 358, 360, 364, 368, 376

F

Faithful representation, 177

Financial statements, 34

Financing non-current assets, 91

Fundamental qualitative characteristics, 176

G

General ledger, 7, 10

Going concern, 171

Goodwill, 92, 94

Gross profit, 389, 390, 393, 400, 409, 413, 420, 423
 margin, 547, 548, 552
 mark-up, 548

H

HM Revenue and Customs, 64, 67, 68, 77, 78

I

IAS 16 – Property, Plant & Equipment, 85

IAS 2, 195, 201, 211

Income, 5
 accruals, 302
 tax, 72

Incomplete records, 478

Input VAT, 65

Intangible non-current asset(s), 92, 97

Integrity, 179

Interest
 on capital, 436
 on drawings, 436, 449

Inventory, 389, 390, 392, 393, 394, 396, 397, 400, 401, 403, 404, 409, 415, 417, 418, 420, 423, 425, 437, 442, 457, 478, 480, 491, 493, 498, 499, 500, 507, 509, 510, 513, 516, 520, 521, 528, 530, 531
 costs of conversion, 202
 purchase cost, 201
 weighted average cost, 203

Irrecoverable debt, 219, 221, 227, 228, 229, 230, 236, 240

J

Journal, 89, 90, 141, 156, 304

L

Ledger, 2, 12, 16, 19, 21, 25, 26
 account, 1, 85

Liabilities, 34, 35, 393, 395, 396, 397, 398, 401, 403, 410, 414, 419, 421, 424

Liability, 3

M

Margin(s), 493, 495, 496, 498, 515, 516

Mark-up, 493, 495, 496, 500, 507, 512, 513, 529

Memorandum (subsidiary) ledger(s), 10, 246

Missing figures, 478

N

Net assets, 479, 480, 481, 482, 505, 515, 525, 526, 531

Net profit, 393, 395, 396, 398, 400, 401, 410, 413, 414, 421, 423, 424
  margin, 549, 554

Net realisable value, 203, 204

Non-current
  asset(s), 3, 82, 83, 84, 86, 90, 91, 92, 94, 95, 134, 136, 142, 149, 150, 153, 394
  asset register, 92, 93, 94, 133
  liabilities, 4, 394, 395
  register, 116, 121

O

Objectivity, 180

Opening inventory, 197, 208

Output VAT, 65

P

Part-exchange, 133, 142, 143, 153

Partnership, 433, 434, 435, 436, 437, 445, 451, 452, 453, 454, 459, 460, 466

Payables ledger, 10, 247
  control account, 257

Payroll - confidentiality, 73

Pension contributions, 73

Personal advantage, 184

Petty cash book, 9

Planning, 552

Prepayment(s), 291, 294, 296, 298, 301, 304, 309, 392, 395, 397, 398, 400, 401, 405, 411, 412, 421, 422, 424

Primary users of the accounts, 170

Professional
  and technical competence, 182
  behaviour, 187
  courtesy, 189
  scepticism, 178, 557

Professionalism, 188

Profit, 3
  appropriation, 435
  for the year, 391
  or loss on disposal, 134, 135
  share, 436, 445, 446, 452, 458

Profitability, 546
  ratios, 546

Prudence, 218, 222, 236

Prudent, 185

Purchase(s), 13, 14, 16, 17, 18, 20, 22, 23, 24, 42, 43, 45, 46, 49
  day book, 8
  invoice, 71
  ledger control account, 485, 487, 492, 507, 508, 525
  returns, 22, 23, 253
  returns day book, 9

R

Rates of VAT, 65

Ratio(s), 546
  analysis, 556

Receivable(s), 217, 218, 220, 225, 226, 230, 231, 233, 236, 395, 396, 398, 400, 401, 403, 406, 410, 421, 424, 455, 459, 460, 477, 479, 486, 488, 492, 511, 512, 518, 522
  ledger, 10, 246
  ledger control account, 256

Reconciliations, 259

Recurring entries, 37

Relevance, 171, 177

Residual value, 103

Return On Capital Employed (ROCE), 550, 554

Revenue expenditure, 82, 97

Index

S

Salaries, 435
  partners, 458, 466

Sales, 14, 16, 18, 20, 22, 23, 24, 42, 43, 45, 46, 47, 48, 49, 389, 390, 392, 393, 397, 399, 400, 402, 406, 408, 409, 411, 412, 413, 420, 422, 423
  commission, 436
  day book, 8
  ledger control account, 485, 486, 489, 490, 492, 503, 505, 507, 509, 511, 512, 525
  returns, 22, 252
  returns day book, 8

Separate entity concept, 2

Settlement discount, 71

Sole trader, 387, 393, 395, 396, 402, 408, 411, 419

Standard rated, 66

Statement of financial position, 4, 34, 35, 387, 393, 454

Statement of profit or loss, 34, 387, 388, 389, 390, 391, 392, 393, 400, 415, 416, 417, 418, 419, 425, 433, 437, 457, 463, 478, 493, 518, 519, 528

Straight line, 106, 109

Subsequent expenditure, 91

Suspense, 313, 319, 320, 321, 322, 323, 324, 325, 330, 332

T

Tangible Non-Current Assets, 91, 92

Taxable
  persons, 64
  supplies, 65

The Cloud, 36

The Code of Ethics for Professional Accountants, 178, 179

The qualitative characteristics, 176

Timeliness, 177

Trade discount, 71

Trading account, 388

Trial balance, 34, 19, 24, 45, 49, 165, 166, 168, 314, 339, 342, 343, 359, 361, 362, 363, 364, 369, 376, 378, 379, 380, 382, 402

U

Understandability, 177

Useful economic life, 103

V

VAT, 78
  exempt, 69
  sales tax, 64
  zero rated, 69

Verifiability, 177

Z

Zero-rated, 67